Productivity, Innovation and Knowledge in Services

Productivity, Innovation and Knowledge in Services

New Economic and Socio-Economic Approaches

Edited by

Jean Gadrey

Professor of Economics, University of Lille 1, France

Faïz Gallouj

Associate Professor of Economics, University of Lille 1, France

Edward Elgar
Cheltenham, UK • Northampton, MA, USA

© Jean Gadrey, Faïz Gallouj 2002

Published by
Edward Elgar Publishing Limited
Glensanda House
Montpellier Parade
ML Cheltenham
Glos GL50 1UA
UK

Edward Elgar Publishing, Inc.
136 West Street
Suite 202
Northampton
Massachusetts 01060
USA

A catalogue record for this book
is available from the British Library

Library of Congress Cataloguing in Publication Data

Productivity, innovation and knowledge in services: new economic and socio-economic approaches/edited by Jean Gadrey, Faïz Gallouj.
    p.cm.
  Includes index.
    1. Service industries – Technological innovations. 2. Technological innovations – Economic aspects. 3. Economic development. I. Gadrey, J. II. Gallouj, Faïz.
  HD9980.5.P758 2002
  338′.06—dc21   2002021986

ISBN 1 84064 969 0

Typeset by Cambrian Typesetters, Frimley, Surrey
Printed and bound in Great Britain by MPG Books Ltd, Bodmin, Cornwall

Contents

PART I   PRODUCTIVITY AND PERFORMANCES IN SERVICES

PART II   INNOVATION IN SERVICES AND THROUGH
          SERVICES

Figures

Tables

Contributors

William J. Baumol is Professor and Former Director at the C.V. Starr Center for Applied Economics, New York University and Senior Research Economist and Professor Emeritus at Princeton University, USA.

Bernard Chane Kune was Associated Researcher to the Centre d'Etudes Prospectives et d'Informations Internationales (CEPII), Paris, France at the time the chapter was written.

Jacques De Bandt is a CNRS Research Director at LATAPSES, University of Nice, France.

Ludovic Dibiaggio is Research Fellow in the Centre for Research in Innovation Management (CENTRIM) at Brighton University, UK, and Affiliated Professor at CERAM, Sophia Antipolis, France.

Jean Gadrey is Professor of Economics at the University of Lille 1, France.

Faïz Gallouj is Associate Professor at the University of Lille 1, France.

Pim den Hertog is Senior Researcher/Partner at Dialogic Innovation and Interaction, Utrecht and at the Department of Innovation Studies, Utrecht University, The Netherlands.

Emmanuel Lazega is Professor of Sociology at the University of Lille 1, France.

Ian Miles is Professor of Technological Innovation and Social Change at the University of Manchester, UK, where he is also co-Director of PREST (Policy Research in Engineering, Science and Technology), and of CRIC (Centre for Research on Innovation and Competition).

Nanno Mulder was Research Economist at the Centre d'Etudes Prospectives et d'Informations Internationales (CEPII), Paris, France at the time the chapter was written.

Pascal Petit is a CNRS Research Director at the Centre d'Etudes Prospectives d'Economie Mathématique Appliquées à la Planification (CEPREMAP), Paris, France.

Maria Savona is PhD Candidate at SPRU (Science and Technology Policy Research), University of Sussex, UK, and Research Fellow at the University of Camerino, Italy.

Edward N. Wolff is Professor of Economics at New York University, USA.

BK Title: L80

Preface

William J. Baumol

It has well been said that economists are qualified to predict anything but the future. But, occasionally, the future is already here, just waiting to be recognized. We can forecast the ethnic composition of the native-born labour force with some degree of confidence because its future members are already alive. In the same way, we can predict the division of tomorrow's industrial economy among agriculture, manufacturing and services because the change is with us already. But it is only inadequately reflected in the writings of journalists and even in the economic literature. Observers worry when their economy falls behind in manufacturing employment, though the evidence indicates clearly that their primary concern should be about their nation's role in the services. The new composition of employment is clear in the USA, for example. Despite the vast volume of its agricultural output, employment in that sector has fallen below 3 per cent of the total. As an industrial economy, it is curious that manufacturing jobs provide far less than an additional 20 per cent to this sum. The rest is services.

Moreover, there is reason to believe that within those services the key to future growth is to be found. Terms such as 'computer programs' and 'the Internet' suggest dramatically that this is so, and the prosperity contributed in locations from Silicon Valley to Tel Aviv indicate how much is at stake. But this is not even the most fundamental point here. It is difficult to dispute that innovation has been the most critical contributor to the economic growth that sets the free enterprise economies apart from all other forms of economic organization known to history. But the crucial point for the current topic is that *innovative activity is fundamentally a service activity.* In other words, there is good reason to conclude that within the services there is to be found the main component of the remarkable growth engine of capitalism.

While I have suggested that the literature on the services has not yet attained a volume commensurate with their importance, recent contributions by economists to analysis of this arena have hardly been negligible. Groups of highly qualified and productive researchers have contributed to a valuable and growing literature that begins to provide a deeper understanding of the issues raised by the role of the service sector. Jean Gadrey and his colleagues have been in the vanguard of this activity and their work has provided much needed additions to the analysis of the subject. This volume is a significant example of their work. And it is significant not only because of the quality of its contents but also because of the particular topic on which the compendium focuses.

The subject, in short, is a fundamental paradox in the relationship between the services and growth in the overall economy. There are two elements in this paradox, the one relating to technological progress within the supply of services themselves, and the other stemming from the role of the services in the growth of the economy as a whole, including that of other sectors.

What I may refer to as the 'within services' part of the paradox is the long-held (and not altogether incorrect) perception that the services are the home to activities in which productivity growth is particularly slow – the productivity-stagnant sectors of the economy. This view was based partly on direct observation of some service activities in which the process of production and supply shows little change over the decades or even centuries (thus, my often-cited example of live performance of a Mozart string quartet). The observation was also based on analysis of the activities in question, citing their handicraft characteristics, their incompatibility with standardization and mass production, and the fact that their quality is often heavily dependent on direct contact between the supplier and the consumer, as in the case of examination of a patient by a doctor. All this seems to make a convincing case, until we look a bit further and note the profound changes in the *quality* of the services supplied. A twenty-first century doctor may not have many labour saving inventions at his/her disposal and may spend as much time per patient as a doctor of the eighteenth century, but the former may well save the patient's life while the latter was very likely to shorten it. Surely that represents a dramatic growth in productivity. And there are other observations that complicate the view that the services are the home of technological stagnancy. As is reported in this volume, investment in computer equipment and activities in recent decades has been some three times as high in the services as in manufacturing.

This, then, is the first part of the paradox – provision of the services seems technologically stagnant and, at the same time, the very opposite. As is, by definition, true of other paradoxes, there is a resolution, fundamentally that both conclusions are different sides of the same truth. In brief, technical progress often provides services of far higher quality than in the past – that is the technologically progressive side of their production. But often, lack of substantially labour saving technology condemns their costs to rise continually and persistently far faster than costs in other sectors of the economy. These issues are among those explored more fully and effectively in this volume.

The other side of the paradox is related to the contribution of the services to other sectors. It has been held for some time that since productivity in the services at least appears to grow more slowly than that in the rest of the economy, as the economy's labour force shifts increasingly toward the services, *average* productivity growth in the economy as a whole will be held back. Two new observations, however, cast substantial doubt upon the substance of this conclusion, even though it may retain some theoretical validity. First, there is a new result (see the Oulton theorem, in chapter 7) that requires us to distinguish between final product and intermediate product services. The new result tells us that for final-product services the slow-down effect upon the economy of the shift of labour to the services remains true. But for intermediate service outputs (business services) that do constitute a very large share of the rise of employment in the sector, a shift of the labour force in the service direction will *add* to overall productivity growth. Second, as already noted, innovation is predominantly a service activity, and what is more important than innovation for overall productivity growth?

In sum, this book deals with a subject of the utmost importance for the future of our economies. And it offers insights that span the range of beneficiaries, from pure theoretical analysis to formulation of practical policy. Who can ask for more?

BK Title!

N/A

Introduction

Jean Gadrey and Faïz Gallouj

By the end of the twentieth century, the developed economies had been characterized, variously, as information economies, knowledge economies, post-industrial economies and, more recently, 'new economies'. In strictly factual terms, however, the characteristic that leaps most noticeably to the eye is the strong and sustained growth over recent decades of the share of services in employment and in nominal GDP. Although economists and other social scientists have been producing noteworthy studies of these activities for a long time, in an attempt both to explain their growth and to examine the economic and social challenges they pose, the relative share of research on services can be said still to be lagging behind that of services in economic activity.

Two of the principal topics that researchers on services have been concerned with are, on the one hand, productivity and, more generally, performance in service activities and, on the other, innovation in and through services. These two questions are obviously connected, if it is accepted that medium and long-term economic performance are strongly linked to the dynamism of innovation. This dual issue lies at the heart of the present book, which has its origins in an international conference held in the northern French cities of Lille and Roubaix in June 2000 and attended by most of the leading researchers on these topics.

All the contributors to this book have long experience of theoretical and empirical research on services. Their extensive empirical knowledge of services has led most of them to identify an often very wide gap between the stylized facts they present and the tools economists have traditionally used to interpret these facts. The productivity question is a puzzle in many so-called 'stagnant services', where the data provided by national accountants show little or no increase in productivity, while closer empirical observations and case studies reveal that some of these sectors are in fact as dynamic as many manufacturing industries. How can these opposing views be reconciled? Several arguments have been put forward, but none seems to account adequately for such a 'cognitive gap'. For this reason, it would seem unwise to reject the hypothesis that many service outputs are being wrongly conceptualized and measured.

It is not our contention that the main economic tools (growth, productivity, or the substitution of capital for labour, among others) currently used for such purposes should be abandoned. Far from it. Many of the current measurement methods could be improved, especially in the vast field of service quality assessment. However, there is some doubt as to whether this type of 'incremental' improvement will be sufficient to capture efficiency and quality gains in sectors such as health, education, social and care services, finance and insurance, and even retailing and eating and drinking places. More 'radical' conceptual innovations are likely to be needed. This book provides some pointers to the innovations – of both types – required if the economic performances of services is to be accurately measured.

The same applies to innovation in and through services. Many of the existing theories and concepts undoubtedly constitute powerful tools for understanding some at least of the innovation processes in services. For example, neo-Schumpeterian theories take account, to a certain extent, of the diversity of technological trajectories in services, while neoclassical approaches may help to understand the impact of innovation and R&D on growth (see Chapter 7).

At the same time, however, most of the existing approaches, and the corresponding measurement methods and classifications used in national surveys and other studies, retain much of their bias towards manufacturing and technology and fail to capture some of the fundamental aspects of innovation in services.

Just as productivity levels are said to be low, so innovation in services is often said to be non-existent or confined to the adoption of technologies originating in manufacturing industries. Thinking of this kind can cause serious difficulties in an economy dominated by services, since it precludes efforts (particularly on the part of the public authorities) to develop ways of energizing an area of activity of great importance for the future of firms, industries and nations.

These misconceptions have their origins in the manufacturing and technological bias of our analytical apparatus. In most neoclassical economics, innovation is perceived through the concept of the production function and is limited to process innovation (as incorporated into technical equipment). From this perspective, it is but a short step to reduce innovation in services to the mere adoption of technical equipment produced by the only driving force supposedly capable of innovation in the economy, that is manufacturing industry. Thus the main body of literature implicitly or explicitly related to innovation in services focuses on the generic theme of the spread and the impact of the new (informational) paradigm on services.

Recent economic analyses (based on evolutionary and neo-Schumpeterian approaches), which are more sensitive to the characteristics of the 'black box' of the firm (that is to learning phenomena and the mediums through which they are enacted – routines – and to the tacit and idiosyncratic aspects of technologies) and more inclined to accept a broader definition of innovation, have not succeeded in ridding themselves of this technological bias. In such analyses, services are generally dominated by the suppliers of their technical equipment.

This general conception of the technological and adopted nature of innovation in services has certain corollaries that it is important to emphasize. Services are, allegedly, as unacquainted with R&D as they are with innovation, despite the large number of engineers and managers now employed in service industries. That this is a widely held view is demonstrated by the fact that national and international indicators of R&D and innovation (the Frascati and Oslo manuals, for example) almost completely ignore the specificities of service activities.

The five chapters of this book devoted to innovation in services may adopt a number of different theoretical perspectives, notably neoclassical and neo-Schumpeterian ones, but they share the common aim of going beyond this technological bias. These chapters not only focus on the specificity of innovation in services, but two of them (Chapters 10 and 11) also reverse the subordinate relationship between manufacturing and services in so far as they focus on the active role played by knowledge-intensive services in their clients' innovation processes (including those in manufacturing industry). William Baumol's chapter goes even further in the rehabilitation of services, stressing as it does that R&D is itself a prominent service activity.

THE MAIN CONCEPTUAL LINK BETWEEN THE TWO PARTS OF THE BOOK: KNOWLEDGE

We have already advanced one argument of a general nature in order to explain why we have seen fit to gather together within one and the same volume chapters focusing, on the one hand, on productivity, growth and performance in service industries and, on the other, on innovation in and by services. The argument runs as follows: medium and long-run economic performance depends crucially on the dynamism and forms of innovation. And since services now account for almost three-quarters of all economic activity in the developed countries, there are good grounds for believing that innovation linked to services is a major factor in determining performance at global level.

In fact, however, the strongest link between the two parts of the book, the link on which its overall coherence is founded, is located on the conceptual level and can be summarized by a few key words: co-production, service quality (and the corresponding innovations and performance) and, above all, knowledge and intelligence.

Most of the contributors to this book are convinced that, in practice, innovation and performance in services flow increasingly from the mobilization of intelligence and knowledge. Consequently, their theoretical analyses must themselves be innovative, bringing new concepts, new methods and new models to bear on the economics and socio-economics of knowledge. Knowledge is a key component of production (for example: how can activities whose principal output is knowledge be rationalized? What is the role of information and communication technologies (ICTs) and knowledge-intensive business services in these processes?), in consumption (how do users contribute to this knowledge economy?) and in the relations between production and consumption: cooperation, market transactions, social transactions and service relationships, and so on.

Of course, intelligence has always been an essential 'factor of production' in economic history. Moreover, it is as decisive a factor in manufacturing or agriculture as in services. However, examination of the facts shows beyond any shadow of a doubt that the intellectual component of economic activity is growing steadily in importance. Services are particularly affected by this trend. Firstly, they have certain specific characteristics, particularly in the area of direct cognitive interactions with users. Secondly, they are extremely revealing of complex situations in which the core of the output becomes a problem-solving activity. Finally, as William Baumol points out in Chapter 7, they include what is perhaps the 'king' of activities in the knowledge economy, namely R&D.

Thus the title of the book, 'Productivity, innovation and knowledge in services', can be understood as expressing, in shorthand, the linkage that exists in services between issues relating to performance and innovation and those relating to knowledge.

A DETAILED SUMMARY OF THE BOOK

Traditional measures of productivity growth suggest that gains in service industries in the United States have been very low since 1979. However, other indices of 'technological activity' show that service industries have actually been more technologically active than goods producing industries over this period. In Chapter 1, Edward Wolff investigates different indicators of technological activity among goods producers and service providers. For example, investment in computerization has been much greater in services than in goods-producing industries (about three times as high since 1977). The educational attainment of the workforce and other skill indices are higher in service than in goods-producing industries over this period. Moreover, the degree of change since 1970 in the occupational composition of employment has been almost as great in service industries as in goods-producing industries.

The upshot of the chapter is that so-called stagnant services, as portrayed in the standard cost-disease model, are *not* technologically inert. Though these industries show up with close to zero productivity growth, they are very active and have undergone major changes over time by other technological indices. Indeed, by some of the indices (mean skills, mean schooling, share of knowledge workers, investment in OCA (Office, Computing and Accounting equipment) and age of capital), these sectors are more technologically active than goods producers or progressive services.

Is the poorer productivity performance of services in recent years due to the fact that their output is becoming increasingly difficult to measure? This could be a substantial part of the explanation. The distinguishing features of service industries in the post-1980 period are both their high rate of computerization and their high degree of employment restructuring. It is likely that both are associated with a more heterogeneous output. The high degree of computerization found in finance, for example, has been responsible for the creation of a bewildering array of new financial products. The same appears to be true of the insurance industry and business services. Likewise, the fact that the degree of employment restructuring increased substantially between the 1970s and 1980s might be associated with an increasing variety of service products. It is possible that the more heterogeneous output has made service output harder to measure over time and that the apparent low productivity growth in services after 1980 is in fact a measurement problem.

But there are two other possible explanations. The first of these could lie in the high adjustment costs associated with the introduction of new technology. According to this line of argument, productivity growth in the so-called stagnant services should increase to more normal levels in the future as the IT revolution reaches maturity.

The second explanation is that service providers are now able to use this new technology to increase profits in other ways besides augmenting productivity. In particular, they may be employing IT for product differentiation rather than productivity enhancement. If this is the case, then the low productivity growth measured for the 'stagnant' services might persist indefinitely.

In Chapter 2, Jean Gadrey shows that certain conceptual issues relating to the definition of output in many 'stagnant' services give rise to serious measurement problems. This chapter summarizes the findings of a research project carried out between 1989 and 1992 in close cooperation with Thierry Noyelle and Thomas Stanback of Columbia University. The aim of the project was to compare productivity in services in France and the United States, and in particular to ascertain whether productivity in services was indeed weaker and productivity gains lower in the United States than in France and whether this could explain the very high levels of job creation in the American service sector and the relatively modest levels in France. This interpretation was very widespread in the early 1990s and is still advanced today. According to Gadrey, this explanation is, for the most part, an illusion and the main answers to the question are conceptual and methodological in nature. Furthermore, by showing the limits of the traditional concepts in the case of an international comparison, useful pointers can be gleaned as to how to interpret the so-called 'productivity paradox' in each country.

In most services the USA appears to have a real technological and organizational lead. Services in France do not lag behind in all their technological characteristics. However, in most of the comparisons undertaken, the gap is significant. How can America's undoubted technological and organizational lead in many services be reconciled with the very poor productivity records of these industries? Gadrey's answer to this paradox has two main thrusts.

Firstly, he advocates what can be described as a functional approach to service activities. Most service industries can be analysed as a combination of three sets of 'production' functions: informational functions, material logistical functions and direct service functions, which involve face-to-face contact with clients, customer care and assistance, advice and so on.

Service industries in the USA seem to have a noticeably higher level of efficiency than their French counterparts in the first two fields (those in which most advanced technologies can be introduced) and to provide a greater volume of direct services to customers, with relatively more people employed to perform this third category of functions. Traditional measurements of output, such as the volume of goods sold in retailing, the number of people admitted to hospitals (possibly supplemented by a complexity index), tons of goods × kilometers carried in air transportation, premiums or losses incurred at constant dollars in insurance and so on, do not take account of the amount of direct service produced; their use is likely, therefore, to lead to the conclusion that overall labour efficiency in the USA is relatively poor.

Secondly, Gadrey develops a new conceptual approach to output in service activities. The core idea behind this approach can be grasped from one question, which arises out of one of the five case studies undertaken by Gadrey and his colleagues. In the supermarket industry, do we get the same output when, for the same basket of goods bought, we get our purchases bagged, delivered to our homes if necessary, or carried to our car on request, when we have 50 per cent more varieties of goods (stock-keeping units) to choose from, when the store's opening hours per week are twice as long, when there is a customer assistance counter, when more scanning systems save our time at the checkout counter and when, in addition to this identical basket, we can also buy hot food 'to go' as well as other kinds of prepared food (from salad bars, for example)? What the French–US comparison shows is that more people are employed in the typical American supermarket for roughly the same volume of goods traded, not because of lower 'productivity' but, if output is analysed as a combination of services associated with the trade of goods rather than simply with the volume of goods themselves (the usual method based on sales at constant prices), because the output of US supermarkets is fundamentally different.

Moreover, if this more complex, service-based approach is adopted, it can be shown that, during the 1980s, the average US supermarket clearly increased its performance in terms of quality and quantity of services delivered, leading to a decrease in its 'productivity' as measured in the traditional way, while its French counterpart was improving 'productivity' by restricting its service component and developing the 'self-service' and large-scale strategy pioneered in the USA during the 1950s, 1960s and early 1970s. This example indicates the general approach: in a service economy, we need thoroughly to reappraise the traditional concepts of output and the methods used to measure it and to evaluate the significance of the rising level of service provided.

In the last part of this chapter, Jean Gadrey shows that improved and more complex procedures might be used in order to provide better estimates of effi-ciency changes in services. In most cases, this involves introducing the main variables neglected in the traditional approaches: service complexity, intensity and outcomes.

In Chapter 3, Jacques De Bandt and Ludovic Dibiaggio deal with the so-called 'learning' economy as a source of conceptual difficulties that make it necessary to develop new theoretical categories for evaluating performance. In developed countries at least, productive systems have been undergoing deep and wide-ranging changes since the early 1970s. Two of the most important of these changes have been the growth of information-related activities (comput-ers and software, information systems and so on) and, particularly from the 1980s onwards, the development of R&D activities and innovation systems.

This chapter puts the emphasis on a set of new phenomena and realities, of which it can be shown that they cannot be handled within the framework of the old industrial paradigm. A new paradigm is required, one that has as its main reference point the role of knowledge in production and value creation. At the core of this analysis is the capacity to produce knowledge in response to specific questions (or problems or needs) when the question, in turn, is a source of knowledge creation. Distinctions have to be made, on the one hand, between different types of knowledge of varying degrees of complexity and, on the other, between different modes of organization in productive systems.

The status of knowledge depends essentially on the context in which it is used. Rather than simply emphasizing knowledge-intensive activities, De Bandt and Dibiaggio focus on the level of commonality in the environment in which knowledge is re-used. Indeed, knowledge standardization – through codification or routinization – depends on the reproduction in similar contexts of actions or decisions that have already been tried and tested. Self-evidently, therefore, the introduction of ICTs may improve knowledge standardization. However, new technologies may also increase the set of problems to be solved, raise users' expectations and open up new opportunities for knowledge creation.

Working within this framework, the authors draw up a typology of contextual situations that affect the nature of the cognitive process as it is implemented. They put forward *simple*, *problem-solving* and *complex situations* as three archetypes of decision-making or learning situations. Each archetypical situation is defined in terms of the agent's familiarity with the question he/she has to answer, the problem he/she has to solve or the situation in which he/she has to behave.

In all situations in which only 'simple' knowledge has to be produced, either because the situation is simple or because it can be simplified, ICTs can perform the tasks and produce considerable efficiency gains. Some progress is equally possible in some of the 'problem-solving' situations, to the extent that certain standardization procedures are feasible. However, there is another, concurrent trend towards contextual specificity, customization and complexity. Because of the competencies required, complex knowledge has to be co-produced through organizational learning processes. As a result, co-production – which is at the heart of the 'service relation' – becomes a central aspect of the new modes of production.

In Chapter 4 Bernard Chane Kune and Nanno Mulder provide an international comparison of productivity in the transportation sector, with a focus on total factor productivity (TFP). Labour productivity is often regarded as an approximate measure of service provider efficiency. Since services are supposed to use relatively little capital, this partial measure is seen as a proxy for overall efficiency. However, in many services such as transport, capital is a major production factor. Thus in order to accurately assess the overall efficiency of these services, labour productivity measures should be complemented by measures of capital and TFP. For France, it has been impossible to date to estimate capital productivity and TFP for the transport sector as a whole for want of any estimates of capital inputs. This chapter aims to fill this gap by providing new, detailed estimates of capital input in French transport from 1970 onwards. These data are used in combination with series on output and labour input to estimate productivity. Finally, the performance of the French transport industry is compared with that of the German, UK and US industries.

In contrast to many other studies of productivity, the contribution of capital to production is *not* measured by the value of the stock of assets but by the volume of services rendered by this stock (this method is also referred to as the 'Jorgenson approach'). Capital services are measured by the product of the volume of capital, approximated by the net capital stock, times its user cost.

The latter is estimated by the sum of depreciation, the real interest rate and capital gains. The net stocks of transport equipment in air and maritime transport are measured by administrative records. The stock of other assets is estimated by the perpetual inventory method, which sums several years of capital formation and deducts assets that reached the end of their service life. Detailed series of investment and discards are compiled for eight different sub-sectors of the transport industry, showing for each a breakdown into infrastructure, transport equipment, and other machinery and equipment.

In the second part of the chapter, productivity results are presented. Total factor productivity is estimated using the Törnqvist discrete approximation to the Divisia index. The variance of productivity patterns across sub-sectors of the transport industry is not unique to France, as is illustrated by a comparison with Germany, the United Kingdom and the United States. Overall productivity gains in Germany and the United Kingdom were similar to those in France. The three European countries outperformed the USA. At the sub-industry level, it turns out that air transport is the industry with the largest capital gains in all countries. The USA is the only country with large productivity gains in railways. France outperformed other countries in terms of productivity growth in air and maritime transport. In the other industries, French productivity growth was below that of the other countries.

In Chapter 5, Pascal Petit analyses the potential for growth and productivity in modern, highly tertiarized economies whose growth regimes are currently being influenced by wide-ranging technological changes driven by ICTs. Such economies offer considerable potential for growth but there are many constraints on the realization of that potential. In particular, the dynamism of certain sectors and the improvement in the welfare of certain social categories has to extend to other sectors and other social categories. This cannot be achieved simply by redistributing productivity gains and the associated incomes but will have to be accompanied by significant changes in activities and in those groups that are lagging behind.

This chapter seeks to clarify the terms of the choices for such a redistribution of income and knowledge, using a sectoral growth model for the main OECD countries that could account for the shift towards knowledge-based economies. This transformation denotes less an abstract accumulation of information and knowledge that is difficult to measure than a general (though uneven) enlargement of the strategic behaviours of economic agents who can access, by means that have to be specified, more information and knowledge. Services to firms and households play a key role of intermediaries in this access. They take advantage for that purpose of the contemporary interdependent developments of three structural changes, initiated decades ago: globalization, education and a new technological system based on ICTs.

Petit attempts to show how services interact with the development of these structural changes constituting some multi-layer network supporting the various externalities that can fuel a process of endogenous growth. For such mechanisms of economic growth to reach some sizeable momentum the role of intermediation of services, for both firms and individuals, has to be comprehensive and lasting. In this perspective the outcomes of various OECD countries in the 1990s are discussed. This discussion underlines that in such transition period the Scandinavian countries may give more insights on what the real dynamics of knowledge-based economies could be than the Anglo-Saxon countries.

In Chapter 6, Emmanuel Lazega also focuses on knowledge and the standardization thereof, but this time from a sociological or 'socio-economic' perspective. He examines the relationship between distributed knowledge and economic performance in a professional or 'collegial' organization. He identifies a few conditions under which the pattern of knowledge flows is most productive for firms providing professional services with an emphasis on quality. In such organizations, the production of services for clients is difficult to routinize, since professional expertise and advice cannot be easily standardized. Consequently, 'internal' transaction costs related to flows of resources, including knowledge, can be assumed to account for a high share of total costs for the firm as a whole. The practical problem for such firms is to find ways of reducing complexity and constructing certainties in order to learn from their own experience and provide high-quality advice for clients. In order to produce such knowledge-intensive work on a regular basis, intelligence is shared in two types of situation at least: in joint work on cases or in case-related advice relationships. Saying that intelligence is 'shared' does not, however, do justice to what really happens in the flows of intelligence. The important characteristic of such flows is shown to be that knowledge as a resource is efficiently distributed/allocated through two processes: selection of exchange partners who share common identities in dense subsets (social niche seeking) and concentration of the authority to know (through competition for status). Some members emerge as having the authority to know, although such status is fragile. This allocation of knowledge is a micro-political learning process, but it is also efficient. Efficiency can be measured, it is argued, by drawing on statistical evidence on the relationship between crude measurements of economic performance and position in social networks concerned with the allocation of knowledge.

An empirical study of a medium-sized corporate law firm in the north-eastern United States is used for this purpose. Distributed knowledge is measured through two types of networks: a network of co-workers, with whom the 'whole picture' of the case is shared, and the advice network within the firm. Members' individual performance data (hourly rates, number of hours worked, fees brought in) are analysed as an effect of position in this network.

Dependence of economic performance on the overall pattern of ties in the two networks is established. This suggests that proxy measurements of productivity based on social network analysis are possible in knowledge-intensive organizations, a thorny issue in contemporary economics.

In Chapter 7, William Baumol reminds us that R&D is a service activity that is likely to be the current 'king of the services and perhaps even of the economy as a whole'. This chapter tells a feedback story, indicating how R&D activity affects the productivity performance of the economy and how, in turn, the economy's degree of success in productivity growth affects the magnitude of R&D activity. The result is the skeleton of a model of the interactions of growth and R&D that is truly endogenous and, moreover, not ahistorical, unlike most theoretical analyses in this arena.

The analysis is conducted in three sequential steps. In the first, the production of new information through R&D activity stimulates productivity growth *in industry*. In the second, the price (real cost) of *information production and dissemination* rises as a result. This is because these activities are 'asymptotically stagnant', that is they are characterized by productivity growth that is initially high but, with the passage of time, tends to lag further and further behind that of industry. In the third step, information grows relatively more costly and, as a result, other inputs tend to be substituted for information in the production process. For example, when R&D costs have risen, a firm that wants to increase its output may decide not to invest more in R&D with a view to increasing the productivity of its machines but to buy additional machines of the current type instead. Thus the rising cost of the innovation process can cut the derived demand for innovative activity. That in turn impedes productivity growth, thus reversing the first of the three steps of the inter-temporal process in its next iteration.

The main implication of this model might be that the very success of the R&D sector may conceivably sow the seeds of a future price impediment to demand for its output. Much depends on the occurrence of significant breakthroughs, either from truly independent innovators or from routine business R&D activities.

In Chapter 8, Ian Miles conducts a survey of studies of innovation in services. Different phases in the evolution of these studies are identified.

1. Services were neglected for a long time. In the early days of political economy, agriculture and manufacturing, not services, were the important areas of economic activity.
2. Services then started to become an important economic phenomenon, accounting for a major share of employment and GDP in developed countries. Nevertheless, the study of innovation in services was suffering from inertia and lagged behind the recognition of the importance of services.

Most of the studies were concerned with explaining the growth of the tertiary sector rather than investigating the meaning of innovation in services, which was regarded as very limited.

3. Barras's model is often considered to be the first attempt to build a theory of innovation in services. Like other models and surveys – especially evolutionary taxonomies of technological trajectories in service industries – it is based on a concept of innovation limited to the technological dimension that has been formalized in OECD manuals.

4. Several more recent studies and surveys have sought to go beyond this technological bias. These studies focus on the specificities of service activities, both in terms of the nature of innovation and of the models of innovation organization.

5. The main conclusion of Ian Miles's chapter, and the last stage in the evolution of studies of innovation in services, is that such studies have undergone a process of 'tertiarization'. The enhanced understanding of issues around innovation in services that should ensue is likely to shed further light on innovation in the economy as a whole, far beyond the service sector itself. There are several reasons for this tertiarization: manufacturers often manage service activities in which they may innovate and KIBS (knowledge-intensive business services) are playing an important and growing role in the whole innovation system.

In Chapter 9, by Maria Savona, the link between demand, innovation and growth in services is empirically addressed, looking at the case of Italy. The analysis attempts to disentangle the role of demand vis-à-vis technological change in explaining the different patterns of growth across services. It is argued that it is the composition of demand for services by different destination markets, besides the widening of technological opportunities provided by the information and communication technology paradigm, which accounts for the diverse patterns of growth in services.

The empirical analysis explores the sectoral composition of demand for services by different destination markets (primary and manufacturing sectors, market and public services, final consumers), which represents the sectoral division of labour between services and other branches of the economy. Further, the main innovative profiles, as a result of the diverse impact of technological change on service sectors' innovative performance, are identified. Finally, the dynamics of growth experienced by service industries in the decade 1991–96 are shown. The three sets of descriptive evidence are then used in a regression framework, to endogenously take into account the role of demand and technological change in explaining sectoral differences in the rate of growth across service industries.

The results of the empirical analysis confirm that a sectoral specialization towards intermediate producer demand (manufacturing sector and business services sector) is a necessary condition for a positive growth performance of services. On the other side, the exploitation of the technological opportunities provided by the new ICT paradigm is not a sufficient condition for a positive growth performance when service industries are specialized in final and intermediate distributive demand (trade and finance sectors).

Chapters 10 and 11 are devoted to knowledge-intensive business services (KIBS). KIBS can be defined as activities in which knowledge is both the input and the main output. These activities pose theoretical problems associated with two fields of economic theory: the economics of service industries and that of information and knowledge.

Before dealing with the role of KIBS, Pim den Hertog's chapter adopts a managerial perspective in order to develop, first, a theoretical model of innovation in services and, second, a typology of innovation patterns in services. The innovation model has four interlinked dimensions: new service concept, new interface, new delivery system and new technological options. On the basis of this model, several patterns of innovation are identified: supplier-dominated innovation, innovation within services, client-led innovation, innovation through services and paradigmatic innovations.

However, the main purpose of Chapter 10 is to examine the role of KIBS in innovation systems. Three different roles are distinguished: KIBS as facilitators (supporting the client in the innovation process), KIBS as carriers (transferring an innovation from a given place to a client) and KIBS as sources of innovation (playing a major role in developing innovation in client firms).

The main conclusion of this chapter is that, in view of the major role they play in transferring, creating and combining knowledge, KIBS should be seen as 'a second knowledge infrastructure', the first being the 'public knowledge infrastructure' made up of research and technology organizations and higher education institutions.

Chapter 11, by Faïz Gallouj, has two main goals. Firstly, it seeks to describe a normal service transaction in terms of the various basic modes of knowledge processing and production used by KIBS firms. The service provider's main activity can be described as the transfer of knowledge from one or several sources to a receiver (the client considered from a different analytical point of view). The term 'transfer' denotes the various interventions of the KIBS provider in the different dimensions of knowledge: its (physical) circulation, its nature (tacit versus codified knowledge), its scope (general versus specific or localized knowledge) and its structure (association and dissociation of knowledge). However, the quality of the previous interventions by the KIBS provider also depends very much on the quality of the sources and the receivers.

Secondly, the chapter seeks to establish the links and boundaries between a normal transaction of this kind and innovation. Two difficulties have to be overcome. Firstly, the same basic knowledge processing mechanisms are mobilized in innovation projects and in normal service transactions. However, this should not lead to the conclusion that all KIBS transactions constitute innovations. Secondly, it is necessary but difficult to distinguish innovation in KIBS from innovation through the use of KIBS, that is the contribution of KIBS providers to innovation in their client organizations. Both forms of innovation draw on the same organizational memory and feed back into the same memory. Moreover, the highly interactive nature of many knowledge-intensive business services disrupts the ownership regimes of certain forms of innovation.

PART I

Productivity and Performances in Services

1. How stagnant are services?

Edward N. Wolff

Traditional measures of productivity growth show very low gains made by service industries since 1979 in the United States. However, other indices of 'technological activity', such as computerization, show that service industries have actually been more technologically active than goods-producing industries over this period. Wolff (1991) called attention to this inconsistency in the case of the insurance industry. This chapter will investigate different indicators of technological activity among goods producers and services. Moreover, it will try to shed some light on this apparent paradox.

As shown in Table 1.1, on the basis of US Bureau of Economic Analysis data on output, labour input and capital stock, conventionally measured total factor productivity (TFP) growth in stagnant services has been virtually zero in the USA since 1979 – indeed, negative, for several service industries (see the Data Appendix for information on measuring TFP). On the other hand, services have invested much more heavily in computerization than goods-producing industries (about triple since 1977). The educational attainment of the workforce and other skill indices are greater in services than goods producers over this period. Moreover, the degree of change in the occupational composition of employment has been almost as great among service industries as in goods industries since 1970.

The first part of the chapter will summarize the underlying 'cost disease' model of the service sector. The next two parts will include descriptive statistics on various indicators of technological activity in service and goods industries over the 1947–97 period in the United States. The indicators in Section 2 include: (1) the change in the skill level of the workforce and (2) the change in the occupational composition of employment. Those in Section 3 include: (3) investment in total equipment per worker; (4) investment in office, computing, and accounting (OCA) equipment per worker; and (5) the change in the average age of capital. The basic data sources for the paper are employment data for 267 occupations and 64 industries which are obtained from the Census of Population for years 1950, 1960, 1970, 1980 and 1990; and National Income and Product Accounts and corresponding wealth and employment data. The level of industry detail is 45 sectors (see Appendix Table A1.1). Section 4 will consider the relation between standard measures of

Table 1.1   Total factor productivity (TFP) growth by major sector, 1947–97
            (Average annual growth in percentage points)

Sector	1947–73	1973–79	1979–97
A. Goods-producing industries			
Agriculture, forestry, and fisheries	1.54	–2.33	5.52
Mining	2.22	–3.41	3.06
Construction	4.00	–4.48	0.49
Manufacturing, durables	1.95	2.19	3.12 ·
Manufacturing, nondurables	0.40	1.07	2.23
B. Progressive services			
Transportation	1.10	0.13	0.88
Communications	2.99	2.94	1.46
Electric, gas and sanitary services	5.35	2.66	0.62
C. Stagnant services			
Wholesale and retail trade	1.08	–1.01	0.86
Finance, insurance and real estate	1.41	0.37	–1.53
General services	0.12	0.25	–0.35
Government and government enterprises	0.59	0.15	–0.03
Total goods and progressive services	2.12	0.25	2.04
Total stagnant services	0.70	0.58	0.07
Total economy (GDP)	1.39	0.38	0.77

Note: See Data Appendix for sources and methods.

productivity growth and these other indicators of technological activity. Concluding remarks are provided in the last section.

1.   BACKGROUND

The cost-disease model, originally developed by Baumol (1967) and later expanded by Baumol et al. (1989), provides the framework for the empirical analysis. Before entering the substance of the discussion, let us first discuss several definitional issues. Generally, a service is defined as an economic activity which yields a product that is not a physical object. Transmission of a telephone call, the litigation of an attorney, and the teaching of a course all have their market prices and are valued by consumers. Each purchaser of such a service may have a good deal to show for the expenditure, but it is not incorporated in a tangible product.

Intangibility of product, however, is probably the *only* attribute common to all services. In particular, there is one way in which they differ from one another that is crucial from the point of view of our analysis, and that is their extreme differences in amenability to productivity growth. Some services, like data processing and telecommunications, are impersonal and electronic and, as shown in Table 1.1, have very high productivity growth. These services with a propensity to rapid productivity growth are referred to as *progressive*, as a description of their technological attributes. Those services for which productivity change is very difficult to achieve are called *stagnant*. Such productivity stagnancy may be virtually endemic to the product (for example, a half-hour string quartet). Or, such a service may be so unstandardized that it is incompatible with mass production methods (for example, medical diagnosis or investigating a legal problem). Or, it may result from the fact that acceptable product quality requires some specifiable minimum labour input (for example, attention by a skilled physician or a teacher). In reality there are gradations between the extreme cases of the progressive and the stagnant services.

The cost-disease model is geared not toward services in general but to stagnant services in particular. The model assumes that the technology (production function) of the stagnant service is fixed over time, while that of the progressive sector (both goods and services) shows rising productivity over time. Several implications follow from this premise. First, if the share of stagnant services in constant dollar GDP is fixed over time, then the share of stagnant services in current dollar GDP will rise continuously over time. Second, the cost and price of stagnant services will rise cumulatively relative to the cost and price of other outputs. Third, stagnant activities will use a share of the economy's labour inputs that grows at a higher rate than the growth in its share of total output.

2.   SKILLS AND OCCUPATIONAL CHANGES

I begin the consideration of alternative indices of technological activity with skill change. I use the fourth (1977) edition of the Dictionary of Occupational Titles (DOT) for my skill measures. For some 12 000 job titles, it provides a variety of alternative measures of job-skill requirements based on data collected between 1966 and 1974. This probably provides the best source of detailed measures of skill requirements covering the period 1950 to 1990. Various measures of workplace skills are developed from this source for each of 267 occupations (see Wolff, 1996, for more details). In this application, I use one of the measures, Substantive Complexity (SC). This is a composite measure of skills derived from a factor analytic test of DOT variables. It was found to be correlated with General Educational Development, Specific Vocational Preparation (training time requirements), Data (synthesizing, coordinating, analysing), and three worker aptitudes – Intelligence (general learning and reasoning ability), Verbal and Numerical.

Table 1.2 shows the average SC scores by major sector over the period from 1950 to 1990 (the periodization is based on data availability). The sectors are divided into two groups. The first includes goods-producing industries and three service sectors transportation, communications and utilities. These service sectors all produce readily measurable output and, in terms of productivity growth, behave very much like the goods producers. The second group are the stagnant sectors. As shown in Table 1.1, these all have had very low (or even negative) productivity growth.

As shown in Table 1.2, cognitive skill levels (SC) are, on average, higher in the stagnant service sector than the goods and progressive services sector. In the 1980–90 period, employees in finance, insurance, and real estate (FIRE) had the highest average SC score (5.25), followed by general services (4.85), communications (4.74) and the government sector (4.61). On the other hand, the growth in mean SC was somewhat higher in goods industries and progressive services (0.53 points) than in stagnant services (0.43 points) between 1950 and 1990. Still SC levels increased in the stagnant service industries as it did among goods producers and progressive services.

On the detailed 45-industry level (see Appendix Table A1.1 for a listing), the five highest ranking industries in terms of SC levels in the 1980s are: professional services and non-profits (5.96), radio and television broadcasting (5.87), insurance (5.51), banking and investment companies (5.41) and educational services (5.32). Of these, four are stagnant services. In terms of the growth of SC over the 1950–90 period, the five highest ranked industries are: tobacco products (1.60), personal services (1.32), insurance (1.02), other transportation equipment (0.93) and banking and investment companies (0.86). Three of the five are stagnant services.

A second measure of worker skill is the mean years of schooling of employees within an industry (see Table 1.3). These are derived directly from decennial Census of Population data for years 1950, 1960, 1970, 1980 and 1990. The pattern is very similar for the mean education of the workforce. Average schooling is higher in stagnant services than the goods and progressive service sector and is led by general services (13.7 in 1980–90), followed by FIRE (13.5), government (13.4) and communications (13.3). The change in mean education over the four decades, as with the change in SC, was larger in the goods and progressive services sector (3.4 years) than in the stagnant service sector (2.6 years).

Table 1.2   Average cognitive skill (substantive complexity) level by period and sector, 1950–90 (period averages)

Sector	1950–60	1960–70	1970–80	1980–90	Change 1950–90
A. Goods industries and progressive services					
Agriculture, forestry and fisheries	3.67	3.64	3.61	3.64	0.01
Mining	3.35	3.71	3.98	4.13	1.02
Construction	3.67	4.02	4.16	4.22	0.80
Manufacturing, durables	3.50	3.71	3.84	3.96	0.65
Manufacturing, nondurables	2.98	3.12	3.34	3.49	0.58
Transportation	3.16	3.25	3.35	3.32	0.11
Communications	4.02	4.26	4.51	4.74	0.93
Electric, gas and sanitary services	3.85	3.87	4.07	4.33	0.56
B. Stagnant services					
Wholesale and retail trade	3.91	3.84	3.88	3.98	0.04
Finance, insurance and real estate	4.63	4.96	5.13	5.25	0.90
General services	4.32	4.46	4.73	4.85	0.52
Government and government enterprises	4.24	4.30	4.46	4.61	0.42
Total goods and progressive services	3.41	3.57	3.73	3.83	0.53
Total stagnant services	4.18	4.26	4.44	4.57	0.43
Total economy	3.78	3.94	4.15	4.30	0.62
Memo: detailed service industries					
32. Wholesale trade	4.05	4.13	4.14	4.22	0.30
33. Retail trade	3.88	3.77	3.82	3.93	−0.01
34. Banking and investment companies	4.71	4.99	5.26	5.41	0.86
35. Insurance	4.94	5.25	5.31	5.51	1.02
36. Real estate	3.98	4.31	4.59	4.66	0.81
37. Hotels, motels and lodging places	2.79	3.04	2.97	3.08	0.71
38. Personal services	2.82	3.10	3.80	4.17	1.32
39. Business and repair services	3.09	2.99	3.55	3.93	0.56
40. Auto services and repair	4.23	4.17	4.17	4.22	−0.02
41. Amusement and recreation services	4.01	4.04	4.30	4.34	0.16
42. Health services and hospitals	5.07	4.49	4.46	4.61	−0.86
43. Educational services	5.51	5.43	5.32	5.32	−0.17
44. Professional services; non-profits	5.91	6.21	6.16	5.96	0.21
45. Public administration	4.24	4.30	4.46	4.62	0.44

Note: Figures for major sectors are weighted averages of individual industries within each major sector.

Sources: See the Data Appendix for sources and methods and Appendix Table A1.1 for detailed sector listing.

Table 1.3   Mean years of education by period and sector, 1950–90
          (period averages)

Sector	1950–60	1960–70	1970–80	1980–90	Change 1950–90
A. Goods industries and progressive services					
Agriculture, forestry and fisheries	8.1	9.1	10.5	11.5	4.02
Mining	9.2	10.4	11.6	12.5	4.21
Construction	9.5	10.3	11.2	12.0	3.11
Manufacturing, durables	10.3	11.0	11.7	12.4	2.90
Manufacturing, nondurables	9.8	10.5	11.3	12.1	3.05
Transportation	9.8	10.6	11.4	12.3	3.21
Communications	11.4	12.0	12.6	13.3	2.52
Electric, gas and sanitary services	10.7	11.2	11.8	12.7	2.79
B. Stagnant services					
Wholesale and retail trade	10.6	11.2	11.9	12.5	2.33
Finance, insurance and real estate	11.8	12.4	13.0	13.5	2.29
General services	11.6	12.3	13.1	13.7	2.72
Government and government enterprises	11.5	12.0	12.7	13.4	2.42
Total goods and progressive services	9.6	10.5	11.4	12.2	3.43
Total stagnant services	11.2	11.9	12.6	13.2	2.60
Total economy	10.4	11.3	12.1	12.9	3.23
Memo: detailed service industries					
32. Wholesale trade	10.9	11.7	12.2	12.8	2.68
33. Retail trade	10.6	11.1	11.8	12.4	2.24
34. Banking and investment companies	12.1	12.5	13.0	13.6	1.84
35. Insurance	12.3	12.7	13.1	13.4	1.33
36. Real estate	10.7	11.7	12.5	13.5	4.06
37. Hotels, motels and lodging places	9.5	10.7	11.4	12.1	3.73
38. Personal services	9.3	10.2	11.4	12.4	3.73
39. Business and repair services	9.8	10.4	11.5	12.5	3.11
40. Auto services and repair	9.7	10.5	11.3	11.9	2.84
41. Amusement and recreation	10.7	11.3	12.2	12.9	2.72
42. Health services and hospitals	13.0	12.6	12.9	13.6	0.68
43. Educational services	13.9	14.4	14.4	14.6	1.54
44. Professional services; non-profits	13.4	13.5	13.8	14.1	0.99
45. Public administration	11.5	12.0	12.7	13.4	2.43

Note: Figures for major sectors are weighted averages of individual industries within each major sector.

Sources: See the Data Appendix for sources and methods and Appendix Table A1.1 for detailed sector listing.

On the detailed 45-industry level, the highest ranking industries in terms of mean schooling levels in the 1980s are: educational services (14.6), professional services and non-profits (14.1), radio and television broadcasting (13.9), banking and investment companies (13.6) and health services, including hospitals (13.6). Again, four of the top five are stagnant services. However, all of the top five industries in terms of the growth in schooling levels are goods producers: coal mining (4.12), real estate (4.06), agriculture, forestry, and fishing (4.02), metal mining (3.91) and lumber and wood products (3.87).

Another dimension of occupational skills is based on the number of 'knowledge producers' in an industry. The basic data are again from the US decennial censuses of 1950, 1960, 1970, 1980 and 1990. In the classification schema, professional and technical workers have generally been classified as knowledge workers, depending on whether they are producers or users of knowledge. Management personnel have been taken to perform both data and knowledge tasks, since they produce new information for administrative decisions and also use and transmit this information (see Baumol et al. 1989, chapter 7, for details on the classification system).

Table 1.4 shows the ratio of knowledge workers to total employment by major sector of the economy. The stagnant service industries as a group are more intensive in their use of knowledge workers than the goods sector, and the leading sector is the government (15.8 per cent in 1980–90), followed by business and other services (14.6 per cent) and FIRE (13.7 per cent). However, the increase in the share of knowledge workers in total employment between 1950 and 1990 was much greater for goods and progressive services industries than stagnant services.

On the 45-industry level, the top industries in terms of the share of knowledge workers over the 1980–90 period are: radio and television broadcasting (43.4 per cent), professional services and non-profits (34.7 per cent), amusement and recreation services (22.8 per cent), other transportation equipment, including aircraft (20.1 per cent), and oil and gas extraction, including petroleum engineers (19.7 per cent). Only two stagnant services appear in the list of the top five. In terms of the growth in the share of knowledge workers over the 1950–90 period, the highest ranking industries are: professional services and non-profits (19.3 per cent), other transportation equipment (15.1 per cent), banking and investment companies (11.0 per cent), telephone and telegraph (11.0 per cent), and oil and gas extraction (10.4 per cent). Once again, only two of the top five are stagnant services.

Another indicator of technological change within an industry is the degree to which the occupational structure shifts over time. For this, I employ an index of similarity. First define:

Table 1.4   *Knowledge workers as a percentage of total employment by*
             major sector and period, 1950–90 (period averages)

Sector	1950–60	1960–70	1970–80	1980–90	Change 1950–90
A. Goods industries and progressive services					
Agriculture, forestry and fisheries	0.7	1.6	2.8	3.5	3.1
Mining	6.0	9.0	11.5	13.7	10.3
Construction	6.0	7.4	7.7	8.9	5.2
Manufacturing, durables	7.0	9.4	10.9	12.2	7.3
Manufacturing, nondurables	5.9	6.8	7.9	9.3	4.5
Transportation	4.5	5.0	5.3	5.9	2.0
Communications	10.1	12.3	15.4	19.6	12.7
Electric, gas and sanitary services	8.7	8.8	10.3	12.9	5.4
B. Stagnant services					
Wholesale and retail trade	9.3	7.5	8.2	10.0	0.1
Finance, insurance, and real estate	9.9	10.6	11.4	13.7	6.2
General services	11.5	11.8	13.1	14.6	3.7
Government and government enterprises	12.1	12.8	14.7	15.8	3.7
Total goods and progressive services	5.3	7.2	8.6	10.0	6.4
Total stagnant services	10.6	10.2	11.4	13.1	2.8
Total economy	7.8	8.8	10.3	11.9	5.4
Memo: detailed service industries					
32. Wholesale trade	10.3	9.3	9.3	10.4	0.4
33. Retail trade	9.0	7.0	7.9	9.9	0.0
34. Banking and investment companies	12.6	14.6	16.1	19.5	11.0
35. Insurance	10.8	9.9	9.5	11.2	1.6
36. Real estate	3.8	3.7	5.1	6.1	1.8
37. Hotels, motels and lodging places	6.0	8.2	8.1	8.0	4.2
38. Personal services	6.4	6.5	8.6	11.1	5.3
39. Business and repair services	11.3	10.3	13.2	16.8	5.0
40. Auto services and repair	5.3	5.5	4.7	4.6	0.4
41. Amusement and recreation services	20.4	20.3	23.7	22.8	−2.0
42. Health services and hospitals	8.9	2.5	3.3	4.5	−10.4
43. Educational services	15.3	14.4	14.2	14.4	−1.5
44. Professional services; non-profits	24.0	32.0	33.0	34.7	19.3
45. Public administration	12.1	12.8	14.7	15.9	3.9

Note: Figures are based on aggregate employment within each major sector.

Sources: See the Data Appendix for sources and methods and Appendix Table A1.1 for detailed sector listing.

M = occupation-by-industry employment coefficient matrix, where m_{ij} shows the employment of occupation i in industry j as a share of total employment in industry j.

The employment data, as indicated above, are for 267 occupations and 64 industries and are obtained from the decennial Census of Population for years 1950, 1960, 1970, 1980 and 1990. The similarity index for industry j between two time periods 1 and 2 is given by:

$$SI^{12} = \frac{\Sigma_i m^1{}_{ij} m^2{}_{ij}}{[\Sigma_i \, (m^1{}_{ij})^2 \, \Sigma_i \, (m^2{}_{ij})^2]^{1/2}} \tag{1.1}$$

The index SI is the cosine between the two vectors s^{t1} and s^{t2} and varies from 0 – the two vectors are orthogonal – to 1 – the two vectors are identical. The index of occupational dissimilarity, DI, is defined as:

$$DI^{12} = 1 - SI^{12} \tag{1.2}$$

where a greater value of the index DI indicates more dissimilarity between the two vectors.

Results for DI are shown in Table 1.5. The DI index for the total economy, after rising slightly from 0.050 in the 1950–60 period to 0.056 in the 1960–70 decade, dropped to 0.019 in the 1970s but then surged to 0.095 in the 1980s, its highest level of the four decades. These results confirm anecdotal evidence about the substantial degree of industrial restructuring during the 1980s. Similar patterns are evident for the major sectors as well. In fact, seven out of the twelve major sectors experienced their most rapid degree of occupational change during the 1980s. The three sectors that experienced the greatest occupational restructuring over the four decades are utilities (0.101), FIRE (0.068) and communications (0.066). Occupational change was particularly low in agriculture (0.005), coal mining (0.028), transportation (0.029) and construction (0.031).

On the 45-industry level, the five highest ranking industries in terms of DI over the 1980–90 period are: amusement and recreation services (0.186), chemicals and allied products (0.172), professional services and non-profits (0.171), business and repair services, except automotive (0.167) and radio and television broadcasting (0.150). Of these, three are stagnant services.

Table 1.5   Dissimilarity index (DI) *of the distribution of occupational employment by major sector, 1950–90*

Sector	1950–60	1960–70	1970–80	1980–90	Change 1950–90
A. Goods Industries and Progressive Services					
Agriculture, forestry and fisheries	0.000	0.001	0.001	0.017	0.005
Mining	0.022	0.025	0.020	0.045	0.028
Construction	0.040	0.025	0.005	0.053	0.031
Manufacturing, durables	0.100	0.039	0.014	0.096	0.062
Manufacturing, nondurables	0.077	0.050	0.023	0.088	0.060
Transportation	0.030	0.024	0.014	0.048	0.029
Communications	0.032	0.061	0.043	0.128	0.066
Electric, gas and sanitary services	0.078	0.169	0.053	0.105	0.101
B. Stagnant services					
Wholesale and retail trade	0.026	0.019	0.029	0.078	0.038
Finance, insurance and real estate	0.043	0.117	0.033	0.080	0.068
General services	0.061	0.091	0.029	0.047	0.057
Government and government enterprise	0.046	0.054	0.042	0.045	0.047
Total goods and progressive services	0.063	0.061	0.014	0.110	0.062
Total stagnant services	0.022	0.056	0.026	0.077	0.045
Total economy	0.050	0.056	0.019	0.095	0.055
Memo: detailed service industries					
32. Wholesale trade	0.428	0.032	0.010	0.117	0.146
33. Retail trade	0.057	0.018	0.034	0.064	0.043
34. Banking and investment companies	0.278	0.297	0.043	0.061	0.170
35. Insurance	0.095	0.037	0.012	0.075	0.055
36. Real estate	0.080	0.016	0.009	0.110	0.054
37. Hotels, motels and lodging places	0.829	0.030	0.027	0.143	0.257
38. Personal services	0.043	0.096	0.130	0.049	0.080
39. Business and repair services	0.097	0.019	0.098	0.167	0.095
40. Auto services and repair	0.009	0.007	0.002	0.019	0.009
41. Amusement and recreation services	0.074	0.183	0.013	0.186	0.114
42. Health services and hospitals	0.536	0.020	0.008	0.011	0.144
43. Educational services	0.117	0.009	0.005	0.004	0.034
44. Professional services; non-profits	0.677	0.047	0.029	0.171	0.231
45. Public administration	0.050	0.054	0.042	0.050	0.049

Note: Figures are based on aggregate employment within each major sector.

Sources: See the Data Appendix for sources and methods and Appendix Table A1.1 for detailed sector listing.

3.   EQUIPMENT INVESTMENT AND CAPITAL VINTAGE

I next consider the investment activity of goods and service industries. As shown in Table 1.6, average annual investment in equipment, machinery and instruments (including OCA) per person engaged in production (PEP) was much higher among the goods and progressive service sectors than among stagnant services – triple overall. The two leading sectors in the 1987–96 period are progressive services – utilities ($34 300) and communications ($27 000) – followed by coal mining ($14 600). The FIRE sector ($10 700) ranked fourth overall. However, the growth in equipment investment per PEP between the 1947–56 and the 1987–96 periods was higher among stagnant services (ratio of 3.6) than in the goods and progressive services sector (ratio of 2.5).

On the more detailed 45-industry level, the five leading sectors in terms of investment in equipment per PEP in the 1987–96 period are all goods producers or progressive services: utilities ($34 300), telephone and telegraph ($31 090), petroleum and coal products ($30 130), metal mining ($21 390), and coal mining ($17 540). However, in terms of growth between the 1947–56 and the 1987–96 periods, the top two industries are both stagnant services – banking and investment companies (ratio of 15.9) and insurance (14.8) – followed by coal mining (10.6), radio and television broadcasting (7.6) and telephone and telegraph (6.8).

The next indicator is average annual investment in office, computing and accounting equipment (OCA) per PEP. As shown in Table 1.7, investment in OCA per PEP grew by a factor of 24 between the 1947–56 and the 1987–96 periods, from $20 (in 1992 dollars) per PEP to $485. Indeed, by 1997, it had reached $2178 per worker. By the 1987–96 period, the most OCA-intensive sector by far was FIRE, at $2571 per employee, followed by utilities ($1468) and communications ($1060). Wholesale and retail trade was a distant fourth ($669). On the whole, the stagnant service sector has been investing more intensively in computer equipment than the goods and progressive service sector (a three-fold difference by the 1987–96 period). Moreover, the former's average annual investment in OCA per worker grew by a factor of 36 between the 1947–56 and the 1987–96 periods, compared to a nine-fold increase for the latter.

On the 45-industry level, the leading industries in terms of investment in OCA per worker in the 1987–96 period are: banking and investment companies ($3290), petroleum and coal products ($2201), insurance ($2060), wholesale trade ($1943) and real estate ($1808). Four out of the five are stagnant services. In terms of the growth in investment in OCA per PEP between the 1947–56 and the 1987–96 periods, the top two sectors are stagnant services – wholesale trade (ratio of 69.5) and personal services (63.8) – followed by

Table 1.6   *Annual investment in equipment, machinery and instruments per person engaged in production (PEP), 1947–97 (thousands, 1992 dollars, period averages)*

Sector	1947–56	1957–66	1967–76	1977–86	1987–96	Ratio of 1987–96 to 1947–56
A. Goods Industries and Progressive Services						
Agriculture, forestry and fisheries	2.4	3.2	7.0	7.6	7.7	3.2
Mining	3.7	6.8	11.1	11.1	14.6	3.9
Construction	2.0	2.0	2.3	1.9	1.6	0.8
Manufacturing, durables	1.8	1.9	2.9	3.0	3.3	1.8
Manufacturing, nondurables	2.0	2.2	3.5	4.3	5.4	2.7
Transportation	4.0	4.9	7.6	8.2	7.3	1.8
Communications	4.4	7.7	13.8	22.0	27.0	6.2
Electric, gas and sanitary services	10.9	12.8	22.4	30.5	34.3	3.2
B. Stagnant services						
Wholesale and retail trade	0.7	0.9	1.3	1.8	2.4	3.3
Finance, insurance and real estate	2.6	2.8	4.6	6.5	10.7	4.1
General services	0.7	1.0	1.5	1.4	1.7	2.5
Total goods and progressive services	2.5	3.0	4.8	5.6	6.2	2.5
Total stagnant services (except government)	0.6	0.8	1.2	1.6	2.3	3.6
Total economy (except government)	1.6	1.8	2.6	3.0	3.5	2.2
Memo: detailed service industries						
32. Wholesale trade	9.6	12.3	22.1	38.9	55.7	5.8
33. Retail trade	6.2	7.2	9.7	10.6	12.8	2.1
34. Banking and investment companies	7.9	10.0	35.4	70.8	124.8	15.9
35. Insurance	4.4	4.1	7.0	31.9	65.0	14.8
36. Real estate	80.6	101.4	129.7	102.1	127.9	1.6
37. Hotels, motels and lodging places	3.6	7.9	10.9	13.9	11.8	3.3
38. Personal services	1.4	3.2	6.1	6.2	6.4	4.6
39. Business and repair services	12.6	19.9	37.4	16.9	28.0	2.2
40. Auto services and repair	89.0	67.5	89.1	96.5	101.7	1.1
41. Amusement and recreation services	20.2	27.6	35.5	26.2	24.8	1.2
42. Health services and hospitals	5.4	5.5	6.9	7.2	10.3	1.9
43. Educational services	9.9	9.4	9.8	22.9	29.8	3.0
44. Professional services; non–profits	1.5	1.1	0.6	2.3	1.9	1.3

Note: Data on equipment investment is not available for the government sector.

Sources: See the Data Appendix for sources and methods and Appendix Table A1.1 for detailed sector listing.

Table 1.7   *Annual investment in office, computing, and accounting*
equipment (OCA) per persons engaged in production (PEP),
1947–97 (1992 dollars, period averages)

Sector	1947–56	1957–66	1967–76	1977–86	1987–96	Ratio 1987–96 to 1947–56
A. Goods industries and progressive services						
Agriculture, forestry and fisheries	0	0	1	2	2	54.7
Mining	6	29	37	36	52	9.2
Construction	5	8	5	4	4	0.7
Manufacturing, durables	38	41	56	62	72	1.9
Manufacturing, nondurables	26	27	31	80	361	14.1
Transportation	40	44	27	51	115	2.9
Communications	42	49	42	176	1060	25.1
Electric, gas and sanitary services	39	51	32	414	1468	37.9
B. Stagnant services						
Wholesale and retail trade	12	17	27	213	669	55.8
Finance, insurance and real estate	110	153	252	861	2571	23.4
General services	16	23	23	87	459	28.7
Total goods and progressive services	23	28	33	63	202	8.7
Total stagnant services (except government)	17	24	36	175	607	35.9
Total economy (except government)	20	26	35	136	485	24.1
Memo: detailed service industries						
32. Wholesale trade	28	41	79	677	1943	69.5
33. Retail trade	6	8	7	45	233	36.0
34. Banking and investment companies	98	146	303	1247	3290	33.7
35. Insurance	140	161	212	620	2060	14.7
36. Real estate	80	153	216	414	1808	22.5
37. Hotels, motels and lodging places	4	9	8	36	71	19.1
38. Personal services	1	2	2	20	72	63.8
39. Business and repair services	41	41	44	210	1408	34.6
40. Auto services and repair	73	52	17	222	503	6.9
41. Amusement and recreation services	20	24	16	127	300	14.7
42. Health services and hospitals	10	10	6	21	145	14.9
43. Educational services	86	148	145	238	1012	11.8
44. Professional services; non-profits	8	11	10	21	72	9.5

Note: Data on investment in OCA is not available for the government sector.

Sources: See the Data Appendix for sources and methods and Appendix Table A1.1 for detailed sector listing.

three goods producers – agriculture, forestry, and fishing (54.7), leather and leather products (43.6) and paper and allied products (38.8).

Another indicator of investment activity is the change in the average age of capital. The vintage model assumes that new capital is more productive than old capital per (constant) dollar of expenditure. As a result, productivity growth should be greater when the average age of capital is dropping more (or growing less).

There is a clear relation between the change in the overall average age of capital and aggregate TFP growth in the time-series data. Over the period from 1947 to 1973, when TFP growth averaged 1.4 per cent per year, the average age of equipment declined from 7.6 to 6.4 years. Indeed, it bottomed out in 1973. From 1973 to 1997, when the annual average rate of TFP growth was 0.6 per cent, the average age of equipment rose from 6.4 to 7.1 years. Likewise, the average age of structures fell by 6.0 years from 1947 to 1973 but increased by 0.2 years from 1973 to 1997.

The cross-industry association is more mixed. During the 1947–57 period, the average age of equipment declined in both the goods and progressive service sector and stagnant services and to about the same degree (see Table 1.8); in the 1957–67 period, it declined in the former but increased in the latter; in the 1967–77 period, it increased in both sectors but much more among the stagnant services; in the 1977–87 period, it increased in the goods and progressive service sector but declined in the stagnant service sector; and in the 1987–97 period, it increased in both sectors and to about the same degree. In both the 1947–57 and the 1957–67 periods, the largest decline in the average age of equipment occurred in transportation; in the 1967–77 period, in agriculture; in the 1977–87 period, in FIRE; and in the 1987–97 period, in agriculture. On the 45-industry level, the largest declines in the average age of equipment over the 1987–97 period were recorded by metal mining (–2.10 years), amusement and recreation services (–1.82), agriculture, forestry, and fisheries (–0.98), business and repair services, except auto (–0.97) and construction (–0.90). Of these, two are stagnant services.

During both the 1947–57 and 1957–67 periods, the average age of structures fell in both the goods and progressive service sector and the stagnant service sector but to a greater extent in the latter (see Table 1.9); in the 1967–77 period, it fell in the former but increased in the latter; in the 1977–87 period, it declined in both sectors but much more among stagnant services; and in the 1987–97 period, it increased in both sectors but less among stagnant services. During the 1947–57 period, the greatest decline in the average age of structures occurred in durable manufacturing; in the 1957–67 period, in construction; in the 1967–77 period, in agriculture; in the 1977–87 period, in FIRE; and in the 1987–97 period, it rose least in general services. On the

Table 1.8 Change in the average age of equipment, 1947–97 (figures are in years)

Sector	1947–57	1957–67	1967–77	1977–87	1987–97
A. Goods industries and progressive services					
Agriculture, forestry and fisheries	0.80	0.01	−0.26	2.42	−0.98
Mining	−0.02	−0.36	0.09	1.06	1.78
Construction	0.45	−0.22	0.50	1.30	−0.90
Manufacturing, durables	−0.35	−0.09	0.58	0.58	0.57
Manufacturing, nondurables	1.10	−0.49	−0.25	0.99	−0.01
Transportation	−1.45	−1.56	0.00	0.20	−0.70
Communications	0.41	0.20	0.63	0.71	0.08
Electric, gas and sanitary services	−1.09	1.44	0.30	−0.30	2.00
B. Stagnant services					
Wholesale and retail trade	−0.03	−0.59	0.17	−0.38	0.09
Finance, insurance and real estate	−0.08	0.50	0.02	−0.55	0.87
General services	−0.99	0.43	0.55	0.52	−0.45
Total goods and progressive services	−0.42	−0.45	0.03	0.72	0.26
Total stagnant services (except government)	−0.44	0.01	0.26	−0.19	0.25
Total economy (except government)	−0.56	−0.49	−0.04	0.21	−0.08
Memo: detailed service industries					
32. Wholesale trade	0.45	−1.00	0.40	−0.40	0.10
33. Retail trade	−0.27	−0.33	0.10	−0.20	0.20
34. Banking and investment companies	−0.58	−1.27	0.97	0.33	1.31
35. Insurance	−0.55	−0.10	−0.47	−0.24	1.25
36. Real estate	−0.09	0.67	0.60	−0.50	0.20
37. Hotels, motels and lodging places	−2.91	−0.22	1.00	0.20	1.00
38. Personal services	−0.36	0.33	0.60	0.70	−0.20
39. Business and repair services	−2.00	−0.22	1.20	1.36	−0.97
40. Auto services and repair	0.27	1.11	0.40	0.00	−0.70
41. Amusement and recreation services	−0.65	0.46	0.11	1.78	−1.82
42. Health services and hospitals	−0.27	0.78	−0.20	0.40	0.10
43. Educational services	−1.18	0.44	2.20	−1.20	1.20
44. Professional services; non-profits	−0.74	0.15	−0.42	0.03	0.81

Note: Figures are for private non-residential capital stock. For major sectors, they are weighted averages of individual industries within each major sector, with total stock of equipment used as weights. Data on average age of capital are not available for the government and government enterprises sectors.

Table 1.9   Change in the average age of structures, 1947–97 (figures are in years)

Sector	1947–57	1957–67	1967–77	1977–87	1987–97
A. Goods industries and progressive services					
Agriculture, forestry and fisheries	–3.10	–2.80	–1.32	2.75	4.75
Mining	–2.73	0.75	0.96	–1.15	3.56
Construction	–1.91	–5.56	–0.60	5.20	5.70
Manufacturing, durables	–4.58	–3.48	0.16	1.85	1.91
Manufacturing, nondurables	–0.03	–1.42	–0.53	2.43	2.38
Transportation	4.27	5.78	2.00	2.30	1.80
Communications	–2.23	–0.44	–0.93	–0.31	1.52
Electric, gas and sanitary services	–3.73	0.44	0.00	1.60	3.00
B. Stagnant services					
Wholesale and retail trade	–1.92	–4.65	–1.00	–0.63	1.32
Finance, insurance, and real estate	–3.81	–4.81	0.69	–1.43	1.83
General services	–1.95	–3.56	0.94	–0.20	0.84
Total goods and progressive services	–2.10	–1.09	–1.50	–0.19	2.09
Total stagnant services (except government)	–3.07	–4.61	0.33	–1.03	1.54
Total economy (except government)	–2.53	–2.76	–1.22	–1.09	1.32
Memo: detailed service industries					
32. Wholesale trade	–2.82	–2.00	1.20	0.10	4.10
33. Retail trade	–1.27	–4.44	–1.20	–0.10	–0.40
34. Banking and investment companies	–4.20	–4.31	–0.31	–2.28	1.49
35. Insurance	–4.81	–2.81	0.55	–3.46	1.45
36. Real estate	–3.73	–4.89	0.90	–0.90	2.20
37. Hotels, motels, and lodging places	0.45	–5.33	2.20	0.30	1.30
38. Personal services	–1.91	–0.67	0.90	3.40	1.10
39. Business and repair services	–1.19	–2.21	–3.03	–4.99	1.99
40. Auto services and repair	–4.36	1.33	2.30	1.50	0.70
41. Amusement and recreation services	1.53	–1.08	0.79	–2.64	–3.31
42. Health services and hospitals	–7.45	–2.22	3.60	–1.40	1.60
43. Educational services	–2.27	–1.89	–13.50	2.60	0.70
44. Professional services; non-profits	–8.16	–1.63	0.49	3.90	3.54

Note: Figures are for private non-residential capital stock. For major sectors, they are weighted averages of individual industries within each major sector, with total stock of structures used as weights. Data on average age of capital are not available for the government and government enterprises sectors.

detailed 45-industry level, the greatest declines (smallest increases) in the average age of structures during the 1987–97 period are found in stagnant services – amusement and recreation services (–3.31 years), radio and television broadcasting (–0.90), retail trade (–0.40), auto services and repair (0.70) and educational services (0.70).

4. PRODUCTIVITY GROWTH AND TECHNOLOGY INDICATORS

The last piece of analysis considers the relation between standard measures of productivity growth and other indicators of technological activity. On the surface, it appears that the two are very loosely connected, since stagnant services show up very low in terms of conventional productivity growth but quite high according to some of these other indicators.

Table 1.10 presents comparisons between TFP growth and skill measures. The goods and progressive service sector led the stagnant service sector in TFP growth in each of the four decades from 1950 to 1990, except for the 1970s, when there was a virtual tie. However, the stagnant service sector scored higher than the goods sector in every decade in terms of the average level of cognitive skills, the mean schooling level and the share of knowledge workers. Cognitive skill levels did increase somewhat faster in the goods sector, though this was not uniform across decades. On the other hand, mean schooling rose noticeably more in the goods sector than the stagnant service sector in each of the four decades. The share of knowledge workers in the goods sector grew considerably faster than in the stagnant service sector in the 1950s and 1960s and over the full 40 years, though it expanded more slowly in the 1970s and at about the same rate in the 1980s. The *DI* index was greater for the goods sector than for stagnant services in the 1950s, in the 1980s, and over the four decades, though it was smaller in the 1970s and about the same in the 1960s.

Table 1.11 presents figures for investment activity. Annual equipment investment per worker was much higher in the goods and progressive service sector in each of the ten-year periods between 1947 and 1997, while investment in OCA per worker was much higher in the stagnant service sector over the full 50 years and particularly in the 1977–87 and the 1987–97 periods. Changes in the average age of equipment were more negative (or less positive) in the stagnant service sector than in the goods sector over the full 50 years and in three of the five ten-year periods. Likewise, changes in the average age of structures were more negative (or less positive) among the stagnant services over the half century between 1947 and 1997 and in four of the five ten-year periods.

Table 1.10   TFP growth and changes in skills and occupational composition in the goods and service sectors, 1950–90

Indicator	1950–60	1960–70	1970–80	1980–90	1950–90
1. Average annual percentage TFP growth					
Total goods and progressive services	2.17	1.51	0.21	2.04	1.48
Total stagnant services	0.94	0.79	0.23	0.12	0.52
Difference: goods sector – services	1.23	0.72	−0.03	1.92	0.96
2. Mean cognitive skill (SC) level					
Total goods and progressive services	3.41	3.57	3.73	3.83	3.63
Total stagnant services	4.18	4.26	4.44	4.57	4.37
Difference: goods sector – services	−0.77	−0.69	−0.72	−0.74	−0.74
3. Change in mean cognitive skills (SC)					
Total goods and progressive services	0.09	0.22	0.10	0.11	0.53
Total stagnant services	−0.06	0.23	0.14	0.12	0.43
Difference: goods sector – services	0.15	0.00	−0.04	0.00	0.10
4. Mean years of schooling					
Total goods and progressive services	9.59	10.51	11.43	12.23	10.89
Total stagnant services	11.20	11.88	12.62	13.23	12.20
Difference: goods sector – services	−1.61	−1.37	−1.19	−1.00	−1.31
5. Change in mean years of schooling					
Total goods and progressive services	1.01	0.85	1.01	0.57	3.44
Total stagnant services	0.71	0.65	0.81	0.42	2.60
Difference: goods sector – services	0.30	0.19	0.19	0.15	0.84
6. Knowledge workers as a percentage of total employment					
Total goods and progressive services	5.30	7.20	8.60	10.00	7.70
Total stagnant services	10.60	10.20	11.40	13.10	11.60
Difference: goods sector – services	−5.30	−3.00	−2.70	−3.20	−3.80
7. Change in knowledge workers / employment					
Total goods and progressive services	1.70	2.13	0.76	1.85	6.44
Total stagnant services	−1.37	0.66	1.68	1.84	2.80
Difference: goods sector – services	3.07	1.48	−0.92	0.02	3.64

Indicator	1950–60	1960–70	1970–80	1980–90	1950–90
8. Dissimilarity index (DI) for occupations					
Total goods and progressive services	0.063	0.061	0.014	0.110	0.248
Total stagnant services	0.022	0.056	0.026	0.077	0.181
Difference: goods sector – services	0.041	0.005	–0.012	0.033	0.067

Note: Statistics are computed for 31 goods and progressive service industries, 14 stagnant service industries, and 45 total industries.

5. CONCLUDING REMARKS

The upshot of the chapter is that so-called stagnant services, as portrayed in the standard cost-disease model, are *not* technologically inert. Though these industries show up with close to zero productivity growth, they are very active and have undergone major change over time by other technological indices. Indeed, by some of the indices (mean skills, mean schooling, share of knowledge workers, investment in OCA and age of capital) these sectors are more technologically active than goods producers or progressive services. The production function for these services does not remain fixed over time.

It still remains to resolve whether the poorer productivity performance of services in recent years is due to the fact that its output is becoming increasingly more difficult to measure. It should be noted from Tables 1.1, 1.10, and 1.11 that the aggregate performance of stagnant services in terms of TFP growth was reasonably strong before 1970 or so. Moreover, both services and goods industries suffered major declines in productivity growth in the 1970s. The major difference between the two sectors is that while productivity growth recovered in goods industries after 1980, it failed to do so in services.

The distinguishing features of service industries in the post-1980 period are both the high rate of computerization and the high degree of employment restructuring. It is likely that both are associated with a more heterogeneous output. The high degree of computerization found in finance, for example, has been responsible for the creation of a bewildering array of new financial products. The same appears to characterize the insurance industry and business services. Likewise, the fact that the degree of employment restructuring increased substantially between the 1970s and 1980s might be associated with an increasing variety of service products. It is possible that the more heterogeneous output has made service output harder to measure over time, and thus the low productivity growth of services after 1980 is a measurement problem.

There are two other possible explanations. The first of these might reflect the high adjustment costs associated with the introduction of new technology.

Productivity and performances in services

Table 1.11   TFP growth and investment activity in the goods and service sectors, 1947–97

Indicator	1947–57	1957–67	1967–77	1977–87	1987–97	1947–97
1. Average annual percentage TFP growth						
Goods and progressive services	2.01	2.11	0.66	1.04	2.12	1.59
Stagnant services	1.86	0.89	0.49	0.04	0.30	0.72
Difference: goods – services	0.16	1.23	0.18	1.00	1.81	0.87
2. Annual equipment investment per PEP (1000s, 1992 dollars)						
Goods and progressive services	2.5	3.0	4.8	5.6	6.2	4.4
Stagnant services	0.6	0.8	1.2	1.6	2.3	1.3
Difference: goods – services	1.9	2.2	3.5	4.0	3.9	3.1
3. Annual OCA investment per PEP (1992 dollars)						
Goods and progressive services	23.3	28.2	32.7	62.6	201.5	69.7
Stagnant services	16.9	24.1	35.8	174.5	607.5	171.8
Difference: goods – services	6.3	4.1	–3.1	–111.9	–406.0	–102.1
4. Change in the average age of equipment (years)						
Goods and progressive services	–0.42	–0.45	0.03	0.72	0.26	0.14
Stagnant services	–0.44	0.01	0.26	–0.19	0.25	–0.11
Difference: goods – services	0.02	–0.46	–0.23	0.91	0.02	0.25
5. Change in the average age of structures (years)						
Goods and progressive services	–2.10	–1.09	–1.50	–0.19	2.09	–2.78
Stagnant services	–3.07	–4.61	0.33	–1.03	1.54	–6.84
Difference: goods – services	0.97	3.52	–1.83	0.84	0.56	4.06

Note: Statistics are computed for 31 goods and progressive service industries, 13 stagnant service industries (excluding the government sector) and 45 total industries.

The paradigmatic shift from electromechanical automation to information technologies (IT) might require major changes in the organizational structure of companies before the new technology can be realized in the form of measured productivity gains (see, David, 1991, for greater elaboration of this argument). Some confirmation of this hypothesis is provided by Brynjolfsson and Hitt (1998), for example, who find that computerization has a positive effect on firm-level productivity only as long as there are concomitant changes in firm organization. According to this line of argument, productivity growth of the so-called stagnant services should increase to more normal levels in the future as the IT revolution is realized.

The second explanation is that service providers are now able to use this new technology to expand profits in other ways besides augmenting productivity. In particular, services may be employing IT for product differentiation rather than productivity enhancement. For example, they can now customize their products for a larger array of potential clients. Computers allow for greater diversification of products, which, in turn, also allows for greater price discrimination (for example, airline pricing systems) and the ability to extract a large portion of consumer surplus. Greater product diversity might increase firm profits, though not necessarily its productivity. Some evidence on the production differentiation effects of computers is provided by Chakraborty and Kazarosian (1999) for the US trucking industry (for example, speed of delivery versus average load). If this is the case, then the low productivity growth measured for the stagnant services might persist into the indefinite future.

DATA APPENDIX

1. NIPA employee compensation: figures are from the National Income and Product Accounts (NIPA), available on the Internet, http://www.bea. doc.gov/bea/dnz/. Employee compensation includes wages and salaries and employee benefits.
2. NIPA employment data: persons engaged in production (PEP) equals the number of full-time and part-time employees plus the number of self-employed persons. Unpaid family workers are not included.
3. Capital stock figures are based on chain-type quantity indexes for net stock of fixed capital in 1992 dollars, year-end estimates. Average age of capital by type of equipment or structures are for the private (non-government) sector only. Source: US Bureau of Economic Analysis, CD-ROM, 'Fixed Reproducible Tangible Wealth of the United States, 1925–97'.
4. Total factor productivity growth (TFPGRTH) for sector j is defined as:

$$TFPGRTH_j \equiv \pi_j = Y^*_j - \alpha_j L^*_j - (1 - \alpha_j)K^*_j,$$

where Y^*_j is the annual rate of output growth, L^*_j is the annual growth in labour input, and K^*_j is the annual growth in capital input in sector j, and α_j is the average share of employee compensation in GDP over the period in sector j (the Tornqvist-Divisia index). I measure the labour input using Persons Engaged in Production (PEP) and the capital input by the fixed non-residential net capital stock (1992 dollars).

Appendix Table A1.1   45–sector industry classification

Industry number	1987 SIC codes
1. Agriculture, forestry and fishing	01–09
2. Metal mining	10
3. Coal mining	11, 12
4. Oil and gas extraction	13
5. Mining of nonmetallic minerals, except fuels	14
6. Construction	15–17
7. Food and kindred products	20
8. Tobacco products	21
9. Textile mill products	22
10. Apparel and other textile products	23
11. Lumber and wood products	24
12. Furniture and fixtures	25
13. Paper and allied products	26
14. Printing and publishing	27
15. Chemicals and allied products	28
16. Petroleum and coal products	29
17. Rubber and miscellaneous plastic products	30
18. Leather and leather products	31
19. Stone, clay, and glass products	32
20. Primary metal products	33
21. Fabricated metal products, including ordnance	34
22. Industrial machinery and equipment, excluding electrical	35
23. Electric and electronic equipment	36
24. Motor vehicles and equipment	371
25. Other transportation equipment	37 [exc. 371]
26. Instruments and related products	38
27. Miscellaneous manufactures	39
28. Transportation	40–42, 44–47

Industry number	1987 SIC codes
29. Telephone and telegraph	481, 482, 484, 489
30. Radio and TV broadcasting	483
31. Electric, gas and sanitary services	49
32. Wholesale trade	50–51
33. Retail trade	52–59
34. Banking; credit and investment companies	60–62, 67
35. Insurance	63–64
36. Real estate	65–66
37. Hotels, motels and lodging places	70
38. Personal services	72
39. Business and repair services except auto	73, 76
40. Auto services and repair	75
41. Amusement and recreation services	78–79
42. Health services, including hospitals	80
43. Educational services	82
44. Legal and other professional services and non-profit organizations	81, 83, 84, 86, 87, 89
45. Public Administration	–

REFERENCES

Baumol, William J. (1967), 'Macroeconomics of Unbalanced Growth: The Anatomy of Urban Crisis', *American Economic Review*, **57**(3), 415–26.

Baumol, William J., Sue Anne Batey Blackman and Edward N. Wolff (1989), *Productivity and American Leadership: The Long View* (Cambridge, MA: MIT Press).

Brynjolfsson, Eric and Lorin Hitt (1998), 'Information Technology and Organizational Design: Evidence from Micro Data', mimeo, MIT Sloan School, January.

Chakraborty, Arreya and Mark Kazarosian (1999), 'Product Differentiation and the Use of Information Technology: Evidence from the Trucking Industry', NBER Working Paper 7222, July.

David, Paul A. (1991), 'Computer and Dynamo: The Modern Productivity Paradox in a Not-Too-Distant Mirror', in *Technology and Productivity: The Challenge for Economic Policy* (Paris, France: OECD), pp. 315–48.

U.S. Department of Labor. *Dictionary of Occupational Titles*, 4th edn. Washington, D.C. Government Printing Office, 1977.

Wolff, Edward N. (1991), 'Productivity Growth, Capital Intensity, and Skill Levels in the U.S. Insurance Industry, 1948–86', *Geneva Papers on Risk and Insurance*, **16**(59), 173–90.

Wolff, Edward N. (1996), 'Technology and the Demand for Skills', *OECD Science, Technology and Industry Review*, 18, 96–123.

2. The misuse of productivity concepts in services: lessons from a comparison between France and the United States

Jean Gadrey

This chapter summarizes the findings of a research project carried out between 1989 and 1992 in close cooperation with Thierry Noyelle and Thomas Stanback of Columbia University. The aim of the project was to compare productivity in services in France and the United States, and in particular to ascertain whether productivity in services was indeed weaker and productivity gains lower in the United States than in France and whether this could explain the very high levels of job creation in the American service sector and the relatively modest levels in France. This interpretation was very widespread in the early 1990s and is still advanced today. According to our findings, this explanation is, for the most part, an illusion and the main answers to the question are conceptual and method-ological in nature. Furthermore, by showing the limits of the traditional concepts in the case of an international comparison, useful pointers can be gleaned as to how to interpret the so-called 'productivity paradox' in each country.

Why to publish, ten years later, a synthesis of these findings? Because almost nothing changed during the 1990s, either on the conceptual issue, or on that of the productivity trends: the average annual productivity gains in services (as actually measured) remained very low and sometimes negative in the United States during the 1990s,[1] and they were lower than in France. The statistical methods of the BLS (Bureau of Labour Statistics) and the BEA (Bureau of Economic Analysis) (or INSEE (Institut National de la statistique et des Etudes Economiques) in France) evolved, but the main part of the improvements concerned durable goods, computers, software, housing and so on, with few or no changes for the services raising the most serious concep-tual issues.

In February 1999, Edwin Dean published a paper in the *Monthly Labor Review*, p. 27 entitled 'The Accuracy of the BLS Productivity Measures'. His judgement was that existing data, showing 'a negative multifactor productivity growth in so many industries over a period of 15 years seems implausible. There is probably something wrong . . . it appears likely that for some industries with questionable productivity trends, the problem originates with faulty output series'.[2]

The five comparative case studies which I carried out with Thierry Noyelle and Thomas Stanback shed some light on this puzzle. These five industries are retailing, eating and drinking (E-D) places, insurance carriers, air transportation and hospitals. In each case, a specific report was published.[3]

At first sight, a comparative study of the economic performances of service industries in France and in the United States should mainly deal with getting and analysing respective national data (or international databases when they exist), trying to break them down (or to gather them) in similar categories, providing comparable assessments of their variations during a given period of time (essentially the 1980s in our case studies), and finally putting forward several explanatory factors of the observed differences.

This rather positivistic method seems appropriate and, actually, this is what most researchers do when they develop international comparisons of economic performance in services: they use as often as possible existing international data series like OECD data for health services, IATA (International Aviation Transport Association) or ICAO (International Civil Aviation Organisation) data for air transportation,[4] SIGMA data[5] for insurance services and so on. If such ready made international data do not exist, they base their analyses on national figures (very often produced by national statistical institutions, either for construction of national accounts or for other purposes) and try to combine them in a common ad hoc classification. An excellent work in this vein is Elfring's comparative study of service employment in advanced economies (Elfring, 1988). All too often, however, inappropriate and inaccurate data and concepts fault the results.

In our study, we systematically analysed, for five service sectors, existing methods in both countries and we compared the corresponding output and productivity data. It appears that no satisfactory interpretation of the differences between the two countries (and no understanding of productivity variations in each country) can be obtained on this first basis. This is also true for the explanation of the so-called 'productivity paradox' in services.

We subsequently show that improved and more complex procedures can be used in order to provide estimates of efficiency changes. This implies, in most cases, reconsideration of the very concepts of output and productivity in services and the introduction of the main variables neglected in the traditional approaches: service complexity, intensity and outcomes.

1.   SERVICES AND THE PRODUCTIVITY PARADOX IN A COMPARATIVE PERSPECTIVE

1.1   What Does the (Existing) Evidence Say about Service Productivity in Both Countries?

In our study comparing France and the United States in five service industries, we have gathered as much as possible existing national and international productivity data on both countries. And if we had taken the data for granted, our conclusions would have been rather simple and quite in harmony with most of the current standards of thinking about service performances:

First, on the basis of those ratios typically cited, the *absolute levels* of US service industry productivity appear either equivalent or below those in France. For example, more workers are needed in a US supermarket to sell the same amount of goods; more people are employed in US hospitals for the same number of beds or patients admitted.

As for air transportation, the traditional criterion of ton-kilometers transported (including mail and passengers) per employee shows, in 1988, exactly the same level of 'productivity' for Air France and for the average of 27 major North American Airlines. The same holds true for the property-liability insurance business where, in 1988, the levels of premiums earned per employee were roughly the same in both countries,[6] if the current exchange rate of the respective currencies is used for the conversion. A notable exception among the industries studied is in the US eating and drinking places where more meals are served per full-time-equivalent (FTE) worker.

Second, and more important, the 'productivity' gains (variation rates) which result from these traditional data appear to be: (*a*) lower in services than in manufacturing (a widely-held view about services), especially in the USA where the gap is more important than in France; and (*b*) systematically much lower in the USA than in France during the 1980s, and even negative in the USA for several service industries.

For example, between 1983 and 1988, the above-mentioned 'productivity' ratio concerning air transportation increased by 6.1 per cent for Air France and 2.3 per cent for North American Airlines (all figures in this paragraph are average annual changes). In the supermarket industry, between 1978 and 1986, the output per labour hour increased by 4.4 per cent in France (and 3.1 per cent for 'hypermarkets'), while it decreased by –0.1 per cent in the USA. In the hospital industry, where truly comparable data are difficult to provide for many reasons (see Gadrey et al., 1991b), our estimation shows, between 1980 and 1988, an increase of the number of hospital admissions per FTE employee in

France (around 1.3 per cent per year) in contrast to a decrease of the same magnitude in the USA (–1.2 per cent). In the eating and drinking place industry, the situation appears to be even worse for the USA. If 'productivity' is measured by deflated sales per labour hour, it decreased in the USA by –1.9 per cent per year over the 1983–88 period,[7] while it increased in France by 1.7 per cent (over 1983–89).

As for the insurance carriers industry, BEA figures provide an average output growth rate of 0.7 per cent over 1977–89, whereas BLS employment figures display a 2.0 per cent employment growth rate. Labour productivity would consequently have declined by –1.3 per cent per year. In France, records are even worse in national accounts, with an hourly productivity decline of –2.4 per cent per year over 1980–88.

Finally, in the property-liability (P-L) insurance industry alone, it appears, on the basis of existing international data provided by the Swiss journal SIGMA and analysed by Mary A. Weiss (1991) that:

1.   In the USA the 'output' (assessed by the amount of losses deflated by the CPI) would have decreased by –4.4 per cent per year between 1975 and 1987 while it would have increased by 0.3 per cent in France;
2.   The multi-factor productivity index calculated by this author over the same period would have decreased by –1.0 per cent in the USA and increased by 0.7 per cent in France (there is no figure concerning labour productivity);
3.   The variation rates, year after year, seem chaotic in both countries, often skyrocketing one year and plummeting in the next.[8] This unbelievable inconsistency does not deserve any comment in the above analysis.

Our own assessments of labour efficiency in the P-L insurance business in France show that the measured labour productivity would have increased, between 1980 and 1988, by 2.5 per cent or 3.3 per cent per year[9] depending on the criterion used as a proxy for 'real' output. In the United States, with a method based on deflated incurred losses per labour hour, we get a 1.7 per cent annual variation rate between 1980 and 1990.

The conclusion from these measures seems to leave little room for doubt. Not only do services in the USA appear to be produced with low efficiency but also rates of improvement in productivity are relatively low.

In other words, the counterpart of the seemingly good performance of the US economy in adding millions of new service jobs in the 1970s and 1980s would appear to be its lack of productivity improvements in these sectors. According to Lester Thurow and Louise Waldstein (1989),: 'If American service productivity had grown at the rate of West Germany, instead of producing 18.7 million service jobs between 1972 and 1983, the US would have produced only 3.6 million jobs.' (p. 8). And, for this author, who bases his analysis on traditional national and international data (notably the OECD publications), 'The problem of slow productivity growth in services is real – not a statistical artifact.' (p. 6).

As will be shown later, our judgement is substantially more balanced on this point. But let us develop a bit more the mainstream theses of service non-progressiveness.

1.2 Why are American Services Supposed to be Non-efficient and Non-progressive?

It has been commonly held that the services in the USA (*1*) fail to attain the *absolute levels of productivity* experienced by some other countries, such as France; and, above all, (*2*) that they lag behind in terms of *productivity gains*. The first point is of course less clear than the second since it is more difficult to secure data to make satisfactory currency conversions of value[10] than to provide in each country time series of productivity gains with reasonably comparable (though not identical) measures of output.

The major explanations of the poor performance of services in the USA are that US services are more labour intensive, make use of more low-skilled employees and are characterized by a slower pace of diffusion of high technologies. These characteristics are said to be traceable to a management of labour that favours low wages, especially in personal services (including retail trade). Not only has this been a tendency in the past, but also the gap between the USA and European countries is alleged to have increased in the 1980s. Again, we quote Lester Thurow, for whom there is a 'foreign willingness to invest in more capital-intensive technologies' (p. 7), because 'with a more rapid rise in general wages, firms in these countries simply had greater incentives to replace labor with capital' (p. 7).[11] This gap concerns service industries in particular because 'service wages are much higher relative to manufacturing wages abroad than they are in the US' (p. 7).

A second explanation of America's particular difficulty in making substantial productivity gains (either in manufacturing or in services) has been expressed in terms of *convergence* (by William Baumol)[12] or *catch-up* (by Moses Abramovitz).[13] In this view levels of productivity are higher in the USA but the margin of superiority is being closed. Both authors consider that a major explanation of the productivity slowdown in the USA lies in the fact that US industries were (and, sometimes, still are) world leaders, whereas other countries (Japan being a typical example) can adopt, under certain conditions, the behaviour of a quickly learning 'laggard', thus leading to superior productivity gains. Abramovitz does not mention specifically the role of services in his analysis of what he calls 'a process of international productivity catch-up'. He deals rather with cross-country data and regressions at a macroeconomic level (real gross product and global input factors liable to explain economic growth or slowdown).

When Baumol and his colleagues treat, in Chapter 6 of their 1989 book devoted to the convergence theory, the specific problems associated with service productivity and the services' rising share of total employment in the United States, the convergence argument disappears. What reappears is a presentation of two earlier well-known theses on unbalanced growth (Baumol, 1967; Baumol et al., 1985) concerning, first, the cost-disease of many services (notably personal services), named stagnant services, and, second, the intermediate situation[14] of some other services, named asymptotically stagnant services. By and large, most service industries are thus considered as stagnant or potentially so.

In other words, services appear globally as a group of activities that can 'impede the overall productivity growth rate of the economy' (p. 140), but nothing is explicitly said regarding whether or not US service industries are leaders or laggards and what role they play in the catch-up game. Despite this fact, it can be thought that the same convergence argument must implicitly be valid for services if it is worthwhile for the overall US economy, since services (in the broad sense of tertiary industries) accounted in 1990 for 71 per cent of this economy in terms of employment,[15] and roughly the same in terms of GDP. Moreover, there is a clear macroeconomic implication of Baumol's theses: if it is true that many services are stagnant (or asymptotically stagnant) sectors, one must assume that the more tertiarized country is liable to experience the lower productivity gains.

To summarize our own interpretation of Baumol's logic: first, in each service industry, America's greater advances in the past may help explain the poorer productivity gains in more recent years (convergence argument), and, second, for the overall economy, the high level of tertiarization in the USA would be associated with low rates of productivity growth (unbalanced growth argument). These two arguments, so to speak would converge: services would be more 'stagnant' in the USA, and the US economy would be more 'stagnant' than the others.

The third existing explanation of the alleged poor efficiency (or slow economic progress) experienced by US service industries is related neither to labour/capital intensity nor to macroeconomic convergence, but to the organizational ineffectiveness in the massive but often incoherent introduction of information technologies in services. Services account for 85 per cent of total private information technology investment,[16] but part of these expenditures have been a wastage of resources insofar as they lead to information overload and other new forms of Parkinson's Law.

This contradiction between the particular importance of information technologies in services and the meagre productivity performances (as traditionally measured) is also underlined by Stephen Roach,[17] who mentions for example the fact that the FIRE sector (finance, insurance and real estate), which is the IT leader, is also one of those experiencing the worst productivity records (in fact an important decline) between 1973 and 1985, a period of huge diffusion of computer and related technologies. According to BEA figures,[18] the 'output' in constant dollars of the FIRE sector increased, between 1980 and 1988, by 2.8 per cent per year on average, while the number of FTE persons working grew by 3.3 per cent, resulting in a measured 0.5 per cent annual decline in productivity.

For Stephen Roach, this 'productivity puzzle' is related, first, to our lack of experience in evaluating correctly 'productivity paybacks from information technology'[19] or more generally 'white-collar productivity', second, to the fact that, most information technologies being relatively recent, managers and information workers are climbing the traditional 'learning curve' (organizational inefficiencies, may be transitional), and, finally, to an over-equipment of computers and related systems in certain service sectors (the theme of 'information overload'). An interesting survey and stimulating research on these themes are provided by Paul Attewell (1990).

These converging arguments do not say much about the comparative situation of the USA and other developed countries like France, but they do suggest that the phenomena of IT over-equipment and information overload might be worse in the American services, explaining part of the poorer US performances (as traditionally measured).

To the above arguments may be added a fourth: that R&D has been weak in the service industries. This complementary argument will not be given much attention in our analysis, not because of lack of interest, but because no usable international data are available. What this argument says is that the low level of R&D expenditures in services should be included among the various explanations of the poor productivity performances of services compared with manufacturing. Nothing can be drawn on such a basis about the productivity performance of US services compared with other countries, however, unless evidence could be adduced to indicate that R&D efforts are lower in US services, which is exactly the opposite of all our comparative field observations.

Moreover, this argument is itself very questionable. First, it is well known that productivity performance by sectors is not linked with the relative importance of R&D expenditures in that sector, many sectors being able to benefit from technologies perfected in other industries and to experience, accordingly, high productivity gains (for example, agriculture, transportation services or communication services). Second, it is now admitted that we know little about what R&D is in services and how much it costs. In 1986, a study by the Battelle Memorial Institute[20] made a reassessment of the previous existing data (based on NSF's (National Science Foundation) definitions and measurement). The result was amazing: Battelle's estimation of total R&D in services was more than 10 times greater than the NSF figures for non-manufacturing industries! It is not unfair in such conditions to say that this last argument about the specific weakness of R&D in services cannot be seriously supported.

1.3 Why the Previous Explanations Are Not Satisfactory

Each of the three categories of arguments mentioned above raises more questions than they answer. Moreover, they are often mutually contradictory and sometimes self-contradictory, even though each reflects in part realities we have observed during our investigations in France and the United States.

The argument that, in the USA, low wages–low incentives to modernize lead to low productivity prompts two observations:

- First, the argument clearly contradicts both the convergence/catch-up theory and the IT overequipment theory. If US service sectors have long been lacking incentives to introduce modern technologies, and if they lag behind their European counterparts in this regard, they cannot be the productivity leaders that others imitate and seek to equal nor will they be IT overequipped or information overloaded.
- Second and more importantly, the argument rests on the critical macro-economic assumption that relatively low wages are correlated with low capital intensity and low organizational efficiency. Such an assumption is sometimes valid and we have had several opportunities to observe that during periods when labour shortage has induced a tendency toward wage enhancement, service firms have been more prompt to further automatize part of their operations (see our E-D places study, Gadrey et al. (1991c), as well as the case of food retailing in the late 1980s, Gadrey et al. (1991a)). Nonetheless, it is our observation that no general linkage exists between the diffusion of modern technologies and the level and variations of wages in a given service sector. Lester Thurow is certainly right when he says that 'the parking lot attendant so familiar in the United States ... is unknown in Sweden where he/she has been replaced by plastic cards' (Thurow and Waldstein, 1989, p. 7) and similar examples can be found. But their extension to the majority of service industries seems a serious mistake. On the contrary, what struck us in our comparative field research was the impressive technological advance of US service firms or organizations in each of the five industries under study, whatever may be the wage level. It is not unlikely that

this gap has slowly diminished during the 1980s, but it was still real at the end of the decade. Many pieces of evidence converge on this point and the reader may easily check our assertions case by case in our reports.

How is it possible then, that even with relatively low wages in services (especially personal services including retailing), the US service firms could be, in technological and organizational terms, in advance of their European counterparts?

Many factors are certainly at play but our research indicates three that are of prime importance: first, the higher level of competition prevailing over the years in US service markets; second, the much larger size of these markets and the corresponding possibility of more readily taking advantage of both economies of scale and scope; and, third, the higher standard of living of the average American consumer, a factor that generally favours service demand.

These three interrelated factors constituted very strong incentives for US service industries to introduce the most modern technologies and organizational structures earlier than in other countries. Firms in these industries were certainly not unaware of labour-cost containing strategies and, indeed, they benefited, at least during certain periods (like the 1970s), from labour market conditions (baby-boom effect, growing female participation in the labour force) which allowed them to pay low wages to millions of new service workers, increasingly hired as part-timers. Nevertheless, they were expanding their networks and chains (a main organizational innovation), at the same time rapidly introducing new technologies (in information, communication and logistics), gaining market share over more traditional service formats. All this was done (in the 1960s and 1970s) under the pressure of a mounting domestic competition so far unknown in Europe, where domestic or local markets were still protected. In Europe competition similar to that obtained in the US began to emerge only in the early 1980s for retailing, banking and insurance, or in the late 1980s for air transportation and to some extent for restaurants. In the hospital industry and in public health insurance such competition had not yet appeared in the early 1990s.

What seems absent in the 'low wages–low incentives to modernize' hypothesis is a recognition that low labour costs occurring during high labour-force supply periods can actually enable service firms to invest more in modern technologies under conditions of strong market competition and opportunities to increase market share.

As is demonstrated case by case in our reports, these conditions were met in many US service industries during the 1970s. In large measure they continued to be valid in the 1980s but under a different context (rapid diversification of products and services, growing segmentation, new stress on service quality, and harsh competition).

It is worth noting that, in the Thurow–Waldstein contribution previously mentioned, Louise Waldstein provides international data[21] contradicting, at least partly, the thesis of a particularly low incentive to modernize in services. The annual growth of high-technology capital between 1970 and 1985, which was 11.5 per cent for all industries, amounted to 29.6 per cent for financial services, 21.7 per cent for insurance and 16.2 per cent for retail trade. Even if one takes account of the relatively rapid growth of employment in these sectors over the same period, there is little to validate the idea that a willingness to modernize is lacking in US services. If we consider the share of total gross fixed investment (excluding dwellings) accounted for by services, it grew apparently very sharply in the USA, from 24.8 per cent in the early 1970s to 38.1 per cent in the early 1980s. In Japan, France and Germany, this growth was much lower (respectively 22.1 to 23.2 per cent, 23.8 to 28.5 per cent, and 23 to 30.5 per cent). Even though these international data are not very reliable, they indicate a probable leadership of US service industries in terms of capital intensity.

The catch-up arguments appear consistent with our investigations, in that, in most services the USA appears to have a real technological and organizational lead. The 'imitation' processes can be observed, in France, and elsewhere in Europe, in supermarkets (despite the originality of the 'hypermarket' French format), in eating and drinking places (where replicas of American chains have recently been gaining market shares), in the European air transportation industry (airport logistics, reservations and ticketing technologies, concentration aiming at larger market size), and even in European hospitals, which try to get, more than ten years later, the very short length of stay, high level of outpatient visits and stricter separation between acute care and nursing care facilities that prevail in the USA, not to mention the sophisticated (DRG-like, Diagnosis Related Groups) information system on hospital 'outputs'. Not all service technological characteristics are lagging behind in Europe, far from it. But, in most of the cases we studied, notably in France, the gap is significant.

Curiously, although the catch-up thesis seems to hold when services are examined sector by sector in the USA and France in terms of production functions, including their qualitative aspects, the findings are blurred or contradictory when traditional economic indicators of output and productivity are applied.

Indeed, the first condition for the convergence thesis is the superiority of absolute productivity levels in the leading country. But this does not seem to be true in many service industries. And, indeed, the opposite result appears to hold in two out of our five cases (food retailing and hospitals). In only one of them (E-D places) is there clear evidence of higher productivity levels in the USA.

Again, the question must be raised: is it possible to have a noticeable technological and organizational advantage and, at the some time, be lagging in terms of productivity ratios? May the third explanation (failures and inefficiencies in the investment and use of new technologies) be the right answer?

The IT misuse or overequipment argument is not consistent with our observations, even though it has the merit of conceding the evidence of a very high level of IT diffusion in most US services, and thus of contradicting the under-equipment argument. At a microeconomic level, it is obvious that computer and communication systems have often been introduced through a trial and error process, and examples of information overloads are not exceptional. But this has little to do with the variations, at a national level, of traditional output and productivity ratios. If one wonders whether or not computer and communication systems have improved labour efficiency, one has to assess how many people would be necessary today without such systems to produce and process the rapidly growing number of banking and finance transactions, orders, invoices and management control data, reservations, ticketing, hospital bills and so on. We have considered, in each case study, the efficiency of informational functions in both countries, and showed that it is in that field that the USA appears to have the greatest superiority over European countries.

Such a superiority in producing and processing information does not prove, of course, that all these information flows are smartly used and that they contribute positively to overall efficiency in getting final service outputs. Some clues do exist, however, indicating that the IT misuse argument is either wrong or at least of negligible significance.

First, if we consider solely the US economy with its main service industries it is not in the more IT-intensive sectors, such as banking, insurance and telecommunication, that existing productivity records[22] are the worst, quite to the contrary. It is rather in less IT-intensive consumer services, such as grocery stores, eating and drinking places or hotels and motels.

In this regard, two kinds of information flows exist: information as a major direct component of the final service (banking, communication, databases) and information as an internal control and management tool. It seems that the information overload argument is mainly applicable to the latter. But in this case, it should concern manufacturing as well. Second, at an international level, one can hardly see why the USA, where IT systems were introduced much earlier, would not be better placed on the 'experience curve': computers are no longer a new technology, but, rather, a fairly mature one.

To summarize, each of the three current explanations of the seemingly bad performances of US service industries offers interesting insights, but none is really convincing and none can account for the differences we observed between the USA and France. Before beginning to develop our own answers, a first series of evidence of what we mentioned as a technological and organizational US advance must be gathered. We want indeed to convince the reader that the argument that there is a low incentive to modernize US services, even though it can be true in particular cases, is globally contradicted by our investigations. France was the national case submitted to special research. But we had complementary opportunities to interview people and gather data from several other European countries, confirming the existence of the same gaps.

1.4 What Does Our Own Evidence Say about the Respective Technological and Organizational Levels?

Let us limit ourselves to the five sectors studied. Three criteria can be used to make meaningful comparisons:

- The degree of diffusion of modern information technologies, a parameter especially important in services;
- The degree of diffusion of modern logistic technologies (in the sense of the operational management of flows of goods). Indeed, for certain services (and, of course, in retailing and transportation), these are core technologies;
- The degree of adoption of organizational structures generally associated with more economic rationality (as compared with traditional service delivery), and greater application of sophisticated management methods.

In every one of these three dimensions, there is absolutely no doubt that, for each of our five industries, the USA was ahead, sometimes slightly, but, in most cases, very markedly. Many examples were presented in our study. I select here some of them.

As for information technologies, the US supermarket industry has been widely using scanning devices (associated with barcodes and with global management information systems concerning stock management, product-line control and so on) many years before France. The proportion of US supermarkets equipped with scanning systems was 14 per cent in 1980 and 65 per cent in 1989, but only 5 per cent in France in 1985 and 21 per cent in 1989. The same holds true for the use of computerized 'Direct Product Profit' methods or EDI (Electronic Data Interchange) linkages, which spread rapidly in the USA during the 1980s while they were still almost unknown in France. In the air transportation sector, where French and US aircraft technologies are among the most advanced, marked differences exist in information logistics. The US airline industry is significantly better equipped in terms of computerized airline schedule and reservation systems than its European counterparts (for more evidence, see Gadrey et al. 1992a). In hospitals, the information technology gap is huge, and one of its consequences is the fact that no comprehensive data about admissions per type of diagnosis exist in France: a DRG-type system, which requires a high level of computerization, is not expected to be available before the end of the 1990s, while it has existed in the US since the early 1980s. Core medical technologies such as MRI (Magnetic Resonance Imaging) scanners and other imaging and electrophysiologic equipment are also more often available – and are heavily used – in the USA. In eating and drinking places, the difference is no less significant, particularly in relation to the importance of chains which is very high in the USA and very low in France: the number of US restaurants equipped, for example, with computerized point of sale (POS) systems began to grow in the late 1970s, largely in response to the increasing importance of chains, with their greater capacity to invest and greater sophistication, about ten years before the same tendency appeared in France.

In the insurance business, we have no solid empirical evidence of a possible gap, except that the diffusion of computers and DP-based management was much earlier in the USA, allowing a greater diversity and flexibility of the contracts and services. With regard to the logistics of goods and related technologies, we have some clues (but less reliable and comparable data) of their superiority in the USA, especially in the supermarket industry (with a greater use of direct store delivery systems and minimal stock strategies), in airport logistics, and in eating and drinking places (again in direct relation to chain organization).

Organizational structures of service industries and service firms are, especially in consumer services (such as E-D places, hotels and motels) and retailing, characterized in the USA by a much greater importance of network, franchise and chain systems, and correspondingly by a comparative lower weight of small firms and 'mom and pop' independent outlets, generally assumed to be less efficient.

A first important example can be taken from our food retailing study. In the USA, the share of grocery store sales accounted for by supermarkets was already very high in the early 1960s (around 70 per cent). In France, the share of food sales by super/hypermarkets grew from less than 10 per cent in 1968 to just over 40 per cent in 1985. In other words, in France, more efficient forms of food distribution had still, in the late 1980s, less important than more traditional ones, such as street-corner butchers and bakers.

In eating and drinking places, a second example, the chains accounted only for about 10 per cent of restaurant sales in France in the late 1980s. In the USA, franchise-type restaurants[23] had already accounted for 26.2 per cent of all eating places sales by 1972 and represented, in 1987, 45 per cent.

1.5 Sorting Out the Productivity Paradox: First Indications

Let us come back to the core issue of this first part: how is it possible to reconcile the undoubted technological and organizational US leadership in many services with its very poor productivity records? Our own answers to this paradox can be summarized in two major points:

1.5.1 The functional approach to service activities

Most service industries can be analysed, in terms of 'production function', as a combination of three sets of functions, each being associated with different types of technologies, organizations and efficiency criteria. These functions are:

- The informational functions, either as direct components of the delivered service or as internal management functions;
- The functions of material logistics, whose importance varies among service industries (they are often core functions in certain consumer services, in transportation and in retailing);
- The direct service functions, associated with the face-to-face contact with clients, with care and assistance to customers, advice and so on.

What appears in the case of the US service industries, as compared with their European counterparts, is a noticeably higher level of efficiency in the first two fields (those where most advanced technologies can be introduced) and a greater amount of direct service provided, with relatively more people employed to fulfil this third category of functions. Thus, if one uses, as is generally the case, traditional output measurement (for example, the amount of goods sold in retailing, number of people admitted in hospital, possibly with a complexity index, ton × kilometers in air transportation, premiums or losses incurred at constant dollars in insurance and so on) that does not take account of the amount of direct service produced, one is likely to conclude that the overall efficiency of labour is relatively poor in the USA. Hence the kind of argument mentioned above, put forward by L. Thurow for example, about a possible weakness of the capital–labour ratio in services, an argument that does not seem to apply for informational and logistic functions in the USA, but that is more realistic for direct service functions.

The question is then: is the output of a US service industry, that delivers much direct service to customers (with the exception of the restaurant industry), of the same nature as the output of its counterpart in France, where the level of direct service is generally inferior? This question leads to our second point.

1.5.2 The conceptual approach to services output

Here are the main difficulties but also the main explanations of the productivity paradox. It is not, as Lester Thurow put it, a 'statistical artifact', but a major conceptual issue. The core idea behind our approach can be grasped from one question, which arises out of one of our five case studies. In the supermarket industry, do we get the same output when, for the same basket of goods bought, we get our purchases bagged, delivered to our homes if necessary, or carried to our car on request, when we have 50 per cent more varieties of goods (stock-keeping units) to choose from, when opening hours per week are twice as long, when there is a customer assistance counter, when more scanning systems save our time at the checkout counter and when, in addition to this identical basket, we can also buy hot food 'to go' as well as other kinds of prepared food (from salad bars, for example)? What the French–US comparison shows is that more people are employed in the typical American supermarket for roughly the same volume of goods traded, not because of lower productivity but, if output is analysed as a combination of services associated with the trade of goods rather than simply with the volume of goods themselves (the usual method based on sales at constant prices), because the output of US supermarkets is fundamentally different.

Moreover, if this more complex, service-based approach is adopted, it can be shown that, during the 1980s, the average US supermarket clearly increased its performance in terms of quality and quantity of services delivered, leading to a decrease in its productivity as measured in the traditional way, while its French counterpart was improving productivity by restricting its service component and developing the self-service and large-scale strategies pioneered in the USA during the 1950s, 1960s and early 1970s.[24] This example indicates the general approach: in a service economy, we need thoroughly to reappraise the traditional concepts of output and the methods used to measure it and to evaluate the significance of the rising level of service provided. The next part is devoted to this issue, which begins with a preliminary question: what is a service?

2. REVISITING OUTPUT AND PRODUCTIVITY CONCEPTS IN SERVICES

It is our contention that, for theoretical reasons, most existing output and productivity data used by economists to analyse the performance of services at a national or international level are either questionable or irrelevant. The first theoretical question is, of course, the nature of a service activity, as compared with goods-producing activity. Indeed, the core of our arguments is that (1) there exist fundamental differences between the two cases,[25] and (2) traditional output measures are biased because they are conceived in industrial terms: what they usually measure ('surrogate output') is not what really matters (the services provided); and this 'surrogate output' per hour worked can be stagnant while the importance of services supplied increases. The importance of the latter is more complex to assess and is unlikely to be restricted to one synthetic ratio.

This second part is organized in two sections. First, a definition of services as processes and transformations is elaborated. Second, the consequences of that definition on the economic evaluation of service output are studied, leading to new concepts, better fitted to services.

2.1   What Is a Service?

For many years, various definitions or characterizations of services have been put forward by researchers or statisticians who faced the kind of issue we are now delving into. Services have, for example, been defined as non-material, or non-stockable, or as products delivered at the very time they are produced. Each of these characteristics provide interesting insights, but it is widely agreed that none encompasses the real world of services and that none is useful enough to allow one to progress toward definition and evaluation of services output. A more complex definition, which is more useful for our present purpose, was given by Peter Hill in 1977. It says that 'A service may be defined as a change in the conditions of a person or a good belonging to some economic unit, which is brought about as the result of the activity of some other economic unit with the prior agreement of the former person or economic unit' (Hill, 1977).

It is this kind of approach, whose merit is first to consider a service as a process, and second to distinguish the economic units involved in this process, that we are going to develop. Without pretending that our own definition covers entirely the vast array of activities gathered under the heading 'services', it concerns a large majority of them. A triangle (Figure 2.1) forms the starting point.

Following Figure 2.1, our definition[26] will be: a service is an operation, aiming at a transformation of a reality *C* owned or used by a customer *B*, with the operation carried out by a provider *A* on the request of *B* (and often in interaction with him), but not ending in a final good likely to circulate independently from *C*.

What is essential for output and productivity analyses is, first, to distinguish *B* and *C* (the service, as an operation, is about the transformation of *C* whereas the service, as a satisfaction, concerns the customer *B*); second, to specify in each case what is the reality *C* and the nature of its transformation, and, third,

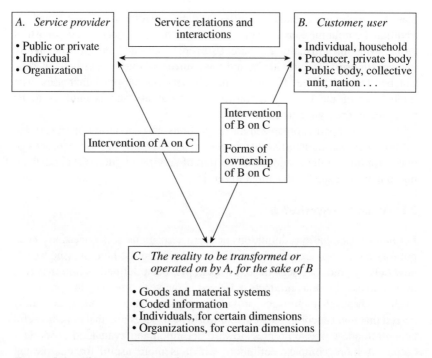

Figure 2.1   The service triangle

to recognize the cases (frequent in services) in which *A* and *B* interact or play a complementary role in bringing about the final result. Four main categories of reality *C* exist, whose transformations raise increasing difficulties of analysis as one passes from one category to the next:

- Goods and other technical systems owned by *B* that *A* is supposed to repair, transport, maintain, secure and so on. Indeed, many service operations deal with goods, machines, systems, buildings and the like;
- Coded and standardized information (including money in its pure symbolic form) that *A* must transfer, process or manage on behalf of *B*;
- The individual *B* himself, for certain of his dimensions: body and health, intellectual capacities, spatial location;
- Organizations and their collective knowledge, competencies or structures, that *A* is supposed to analyse, transform or improve, under the request of *B*, and often with his participation. *B* can be a member or a sub-organization of *C*, or another body.

2.2 Toward New Economic Analyses of the Results of Service Activities

The above conceptual approach of a service as an operation may help analyse its results in a new fashion. In our view, this process must be carried out according to four stages (sections 2.2.1–2.2.4).

2.2.1 What reality *C* is to be transformed and operated on?

Answering this question at certain levels of globality (a sector, or even a firm) means specifying first the nature of *C* (sometimes a set of intricate realities) and second the quantity of the various realities treated (for example, the quantity of goods traded in retailing, the number of people or tons of goods in transportation services, of people admitted in hospitals, of files or transactions processed or money transferred in informational services and so on).

The traditional measurement of retailing output variations (including the case of eating places) on the basis of deflated sales goes hardly further than this stage, except that, for the sake of aggregation, the 'quantity' of goods is not defined as the number of items, but rather as a weighted combination of such product-line numbers. In insurance, the use of premiums or losses incurred (at constant dollars) as an output proxy falls into this category, where nothing like a service (operation or transformation) is taken into account. Not surprisingly, the results may be deceptive or paradoxical.

Not all output measures in terms of deflated sales, however, are necessarily misleading as a measure of the output of services. If, for example, the price index reflects fairly accurately the prices and weights of the service mix itself, and if the service production costs account for the bulk of the sales, a fairly good estimate may be obtained. This is obviously not the case with retailing, where the service itself (whose value is roughly reflected by margins) accounts generally for a minor share of the sales, whereas the deflator concerns the prices of goods sold and not the cost of retailing services of a given quality.

2.2.2 What operations or transformations are fulfilled on *C*, and how to evaluate them?

Indeed, viewing services as operations leads to a conceptualization of their output which we will name the direct output or operational output, associated with particular productivity concepts named either direct productivity, or, better, operational efficiency. In that sense, service operational efficiency increases when the same transformation can be carried out with less labour input.[27]

The main difficulty, at this stage, is to evaluate in 'real' terms the amount of transformations and its variation over time. In principle, such an evaluation method means resolving the following:

1. In the same way that there is needed an accurate classification of the real-
    ities C under transformation, as well as their quantification, the transfor-
    mations themselves must be classified if a 'direct output' measure is
    wanted. The term 'transformation' covers a wide range of other terms,
    specific to individual sectors. Examples are 'case', 'operation', 'treat-
    ment', 'intervention', 'assignment', 'repairing', 'procedure', but also
    transportation, transfer, delivery and so on. None of these designates an
    object or a good, nor other fixed material system. All concern processes,
    transformations, changes of state[28] of given material, informational or
    organizational realities.

2. In order to get an evaluation, in real terms, of the increases or decreases
    in the amount of transformations fulfilled or cases treated, when these
    cases are diverse, a theoretical method consists of weighting them, after a
    breakdown by categories as homogeneous as possible. This 'case mix
    approach' resembles (on a purely formal ground) conventional output
    measures in goods-producing sectors, but in most service industries it
    appears to be much more difficult to carry out, because classifying and
    weighing transformations or changes of state raises more problems than
    classifying and weighting material products. Nonetheless, such a task
    must be undertaken as long as data exist. This can result in two separate
    indices:

    - First, a rough 'quantity of cases' index, q, that does not take into
      account changes in the variety and complexity of cases treated;
    - Second, a 'case-mix complexity' index, c, that attempts, on the basis
      of detailed classifications and adequate weights, (or other methods like
      deflation procedures whenever they seem relevant) to capture the vari-
      ations of the average case complexity. The resulting index, $q \times c$,
      provides, at least theoretically, an initial estimate of direct output vari-
      ations, insofar as it is admitted that direct output is associated with the
      amount of 'cases treated'.

A first illustration is given by the evaluation of hospital outputs. The 'quantity of cases' can be measured either by the gross number of admissions or by
a combination of admissions and outpatient visits ('adjusted admissions'; for
more details, see Gadrey et al. (1991b)). As for the 'case-mix complexity'
changes, it must be estimated after an attempt, first, to classify admissions by
degree of complexity of the corresponding treatments, and, second, to weight
them accordingly. This is a highly complicated exercise, where the availability of DRG-like data[29] and base-year costs per DRG is helpful, although not
entirely conclusive as will be shown. Such data are available at a national level
in the United States, but not in France. When this is done, the exercise is likely

to bring about a first important revision of conventional ideas about the drop in US hospital productivity during the 1980s (about –1.2 per cent between 1980 and 1988 in terms of 'adjusted admissions' per FTE employee), as it appears that, over this period, the case-mix complexity would have grown substantially (about 1.7 per cent per year). The combined result of these two changes (an average gain of 0.5 per cent) does not indicate a large improvement in productivity, but, at least, there is an increase.

A second illustration concerns air transportation, where the most widely used output measurement method, expressed in terms of persons transported × kilometers or tons × kilometers, seems to correspond to the characteristics of a case-based approach. The 'transformation' under study is, here, the transportation service itself. The measure of the amount of direct service delivered is based on two assumptions: first, that output is proportional to the number of people (or tons of freight) concerned, and second that it is proportional to the distance. In other words, the quantity of cases resembles the 'people admitted' variable used in hospitals, whereas the complexity per case index is assumed to be the distance travelled per passenger or per ton of freight. As will be demonstrated in the next paragraph, such an assumption is likely to oversimplify the service delivered in this sector.

2.2.3 The amount or intensity of services provided per case, at a given level of case complexity (the residual component of service output)

The point reached above is that combining quantification by line of 'products' with an appropriate weighting procedure is necessary. Such a method is, in principle, very close to existing industrial output measures. The only difference would be that, in goods-producing sectors, the lines are distinguished according to the types of goods, whereas in services they would be distinguished according the types of cases or transformations carried out.

We will at this stage put aside the question of whether or not, in manufacturing, the evaluation of output takes account of material inputs and deducts them in such a way as to get a closer assessment of what the manufacturing unit or sector actually adds in current or real value. This 'double deflated' value added method may be regarded as an attempt to measure in real terms a transformation of material inputs into final goods. We concede for the moment that, in most manufacturing sectors, the major part of the measured output changes is given by an index of the (deflated) volume of goods sold (based on weighted quantities of goods per line). Such a method would not appear at first glance to be defective in the case of services since it goes straight to the measurement of the transformations being effected. Thus, the possibility of estimating productivity would appear to be favourable and the only remaining difficulties would seem to be practical (getting classifications and data) rather than theoretical.

This is not true, for one and only one reason: because we are in the domain of services, and because, consequently, analysing output as an amount of cases or transformations raises several difficulties unknown or marginal for the bulk of goods production. Before considering the main types of difficulties encountered, let us begin with three examples, the first of which (air transportation) displays some of the limits of the conventional methods but provides room for possible adjustments, the second (hospitals) presents greater difficulties, and the third (business and professional services) even more.

Let us assume that, for an airline company A, the average distance flown by passengers is higher than for a company B, everything else being equal in terms of size of aircraft, passenger comfort, the size of the fleets, as well as airport facilities and services rendered (freight being put temporarily aside). It is well known that, in this sector, the longer the average haul, the fewer the personnel (flying and ground personnel) per passenger × kilometer is likely to be, due to obvious reasons having little to do with labour efficiency. In such a case, the conventional productivity ratio will show a seemingly higher efficiency of A, whereas the truth is that the output of A differs from the output of B in qualitative terms: the 'mix' of services rendered per worker (per passenger × kilometer) is not the same (long nights require relatively less labour of flying attendant and of ground personnel) and the data need to be adjusted for average length of flight. Moreover, insofar as a multi-variable statistical analysis is capable of taking account of the other important parameters liable to define this 'mix of services', further improvements of the method can be obtained. The rough measurement of the output in terms of persons × kilometers or tons × kilometers is not meaningless, but it is nonetheless largely biased because it relies on a very crude representation of what the service is, as a transformation or a change of state. It represents the service provided to a passenger as a number of kilometers flown, which is certainly important but narrow. Besides the pure spatial transfer, an array of services is combined to provide the global air transportation service. Integrating these various services in the analysis, at least the most important ones, is crucial to judge the result of such an activity. This is what we call the importance or intensity i of services delivered per case, a case being what has been defined in the above paragraph. This variable i is always a combination of various parameters. Even if it appears often as a residual (or forgotten) factor in many studies of services productivity (it is usually named service quality), its role is crucial in most of our international comparisons. As far as air transportation is concerned, we have shown, for example, that, once the first crude ratios have been adjusted to take account of the distance effect and another source of bias (the 'weight load factor'), 'productivity' would appear to have grown faster among American than Western European airlines between 1983 and 1988, which is the opposite of what was shown by the crude ratios.

The hospital case is more complex, due, first, to the huge diversity of typi-cal 'cases' or 'treatments' and, second, to the variety of individual situations or complications that may occur within a given case. In the USA but not in France, some headway can be made in measuring complexity. The existence of DRG-based data since the early 1980s is a remarkable asset, as each DRG can be treated as a 'case' or a type of transformation, associated with a mix of services or procedures. On such a basis, it is possible to estimate the changes over time in the complexity of the mix of cases, named 'across-DRG case complexity changes' (Ashby, 1990). This can be done by weighting each DRG by an appropriate base-year cost. In other words, the DRGs represent a complex classification with a built-in consideration of several of the parame-ters or service characteristics similar to those that were lacking in the above example of the crude air transportation output. In hospitals, equivalents of the crude air transportation output measure exist and were used before the imple-mentation of DRGs: hospital days (an idea close to the distance flown crite-rion), or hospital beds (the rough equivalent of the number of seats in planes).

Does that mean that the newer DRG-based output measures are completely satisfactory, if appropriate weighting coefficients exist? Unfortunately, no, for two reasons. First, the fact is that within a given DRG are gathered a wide range of individual treatments and care. Even if they belong to an identifiable group, these internal cases can experience severity changes or 'within-DRG case complexity variations'. This is not negligible: Ashby's (1990) estimation of this internal complexity variation in US hospitals between 1980 and 1988 is 0.5 per cent per year.

Second, there exist other service characteristics that are not taken into account in the previous estimates of case complexity variations. For a given 'case' (DRG), hospitals can, for example, increase or decrease their nursing services, the time spent in providing patients and relatives with information, accommodation and food services. These other service components can be significant. Thus, a 'residual factor' that we called service intensity (service quality would also be appropriate) must still be considered, although the DRG classification of the cases in terms of complexity does reduce this residual factor. In US hospitals, a rough estimate of the changes in service intensity between 1980 and 1988 is 1.0 per cent per year (Ashby, 1990), while the case complexity would have increased by 1.7 per cent (including the 0.5 per cent for within-DRG case complexity noted above). Once the two effects (complexity and intensity) are combined in measuring average variation in output, the oper-ational efficiency ('productivity') of labour would have increased, in US hospi-tals, by 1.5 per cent per year, nearly the opposite of what was given by the crude indicator of adjusted admissions per FTE employee. What this example tells us is that there is no way of obtaining for hospitals measures of output that are as representative as those used in most goods-producing sectors. The unavoidable singularity of patients' problems and treatments is not incompatible with a (complex) classification method according to diagnoses and patient character- istics, but each class so obtained remains a class of different cases associated with different services and with severity changes: it is not like a given group of products, since flexible transformations of living realities are involved. Going as far as possible to seize these transformations is useful, but this has to leave the brave old world of standardized products (or services), to grasp the exceptional diversity of the customized and professionalized services that hospital services are.

The third example concerns business and professional services, and espe- cially consultancy-like services. Traditionally, national and international data, when they existed, have not made use of an output measurement method other than the deflation of turnover (fees) by a labour cost index (average cost of a consultant's hour), or even a straight measure of labour hours, considering implicitly that the real service unit is one hour of consultancy services. Of course, such a definition results in a near stagnation of measured productivity. In the early 1990s, there has been a tendency for national statistical institutions to improve output estimates through double deflation procedures and some effort to launch research programmes aiming at building DRG-like classifica- tion of consultancy services. A first project was begun in 1991 in France for field survey services, and a complex price index exists in Canada for engi- neering services. Both rely on a classification by type (and price) of contracts (see Gadrey et al. (1992b) for more details on contract-based approaches). It seems reasonable to expect that with most consultancy services, the likelihood of getting workable output types (categories of contracts combining 'diagno- sis' classes and client classes) is much worse than with hospital services. Moreover, the question would remain whether the output to be evaluated is the contract or the results of its implementation in the client organization (see the next section: output versus outcome).

From these three examples, it follows that a complex method of 'direct output' (or 'operational output') evaluation is needed. It consists, assuming that acceptable classifications and data exist, in multiplying three indices:

o (service output index) $= q$ (quantity of cases) $\times c$ (case mix complexity) $\times i$ (service intensity or quality per case, or residual component).

The main difference between c and i is not conceptual but rather practical: c takes account of the sub-categories of services that can be distinguished and quantified at a sectoral level depending on the quality and availability of such classifications within the sector (for example, DRGs, if such a classification scheme is available, which is the case in the USA, but not in France); i repre- sents an attempt to say more and to evaluate, with generally less quantifiable data, which service dimensions are not taken into account in the c index, and how they vary (over time, or across countries).

It would seem that we have now, at least theoretically, a fairly comprehensive view of the multiple dimensions of service output. But this is not yet the case: a fourth category for the analysis of results cannot be ignored in many services. It is no longer an issue of output, but rather one of outcome.

2.2.4   From output to outcome and from operational efficiency to service effectiveness

Up to now, we have defined the service output as a transformation, or a change of state, with examples of 'immediate' or 'direct' transformation undergone by the reality C, during the service operation.

But these direct transformations have further effects, namely outcomes. Educational and training services, and more generally services based on knowledge transfers (a major category of activities in developed countries) have certain immediate outputs to be analysed (short-run transfer criteria). But the evaluation of their medium- and long-run outcomes is often more important. This holds true for many business and professional services. Some of them are, in fact, charged and paid for on an outcome basis, in the (relatively rare) cases in which the outcome (or a proxy) is easily quantifiable. Lawyers can either charge for their services on a direct output basis (complexity of the legal work to be undertaken, intensity of the services provided, time devoted) or on an outcome basis (a given proportion of the client's financial gains from litigation).

Health services are a second example of the difference between the direct service output and the possible categories of outcomes, expressed in terms of well-being, with diverse available indicators such as infant mortality rate, life expectancy, rate of readmission, relapse or complications, prevalence of diseases and so on.

A third example, close to the first one, is the rapidly growing sector of informational activities, including the bulk of internal administrative functions of firms and other organizations. Indeed, if the immediate output of these activities is made up of information produced, processed and transformed (hence the possibility, in certain cases, of quantifying this output by categories of processes, files, standardized policies or transactions, time of online consultation of a database and so on), their outcomes depend on their relevance for the customer's needs for his or her own decision-making process (if information is required in order to make a decision) or to deal with the problems he or she has to tackle.

In services there are likely to be greater difficulties in assessing outcomes than in the case of goods: first, because there is not always a clear-cut discontinuity between short-run transformations (direct service output) and medium or long-run effects; second, because customers may become more demanding in terms of outcome assessment, to the point of requesting guarantees or other forms of integration of outcome performance standards as a part of the 'package' that they buy. When, for example, people buy and sell HMO (Health Maintenance Organizations) services, they put the stress on health outcome (effectiveness) more than on health service operational efficiency in each admission or treatment. They pay to get 'functioning systems', the same being true for companies buying data processing services, and for a large array of preventive or maintenance services, as well as for many insurance services. We are not going to delve any longer into this issue which is certainly of utmost importance insofar as societal and political issues are at stake.

CONCLUSION: THE DIMINISHING RETURNS OF PRODUCTIVITY CONCEPTS?

In the future, the main issue will probably not be how to improve productivity measurement in order to get the acceptable single indicator of productivity. Rather it is likely to be how to go beyond a simplistic concept and correspondingly simplistic measures in order to observe, first, the operational efficiency in the provision of service (recognizing complexity and intensity changes), and, second, the indirect results (or outcomes) of the transformations under study.

The more complex are the problems tackled (for example, business and professional services, hospital services, educational services, R&D and so on), the more unlikely is any synthetic productivity ratio to summarize the efficiency and effectiveness of the corresponding services, and the more useful it becomes to build and to implement complex evaluation procedures. Productivity analyses remain useful analytical tools, however, as long as, for a given sector or function, the share of standardized productions and transformations is substantial. This is still the case for certain service sectors or functions, but the general tendency is of the opposite sort: toward diversification, de-standardization, multi-service offerings, customization and tailorization of both demand and supply, and toward a growing demand for interactive procedures.

In each service sector, it is necessary to evaluate the importance of this shift toward increasing complexity and to determine what conventional productivity approaches are able to say when one wants to assess the changes in a sector's performance and competitiveness. In general, we seem to be witnessing diminishing returns of productivity concepts as they are applied to increasingly complex economies.

NOTES

1. According to Robert Gordon (1999), during the second half of the 1990s, the productivity growth acceleration was limited to the sector of durable goods (especially computers). Between 1987 and 1998, the food store industry (SIC 54) experienced a –1 per cent average annual decline of output per hour (BLS website www.bls.gov/home.htm).
2. Almost all of them are service industries.
3. All publications by Jean Gadrey, Thierry Noyelle and Thomas Stanback, published as joint reports and working papers of the University of Lille 1 (France) and the Eisenhower Center for the Conservation of Human Resources (Columbia University, New York). See references.
4. See our report on productivity in air transportation (Gadrey et al., 1992a).
5. SIGMA is a review of the "Compagrie Suisse de Réassurance' (Geneva).
6. In France, in 1988, the amount of gross premiums per employee (excluding independent brokers and agents, and their own employees) was 181 066 millions FF/103 700 = 1.74 million FF in P-L insurance. In the United States, in 1988, the total of premiums earned amounted to 193.3 billions of dollars (*Statistical Abstract of the US, 1991*), while employment (accounting for 45 per cent of the total insurance carriers industry) was about 649 000. Hence a 'productivity level' by 0.3 million dollars per employee or, expressed at the 1988 exchange rate (1\$ = 5.96 FF), 1.77 million FF. In terms of PPP rate of change (1\$ = 6.64FF in 1988), this amount is 1.99 million FF, that is 14 per cent higher in the US.
7. Reliable data do not exist in France before 1983 for restaurants. Only in 1983 was an enterprise survey organized in this sector.
8. For example, in France, the multi-factor productivity growth was 48.7 per cent in 1982 and –36.9 per cent in 1983. In the US it was 193.2 per cent in 1984, –29.1 percent in 1985 and –146.4 per cent in 1986!
9. Actually, the range of the possible estimations is even larger than this interval (see Gadrey et al., 1992b).
10. It is not obvious to compare one 'meal' in the US E-D places industry and one 'meal' in an average French restaurant, or to convert (either with PPP index or with current exchange rates) the respective levels of losses incurred in the property-liability insurance.
11. What is important here is, in fact, the relative cost of labour to capital.
12. See Baumol et al. (1989) and Baumol (1986).
13. Moses Abramovitz has developed his themes of catch-up and convergence over some time (see Abramovitz, 1986 and 1990).
14. In the sense that their production factors contain two components: the first of a hardware type, whose relative cost is decreasing because it is produced in the progressive sector; the second of a software or service type, whose relative cost increases because there is no productivity gain in its own production.
15. According to OECD figures and classifications. US data give higher levels.
16. Gary Loveman, quoted in *The Economist*, 24 August 1991. This figure is quite in line with the estimates provided by Stephen Roach (in Guile and Quinn, 1988) for 1985 about the information technology capital, 84 per cent of which was then located in service-providing sectors.
17. Stephen Roach (in Guile and Quinn, 1988). See also Stephen Roach (1989).
18. *Statistical Abstract of the United States*, 1991, p. 494.
19. An illustration is given by banking services where, depending on statistical methods, productivity gains are either poor (even negative) or very substantial (see Gadrey, 1996).
20. See Battelle Memorial Institute, Probable Levels of R&D Expenditures in 1987: Forecast and Analysis, Columbus, OH.
21. Sources of these data not given.
22. These records obviously depend on the definition and measurement method of the output. In the case of banking, for example, the results are sharply different according to whether one uses a 'transaction approach', displaying substantial productivity gains, or a 'liquidity approach' (based on a bank's financial results in constant dollars), often associated with poor

productivity performances (Gorman, 1969). While BEA uses the latter, BLS produces alternative figures based on the first type of method (Dean, 2000).

23. They constitute the bulk of limited-menu restaurants, but they exist also in eating places other than limited menu (especially what is called 'restricted menu').

24. It is worth noting that US food store productivity as traditionally measured by real sales per hour worked rose sharply from 1948 to a peak in 1972 (2.4 per cent annual rate of change). See Gadrey et al. (1991a).

25. However, in modern manufacturing, traditional output approaches are also often difficult to extend as far as use value is concerned. The case of computers is well known in this respect.

26. I subsequently reconsidered and modified this definition in a paper published by the Review of Income and Wealth (September 2000), but for the sake of productivity analyses, this 'triangle' approach remains valid.

27. We limit ourselves to labour productivity.

28. Interestingly, there is no change of state in the case of particular services of a preventive type, whose aim is precisely the protection against undesirable changes that are likely to occur in their absence.

29. 'The analysis resulted in the formation of 467 distinct patient classes referred to as DRGs. Each DRG is defined in terms of one or more of the following variables: principal diagnosis, operating room procedures, comorbidities and complications (secondary diagnoses), age, and in a few cases discharge status. As such, the DRGs represent a multivariable system for classifying hospital discharges from acute care hospitals into patient groups or types of cases with similar expected patterns of resources use. Thus, the DRGs operationally define the products of the hospital in terms of classes of patients with similar sets of services' (Fetter and Freeman, 1986).

REFERENCES

Abramovitz, Moses (1986), 'Catching Up, Forging Ahead and Falling Behind', *Journal of Economic History*, 46, June, 385–406.

Abramovitz, Moses (1990), 'The Catch-Up Factor in Postwar Economic Growth', *Economic Inquiry*, **28**(1), January, 1–18.

Ashby, John L. (1990), 'The Trend in Hospital Output and Labor Productivity, 1980–1988', PROPAC (Prospective payment assessment commission), Washington DC, July.

Attewell, Paul (1990), 'Information Technology and the Productivity Paradox', working paper, Graduate Center of the City University of New York, December.

Baumol, William (1967), 'Macroeconomics of Unbalanced Growth: The Anatomy of Urban Crisis,' American Economic Review, 57(3), 415–26.

Baumol, William J., Sue Anne Batey Blackman and Edward N. Wolff (1985), 'Unbalanced Growth Revisited: Asymptotic Stagnancy and New Evidence,' *American Economic Review*, 4, 806–17.

Baumol, William J. (1986), 'Productivity Growth, Convergence and Welfare : What the Long-Run Data Show', *American Economic Review*, 76, December, 1072–85.

Baumol, William J., Sue Anne Batey Blackman and Edward N. Wolff (1989), *Productivity and American Leadership. The Long View* (Cambridge, MA: MIT Press).

Dean, Edwin R. (1999), 'The Accuracy of the BLS Productivity Measures', *Monthly Labor Review*, February, 24–34.

Elfring, Tom, 1988, *Service Employment in Advanced Economies* (Groningen, NL: University of Groningen Press). See also, by the same author, a summary of this study: 'New Evidence on the Expansion of Service Employment in Advanced Economies', *The Review of Income and Wealth*, **35**(4), December 1989, 409–40.

Fetter, Robert B. and Jean L. Freeman (1986), 'Diagnosis Related Groups: Product Line Management Within Hospitals', *Academy of Management Review*, **11**(1), 41–54.

Gadrey, Jean (1996), *Services: la productivité en question* (Paris: Desclée de Brouwer).

Gadrey, Jean, Thierry Noyelle and Thomas M. Stanback (1991a), 'Productivity in Retailing', report, University of Lille 1, France, and the Eisenhower Center for the Conservation of Human Resources, Columbia University, New York, February.

Gadrey, Jean, Thierry Noyelle and Thomas M. Stanback (1991b), 'Productivité et emploi dans les hôpitaux français et américains', report, University of Lille 1, France, and the Eisenhower Center for the Conservation of Human Resources, Columbia University, New York, February.

Gadrey, Jean, Thierry Noyelle and Thomas M. Stanback (1991c), 'Productivity in the Eating and Drinking Places Industry', report, University of Lille 1, France, and the Eisenhower Center for the Conservation of Human Resources, Columbia University, New York, August.

Gadrey, Jean, Thierry Noyelle and Thomas M. Stanback (1992a), 'Productivity in Air Transportation', report, University of Lille 1, France, and the Eisenhower Center for the Conservation of Human Resources, Columbia University, New York, March.

Gadrey, Jean, Thierry Noyelle and Thomas M. Stanback (1992b), 'Productivity Gains in Life and Property/Casualty Insurance', report, University of Lille 1, France, and the Eisenhower Center for the Conservation of Human Resources, Columbia University, New York, April.

Gadrey, Jean (2000), 'The Characterization of Goods and Services: on Alternative Approach,' *Review of Income and Wealth*, **46**(3), September, 369–87.

Gordon, Robert (1999), 'Has the "New Economy" Rendered the Productivity Slowdown Obsolete?', June, http://Faculty-web.at.northwestern.edu/economics/garden/indexrise.html.

Gorman, John A. (1969), 'Alternative Measures of the Real Output and Productivity of Commercial Banks', in Victor R. Fuchs (ed.), *Production and Productivity in the Service Industries* (New York: Columbia University Press).

Guile, Bruce R. and James Brian Quinn (eds) (1988), *Managing Innovation: Cases from the Service Industries*, (Washington DC: National Academic Press).

Hill, Peter (1977), 'On Goods and Services', *The Review of Income and Wealth*, **23**(4), December, 315–38.

Roach, Stephen (1989), 'Pitfalls on the New Assembly Line: Can Services Learn from Manufacturing?', OECD International Seminar on Science, Technology and Economic Growth, Paris, June.

Statistical Abstract of the US, various years, US Census Bureau, Washington DC.

Thurow, Lester (1989), 'Toward a High-Wage, High-Productivity Service Sector', Economic Policy Institute, Washington DC.

Weiss, Mary A. (1991), 'International P-L Insurance Output, Input, and Productivity Comparisons', *The Geneva Papers on Risk and Insurance*, **16**(2), December.

3. Informational activities as co-production of knowledge and values

Jacques De Bandt and Ludovic Dibiaggio

INTRODUCTION

At least in developed countries, productive systems have been undergoing, since the beginning of the 1970s, deep and wide-ranging changes. Of particular importance, among these changes, has been the growth of service activities, particularly of financial and business services. Significant among these have been the growth of activities related to information (informatics, information systems and activities) and, particularly in the 1980s, R&D activities and systems of innovation.

This chapter aims at analysing those evolutions and at proposing a consistent interpretation, with reference to a specific representation of the 'new economy'. The 'learning economy', in which knowledge is supposed to play a new and much increased role, is implying both new 'ways of doing' in the various domains and new types of relations to space and time. If so, what is at stake is the interpretation of the actually observed evolutions of production activities in this perspective.

The emphasis will be on a set of new phenomena and realities, of which it can be shown rather easily that they cannot be handled within the framework of the old industrial paradigm, which was referring mainly to the energetic transformation of raw materials. Their novelty has to be highlighted, so as to show that in order for these new phenomena and realities to be understandable, a new paradigm or system of interpretation is required, referring essentially to the role of knowledge in production and value creation.

An attempt will be made in order to show that the above mentioned evolutions are converging or – what is maybe more correct – are to a large extent overlapping. The common denominator is the capacity to produce knowledge as a response to specific questions (or problems, needs and so on) where the question in turn, in its context, is a source of knowledge creation. It then becomes important to insist on the central role of knowledge production processes. Distinctions have to be made between different types of knowledge with various degrees of complexity and between different forms of organization of productive systems. It is in this framework that the growth of informational activities can be shown to constitute a major aspect of the actual transition as concerns the organization of productive systems.

1. EVOLUTIONS, AS OBSERVED AND ANALYSED

1.1 The Growth of Service Activities, of Informational Activities, and of R&D Activities within the Framework of (National) Innovation Systems

The main aspects of these evolutions are well known. But the way they are presented matters. The growth of *services* follows a secular path, as formalized in the Fisher–Clark model: the growth of tertiary activities (actually in the order of 70 per cent of both GDP and employment) is the consequence of the combined action of productivity growth and of the changing composition of demand resulting from the parallel growth of incomes. The origin of the growth of *informational activities* and jobs is somewhat more difficult to identify.[1] While growth has been rather progressive, a strong acceleration has become evident in the years ending the high growth period (of the 1950s and 1960s) and later. Even while *national systems of innovation* have emerged and become visible after World War II (at least, strongly related to defence objectives, in some countries), the growth of R&D activities has been strongly accelerated in the 1970s and 1980s.[2]

Whatever the origins of these evolutions, the rather recent awareness of their importance corresponds typically to the 'transition crisis' starting around 1970. Because of the apparent disappearance of industry as the central driving force of the system, questions were being raised about the future of growth in the developed countries.

It rapidly became clear, in the course of the 1970s, that only service activities and jobs were continuing to grow. But because the image of services was not very positive – they were not seen as likely to contribute much to growth – it was only somewhat later, particularly with the opening of the Uruguay Round, that the importance of service growth became really visible. As concerns informational activities, Porat's seminal work of 1977 was already quite elaborated, suggesting the development of new forms of labour organization and new ways of doing in the production sphere. Parallel to this, the new importance of non-material investments, representing such new ways of doing, became increasingly visible. Finally a whole body of literature on R&D expenditures and activities was illustrating the widespread belief in the possibility to develop new technologies and, on that basis, new production activities and jobs.

But, at the same time, even while these evolutions were becoming apparent more or less simultaneously, their analyses have been kept totally separate, at least until recently. The explanation seems to be that their observation was referring to totally divergent representations of the world of production.

The growth of services, seen as poorly productive, was leading to rather pessimistic forecasts of some kind of stagnation. On the contrary, the growth of informational activities was seen as the emergence of new ways of doing. As concerns R&D and innovation processes, most analyses – mainly of the evolutionary type – were considering essentially innovation and technological change processes and mechanisms, independently of any relation with the growth regime.

Many analyses of these evolutions have thus been developed, but separately and, but for exceptions, without any link. A major proportion of such (including multidisciplinary) analyses has been devoted to innovation processes, because they were considered as the most important stakes. Somewhat paradoxically, analyses of service activities have been, quantitatively, more important than those of informational activities.

1.2   The Existing Links between the Respective Growth of Services, of Informational Activities and of R&D Activities

These three evolutions have thus been considered separately and their analyses have been referring to independent representations of the world of production. This being said the question is whether these evolutions are indeed separated or what, on the contrary, their links or common elements are.

One important link, organic as it were, exists between these evolutions. This has led (i) to pinpoint the notion of non-material investments, in relation with R&D activities (De Bandt, 1981), (ii) to identify, within the overall service category, the specific category of informational service activities, corresponding to another type of production logic (De Bandt, 1996a), and (iii) to relate informational activities to innovation processes (for instance Cohendet, 1994).

But we are still far from a situation in which this link could be considered as being generally accepted and there are many reasons for this. The discussions about service activities have been dominated by a number of difficult debates about rather second-order issues:

- The question whether services are rather similar to or rather different from goods varies according to authors and circumstances, opinions have fluctuated from one extreme to the other.

- The question whether services are rather material or rather non-material, compared to goods which are essentially material. Of course services can have a more or less important material basis.
- The distinction between traditional services (externalized domestic services and transports) with low skill levels, and modern services with high skill and value added levels.

Different typologies and classifications have been developed, referring to a limited number of criteria.

It could safely be said that these are all attempts aiming at proposing some needed distinctions within a field whose unity one tries to maintain, more or less artificially. But even so, those distinctions tend to question this unity, because of the convergence of a number of important lines of opposition. Catchwords tend to be associated along two lines:

- Standardized goods and services, materiality, traditional services, low skills or automation.
- Specific goods and services, co-production, non-materiality, new services with high skills and high value added.

In order to go further, one would need to make an *n*-dimensional analysis, referring to *n* possible characteristics of all productive activities (weighted by their value added). This would probably lead to significant classifications. But the interest of such classification can only be limited: on the one hand, because enterprises do include hybrid subsets of activities of different kinds (making still more detailed analyses necessary), on the other hand, because enterprises are interpenetrating each other increasingly, and finally, because, in a dynamic perspective, the activities which are internalized within enterprises and the nature of the various activities are changing continuously.

But is the reason why the search for well-defined categories of activities is hopeless not the very simple fact that the modes of production are changing? What are changing are the ways of doing in the production of products and values.

If so, shouldn't we abandon the idea of making one or more distinctions and of building classifications, which would be somehow perfect and sufficiently stable. Shouldn't we concentrate our attention on what, within the evolution of services, reflects those new modes of production.

We have here to stop for a while at the notion of 'service relation', which has been put forward (De Bandt and Gadrey, 1994), as reflecting also some typical feature of the new ways of doing. The integration of the client/customer within the production process, that is co-production, represents indeed a fundamental change of the ways of doing, whose consequences may be considerable.

Highlighting the service relation was obviously a good idea, and has met with considerable interest. The use of this notion has become widespread. But it was probably, from different respects, not such a good idea. Of course the idea of co-production is important. But by using the term 'service relation', it was as if this was referring to service activities as such, which was a mistake. Proof of this is the fact that is has immediately been felt necessary to insist on the possibility for the service relation to characterize any kind of production activity, including industrial activities. What is important in what has been called the service relation, is not co-production per se. Co-production doesn't raise any problem in those cases in which processes and products are prede- fined and reproduced identically. Co-production becomes important when this implies some co-production of more complex knowledge, requiring some kind of cognitive interaction between complementary competencies. Moreover, this is the reason why those informational activities are increasingly performed within what can be called the mixed model combining 'buy' and 'make' on the basis of narrower and deeper specialization, instead of the traditional either 'buy' or 'make' model.

Research on informational activities and jobs has not been any more successful, if one may say so. In hindsight, it seems clear that the intuitions and seminal work of Porat has not had the success and the follow-up, which it obviously deserved. The explanation may be that his work has been the object of a double 'recuperation' process: due to the emphasis which has been put both, practically, on the handling and circulation of data (databases, data flows, including transborder flows and so on) and, theoretically, on the theory of information, formalizing the mechanics of data and signal flows.

It is true that the literature on the information society or economy has insisted much more on the volumes of data to be handled, than on the produc- tion of knowledge. This literature has been punctuated by some important reference points. Porat (1977) himself had a certain propensity to look mainly at the volume of data corresponding to the endless increasing multiplicity of transactions. With the 'control revolution' of Beniger (1986), the emphasis is put on the possibility to follow, on a real time basis, all possible flows within enterprises, to develop systematically management controls and to push to its extreme limits the rationalization of all aspects of the functioning of enter- prises.[3] It is only with the 'knowledge jobs' (as distinct from 'data jobs') of Baumol et al. (1989) that informational activities consisting in producing more complex knowledge come to the fore. But this category was not used for analysing the transformations of the modes of production.

This all means that the capacities for storing and transmitting information remain central. As a matter of fact, the increased capacities for handling infor- mation at decreasing costs, or even at zero costs, have initiated strong cumulative processes leading to new needs and demands for more detailed, more varied, more sophisticated information, requiring more important handling capacities, and so on. Increased knowledge production leads to new types of software, allowing for more elaborated knowledge productions. But while, in real life, the second aspect is progressively gaining momentum, software becoming more and more important relative to hardware, the tenants of the information society or economy have kept their eyes fixed mainly on the first aspect.

As concerns R&D activities and innovation processes, the link between their development and the above mentioned evolutions would seem to be rather obvious. R&D activities are part both of informational service activities and of non-material investments, and are of course typical informational activities. And other informational activities may be contributing to innovation processes. But this very obvious junction has not happened, at least until rather recently. The abundant literature devoted to R&D activities and innovation, while rightly insisting on the various components of innovation processes (competencies, organizational learning and so on), has not dealt adequately with value creation.

A careful look at those evolutions, however, shows that some of their components are clearly overlapping:

- In the case of service activities, not services as such, even while it is in relation with services that co-production has been highlighted, but co-production, which takes all its importance when what is at stake is the co-production of knowledge.
- In the case of informational (service) activities and jobs, not just information handling, but, beyond, knowledge production activities, contributing to non-material investments.
- As concerns R&D activities, they are part of informational activities at large which produce innovation processes.

This tends to show that the common denominator is made of informational activities: the dynamic aspect corresponds to more or less complex knowledge production requirements.

The way they are labelled is of course of secondary importance: as industrial activities if they are performed within 'industrial' enterprises, or as services activities, if they are performed by external service providers, or as non-material investments and assets. The important question is not whether they are classified as secondary or tertiary activities, by way of convention. Taking account of the nature of those activities and of the relations between actors and of the ways of doing which they represent, and taking account, more fundamentally, of their decisive role in the production of products, values and wealth, the question is whether we shouldn't abandon actual classifications in which activities can only be classified either as secondary or tertiary.[4]

Of course, the central question is about the reasons for this new, decisive, importance of those knowledge production processes, for the production not only of products, but of values and wealth.

The pure reproduction of material production operations, which can be done at decreasing costs, either because they are completely automated, or because they are performed with low wages outside, is less and less a source of value and profits. Such operations represent in any case a decreasing share of GDP. If so, what are the new sources of value and wealth? Of course, we have generic information and communication technologies, with widespread application possibilities. Their considerable potentialities allow for many cost savings at the level of flows and transactions: from handling information to producing knowledge, from rather simple to progressively less simple knowledge.

But beyond this, potentially the main sources of value are related to the necessity and the possibility to face the much-increased complexities of productive realities. These complexities are translated into limits to growth, decreasing returns and negative externalities, which have to be compensated for by continuous flows of new solutions, on the basis of complex knowledge production processes.

What is at stake is the capacity to effectively face those complexities. Complex knowledge production has various difficulties to meet competence and organizational requirements. Centrally, they usually have to be co-production or organizational learning processes, because of the variety of complementary competencies, which are required. Because of these requirements, complex knowledge production processes are known not to be very efficient or effective.

The problem then is how they can be made to be more efficient and effective. We thus need to know more both about the type of knowledge, which has to be produced and about the possible contribution of information technologies and cognitive sciences to building up the required capabilities for complex knowledge production. But we also need to know more about the way the various organizational requirements of learning processes can be met.

2. KNOWLEDGE AT THE CENTRE OF THE PRODUCTIVE SYSTEM

The previous section clearly showed that knowledge production and diffusion have progressively become key parts of economic activities. It is not clear, however, what analysts mean by knowledge and to what extent its increasing intensity constitutes a structural transformation of productive systems. One aspect of the answer is that technological advances and the reduced cost of computers and of digital communication (information and communication technologies – ICTs) have allowed service industries (in particular banks, telephone and telecommunication networks, and distribution and retailing firms) to benefit from economies of scale as manufacturing did 100 years ago, thus favouring the emergence of global-scale service.

Additionally, there is a general belief that such rapid technological progress favours the widespread diffusion of knowledge, leading us towards a 'frictionless' economy. This simple – maybe simplistic – idea is that electronic interactions will permit knowledge about products and about other agents' behaviours to be shared faster and more reliably. Consequently, transaction costs (due to information search and to information asymmetries) will drop and induce a better (and maybe more efficient) use of knowledge, which naturally leads towards perfect market conditions. In other words, the simplification of knowledge – that is made reusable by digitizing it – and the standardization of intangible assets facilitate access to information that was previously hidden or expensive to acquire and have subsequently promoted information intensive market transactions. And indeed, it is clear that customer–suppliers relationships have changed dramatically with the implementation of electronic supply chain links, essentially because of cost reduction and reliability improvements (Brynjolfsson and Hitt, 2000).

At the same time, ICTs have had a dramatic impact on the organization of activities within the firm: information processing systems and communication technology induce a higher decentralization of activities and annihilate the role of managers as both controllers and information processors between different hierarchical levels. Then, bureaucratic companies are being replaced by '*network organisations*' and virtual corporations that communicate by using electronic information systems, thereby favouring the decentralization of their decision-making systems. In this perspective, economic activity tends to converge towards exchange involving either internal (within firm) or external (between firm) networks of small, autonomous production or service units (Zenger and Hesterly, 1997).

On the other hand, it has been stressed and widely recognized that there are some difficulties in transmitting (and thus trading) knowledge that is firm specific, idiosyncratic and tacit such as know-how (Teece, 1981, 2000; Winter, 1987). This promotes the argument that knowledge should be distinguished from information. While information can be codified and thereby be easily transmitted, knowledge is not a simple flow of input that can be processed but is rather a structure that relies on cognitive mechanisms (Dibiaggio, 1999). Along with this view, knowledge-based arguments suggest that organizational knowledge provides a synergetic advantage not replicable in the market. As a consequence, knowledge is presented as an irreducible friction: for knowledge to co-locate with decision-making some personal relationships are required.

While this argument justifies the importance of team working (Nonaka and Takeushi, 1995) and of close personal relationships between customer and suppliers (Lundvall and Johnson, 1994), it does not completely explain the observed complementary relationship between ICT investments, electronic relationships and the increase of knowledge workers and of knowledge-intensive service providers. In particular, a series of articles published by Bresnahan and his colleagues (Bresnahan, 1999; Bresnahan et al., 1999; Autor et al., 2000; Brynjolfsson and Hitt, 2000) show that at the firm level the result of the introduction of ICTs have different and sometimes contradictory effects on work's organization and on skills and knowledge required to use them. Their case studies stress a strong interdependence between technological and organizational changes in two different ways. On the one hand, ICTs enhanced standardization and greater specialization in activities with stable characteristics, that is highly prescribable, giving rise to a computer–labour substitution in line with Rifkin's (1995) predictions. But on the other hand, they find that greater levels of information technology are associated with greater levels of skill and education in the workforce and with an increase of labour intensity in activities with unpredictable problems to be solved.[5] At organizational levels, results are balanced. Bresnahan et al. (1999) surveyed 400 companies that invested in ICTs and found an increase in delegation of authority to individuals and teams. But other qualitative studies (Alvesson et al., 2001) show that some knowledge-intensive and project-oriented firms, such as consulting groups or biotech companies do not reduce their level of bureaucratization and, conversely, tend to standardize their activities and to increase the centralization of responsibilities.

This section will argue that a further investigation in knowledge characterization will help us understand these phenomena better. Knowledge status actually depends essentially on the context of its use. Rather than simply emphasizing knowledge-intensive activities (with high degree of know-how and of '*unarticulable*' knowledge – to use Winter's (1987) terms), we shall focus on the level of commonality of the environment of knowledge re-use. Indeed, knowledge standardization[6] – through codification or through routinization – depends on the reproduction of experimental actions or decisions in similar contexts. As a consequence, introducing ICTs may of course improve knowledge standardization. But new technologies may also increase the set of problems to be solved – users' expectations and opportunities for knowledge creation – so that standardization may go along with higher uncertainty and complexity of activities inducing new activities and new forms of organization.

2.1   Knowledge in a Cognitive Economy

A knowledge-based economy relies on the recognition that knowledge – and not mere information – is at the centre of contemporaneous economic activities, so that learning becomes crucial to the process of economic growth (Foray and Lundvall, 1996). But what does knowledge mean? As Dosi (1996, p. 84) explains, while information entails well-stated and codified propositions about 'states of the world', that is objects or events, or explicit mechanisms, recipes or laws, knowledge includes cognitive categories, codes of interpretation, tacit skills, and problem solving and fuzzy defined search heuristics. As such, knowledge is a capacity to interpret information (a state of the world) and to select an action that is supposed to induce expected consequences. This presentation conforms to the traditional information processing perspective of cognitive systems (for instance Simon, 1982). But as Steinmuller (1999) suggests, knowledge is also a capacity to produce more knowledge and information, that is to create new interpretation frames, and even create new actions in unknown environments.

2.1.1 What knowledge is and how to deal with it

To integrate this creative dimension, knowledge should not be assimilated to a pure adaptive process. To make it simple, let us define knowledge as a cognitive structure that is able to make the link between a recognized question (a problem) and a possible answer (a solution or an action). This process is traditionally asserted by most learning models to be a linear sequence: perception – representation – judgement – choice – action (Dosi et al., 1996), where representation, as the cognitive counterpart of external world, plays a central role. This representation theory, as set up by the 'computation–representation paradigm' considers mind as a system processing symbols based on the existence of 'states of mind' and on their transformation. Then, decision-making or problem solving can be interpreted as the output of a logic succession of transformation rules implemented properly. As a consequence, representations (states of mind) are logically related to external entities[7] and knowledge is modelled as a transferable construct (cf. Gardner, 1985).

Another stream of research relies on a different tradition that views knowledge as a creation process rather than as a representation (Maturana and Varela, 1980). This approach focuses more on the process of knowing than on knowledge. Knowing and learning are viewed as the evolution of the structure of cognitive systems. Learning is no longer viewed as an adaptation to environmental changes but as a construction of the cognitive system that aims to maintain its identity. The cognitive system's behaviour is guided by the search for a required stability: when recognizing a transformation of its structure, the system defines a strategy that restores its structural stability and maintains its identity.[8] Recognition capabilities are dependent on experiences provided by specific and contextual actions. It is embodied in individuals embedded in social networks that stock implicit common understanding and insure similar or compatible behavioural patterns in commonly recognized situations.[9] The creation of meaning results from ongoing social interactions grounded in collective practices and in the specifics of the social and cultural setting (Blackler, 1995; Galunic and Rodan, 1998).

2.1.2 A typology of situations

Following this framework, we can define a typology of contextual situations that affect the nature of the cognitive process as it is implemented. The argument is that agents will exhibit specific kinds of rationality (implement different cognitive mechanisms) regarding the complexity[10] of the problem to solve or the question to answer; that is, according to the recognition of the problem to be solved, related to experience of effective actions in this context. We put forward *simple*, *problem-solving* and *complex situations* as three archetypes of decision-making or learning situations that induce different behavioural patterns. Each situation-type depends on the familiarity of the agent with the question to be answered, the problem to be solved or the situation in which he or she has to behave. Rather than considering agents endowed with (limited) cognitive capabilities, we describe agents that behave in different levels of '*bounded uncertainty*' related to a level of '*disbelief*' about specific events, following Shackle's terminology (1961). In case of certainty, *disbelief* is nil, this means that agents have a complete knowledge of the consequences of each possible actions given the observed state of the world. At the opposite extreme, in the case of *radical uncertainty*, certain states of the world are not within the scope of the agent's *structural knowledge*. Consequently, agents are necessarily unaware of the possible occurrence, which gives rise to a complete *surprise*.

Simple situations characterize a decision-maker facing a problem or a question that he or she estimates or judges to be simple because the answer to the recognized question is directly available. An extreme case is a *Pavlovian* stimulus–answer process such as braking when the red light shows. This is pure routine.

Problem-solving situations apply when the problem encountered is recognized, but there is no automatic available action to solve it. Deliberation and problem-solving strategies (heuristic implementation) are required. A *problem-solving situation* is characterized by a closed problem space so that procedural rationality as defined by Simon (1982) can be implemented (Dosi and Egidi, 1991). Since the question is clear and the solution is known to exist but cannot be reached automatically, the problem is decomposed in sub-problems that can be solved independently and sequentially. Learning (about the nature of the problem to be solved) and solving the problem in such a situation rely on a combination of inductive and deductive rules. In this situation, learning does not affect *structural knowledge* consistency but may extend its size, possibly by adding new categories of *specific knowledge*.

A *complex situation* results from an ill-defined problem, a desired end-result to which the solution cannot be found by implementing logical transformation rules or heuristics from initial conditions. There is no clear possible representation (recognition) since we are typically in a meaningless situation. The problem space is open, that is agents are *ignorant* (in the sense of Knight, 1921) about the existence of a solution. Indeed, the existence of a solution is pure conjecture. As there is no relevant cognitive structure in the system, the strategy followed is lateral learning relying on *abductive* reasoning rather than inductive or deductive rules. This consists in looking for analogies: try to find similarities with previous experiences, models, rules and so on (Richard, 1995). Learning in *complex situations* is likely to affect the consistency of *structural knowledge*. Creation is a process of redefining the structure of the knowledge system.

Learning and problem solving develop through repetitive trial and error processes as corroborated both by studies of engineering activities (Vincenti, 1990; Constant, 2000) and of children's learning by experimental psychologists (compare Richard, 1995). They both describe learning and problem solving as recursive practices that yield reliable knowledge in the sense that it proves to be effective in the context of its use.

This process of 'recursive Popperian falsification' by experimentation results in a strongly corroborated *problem space* that defines a relation between a class of problems and a class of solutions. This problem space, therefore, consists of a set of knowledge delimited by their application domain. It comprises knowledge of the properties of elements and the relationships among them (Stankiewicz, 2000). This stabilization of a knowledge base constitutes the structure of the knowledge system's organization. It tends to abstract from its contextual applications and to form an implicit self-contained structure of recognition. This structural knowledge is distinguished from specific knowledge (Nelson, 1991; Iansiti, 1998; Constant, 2000) that remains problem- and context-specific, highly dependent on practical know-how.

The level of complexity of a situation is related to the extent to which the consistency of the knowledge base is likely to be challenged by the potential answer suggested by a question. To put it differently, in *simple situations*, the relation between a recognized question and an answer is implemented automatically. In *complex situations*, the question is ill defined and the existing knowledge base does not provide the required structure of recognition. Then, the problem-solving strategy is to modify the problem space by testing new solutions and creating new question–answer relations. This will affect the structure of the knowledge base.

2.2 Standardization, Increasing Complexity and Organization Dynamics: Co-Production as an Organizational Answer

For the division of labour to be possible, problems have to be partitioned. Problem partitioning requires two constraints. First, the general problem has to be clearly defined and to remain stable over time. Otherwise, the nature of the complementarities between different activities may be modified and partitioning should be reconsidered. Second, partition requires information exchange both because sub-tasks may require information generated elsewhere and because sub-tasks' outputs have to be integrated effectively at a higher level. This may be difficult for two reasons: situation complexity and knowledge stickiness. Complexity because in *complex situations*, partition is not possible *ex ante*. The nature of the problem is evolving during the course of the problem solving process. Difficulties in 'unsticking' knowledge results from strong complementarities between different bodies of knowledge that cannot be unbundled. Moreover, there may be knowledge asymmetries across knowledge producers and knowledge users, and knowledge transmission can be limited by tacitness and limited incentives to reveal knowledge (compare von Hippel, 1998).

The central hypothesis of studies testing the impact of ICTs on organizations, is that the introduction of ICTs reduces co-ordination and transaction costs and subsequently promotes both market relations and virtual or 'disaggregated' organisation (Zenger and Hesterly, 1995). As Coase (1937) explained, gathering the required information to make transactions (such as determining design, price, quantity, schedule, and so on) is costly. Williamson (1975, 1985) further explained that transaction costs tend to be higher when assets are specific and transactions infrequent because of the cost of searching for appropriate suppliers, specifying contracts, enforcing the contracts, and handling financial settlements. Malone et al. (1987) show that product complexity is a strong factor of transaction costs because the customer requires a large amount of information to simply use it and monitoring product quality is expensive.[11] At market level, the introduction of ICTs contributes to reducing those information costs since information access is made easier, faster and more reliable and thereby favours market relations rather than internalization (Argyres, 1996)[12] and thus reduces adverse selection and the risk of investments being held up.

At firm level, ICTs have a great impact on organization because they improve information processing capacities and thereby solve some co-ordination problems in case of uncertainty, reducing the need of interpersonal relationships. However, these developments tend to consider only one dimension of the problem, namely the reduction of uncertainty and of information ambiguity due to better and more reliable communication and greater information processing capacities. These arguments rely on the hypothesis that ICTs tend to make situations *simpler* (that is they increase recognition capacities and reduce uncertainty) by standardizing knowledge and intangible assets in order to make them reusable at a lower cost. They do not consider the increasing complexity and knowledge stickiness that ICTs directly and indirectly induce.

The driving force of this evolution is of course the combination of techno-logical change, which approximately follows the famous Moore's law,[13] and the increasing connectivity made possible by the Internet. This dramatic price reduction combined with the rise of transmission and processing capacities together permit a greater automation of information gathering, processing and storage and of decision-making. This gives rise to new opportunities for scale economies and decreases the need for monitoring, making intermediate management useless. Indeed, standardization enhances both information reli-ability and compatibility of different aspects of *specific knowledge*. By stan-dardizing (reducing variety) *structural knowledge* it facilitates knowledge transfers (Tassey, 2000).

In other words, nothing new since Adam Smith's pin manufacture. Task partitioning and the subsequent specialization give rise to increasing returns so far as sub-tasks remain compatible. Further, Taylor's scientific organization of work and Ford's chain production are organizational methods that make situ-ations *simpler* by standardizing and even rigidifying *structural knowledge*. This increases the prescribability and reliability of tasks and reduces monitor-ing costs and information exchange requirements. Mass production is a conse-quence of the standardization of consumers' choice (we all remember the Model T) and of production and distribution (logistics) providing economies of scale, scope and speed. Finally, programmable machine tools move a step further in making flexible situations *simpler* by automating the adaptation process (Rosenberg, 1982), reducing the possibility of the occurrence of unex-pected problems.

This is what information activities are currently experiencing as structural knowledge is made rigid and information processing is automated. Consequently, organizations experience strong learning effects in information activities, thereby reducing knowledge transmission costs (Bolton and Dewatripont, 1994). Moreover, increasing communication capacities favour parallel information processing, thereby reducing the need of centralization (Radner and van Zandt, 1992). These elements, combined with the reduction of agency costs, essentially due to the decreasing costs of monitoring and of the implementation of incentive systems, together permit a greater decentral-ization of organisations.[14] The make or buy decision is affected in the same way. Information standardization and increasing specialization reduce trans-action costs and give the opportunity to specialists to provide and enjoy scale economies and learning effects on specific information services.

Standardization eventually contributes to the emergence of a mass market for information services at various levels: online interactions substitute for traditional customer–supplier relations,[15] it enables movement of orders and delivery management online and customers can be provided with online support.[16] ICTs have also enhanced greater division of labour in R&D, promoting markets for technologies (Arora et al., 2000), and have initiated strong economies of scale in research projects. Additionally, by putting their supply chains online companies expect major cost savings. They claim that these gains range between 2 and 40 per cent of total input costs depending on the industry and could lead to an economy-wide price reduction of almost 4 per cent (Bassanini et al., 2000).

These trends towards *commodification* and simplification of situations have two consequences for the organization of production systems. First, within firms ICTs indeed lead to flatter organizations and to a destruction of bureaucracies by reducing intermediate management. But unlike traditional hypotheses, ICTs do not favour delegation and bottom-up information systems. On the contrary, standardization improves managers' powers to prescribe and control operational works. Second, on the market place, there is a clear trend towards disintermediation and outsourcing leading firms to focus on their core competencies. Tacitness and learning-by-doing in R&D activities for instance happens also to be the justification for outsourcing, in particular when the output may be used as a turnkey solution, permitting a simplification of knowledge reuse.

ICTs, however, also induce increasing complexity, generating re-intermediation, the emergence of new activities and modifications of production processes. Increasing complexity can be interpreted in two ways. On the one hand, complexity occurs as a natural counterpart of standardization: stabilization of structural knowledge and of (knowledge) production processes favours a vertical division of labour relying on higher skills and competencies in emerging specific domains (information systems security and maintenance, software development and so on). Further, this leads to the standardization and the automation of control functions (Beniger, 1986). But as mentioned earlier, the division of labour may be questioned at all times when new knowledge is likely to change the nature of complementarities between activities. There are specialists who actually tend to increase knowledge obsolescence by constantly proposing solutions that affect technical systems' structure in order to overcome potential systemic bottlenecks, an outcome described as reverse salient by Hughes (1992). In other words, while information works tend to be automated, there is a complementary need for unprescribable activities relying on ever changing *specific knowledge*.

The other factor of increasing complexity is, in a sense, the counterpart of Moore's law. While innovation (in semiconductors' capacities) goes at a regular pace, complementary innovations and functional complexity increase exponentially. This dramatically affects the whole value chain and increases knowledge production in *complex situations*. Knowledge production in *complex situations* requires specific organizational design: more than simple decentralization of work, it requires a decentralization of responsibility. Because knowledge production in *complex situations* is closely related to recognition capabilities, only those teams that are involved in the context of knowledge production can understand their environment and take relevant decisions. Unlike the interpretation paradigm that considers middle managers as translators for top managers, so that organizations can be represented as information processors, translation would be too costly (or impossible) given the lack of common language between different contexts. Networks of autonomous teams based on knowledge co-production processes happen to be the most effective organization. Co-production means the production of knowledge based on co-operation. The make or buy decision is no longer the main question in organization setting. Rather it is to set up teams that can at any time mobilize different bodies of knowledge that are likely to be complementary in the context of the project. As projects are renewing regularly, functional or hierarchical organizations are constantly limited by complexity (compare Powel et al., 1996, 1998; Hansen, 1999).

This also changes the traditional hypothesis regarding the frictionless economy. Rather than considering the market and organizations as the two polar solutions for a problem of organization of activities, they appear to be parts of the same dynamic. Eventually, it may be that the make or buy dilemma is not the good question since in complex situations transaction costs are just unforeseen *ex ante*. The question is rather finding the relevant setting to organize sustainable networks relying on trust. Because, indeed, knowledge asymmetries give rise to free-riding. But there is no way that any contract nor any bureaucracy can sort this problem out. The only criterion is knowledge sharing in order to motivate agents with great 'cultural distance' (to use Lundvall's term, 1991) to co-produce value. Faulkner and Senker's study (1995) is a good illustration of this phenomenon. They show that engineers and researchers need to establish personal relationships and strong ties with external partners because of the progressive extension of research programmes that tends to integrate dimensions beyond their domain of expertise. While they do not belong to the same institution and not necessarily to the same research tradition, they have to create a new language (structural knowledge) because they increasingly need to co-produce specific knowledge to solve *complex problems*.

More generally, this confirms the idea stressed by Gibbons et al. (1994) that there are important changes in the social conditions of the production of knowledge that result in the emergence of a distributed knowledge production system. Knowledge production and dissemination are no longer self-contained in specified domains carried out in well-identified institutions or private research labs. Rather, knowledge is created through complex interactions organized around projects and problems to be solved. While, these authors insist on the implications for education and institutions such as the university that will have to work hand in hand with industry, the whole knowledge productive system is actually affected. Because *complex situations* become critical, those knowledge workers (defined as problem identifiers, problem solvers, and problem brokers by Gibbons et al.) develop an increasing variety of knowledge that can potentially be related in projects. They will need more and more opportunities for interaction that are not limited by the boundaries of the firm. Those relations cannot be anticipated before projects are defined so that organizations will have to work with networks that are trust related rather than contract related and that will require continual processes of making languages (structural knowledge) cohere.

CONCLUSION

Clearly, informational activities, and among them R&D and innovation related activities, are developing fast within the world of production, both inside and outside user firms: they are widely diffused and quantitatively becoming dominant. Non-material investments, on the basis of such informational activities, typically represent new ways of doing within the production sphere. What is at stake is the production of value and wealth by solving series of actual problems on the basis of relevant knowledge. Such relevant knowledge has to be produced and, increasingly, co-produced, on the basis of complementary competencies.

As a matter of fact, speaking of the production of knowledge and of the application of ICTs to the production of knowledge, very different or even contradictory trends are to be observed, both the automation of simple knowledge in rather simple or simplified situations and the co-production of complex knowledge in increasingly complex or uncertain situations. And this is thus explained by the type of knowledge that has to be produced according to the level of complexity of the situation or problem that has to be tackled.

There is on the one hand a general trend towards simplification, standardization, division of tasks and so on. This has, in the past, made up for huge productivity increases in the manufacturing sector. This trend has been more recently at work in informational activities. In all situations in which only 'simple' knowledge has to be produced, either because the situation is simple or because it can be simplified, ICTs can perform the tasks and induce considerable gains. Some progress is equally possible in some of the 'problem' situations, to the extent that some standardization procedures seem feasible. But there is simultaneously another trend, towards contextual specificity, customization, complexity and the like. The world of production is structurally characterized by increasing complexity and uncertainty and, given the possibility of reaching higher levels of complexity such situations require the production of complex knowledge. Because of the competence requirements, complex knowledge needs essentially to be co-produced within organizational learning processes. Co-production, which is at the heart of the 'service relation', thus becomes a central aspect of the new modes of production.

NOTES

1. According to Baumol et al. (1989), in the USA, in 1980, 52 per cent of all jobs were informational jobs. According to J. De Bandt (1996), in France, in 1995, informational activities represented 35 to 40 per cent of jobs and 40 to 45 per cent of GDP.
2. This was however followed by slower growth or even decline in the 1990s (even if private R&D has been compensating partly for the decrease in public R&D). Serious doubts have risen as concerns the efficiency or effectiveness of the resources allocated to R&D activities (see for example, the so-called 'European Paradox'). Such doubts are raising questions concerning the future of the knowledge or learning economy: what if knowledge production activities are not efficient?
3. In the present phase, Internet (B to B, Business to business) allows for the same kind of utmost rationalization of inter-enterprise relationships.
4. From that standpoint, the idea of 'quaternary' activities, which was suggested many years ago, but which is not used any more, was maybe not bad, after all.
5. These studies are meant to explain the observed rise of wage disparities.
6. By knowledge standardization, we mean setting up a context so that knowledge can be re-used at no adapting cost.
7. Representations rely on an informational or a functional description, which cannot necessarily be explained by a physical description.
8. The system's identity lies in its performance system, internally defined, and in its actions, implemented according to internal laws.
9. Which does not necessarily mean isomorphic cognitive structures (compare Dibiaggio, 2000). This simply means that 'if two people have been exposed to different experiences in the past, with resulting differences in the stock of conceptual representations they have formed, they may act on the same data differently' (Arthur, 1992, p. 8).
10. Complexity is here used as a description of the relation between available answers and recognized questions, quite close to Shackle's *potential surprise*.
11. Quoted by Argyres (1996).
12. Notice that those theoretical arguments are only supported by a series of case studies cited by Malone et al. (1987). Kraut et al. (1997) made a survey of 250 firms in four different industries and found no evidence supporting the informational impact (that is the cost of searching for or describing the input) on the make or buy decision.
13. In 1965, Gordon E. Moore made the prescient observation that chips would contain twice as many transistors every 18–24 months, that is a growth of chip capacity at 35–45 per cent per year. In the meantime (between, 1974 and 1996), prices of memory chips have decreased at about 40 per cent per year and prices of logic chips have decreased at about 54 per cent per year.
14. More precisely, ICTs and parallel information processing contribute to the reduction of *ex ante* uncertainty and measurement costs such as information asymmetries, and therefore

adverse selection. They also diminish *ex post* measurement costs as moral hazards by making work more prescribable. This does not mean that workers' efforts are more foreseeable but that the expected output is standardized.

15. Beyond electronic bookshops such as Amazon, traditional companies such as banks, package deliverers and so on are gaining operational leverage. For instance, Federal Express has set up a system that enables online management of all customer services from initial order to delivery.

16. It is estimated that in 1997, online support had eliminated a quarter-million phone calls a month (about $500 million), that is about 9 per cent of total revenue.

REFERENCES

Alvesson, M., D. Kärreman and S. Sveningsson (2001), 'The Return of the Machine Bureaucracy – Management Control and Knowledge Work', paper presented at the Managing Knowledge: Conversations and Critiques Conference, Leicester, 10–11 April.

Argyres, N. (1996), 'The Impact of Information Technology on Coordination: Evidence from the B-2 "Stealth" ', mimeo, School of Business Administration, University of South California Los Angeles.

Arora, A., A. Fosfuri, and A. Gambardella (2000), 'Markets for Technology (Why Do We See Them, Why Don't We See More of Them and Why We Should Care)', mimeo, SPRU seminar presentation.

Arthur, W.B. (1992), 'On Learning and Adaptation in the Economy', mimeo, Institute for Economic Research.

Autor, D.H., F. Levy and R.J. Murnane (2000), 'Upstairs, Downstairs: Computer-Skill, Complementarity and Computer-Labor Substitution on Two Floors of a Large Bank', National Bureau of Economic Research Working Paper, n. W7890.

Bassanini, A., S. Scarpetta and I. Visco (2000), 'Knowledge, Technology and Economic Growth: Recent Evidence from OECD Countires', presentation paper at the 150th Anniversary Conference of the National Bank of Belgium: How to Promote Economic Growth in the Euro Area, Brussels, 11–12 May

Baumol, Willam J., Sue Anne Batey Blackman and Edward N. Wolff (1989), *Productivity and American Leadership: The Long View* (Cambridge, MA: MIT Press).

Beniger, James R. (1986), *The Control Revolution: Technological and Economic Origins of the Information Society* (Cambridge, MA: Harvard University Press).

Blackler, F. (1995), 'Knowledge, Knowledge Work and Organizations', *Organization Studies*, **16**(6), 1021–46.

Bolton, P. and M. Dewatripont (1994), 'The Firm as a Communication Network', *The Quarterly Journal of Economics*, **509**(4), 809–39.

Bresnahan, T.F. (1999) 'Computerization and Wage Dispersion: An Analytic Reinterpretation' *Economic Journal*, June, 390–415.

Bresnahan, T.F., E. Brynjolfsson and L.M. Hitt (1999), 'Information Technology, Workplace Organization and the Demand for Skilled Labor: Firm-Level Evidence' National Bureau of Economic Research Working Paper, n. W7136.

Brynjolfsson, E. and L.M. Hitt (2000), 'Beyond Computation: Information Technology, Organizational Transformation and Business Performance', *Journal of Economic Perspectives*, Fall, **14**(4), 23–48.

Clark C., (1957), *The Conditions of Economic Progress* (London: Macmillan).

Coase R.H. (1937), 'The Nature of the Firm', *Economica*, **4** (13–16), 386–405.

Cohendet, Patrick (1994), 'Relations de service et transfert de technologie', in Jacques De Bandt et Jean Gadrey (eds), *Relations de service, marchés de servcies* (Paris: CNRS Editions), pp. 201–13.

Constant, Edward (2000), 'Recursive Practice and the Evolution of Technological Knowledge', in John Ziman (ed.) *Technological Innovation as an Evolutionary Process* (Cambridge: Cambridge University Press), pp. 219–34.

De Bandt, Jacques (1981), 'Les impacts macro- et micro-économiques', in Commissariat du Plan, *Investissement non matériel et croissance industrielle* (Paris: La Documentation Française), pp. 145–72.

De Bandt, Jacques (1995), *Services aux entreprises : Informations, produits, richesses* (Paris: Economica).

De Bandt, J. (1996a), 'Business Services: Markets and Transactions', *Review of Industrial Organisation*, **11**(1), 19–33.

De Bandt, Jacques (1996b), 'Coopération, accords inter-entreprises, concurrence', in Jacques Laurent Ravix (ed.), *Coopération entre les entreprises et organisation industrielle* (coll. Recherche et Entreprises) (Paris: CNRS-Editions), 195–229.

De Bandt, Jacques (2000), 'Emergence and Development of the Service Economy in the European Union', in Lionello Punzo (ed)., *European Economies in Transition* (London: Macmillan), pp. 67–84.

De Bandt, Jacques and Jean Gadrey (eds) (1994), *Relations de service, marchés de services* (Paris: CNRS Editions).

Dibiaggio, L. (1999), 'Introduction' special issue on Knowledge Economics, *Revue d'Economie Industrielle*, 88, 11–22.

Dibiaggio, L. (2000) 'Hierarchy of Knowledge and Coordination. A Cognitive Perspective', Workshop on Cognitive Economics, Turin-Allessandria, 15–18 November 2000.

Dosi, Giovanni (1996), 'The Contribution of Economic Theory to the Understanding of a Knowledge-Based Economy', in OECD *Employment and Growth in the Knowledge-Based Economy*, pp. 81–100.

Dosi, G. and M. Egidi (1991), 'Substantive and Procedural Uncertainty. An Exploration on Economic Behaviours in Changing Environments', *Journal of Evolutionary Economics*, 1, 145–68.

Dosi, G., L. Marengo and G. Fagiolo (1996), 'Learning in Evolutionary Environments' IIASA (International Institute for Applied Systems Analysis), Working Paper.

Foray, Dominique and Bengt-Åke Lundvall (1996), 'The Knowledge-Based Economy: From the Economics of Knowledge to the Learning Economy', in OECD *Employment and Growth in the Knowledge-Based Economy*, pp. 11–32.

Faulkner Wendy and Jaqueline Senker (1995), *Knowledge Frontiers*, (Oxford: Clarendon Press).

Fisher, A.G.B., (1935) 'The Clash of Progress and Security', Kelley, London.

Galunic, D. C. and S. Rodan (1998), 'Resources Recombinations in the Firm: Knowledge Structures and the Potential for Schumpeterian Innovation', *Strategic Management Journal*, 19, 1193–1201.

Gardner, H. (1985), *The Mind's New Science. A History of the Cognitive Revolution,* (NewYork: Basic Books).

Gibbons, Michael, Camille Limoges, Helga Nowotny, Simon Schwartsman, Peter Scott and Martin Trow (1994), *The New Production of Knowledge*, (London: Sage).

Hansen, M.T. (1999), 'Combining Network Centrality and Related Knowledge: Explaining Effective Knowledge Sharing in Multiunit Firms', Harvard Business School Working Paper.

Hippel, E. von (1998), 'Economics of Product Development by Users: The Impact of "Sticky" Local Information', *Management Science*, **44**(5), 629–44.

Hughes, Thomas P. (1992), ' The Dynamics of Technological Change: Salients, Critical Problems, and Industrial Revolution', in Giovanni Dosi, Renato Gianetti and Pier Angelo Toninelli (eds), *Technology and Enterprise in a Historical Perspective* (Oxford: Clarendon Press), pp. 97–118.

Iansiti, Marco (1998), *Technology Integration: Making Critical Choices in a Dynamic World*, (Boston, MA: Harvard Business School Press).

Knight, Frank (1921), *Risk, Uncertainty and Profit* (Chicago: University of Chicago Press).

Kraut, R, C. Steinfield, A.C Plummer, B. Butler and A. Hoag (1997), 'Coordination Modes and Producer-Supplier Integration: Empirical Evidence from Four Industries', OECD Workshop n. 6 on the Economics of the Information Society, London, March 19–20.

Lundvall, B.Å, (1991) 'Innovation, the Organised Market and the Productivity Slowdown,' in *Technology and Productivity. The Challenge for Economic Policy*, OECD, Paris.

Lundvall, B.Å. and B. Johnson (1994), 'The Learning Economy', *Journal of Industry Studies*, **1**(2), 23–42.

Malone, T., J. Yates and R. Benjamin (1987), 'Electronic Markets and Electronic Hierarchies', *Communications of the ACM*, 30, 484–97.

Maturana, Humberto and Francisco Varela (1980), *Autopoiesis and Cognition: The Realizing of Living* (London: Reidl).

Nelson, Richard R. (1991). 'Why do Firms Differ, and How does it Matter?' *Strategic Management Journal*, 12, 61–74.

Nonaka, Ikujiro and Hirotaka Takeushi (1995), *The Knowledge Creating Company: How Japanese Companies Create the Dynamics of Innovation* (New York: Oxford University Press).

Nightingale, P., T. Brady, A. Davies and J. Hall (1999), 'Economies of System', CoPS Working Paper, Sussex University, UK.

Porat, M.U., (1977), 'The Information-economy: Definition and Measurement, U.S.' Department of Commerce, Washington.

Powell, W.W., Koput, K.W. and L. Smith-Doerr (1996), 'Inter-Organizational Collaboration and the Locus of Innovation: Networks of Learning in Biotechnology', *Administrative Science Quarterly*, 41, 116–45.

Radner, R. and T. van Zandt (1992), 'Information Processing in Firms and Returns to Scale', *Annales d'Economie et de Statistiques*, 25/26, 266–98.

Richard, Jean-François (1995), *Les activités mentales. Comprendre, raisonner, trouver des solutions* (Paris: Armand Colin).

Rifkin, Jeremy (1995), *The End of Work: The Decline of the Global Labor Force and the Dawn of the Post-Market Era* (New York: G.P. Putnam's Sons).

Rosenberg, Nathan (1982), *Inside the Black Box: Technology and Economics* (Cambridge: Cambridge University Press).

Shackle, George L.S. (1961), *Decision, Order and Time* (Cambridge: Cambridge University Press).

Simon, Herbert A. (1982), *Models of Bounded Rationality* (Cambridge, MA: Harvard University Press).

Stankiewicz, Rikard, (2000) 'The Concept of "Design Space" ' in John Zimon (ed.), *Technological Innovation as an Evolutionary Process*. Cambridge, Cambridge University Press, 2000.

Steinmuller, Edward W. (1999), 'Networked Knowledge and Knowledge-Based Economies', Telematica Institute, Delft, February.

Tassey, G. (2000), 'Standardization in Technology-Based Markets', *Research Policy*, 29, 587–602.

Teece, D.J. (1981), 'The Market for Know-How and the Efficient International Transfer of Technology' *Annals of the Academy of Political and Social Science*, 458, 81–96.

Teece, David J. (2000), *Managing Intellectual Capital* (Oxford: Oxford University Press).

Vincenti, Walter G. (1990), *What Engineers Know and How They Know It: Analytical Studies from Aeronautical History* (Baltimore: Johns Hopkins University Press).

von Hippel (1998), 'Economics of Product Development by Users: The Impact of "Sticky" Local Information', *Management Science*, 44, 5, 629–44.

Williamson, Oliver E. (1975), *Markets and Hierarchies – Analysis and Antitrust Implications* (New York: The Free Press).

Williamson, Oliver E. (1985), *The Economic Institutions of Capitalism* (New York: Free Press).

Winter, Sidney G. (1987), 'Knowledge and Competence as Strategic Assets', in David J. Teece, (ed.), *The Competitive Challenge: Strategies for Industrial Innovation and Renewal* (New York: Harper and Row).

Zenger, T. and W. Hesterly (1997), 'The Disaggregation of Corporations: Selective Intervention, High-Powered Incentives and Modular Units', *Organization Science*, 8, 209–222.

4. Capital stock and productivity in French transport: an international comparison

Bernard Chane Kune and Nanno Mulder[1]

INTRODUCTION

The efficiency of service providers is often approximated by labour productivity. This partial measure is seen as a proxy of overall efficiency as services are supposed to use relatively little capital. However, in many services such as transport, capital is a major production factor. To judge the overall efficiency of these services, labour productivity measures should therefore be complemented by measures of capital and total factor productivity (TFP). For France, it has not been possible to estimate capital productivity and TFP at the sectoral level of transport as no capital input estimates have been available.

This chapter aims to fill this gap by providing new detailed estimates of capital input in French transport from 1970 onwards. These data are used in combination with series on output and labour input to estimate productivity. Finally, the French performance is compared with that of Germany, the United Kingdom and the United States.

In contrast to many other studies on productivity, the contribution of capital to production is not measured by the value of the stock of assets but by the volume of services rendered by this stock (also referred to as the Jorgenson approach). Capital services are measured by the product of the volume of capital, approximated by the net capital stock, times its user cost. The latter is estimated by the sum of depreciation, the real interest rate and capital gains. We measured the net stocks of transport equipment in air and maritime transport by administrative records. The stock of other assets was estimated by the perpetual inventory method which sums several years of capital formation and deducts assets that reached the end of their service life. Detailed series were compiled of investment and discards in eight different transport areas, showing for each a breakdown into infrastructure, transport equipment and other machinery and equipment.

In the second part of the chapter productivity results are presented. Total factor productivity is estimated using the Törnqvist discrete approximation to the Divisia index. The variance of productivity patterns across transport sectors is not unique for France, as is illustrated by a comparison with Germany, the United Kingdom and the United States. Overall productivity gains in Germany and the United Kingdom were similar to those in France. The three European countries outperformed the USA. At the sectoral level, it turns out that air transport is the branch with the largest capital gains in all countries. The USA is the only country with large productivity gains in railways. France outperformed other countries in terms of productivity growth in air and maritime transport. In the other branches, French productivity growth was below that of the other countries.

CAPITAL IN FRENCH TRANSPORT

How to Measure Capital Input: Stocks or Services?

The scope of capital input is very different between studies. The Australian Bureau of Industry Economics (1995) adopted a narrow definition as they only included fixed capital goods. Others, such as the System of National Accounts, on the contrary, include a much wider range of assets, such as natural resources and intangible capital (computer software, patents and purchased goodwill). This study considers fixed assets as defined by the System of National Accounts (1993): the value of acquired assets by resident production units used for at least one year in the production process; as well as incorporated goods and services in existing fixed capital goods. Excluded from capital formation are expenses related to research and development and marketing.

A controversial issue in the national accounts and productivity analysis is whether the contribution of capital stock to production is best measured by the gross stock, the net stock or by the services rendered by the capital stock. The gross stock equals the value of all fixed assets in use, evaluated as if they were new, that is without taking account of obsolescence, depreciation, deterioration and price changes. The gross stock concept has been used in prior studies on productivity, which assumed that the productive capacity of assets remains constant over time. This seems realistic for some goods such as computers. However, the productive capacity of most assets decreases over time and the gross stock is therefore a concept of little relevance. Nevertheless, the gross stock is a useful intermediate statistical measure which is used to estimate net capital stocks.

The net capital stock equals the gross stock less depreciation or the decline in value of the assets as they age. An inconvenience of using (gross or net) capital stocks for productivity analysis is that they are stocks whereas all other variables (such as value added, intermediate consumption and hours worked) are flows. Some consider changes in gross or net stocks as flows, but these are first-order flows while changes in the other variables are second-order flows. For the purpose of productivity analysis we are thus interested in the services rendered by the capital stock.

Many growth accountants, such as Edward Denison and Angus Maddison (1987), have assumed that services are proportional to the size of the capital stock. This is unrealistic. Another proposed proxy of capital services is the depreciation rate. This measure is, however, also unsatisfactory as it leaves out the net return of capital assets as well as capital gains. The best-known approach that incorporates all aspects of capital services is that of Jorgenson and Griliches (1967). He measures capital services by the product of the volume of capital services times the user cost of capital. This is analogous to the contribution of labour to production, that is the number of hours worked times the wage rate. He measures the volume of capital services by the (net) stock measured by the perpetual inventory method (PIM), using geometric depreciation. The user cost S_t is determined as follows:

$$S_t = \left(\frac{1 - u_t z_t - k_t}{1 - u_t}\right)[q_{t-1}r_t + q_t d - (q_t - q_{t-1})] + q_t T_t \qquad (4.1)$$

where:

u_t = corporate tax rate at year t
z_t = present value of depreciation deductions for tax purposes on one currency unit's worth of investment over the life-year of the investment at year t
k_t = investment tax credit at year t
q_t = asset price index at year t
r_t = opportunity cost of capital at year t
d = depreciation rate of asset reflecting economic life
T_t = property tax rate at year t

The first term in brackets corresponds to the cost of capital, the second to the replacement cost (depreciation) and the third to the capital loss or gain of the asset. In summary, to determine the service price, one should take account of the corporate income tax, savings in corporate income tax due to capital cost allowances, investment tax credit, interest (that is opportunity) cost of capital incorporated in the asset, economic depreciation, capital gains or losses due to asset price changes and the property tax rate.

For coherency with the other measures in our productivity analysis, we adopted the Jorgenson approach here for the measurement of capital input. As the volume of capital services is assumed proportional to net capital stocks, we will explore below different methods of their empirical measurement.

The Empirical Measurement of Capital Stocks

Different methods are available to measure gross and net capital stocks. The first and best method is surveys. Firms are asked to report historic values of their assets and the dates when they were installed. Assets are subsequently revalued to constant prices using revaluation coefficients. An advantage of surveys over other methods, is the possibility of including leased assets. The reliability of surveys depends on the quality of the survey procedures and the ability of firms to supply the necessary information. Within the OECD, surveys are used in Japan, Korea and The Netherlands but not in France. As the experience of these countries show, surveys are not without problems, as firms often do not register small amounts of investments, alterations to existing assets and the new or second-hand character of the investment.

Secondly, stocks can be approximated by physical measures. Examples include the length of canals, the number of ports and airports, the area of office buildings and the number of trucks and buses. Data on physical measures are readily available in most countries. For historical analyses, especially for the pre-World War II period, capital stock data are also often restricted to physical measures. The major inconvenience of physical measures is that they are not additive and it is therefore impossible to estimate aggregate capital stocks. Moreover, with physical measures it is impossible to distinguish different vintages, each having a different technology, within a capital stock. Therefore one has to assume that all capital goods are strictly identical in terms of productive capacity. This seems very unrealistic.

A third way to estimate stocks is the use of administrative records. In many countries records exist of most types of transport equipment such as aircraft, buses, ships and trucks. These records can be used to measure the stock in one year as well as flows of investment and discards. In combination with data on price assets from statistical offices or international agencies, the build year of assets and price deflators, the value of gross stocks can be estimated. This approach is particularly interesting in activities where equipment is an important part of capital, such as air and maritime transport.

Fourthly, balance sheets are frequently used as they register assets on a net basis. For corporate firms, these are readily available. Unfortunately balance sheets have various disadvantages which render their use almost impossible. Companies register assets at their historical values which means that the capital stock is valued at a mixture of prices. Moreover, depreciation is estimated using fiscal accounting principles which are superior to economic depreciation rates. This means that even though the residual value of assets equals zero according to tax authorities, assets continue to be used in production. Moreover, accounting rules vary from country to country and net stocks therefore are not internationally comparable. From balance sheets it is also difficult to know of the vintages of which the capital stock is composed.

Finally, the most frequently adopted method to measure stocks is the 'perpetual inventory method' (PIM). The PIM sums several years of investment and deducts assets that reached the end of their service life. The PIM was developed by Raymond Goldsmith (1951) in the United States. Growth accountants such as Simon Kuznets, Edward Denison and Angus Maddison have subsequently used it. In France, this method was embedded in the French national accounts by Mairesse (1972).

The PIM has several advantages. Firstly, it requires only investment data, which are more easily available than capital stock data. Secondly, the PIM produces many characteristics on capital stocks, such as gross stocks, capital consumption, net stocks and the average age of capital assets. Thirdly, the PIM is simple to apply and is fully transparent. Finally, identical retirement and depreciation patterns render capital stocks internationally comparable.

A major inconvenience is that the application of the PIM requires various assumptions on the length of asset lives, retirement and depreciation patterns, which are often not very robust. Moreover, the PIM produces biased stock estimates when firms sell investment goods before they reach the end of their service life, as these sales are often not recorded. This occurs often in the case of transport equipment.

The Measurement of Capital Stocks and Services in France

(A)   Gross and net stocks

Two methods were used to estimate capital stocks: administrative records and the PIM. The PIM produces biased capital stock measures in sectors characterized by a large turnover of capital assets and important shares of leased and rented assets.[2] This is the case for most types of transport equipment. For the stock of aircraft and ships, we could correct this bias by using administrative records instead of the PIM (see Box 4.1).

The PIM for gross stocks consists of summing gross fixed capital formation over the life of assets. The PIM requires assumptions on asset lives and discard patterns. For France, estimates are available only by large groups of asset types without a breakdown by sub-sector of transport. Instead we used very detailed assumptions by asset type and sub-sector of transport of the US Department of Commerce, Bureau of Economic Analysis (1999). These are based upon a large body of empirical research and are summarized in Fraumeni (1997). The specific asset-life assumptions were converted to sector-specific

BOX 4.1   THE USE OF ADMINISTRATIVE
RECORDS TO MEASURE CAPITAL
STOCKS IN AIR TRANSPORT

International competition forces air companies to update their fleets regularly and therefore they sell most of their aircraft long before the end of their service life. Moreover, instead of purchasing, companies increasingly lease or rent their aircraft. Administrative records present information on each asset: when assets enter and leave the capital stock, when the asset was built and whether it is owned or not by the operator. Administrative records of aircraft are taken from the Airclaims database.[3] The Airclaims database provides no data on (historical) construction cost. These were mostly taken instead from the *Airliner Price Guide* which contains prices paid by the first purchaser of each type of aircraft in US$. After the conversion to French francs, these historical cost data were deflated to constant prices using the French deflator of aircraft in capital formation of the transport sector.

Robust estimates of the gross stocks can be made with the register data. This is because, contrary to the PIM, no assumptions are necessary on the length of asset lives and retirement patterns, as the registers shows exactly when assets enter and leave the stock. Moreover, not all aircraft are new when they enter the fleet. The estimation of net stocks is more difficult than gross stock as little, easily exploitable information is available of how the market prices of particular aircraft develop over time. Assumptions have to be made on depreciation patterns. The evolution of second-hand prices of transport equipment follows a geometric pattern, as illustrated by Fraumeni (1997). We did, however, not use this pattern, as the register data exclude an important element of capital formation in aircraft, for example major maintenance and revision. Therefore the net value of the aircraft is underestimated over its life time. To compensate for this, we assumed straight-line instead of geometric depreciation, which produces smaller reductions in the constant replacement value during the early life of the aircraft.

These records provide better measures than the PIM for two reasons. First, the PIM values new and used aircraft at market prices and not at their new prices, as one would like for the estimation of gross stocks, or depreciated values, as required for net stock estimation. Instead administrative records allow for the 'correct' valuation of assets. It turns out that, compared to the administrative records method, the PIM systematically overestimates gross capital stocks as it underestimates the value of disposals. Secondly, the PIM does not or only partially accounts for leased and (long-term) rented assets. Chane Kune and Mulder (2000) show that leased or rented assets account for more than four-fifths of new aircraft in France in 1998 and more than 60 per cent of the capital stock. A third of the stock of aircraft is leased from foreign lease companies, which are not taken into account in official statistics of capital formation and PIM-type capital stocks.

asset lives using detailed investment data by sector and asset for the United States (see O'Mahony, 1999). Non-residential structures, transport equipment and other machinery and equipment each consist of several asset types. Non-residential structures comprise different types of buildings (commercial, industrial and so on), but also pipelines, railway structures and railway replacement track. Within transport equipment are distinguished aircraft, cars, ships, tractors and trucks and buses. The other machinery and equipment category includes communication equipment, different types of computer and office equipment, furniture and fixtures. Asset lives for the three asset categories within each sector were calculated as a weighted average.

Suppose that transport equipment T in sector J is composed of i types of assets and let A equal the asset life for asset i. Then the asset life A for transport equipment T in sector J is given by:

$$A_{TJ} = \sum s_{ij} A_{ij} \qquad (4.2)$$

Where $s_{ij} = I_{ij} / \sum I_{ij}$ is the share of asset i in total real transport equipment investment. The average investment shares for non-residential structures were estimated for the period 1950–97 and for transport equipment and other machinery and equipment for the period 1970–97. The results of the weighting procedures show that asset lives of non-residential structures and other machinery and equipment are similar across sectors. On the other hand, service lives of transport equipment are very different across sectors because of the different composition of this asset group by sector as well as the large differences in service lives of components: trucks (10 years) are the largest part of transport equipment in road goods transport whereas rolling stock (28

Table 4.1 Asset life assumptions in transport (years)

Sector	This study			O'Mahony (1998)	
	Non-residential structures	Transport equipment	Other machinery and equipment	Non-residential structures	Transport and other equipment
Railways	45	27	16	45	23
Road passenger transport	40	16	14	38 ⎫	14 ⎫
Road goods transport	38	10	14	⎭	⎭
Water transport	39	26	13	38	24
Air transport	39	20	13	39	15
Transport services	36	25	12	39	12
Total	42	17	14	43	17

Sources: Department of Commerce, Bureau of Economic Analysis (1999) and O'Mahony (1998).

years) is the main asset in railways. Our estimates are similar to those of O'Mahony, as the same method and data were used (see Table 4.1). Small differences are due to the use of US data up to 1994 by O'Mahony (1998) in this study. Retirements were spread over several years around the average service life of an asset category.

The net stock equals the gross stock minus depreciation. Among the large variety of depreciation functions, the one that seems best empirically justified is geometric depreciation. Detailed depreciation rates from Hulten and Wykoff (1981) and Fraumeni (1997) were transformed into sectoral depreciation rates in the same way as was done to estimate sectoral service lives. For this purpose, A_{ij} was replaced in equation (4.2) by asset specific depreciation rates D_{ij}. The depreciation rates by sector and asset group used here are similar to those of O'Mahony (1999) as illustrated in Table 4.2.

Figure 4.1 shows the composition of the net capital stock of the three asset types distinguished in this study. Railways and transport services (which include airports, ports and toll highways) account for the largest part of the gross capital stock of infrastructure (see panel A). Their shares changed little over time. The share of Parisian passenger transport (RATP) has risen and that of air transport declined somewhat over the past decades. The composition of the stock of transport equipment changed radically with rising shares of air transport and trucking and declining shares of maritime and inland water transport (see Panel B). The stock of other equipment is dominated by railways; only the airline branch increased its share.

Table 4.2   *Geometric depreciation rates in transport (annual average growth rates)*

Sector	This study			O'Mahony (1998)	
	Non-residential structures	Transport equipment	Other machinery and equipment	Non-residential structures	Transport and other equipment
Railways	0.0229	0.0523	0.1134	0.0228	0.144
Road passenger transport	0.0238	0.1120	0.1225	0.0242 ⎫	0.144 ⎫
Road goods transport	0.0240	0.1716	0.1207	⎭	⎭
Water transport	0.0239	0.0638	0.1437	0.0248	0.078
Air transport	0.0238	0.0817	0.1220	0.0234	0.135
Transport services	0.0250	0.0564	0.1300	0.0237	0.158
Total	0.0235	0.0481	0.1213	0.0261	0.134

Sources: Department of Commerce, Bureau of Economic Analysis (1999) and O'Mahony (1999).

(B)   Capital services

Capital services equal the volume of capital services, approximated by the net capital stock, times the user cost of capital. The latter is estimated in a simplified version of equation (4.1):

$$S_t = [q_{t-1}r_t + q_t d - (q_t - q_{t-1})] \tag{4.3}$$

The user cost S_t equals the real interest rate ($q_{t-1}\ r_t$) plus depreciation ($q_t\ d$) minus real capital gains ($q_t - q_{t-1}$). It was assumed that the real interest rate equalled 5 per cent for all countries and all sectors. Real capital gains are estimated by the increase in the price of asset i minus the price increase of all assets.

For individual assets, the growth rate of capital services is the same as that of the net capital stock. This is not the case for the total capital stock, as the net stock of non-residential structures is weighted by its user cost, as well as the net stock of transport equipment and other machinery and equipment. For the total transport sector, the use of capital services instead of the gross or net stocks does not yield very different growth rates (see Figure 4.2).

However, on the level of branches, capital services grew at a slower pace particularly in RATP and to a lesser extent in maritime transport (see Figure 4.3). The result for the RATP is explained by the large investments in infrastructure. These have long asset lives and therefore low depreciation rates.

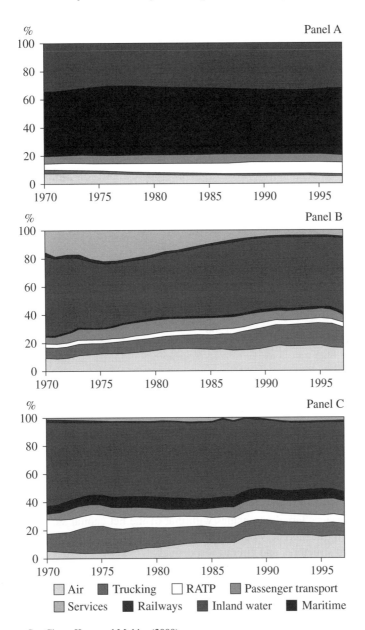

Source: See Chane Kune and Mulder (2000).

Figure 4.1   Net stock composition: infrastructure (Panel A), transport equipment (Panel B) and other equipment (Panel C)

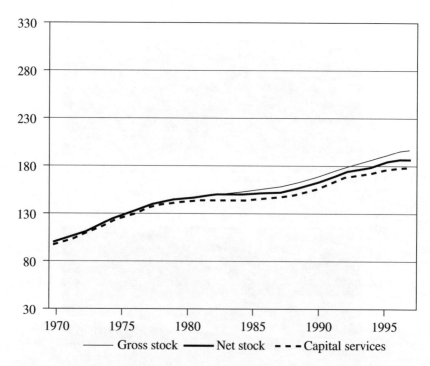

Figure 4.2   Total transport: indices of gross capital stock, net capital stock and capital services (1970 = 100)

The growth of capital stocks depends on new investment, while the growth of capital services is largely determined by depreciation rates. As the former was relatively high, the capital stock grew fast. On the other hand, as depreciation rates were low capital services grew slowly.

When most of the investment is in only one type of capital, the growth of capital services largely coincides with that of the net capital stock. This was the case in transport services and air transport, which invested mostly in non-residential structures and aircraft respectively.

From 1970 to 1997, capital input grew most rapidly in the RATP, followed by road freight transport. The largest decline in capital services occurred in inland water and maritime transport. The latter result should be interpreted with care, as the stock of capital decreased less than shown in Figure 4.3. The large fall in the stocks and services of owned ships was partly compensated by an increase in the use of ships under flags of convenience and leases. Due to data constraints, these were excluded from the capital stock and services estimates of this study.

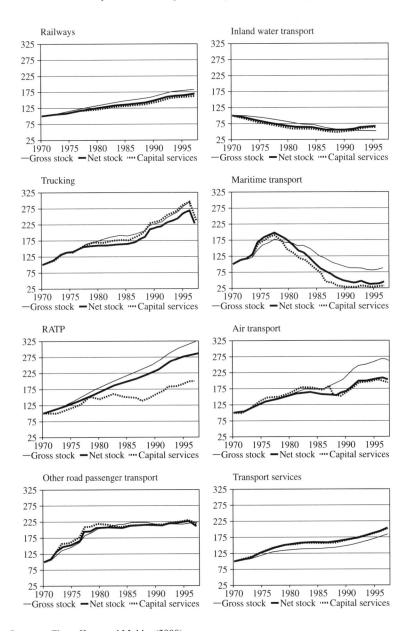

Source: Chane Kune and Mulder (2000).

*Figure 4.3   Indices of gross capital stock, net capital stock and capital
services 1970 = 100*

PRODUCTIVITY COMPARISONS

Introduction

The series of capital services as presented above are used here to measure capital, labour and total factor productivity (TFP). Capital and labour productivity measure the relative efficiency at which those inputs are used, while total factor productivity indicates how well labour and capital are jointly used. TFP is also interpreted as the contribution of technology to production, although it also captures other determinants of production not accounted for by capital and labour productivity such as international trade and structural change.

TFP is measured using traditional growth accounting, following O'Mahony (1999). Suppose country J has the following production function:

$$Q_{Jt} = f_{Jt} (L_{Jt}, K_{Jt}) \qquad (4.4)$$

where Q is real value added, L is labour input (measured by hours worked) and K is capital input (measured by capital services). Under neoclassical assumptions, perfect competition and payments of factor inputs equal their marginal productivity. Total factor productivity growth can thus be estimated using the Törnqvist discrete approximation to the Divisia index:

$$\ln(TFP_t^J / TFP_{t-s}^J) = \ln(Q_t^J / Q_{t-s}^J) - \alpha^J(t, t-s)\ln(L_t^J / L_{t-s}^J) \\ - (1 - \alpha^J (t, t-s))\ln(K_t^J / K_{t-s}^J) \qquad (4.5)$$

where $\alpha^J (t, t-s)$ is the average of the shares of labour compensation in value added in period t and $t-s$. The growth accounting methodology is embedded into the neoclassical theory of production.

This section will compare the French performance by sub-sector of transport in the period 1970–96 to that of the Germany, the United Kingdom and the United States.

International Comparisons of Productivity in Transport

To evaluate its productivity performance, France is compared to three countries with similar levels of economic development: (former Western) Germany, the United Kingdom and the United States. Compared to the European countries, the United States can realize more scale economies, in particular in railways, due to its larger size.

Data for the three other countries were taken from O'Mahony (1999) who presents a four sector breakdown: railways, water (that is maritime and inland water) transport, air transport and 'other transport' (that is trucking and urban and interurban transport and services related to transport). Due to data problems, no series were available for water transport in the UK and air transport in Germany or for 'other transport' in both countries. O'Mahony's series start in 1950 compared to 1970 in this study. She provides a breakdown into two types of capital assets: non-residential structures on the one hand and machinery and equipment on the other.

Total transport
France had the highest growth rates of output in the 1970s and 1980s but the lowest ones in the 1990s. Germany was the output growth leader in the 1990s. During most of the period 1970–95, the volume of labour services shrank in all three European countries as opposed to the United States where employment grew at modest rates throughout. The largest employment cuts were in France, although capital services grew faster in France than elsewhere (see Table 4.3 and Figure 4.4).

French productivity performance was mixed compared to the other countries: France performed better in terms of labour productivity growth but worse in terms of capital and total factor productivity gains. Labour productivity growth in France was amongst the highest in the 1970s and 1980s, after which it dropped. The UK showed the highest capital productivity growth in the 1970s and 1980s. France performed poorly with respect to capital productivity and showed a mediocre total factor productivity performance.

Railways
Railways are very different in Europe and the United States. In Europe, most revenue is generated by passenger transport, whereas in the United States, freight transport accounts for almost all output. In the United States, geographical distances are the most important reason for the low share of passenger travel as most people travel by air. Its size also allows for economies of scale as the average distance over which freight is carried is much longer than in the European countries. As such, the Europeans need relatively greater loading and unloading services to generate the same number of ton kilometres as the USA.

In all countries, the volume of labour services has been cut. This is mainly due to the closure of many regional rail tracks in all countries and the large cuts in passenger travel by trains in the United States (see Table 4.4). In the European countries, employment in rail freight transport has been cut as trucks have taken over a large part of freight transport. Finally, modern rolling stock requires less maintenance which reduced the number of mechanics.

Capital services grew most in France (see Table 4.4 and Figure 4.5). This is mostly explained by the massive construction of fast speed train (TGV)

Table 4.3 Total transport: growth of output, factor inputs and productivity (annual average growth rates)

	Value added				Labour productivity			
	France	Germany	UK	USA	France	Germany	UK	USA
1973–79	2.9	2.9	0.4	2.5	3.3	4.2	1.0	1.3
1979–89	2.7	2.0	2.6	1.8	3.0	2.4	4.1	0.6
1989–95	1.4	4.0	2.6	3.7	0.2	3.5	3.6	1.3

	Hours worked				Capital productivity			
	France	Germany	UK	USA	France	Germany	UK	USA
1973–79	−0.3	−1.2	−0.6	1.2	−0.8	1.3	−1.1	0.7
1979–89	−0.3	−0.4	−1.4	1.3	2.0	1.5	3.5	2.7
1989–95	1.2	0.5	−1.0	2.4	−1.1	3.3	−0.1	4.6

	Capital services				Total factor productivity			
	France	Germany	UK	USA	France	Germany	UK	USA
1973–79	3.8	1.6	1.4	1.8	1.8	3.3	−0.1	1.1
1979–89	0.7	0.5	−0.9	−0.8	2.7	2.1	3.6	1.2
1989–95	2.5	0.7	2.6	−0.9	−0.4	3.4	1.7	2.2

Sources: France: value added, employment and labour income from Ministry of Transport (Ministère de l'equipment et du logement, Direction des affaires economiques et internationales), *Les comptes de transports* (various issues), Paris. For capital services, see Chane Kune and Mulder (2000). For other countries: author's calculations based on O'Mahony (1999).

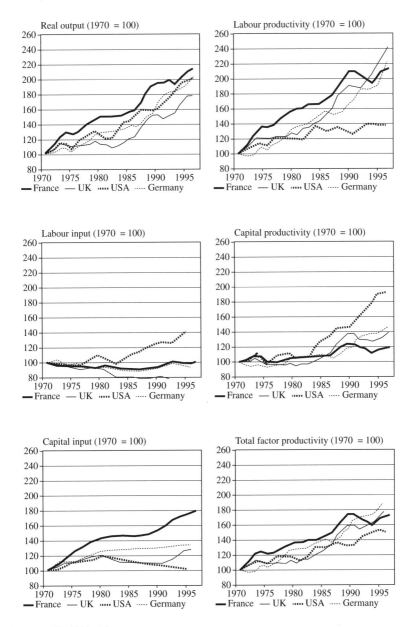

Sources: See Table 4.3.

Figure 4.4   Total transport: indices of output, factor inputs and productivity (1970 = 100)

Table 4.4 Railways: growth of output, factor inputs and productivity (annual average growth rates)

	Value added				Labour productivity			
	France	Germany	UK	USA	France	Germany	UK	USA
1973–79	1.0	−1.8	−1.2	1.8	3.3	2.6	1.0	3.7
1979–89	0.5	−0.9	−0.2	1.3	3.7	2.8	3.6	7.8
1989–95	−3.1	−1.6	−2.7	7.5	−0.9	2.7	0.2	10.2

	Hours worked				Capital productivity			
	France	Germany	UK	USA	France	Germany	UK	USA
1973–79	−2.2	−4.2	−2.2	−1.8	−1.2	−2.3	−0.3	−2.0
1979–89	−3.0	−3.6	−3.6	−6.0	−1.0	−0.9	−0.1	3.1
1989–95	−2.2	−4.2	−2.9	−2.5	−5.3	−1.6	−6.6	7.5

	Capital services				Total factor productivity			
	France	Germany	UK	USA	France	Germany	UK	USA
1973–79	2.3	0.5	−0.9	3.9	2.0	0.9	0.3	2.1
1979–89	1.5	0.0	0.0	−1.7	2.3	1.6	1.5	6.1
1989–95	2.4	0.0	4.2	−0.1	−2.1	1.4	−3.4	8.9

Sources: See Table 4.3.

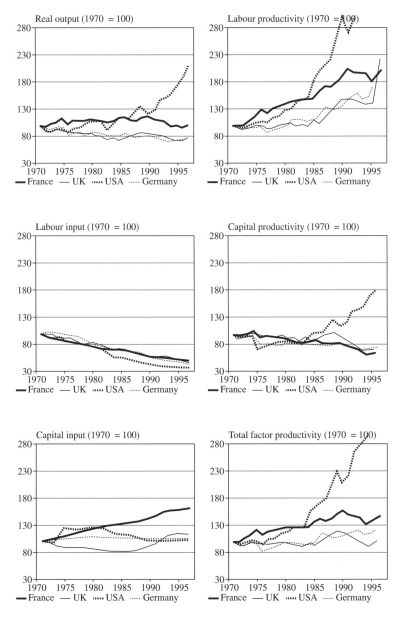

Sources: See Table 4.3.

Figure 4.5 *Railways: indices of output, factor inputs and productivity*
(1970 = 100)

networks which is unprecedented in the other three countries. Nowadays most of the intercity travel is by TGVs running at 300 km per hour. The modernization of the rail network in the other countries was much slower.

The USA outperformed the European countries in terms of labour, capital and total factor productivity mostly because of scale economies. Moreover, as freight transport requires relatively less labour and capital than passenger transport, the USA has an advantage over the European countries where the share of passenger transport in total output is a lot higher. Among the European countries, France performs rather well in terms of labour productivity but poorly in capital and total factor productivity.

Water transport
Water transport consists of inland water and maritime transport. In all three countries studied France, Germany and the USA, inland water transport is by far smaller than maritime transport. Moreover, inland water transport is slowly disappearing in France and Germany as their goods transport is taken over mostly by trucks. Maritime transport is also in decline in the three countries. Output growth was close to zero in all three countries. Employment in the two branches combined fell by more than 50 per cent in France and Germany, while the decrease in the United States was somewhat smaller in the period 1970–95. In France, the capital stock in water transport was also reduced by half, while in Germany and the United States, it increased slightly between 1970 and 1995 (see Table 4.5 and Figure 4.6).

Germany was the country with the largest labour productivity increase, followed by France. Productivity increased very little in the USA. In terms of capital and total factor productivity, France outperformed Germany and the USA. The French performance was achieved through a large reduction of the shipping fleet while it managed to maintain output.

Airlines
The main results for airlines are summarised in Table 4.6 and Figure 4.7. Between 1973 and 1979, labour input and capital input grew faster in France than in the UK and the USA. From 1979 onwards, labour input increased most in the United States. In the 1970s, the growth of employment in France was accompanied by substantial labour productivity growth. In the 1980s and 1990s, French airlines continued to improve their labour productivity at higher rates than those in the UK and the USA. However, in the 1990s, productivity growth went together with a large personnel cut by 20 per cent. In the UK and the USA, employment continued to increase, albeit at lower rates than in the 1980s.

In France, the growth of capital services in the 1970s was higher than that in other periods, as well as higher than in other countries. In the 1980s, capital

Table 4.5 *Water transport: growth of output, factor inputs and productivity (annual average growth rates)*

	Value added			Labour productivity		
	France	Germany	USA	France	Germany	USA
1973–79	3.5	3.7	2.0	6.0	9.0	2.1
1979–89	−4.9	−2.2	−1.6	1.6	2.6	0.2
1989–95	2.4	1.8	0.7	4.5	4.6	−0.3

	Hours worked			Capital productivity		
	France	Germany	USA	France	Germany	USA
1973–79	−2.4	−4.9	−0.1	−1.1	2.1	−2.4
1979–89	−6.5	−4.6	−1.8	8.0	−0.5	0.8
1989–95	−2.0	−2.7	1.0	4.4	2.7	2.6

	Capital services			Total factor productivity		
	France	Germany	USA	France	Germany	USA
1973–79	4.6	1.6	4.5	3.2	5.5	0.8
1979–89	−12.0	−1.6	−2.3	3.3	0.8	0.4
1989–95	−1.9	−0.9	−1.9	4.7	3.7	0.5

Sources: See Table 4.3.

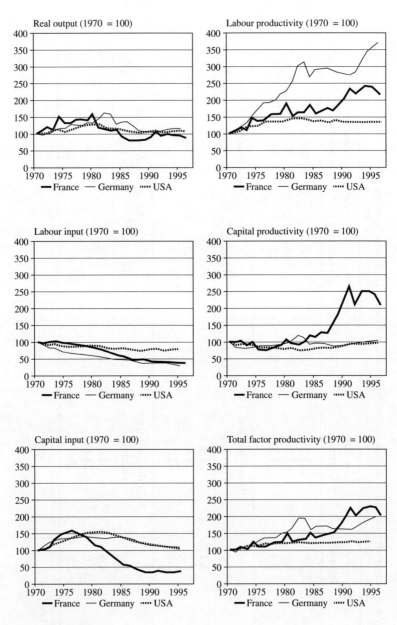

Sources: See Table 4.3.

*Figure 4.6   Water transport: indices of output, factor inputs and
           productivity (1970 = 100)*

Table 4.6 Airlines: growth of output, factor inputs and productivity, (annual average growth rates)

	Value added			Labour productivity		
	France	UK	USA	France	UK	USA
1973–79	6.8	9.1	6.7	4.3	7.1	4.2
1979–89	7.4	4.0	4.8	4.7	1.8	0.6
1989–95	2.4	7.9	6.2	6.5	5.6	3.9

	Hours worked			Capital productivity		
	France	UK	USA	France	UK	USA
1973–79	2.5	1.9	2.4	2.0	6.8	3.7
1979–89	2.5	2.2	4.3	7.4	7.8	2.9
1989–95	–3.9	2.1	2.3	–1.7	2.1	5.8

	Capital services			Total factor productivity		
	France	UK	USA	France	UK	USA
1973–79	4.8	2.2	2.9	3.6	6.4	3.8
1979–89	–0.1	–3.5	1.9	5.7	4.4	0.8
1989–95	4.2	5.7	0.4	3.8	3.5	4.3

Sources: See Table 4.3.

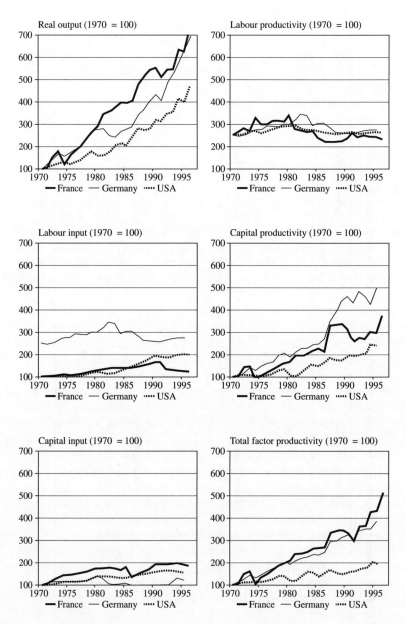

Sources: See Table 4.3.

Figure 4.7   Airlines: indices of output, factor inputs and productivity
            (1970 = 100)

services grew more slowly in all countries and even became negative in the UK; in the 1990s growth recovered except for the United States where it dropped to almost zero. Capital productivity grew fastest in France and the UK in the 1980s, compared to the 1990s in the United States. In France, capital productivity fell until 1995 when it started to grow again.

Total factor productivity always grew at rates above 3 per cent, except for the USA in the 1980s. France experienced very high TFP growth in the 1980s, while British airlines showed rapid progress in the 1970s.

CONCLUSION

The main novelty of this study is the construction of a series of capital stocks and services for eight sub-sectors in transport, hitherto unavailable, and the comparison of the productivity performance between transport sectors and different countries from 1970 onwards. Within a productivity framework, all variables are flows and therefore capital input should be measured by capital *services* and not by *stocks*. Only the former is coherent with other measures such as GDP and hours worked. Capital services are the product of the volume of capital services. The PIM has been used to measure net capital stocks in all sectors except for the stock of transport equipment in air and maritime transport.

For each of the eight sub-sectors of transport, the net stocks of infrastructure, transport equipment and other types of machinery and equipment were estimated for the period 1970–97. In fact, railways account for one-third and transport services (airports, ports, toll roads) for half of all transport infrastructure. Half of the stocks of transport equipment and other types of machinery and equipment are part of railways. In the 1970s to the 1990s, the shares of air transport and trucking in transport equipment increased, whereas that of water transport decreased. Capital services, that is the sum of net stocks of non-residential structures, transport and other equipment weighted by their user cost, grew fastest in air transport and trucking, whereas in inland water and maritime transport the volume of capital services fell.

The capital services estimates were used to analyse the productivity performance since 1970s. Total factor productivity is estimated using the Törnqvist discrete approximation to the Divisia index. However, the net capital stock and services estimates presented here may be refined in various ways. Firstly, in the absence of specific information on asset lives and depreciation patterns by sub-sector of transport in France, American assumptions were used. This bias could be corrected if more information were to be collected if more information were to be collected on the practices of French firms. Secondly, the use of administrative records to estimate stocks, which is more reliable than the PIM, could be extended to other sectors, such as railways, trucking and urban and interurban passenger transport. Thirdly, the estimation of benchmark stocks could be improved by extrapolating further backwards the GFCF (Gross Fixed Capital Formation) series or by reviewing information contained in company balance sheets. Fourthly, the estimation of capital services can be refined by including sector-specific data on interest and tax rates.

NOTES

1. Centre d'Etudes Prospectives et d'Informations Internatioles (CEPII), 9, rue Georges Pitard, 75740 Paris CEDEX 15. We are grateful for comments from Mary O'Mahony and Philippe Poudevigne. This study has benefited from financial support of the French ministry of transport (Ministère de l'équipement, des transports et du logement).
2. Rented assets are ignored in the capital stocks estimates of the national accounts of most countries. However, for productivity and other types of analyses it is necessary to estimate the total capital stock used in production. These should include assets rented for at least a year. In various industries, such as air transport, long-term rentals are increasingly common. The omission of these assets leads to an underestimation of the available capital stock.
3. Airclaims is one of the major insurance companies of aircraft. Their monthly updated database contains data on the stock of aircraft of most countries in the world starting in the 1950s. It presents detailed information on all aircraft *operated* by resident companies of each country, including those leased and rented from domestic and foreign firms.

REFERENCES

Australian Bureau of Industry Economics (1995), 'Overview 1995 – International Benchmarking', Report, No. 95/20, AGPS, Canberra.
Chane Kune, B. and N. Mulder (2000), 'Capital Stock and Productivity in French Transport: An International Comparison', Working Paper. No. 00–18, CEPII, Paris.
Denison, E.F. (1967), *Why Growth Rates Differ* (Washington DC: The Brookings Institution).
Department of Commerce, Bureau of Economic Analysis (1985), 'Fixed Private Capital in the United States', *Survey of Current Business*, 7, July, 36–47.
Department of Commerce, Bureau of Economic Analysis (1999) 'Fixed Reproducible Tangible Wealth of the United States, 1925–97', CD-Rom, Washington DC.
Fraumeni, B.M. (1997), 'The Measurement of Depreciation in the U.S. National Income and Product Accounts', *Survey of Current Business*, July 1997, 7–23.
Goldsmith, R.W. (1951), 'A Perpetual Inventory of National Wealth', Studies in Income and Wealth, 14, National Bureau of Economic Research, New York.
Hulten, C.R. and F.C. Wykoff (1981), 'The Measurement of Economic Depreciation,' in C.R. Hulten (ed.), *Depreciation, Inflation, and the Taxation of Income from Capital*, (Washington, DC: The Urban Institute Press), pp. 81–125.
Inter-Secretariat Working Group on National Accounts of EUROSTAT, IMF, OECD, UN and World Bank (1993), System of National Accounts 1993, Luxembourg, New York, Paris and Washington, DC.
Jorgenson, D.W. and Z. Griliches (1967), 'The Explanation of Productivity Change' *Review of Economic Studies*, 34, 249–83.

Maddison, A. (1987), 'Growth and Slow down in Advanced Capitalist Countries: Techniques of Quantitative Assessment,' *Journal of Economic Literature*, 25, June.

Mairesse, J. (1972), 'L'évaluation du capital fixe productif: méthodes et résultats', *Les Collections de l'INSEE*, No. C18–19/1972, INSEE, Paris.

O'Mahony, M. (1998), 'Capital and Productivity', mimeo, NIESR, London.

O'Mahony, M. (1999), *Britain's Productivity Performance 1950–1996 – An International Perspective* (London: NIESR).

5. Growth and productivity in a knowledge-based service economy

Pascal Petit[1]

The growth regimes of developed economies are currently strongly influenced by a broad technological change centred around the information and communication technologies (ICTs). This transformation takes full advantage of the internationalization and tertiarization experienced by these economies. More precisely the diffusion of these new technologies contributes specifically to the present phases of the long-term trends of expansion of international transactions and service activities.

The accumulation regimes of such economies present strong growth potentials but realization of these potentials is severely conditional. It requires in particular that the impetus of some sectors diffuses to other activities and that, conversely, the welfare improvement obtained by some social classes spreads as well to others. It is a straightforward matter of the growth process gaining some momentum, but it cannot be achieved by a sheer redistribution of incomes and requires important improvements in information and knowledge of the industries and of the people lagging behind. As we shall stress hereafter, emerging growth regimes, whether classified as 'New Economies' or knowledge-based economies, have not really delivered their promises. For all medium and large countries, including the most celebrated case of the United States, growth rates remained rather modest over the 1990s. The bursting of the new technology bubble, initiated in spring 2000, that halved their stock market values within a year, complicates the issue, given that the rise of productivity gains in the USA in the late 1990s had led to the hope that a new era of strong and steady growth was beginning.

Such a rosy future is not necessarily out of reach for ever, its occurrence may only be postponed, but it is also by no means guaranteed. Much depends on a lengthy learning process by which various countries try to extend the bases of rapid economic growth. The notion of a network has often been used as a metaphor of this new growth process. Much as in a network the 'value' of a modern economy (that is, an economy open to new technologies, external competition and massive education) depends on the number and quality of people and activities connected. In effect the development of new economies can be strongly hampered by their inability to get some activities and people connected and interested. The permanence of some dualism, and *a fortiori* its deepening can severely limit economic growth.

The aim of this chapter is precisely to feature the terms in which the above issue of dualism and development can be raised.

In order to do that we shall first consider the fact that the modern economies we are speaking of are tertiary economies, meaning that between two-thirds and three-quarters of their employment is in service activities. A large part of these activities are social and household services. But a rising, and now quite important share, also consists of intermediate services. If the former contributes in a broad sense to an enlargement of the labour force (in other words to an expansion of human capital), the latter are at the root of an extended division of labour between firms that is a strong characteristic of contemporary economies.

We shall base our approach to emerging growth regimes on the assumptions that both mechanisms are bound to be key factors in the coming growth process, renewed as they may be in the current process of modernization.

Still why do we qualify such modernization process as a move towards a knowledge-based economy (KBE)? Our understanding of this common qualifier refers less to an abstract accumulation of information and knowledge than to a significantly enlarged scope for all economic agents (firms and workers alike) to have access to more information and knowledge and to act consequently in more strategic ways. This microeconomic definition leads step by step to a full set of consequences in industrial organization (see Petit, 1999), ranking from an extended division of labour to increased differentiation of products and capabilities of agents, providing that the initial abilities to take advantage of the new context were different. This microeconomic perspective though requires that one can assess whether a new context has been effectively reached or not. In other terms this reference to a modernization process as some structural change modifying the environment in which economies operate has to be defined. We shall for that purpose refer to a trilogy of interdependent structural changes combining long-term trends in developed economies: internationalization, education and the diffusion of a new technological system centred around the information and communication technologies. These evolutions, even if they have been initiated long ago at the outset of the previous growth regime, are not external to the present growth process but are, on the contrary, at the heart of its mobilization of capital and labour. These developments are uneven and offer no panacea, but they constitute opportunities that economies can exploit under some conditions that we aim to precise. Such assessment remains highly tentative as so far no medium or large economy has displayed sustained economic growth that could stand as a model of a successful KBE. The success of small economies in the 1990s, like

Ireland, can bring useful insights but are much less open to generalization, precisely because they were able to take very specific advantage of the new context (its international position in the case of Ireland).

To proceed in our assessment we shall first analyse the three interdependent structural changes that represent the cornerstone of the transformation (section 1). We shall then try to see how these changes are combined with the main factors of an endogenous growth process (section 2). This will allow us to comment broadly on the sectoral dynamics of productivity and output that have been observed in the main developed economies in order to appreciate the relative successes, failures and potentials displayed by these contemporary tertiary economies (section 3).

1.   A TRIANGLE OF INTERDEPENDENT STRUCTURAL CHANGES

We retain three structural changes as foundations of the present change of context. The development of a technological system centred on information and communication technologies can be cited first, as it is often claimed to be the core of the present transformation. This technological development, which started with the development of computers and telecommunications and reached a new scale of development with the PC and the Internet in the last two decades, is only one aspect of the structural change which combines with a growing internationalization and a steady rise in education.

The idea is that these three structural changes which date back from the previous growth regime, and thus appear as rather exogenous and independent, turn out in their present developments to be strongly interdependent and influenced by the various contemporary policies.

Even Moore's law, which refers to the miniaturization of microprocessors (multiplying density by two every eighteen months) and is a key factor accounting for the diffusion of ICTs, echoes this interdependency. This law stems less from some intrinsic physical characteristic of semiconductors than from some common expectation shared by the small world of international manufacturers competing on the technology frontier (an aspect of the present phase of internationalization), a prophecy which they have been able to pursue thanks to close cooperation between science and industrial R&D (an aspect of the development of knowledge born out of the expansion of education and research systems).

The present phase of internationalization has its specific features. It cannot be reduced to an expansion of trade and foreign direct investments, which is not unprecedented in percentage points of GDP.[2] But the range of international transactions has significantly widened in the current period. More countries are involved and many more products are traded, including differentiated types of goods but also including services. Moreover the range of relations and transactions which do not lead to any precise monetary transaction (and therefore are not recorded in balances of payments) has tremendously enlarged, whether these relations concern accords of all kinds between firms, or academic relations, or all the international diffusion of information and knowledge by the media. Most transactions in a developed economy thus presently take into account a wide set of international alternatives and this enlargement of the strategies of agents bears on the nature of competition even at local or national levels.

The last structural change under review concerns the wider diffusion of education. This is a long-term rise which was largely confirmed and legitimized in the aftermath of WWII. The slowdown in economic growth from the mid-1970s onwards did not reduce the pace of this trend. This rise in school enrolment is especially clear with women who are now displaying schooling rates close to the ones experienced by their male colleagues. Education is praised for giving more autonomy and choices to individuals and for providing a capital of knowledge to economies, capital which is directly put to use in a closer relation between science and industries. Still these relations are complex and evolving. Individual capabilities are in effect subject to obsolescence[3] and all the more so given that the development of science and of its relations with industries is spurred by international competition and cooperation. In that respect lifelong training has become a crucial issue.

All these structural changes were already at work during the period of sustained high growth of the 1950s and 1960s, but their weight and effects were not as significant for the strategies of economic agents as they have now become, when the opening of economies greatly enlarges the room for manoeuvre of agents and when the reservoir of educated people impinges noticeably on the organization of work.

Progressively, and in a cumulative way, a threshold has been overtaken in this transformation of the structural context as shown by the growing interdependence between the structural changes under view.

The relation between the diffusion of ICTs and the levels of education is itself at the core of a debate over the biased nature of contemporary technological change. The diffusion of ICTs seems effectively to be accompanied by a rise in the share of qualified workers required (see Machin and Van Reenen, 1998).[4] Such a phenomenon is indeed more pronounced in the manufacturing sector. Basically four types of factors could lead to such effect.

1. It may in the first place stem from a genuine complementarity between the design of ICTs and the capabilities developed by educated workers (see Acemoglu, 1998). The role played by personal computers and abstract operating principles backs this assumption.

2. It may also be the case that the uncertainty on product markets in a more competitive world or regarding the rapid evolution of technologies can induce firms to opt for more qualified workers, supposed to be more reactive, more adaptable to a new environment. Externalization of non-qualified tasks and outsourcing of qualified collaborations can help such reorganization.
3. Still the rise in the magnitude of the supply of educated people may also lead to increase their demand and to adjust work organization accordingly.
4. Finally the trade specialization of developed economies in products using more skilled people can also be a factor of this apparent skill bias.

All the above factors can combine their effects in specific ways to account for a skill bias at the level of each industry. Still the aggregated effect of all these changes on the over all demand for qualified labour may paradoxically reduce it, depending on the relative size and growth rates of the various sectors where the ratio of qualified labour is rather low. In fact this composition effect is largely determined by the speed and nature of the expansion of service activities, which in turn, at least for the intermediate and business services, depend on the reorganization of work undertaken in the above conditions.

All these effects concur to create a radically new economic environment. How are we to appreciate its impacts on the dynamics of developed economies?

It would be misleading to think in the first place that the structural changes under view are accomplished changes across the board of all developed economies, with ICTs diffusion being uniform and comprehensive, internationalization equalling a complete globalization in all activities and education leading to a widespread and sustainable distribution of human capital. One may observe by the end of the 1990s some general achievements in terms of ICTs diffusion and in terms of international access to market and technologies, where most firms are concerned. Levels of school enrolments have reached some similar significant levels, for instance for the class of 20–25 years of age. By and large the sort of 'taking off' condition that we are hinting at seems to have been met by most developed countries (see Table 5.1 for a recapitulation of this general achievement).

Still economic agents, for example, firms and workers, do not have the same experience, some are larger and richer than others. In other words the stocks of education and learning differ deeply and this difference translates all the more into differences between countries so that some countries that were lagging behind have drastically caught up in a recent period (be it concerning schooling rates of younger generations, diffusion of ICTs in SMEs or access to international markets and techniques). As we stressed, this experience mattered in this broad process of transformation which not only concerned the

Table 5.1   *Indicators of structural change in developed economies*

	Diffusion ICT			Education		Internationalization			
	1	2	3	4	5	6	7	8	9
EU-15	–	–	–	–	–	–	–	–	–
B	6	0.5	10	55	22.0	58.4	11.5	3.3	4.9
DK	6.5	1	26	65	26.6	27.0	8.9	2.2	0.0
D	5.5	0.6	10	80	18.7	22.7	4.9	1.6	1.7
E	4	0.6	11	32	22.9	20.9	6.5	1.9	1.0
F	6.3	0.4	10	60	22.1	19.4	5.2	2.6	1.4
IRL	5.8	1.8	14	50	27.1	62.9	14.5	1.4	3.7
I	4.3	0.3	20	40	10.1	18.8	6.6	1.1	0.3
NL	7	1	11	60	23.9	43.3	13.4	5.5	2.5
A	5	1.4	14	63	8.6	29.5	14.1	0.9	1.2
P	5	0.2	15	30	11.2	28.8	6.9	1.6	1.7
FIN	6	1.6	45	63	20.6	29.1	6.4	4.1	1.7
S	8	2	35	70	26.5	32.6	8.2	5.1	4.3
UK	7.5	1.5	14	72	22.8	22.2	6.4	4.9	2.8
US	7.8	6.2	22	82	43.3	9.6	2.6	1.5	1.2
JP	7.4	0.4	30	–	30.6	8.5	2.3	0.6	0.1

Notes

Colume 1:   ICT spending as percentage of GDP in 1997.
Colume 2:   Web sites for e-trade per 100 000 inhabitants 1998.
Colume 3:   Mobile phones per 100 inhabitants 1997.
Colume 4:   Percentage of the population aged 25–64 with at least secondary education in 1996.
Colume 5:   Tertiary levels of education (as percentage of labour force over 15 years old) 1996.
Colume 6:   Trade in goods (as percentage of GDP) 1997.
Colume 7:   Trade in services (as percentage of GDP) 1997.
Colume 8:   FDI as percentage of GDP outflows 1997.
Colume 9:   FDI as percentage of GDP inflows 1997.

Source: OECD (1999).

organization of the firms but at the same time the fabric of interfirm relations. The positions of countries, their abilities to take advantage of the new context, are rather dispersed, to a greater extent than the differences in levels of GDP per head might suggest. A similar phenomenon occurs within each country where the abilities to benefit from the changes are more dispersed than one could have expected from past income and skill differences. The widespread observation (see Atkinson et al., 1995) that income inequalities (before transfers) have increased confirms the above assessment. The widening of the wage gap between skilled and unskilled labour contributes to this last trend.

Indeed the developed economies are in many respects in an intermediary phase of their evolution and this widening of inequalities may be transitory or durable. Much depends on the way in which countries adapt the key structural changes mentioned above in order to cope with the limited capabilities of some to access and fully use new technologies, international markets and education services.

This transformation is analogous to the building up of a multi-layer network with highly differentiated conditions of access. Beyond its metaphorical aspect this reference to a network architecture contains two essential elements regarding the working of our economies. For both firms and workers this network structure helps to generate some positive externality effects, linked with the mutual advantage brought to those connected. Providing firms or workers each meet some specific conditions of access, they can, through this network structure, benefit from more information and knowledge. There are drawbacks in this process and to speak of conditions of access is an euphemism when it refers precisely to problems of obsolescence of information and knowledge. It follows that the end result is not straightforward, when the conditions of access are selective and when the speed of innovation implies a rapid obsolescence of knowledge.

The result of this algebra of positive and negative effects assesses the specific impact of the new environment on the working of each economy.

Our hypothesis is that services are highly instrumental in this result. They do, in each country, adjust the three broad structural changes under view fostering the future engine of economic growth.

This role is obvious concerning the large network services of intermediation. Systems of transportation, of communication, finance and distribution have for a long time represented the backbones of economic development (see the 'visible hand' of Chandler (1977), not to mention Braudel's (1985) long-term view on transportation, distribution and finance). But their present characteristics, from highly differentiated and efficient servicing to yield management pricing, bring their contemporary imprint to this action. The last two decades have also been specially marked by the rise of a set of business services, playing a key role in facilitating information and knowledge transfers, but also some deepening of learning and specialization thanks to externalization and outsourcing. The rise of these new intermediaries favoured a broad reorganization of work within and between firms, more or less connected with the diffusion of ICTs and the resources brought by internationalization (as the knowledge-intensive services are highly internationalized – either belonging to a global network or being closely in touch with international developments). The same process includes the externalization by firms of simple peripheral tasks to specialized firms which are in a better position to rationalize and innovate (an issue which may depend on the state of the labour market of the country under view).

Personal and social services (and also intermediation services which by definition concern both firms and individuals) offer, more than ever, possibilities for people to access knowledge and information, through personal training or via relevant intermediaries. And again ICTs and internationalization have their part to play in this process.

We thus see the whole fabric of service activities at the core of the logistics forging the adjustments of our three long-term structural changes to fuel an engine of growth, relying in great part on an enlarged access of firms and individuals to knowledge and information. The next section will pin down the proper mechanism of this growth engine and it will be followed by a section reviewing the role of services in this process and how successful various countries seem to have been in that respect.

Figure 5.1 recalls the three interdependent structural changes and evokes the role played by the service activities in this node.

2. EXTERNALITIES AND ENDOGENOUS (OR CUMULATIVE) GROWTH

Thus if an economy based on knowledge is an economy which benefits from the effects of such multiform network structure to organize and develop access to information and knowledge, one has to appreciate how the externalities induced by this configuration concur in the process of economic growth. For that matter one should question the true nature of these externalities and the extent to which they are new in essence. One can refer for this purpose to the analytical framework developed by the endogenous growth theory (which originated in the work of Kaldor (1972) on cumulative causation).

The literature on endogenous growth leads us to distinguish two types of approach according to the factors channelling the externalities which concur to increase the productivity of all agents. The first factor concerns the quality of the labour force, that is, the human capital embodied in the workforce. The second factor depends on various logistics close to the ones mentioned above with the intermediation services. The studies on endogenous growth refer more or less to one or the other of these two approaches.

Lucas (1988) gives the most standard expression of the first perspective in retaining education as the main source of positive externality. Romer (1986) in the same spirit chose the training experience gained on the job which is supposed to grow as quickly as the stock of fixed capital (which also implies some obsolescence of this experience over time). Romer (1990) changed this rather ambiguous formulation for a more standard and specific variable such as R&D spending.

The second perspective is rather heterogeneous as one can find all kinds of infrastructures chosen as source of externality. Röller and Waverman (1996)

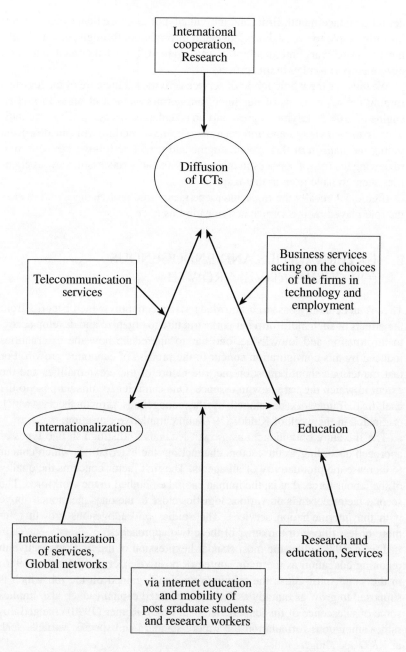

*Figure 5.1   A triangle of structural change deeply transformed in the last
decades by the development of services*

retained telecommunications, Amable et al. (1997) the financial sector, Ashauer (1989, 1994) and Barro (1990) the whole of public expenditure, while Berndt and Hansson (1992), Munnell (1992) as well as Morrison and Schwartz (1996) only considered public investments. Finally Bradford De Long and Summers (1991) selecting the whole of public and private investment developed the idea that infrastructures in general were the proper ground for positive externalities.[5]

In effect the two perspectives are partly overlapping as one concentrates on the formation of human capital (in-house source of knowledge and information) and the other on the organization of specific logistics (outsource of information and knowledge) when obviously both are inputs in the construction of the other.

These works on endogenous growth are often thought of (see Pack, 1994) as having too weak empirical support. Most of them do take a partial view and do not discuss the relative importance of the two perspectives distinguished above, assuming implicitly that these perspectives are more or less complementary and that they have selected the binding factor.[6]

This is unclear for at least two reasons. The first is that one usually consider gross factors when obsolescence of all kinds should be accounted for before assessing which factor is the more binding. The second may be that the effects of the factors are likely to be discontinuous and education or infrastructures really challenged when an economy is faced with the necessity to adjust to some external change.[7] Therefore not only should one retain the two types of factors but also account for their quality and check their conditions of operation. It is a broad programme to which one may only bring partial answers.

Basically the quality of education (that is, how one can incorporate knowledge and information throughout one's life) and of the infrastructures giving access to information and knowledge depend greatly on the use they make of ICT, internationalization and . . . education.

We shall hereafter explicit a scheme of endogenous growth which accounts for some of the previous critics and helps to point at some key issues.

At this stage we finally have a growth model with two sectors, one of them playing specifically the role of a networking infrastructure (largely based on intermediation and business services as hinted at previously). The quality and extent of this sector of infrastructure or of intermediation has positive external effects on the working of the other part of the economy, meaning that it boosts the efficiency of the other sector beyond any effect of prices. A second assumption of this model is that the quality and importance of the education of the labour force affects also positively the efficiency of both sectors.

Let $i = 1,2$ be the indexes of the two economic sectors, with 1 for a broad sector of activities working mainly to satisfy final demand (be they manufacturing or service activities[8]) and 2 for an intermediation sector, broadly defined in order to gather most of the networking activities that could foster positive externalities.

Let us, for sake of simplicity, make the Smithian assumption that productivity gains in both sectors are influenced by the size of markets.[9]

Our previous assumptions lead to the following expression of the productivity gains in both sectors:

$$(E1)\ z_1 = f_1\ (x_1,\ Ip_2,\ Ih_1) \tag{5.1}$$

$$(E2)\ z_2 = f_2\ (x_2,\ Ih_2) \tag{5.2}$$

where z_i and x_i represent respectively the productivity gains and the growth of production over the period under view; Ip_2 is an indicator on the efficiency of the sector of intermediation and Ih_i is an indicator on the quality of the labour force in sector i. Ih_i would not have had to feature in the expression of the productivity gains in the Fordist period. Its introduction aims to account for a new relation between sciences and technologies (see Gibbons et al., 1994) leading to a new relation between human capital and productive efficiency. The skill bias of the contemporary technological change gives a composite illustration of this new relation (as explained in section 1).

Conversely the effect of the efficiency of the intermediation sector on the dynamics of productivity in section 1 is supposed to convey the importance of the redefinition of the division of labour among firms.

Let us now turn to the expression of demand. To the standard determinant of household demand that income constitutes, contemporary economists tend to add a component based on the information and knowledge acquired by the consumers. The income effect on household demand can be directly summarized by the productivity gains in both sectors, providing that these productivity gains remain an important determinant of real wage increases.[10] The question is now to account for the role of learning process taking place on the side of the consumers. This process is at the core of the transformation of the laws of markets[11] whereby quality issues are becoming more important, leading to product differentiation and rapid innovation. The rise in education is certainly a factor in the origin of such change, but it is only one part of the story. Another factor supporting a stronger influence of demand on the dynamics of household consumption is said to be a closer user–producer relationship (Lundvall, 1988). But such a relation is largely mediated by specific service activities, even if a broad set of services is concerned from distribution, communication, transportation and finance, not to speak of the business services closely concerned, for example, marketing and advertising. Once this mediation is evoked, it becomes clear that the learning process on the demand side is influenced by the learning process on the producer side and vice versa.

As a matter of fact this mediation realized by the service activities and the constant innovation that goes with it (as stressed by Gallouj and Gallouj, 1996) is an integral part of the process of product differentiation and innovation that underlies the qualitative turn of the working of product markets in our contemporary economies. To account for this interdependence of the learning processes and for their influence on consumption we retain as a determinant a quality indicator of the intermediation sector with respect to the consumers, Ic_2. This indicator is the equivalent of the quality indicator of the intermediation sector vis-à-vis producers that we introduced previously. Both are certainly linked; still the question of their difference, implying that an intermediation sector could be more or less consumer or producer oriented is interesting.

Finally the relation accounting for final demand of sector 1 (q_1) could be expressed as follows:

$$q_1 = g_1 \left(z_1, z_2, Ic_2, Il \right) \tag{5.3}$$

where z_i stand for the productivity gains in sector i and Il for the quality of the learning process on the consumer side, which depends on the building up of 'human capital' and is in that respect closely linked with education.

The demand in sector 2, which mixes consumer demand[12] and the intermediate demand of sector 1 could be expressed by simply adding that the level of demand in sector 1 is a determinant of the demand in sector 2.[13]

$$q_2 = g_2 \left(q_1, z_1, z_2, Ic_2, Il \right) \tag{5.4}$$

This short two-sector model retains many elements that characterize the new growth regime (see Petit, 1999), although its main purpose is to raise in a more precise way some questions on the new growth process of our highly tertiary contemporary economies.

Let us remark in the first place that two elements underlined in section 1 do not seem integrated so far in the scheme. The first one is the internationalization of the economies which constitutes, beyond its part in the determination of supply and demand, a source of information and knowledge influencing all activities, externalities which should be taken into account in defining the quality indicators that we retained.

The second element missing so far has to do with the effect of latent dualism in the economy whereby firms are not all in the same position, and consumers are not all in the same position to take advantage of the new context, all of which can affect the overall dynamics of the economy.

In fact the whole object of this schematization of the growth process was to see how important stylized facts, such as those two mentioned above, could be

Table 5.2   On the quality of externalities: main indicators

	Diffusion of ICTs	Internationalization	Human capital	Other structural issues
Ip_2 indicator Externalities generated by sector 2 on all production processes	Importance of ICTs equipment or spending relative to sector 2 equipment or production	Internationalization in terms of trade in KIBS or foreign direct investment	Importance of skilled workers in sector 2 Importance of R&D	Relative diversification of the services concerned Initial levels of productivity Share of services
Ic_2 indicator Externalities generated by sector 2 on all consumption processes	Importance of e-trading, and electronic trans-actions with customers	Importance of international networks Inwards FDI in sector 2	Importance of education and lifelong training in sector 2 Importance of urban environment	Relative diversification of the services concerned Initial levels of productivity Share of services
Ih Effect of human capital on all production processes	Average importance of ICTs equipment or spending in the whole economy	Transborder flows of information and knowledge	Levels of education in the labour force Importance of lifelong training schemes	Relative diversification of training Distribution of human capital
Il Effect of human capital on all consumption processes	Use of PCs and Internet at home	Importance of foreign relations, travels and mobility Importance of foreign products	Levels of education Social practices Urbanization Knowledge-intensive leisure	Diversity of social groups and ways of life

taken into account in a straightforward growth pattern, such as that provided by the endogenous growth framework.[14] This leads us to consider that the extent and the distribution of the possibilities to be provided with an international reach, an efficient use of ICTs and to maintain a high level of human capital should be important dimensions of the quality indicators we retained. As the purpose of this schematization was to raise in a coherent and relatively comprehensive way questions on the various externalities at work, we can present them in a systematic way in a table (see Table 5.2), where the five quality indicators used in the model (Ip_2, Ih_1, Ih_2, Ic_2, Il) are crossed with the issues raised around the nexus of structural changes examined in section 1. It should give as well some hints on the available indicators that could be used, at least in a comparative perspective. Beforehand one could question whether or not five indicators or less should be distinguished at such level of aggregation. If the nature of the externalities born by the intermediation sector are bound to be different when regarding the production side, Ip_2, or the consumption side Ic_2, it may not be so clearly the case when looking at the effects of human capital which roughly can be thought of being of the same kind in the production of sector 1, Ih_1, and in the production of the sector of intermediation Ih_2.[15] A similar simplification cannot be extended to assimilate the impact of human capital on the production processes, Ih, with its impact on the consumption processes, Il; even if they interact, consumer skills remain different from worker skills (see Petit and Soete, 2001; Storper, 2000). Under this assumption we only need to characterize four types of externalities.

We can now proceed and see whether the performances of the developed economies in the last decade were roughly in line with the broad hints given by the quality indicators we distinguished in this section to characterize the externalities at work in each country.

3. WHAT CAN WE LEARN FROM THE GROWTH TRAJECTORIES OF THE 90S?

Looking at the evolution of productivity gains in a long-term perspective, it is clear that the great majority of countries did not catch up at the end of the 1990s with the growth rates of the 1950s and 1960s. Thus in the 1990s one finds only a small set of countries displaying growth rates of productivity (real GDP per person employed) above 2 per cent (a rather modest rate still if compared with the 1960s where the rates were closer to 3 and 4 per cent on average): Australia, Finland, Ireland, Korea, Norway, Sweden and Turkey (see Table 5.3).[16]

This subset corresponds to various situations. For some countries like Portugal, Turkey and Korea it may correspond to a classic case of catching up

Table 5.3 Productivity growth in OECD countries (per cent, yearly average)

	1		2		3		4		5	
	79–89	89–99	79–89	89–99	79–89	90–97	79–89	90–97	79–89	90–97
Australia	1.0	2.2	0.7	–	0.1	1.0	3.6	5.4	-0.6	0.6
Austria	1.2	1.2	–	-0.1						
Belgium	2.2	1.7	1.0	1.3	0.7	1.6	3.1	2.2	0.2	0.5
Canada	0.9	1.1	0.3	0.8						
Denmark	0.7	1.8	-0.2	1.5						
Finland	2.6	2.5	1.3	1.5	2.5	0.9	3.1	4.7	0.2	2.9
France	2.2	1.3	1.8	0.3	1.2	0.3	3.8	2.7	0.1	0.1
Germany	1.5	–	1.2	–	0.9	0.4	3.1	3.9	1.6	2.8
Ireland	3.6	3.1	–	–						
Italy	2.0	1.7	0.5	–	0.4	1.4	2.0	4.8	0.0	2.5
Japan	2.6	1.1	2.4	–	4.4	1.0	4.1	0.5	2.3	1.8
Korea	4.8	4.6	2.3	1.9						
Netherlands	-0.3	0.6	-0.9	0.0	1.6	0.3	2.6	2.5	0.7	-0.9
New Zealand	0.5	0.6	–	–						
Norway	1.9	2.3	0.8	1.1						
Portugal	1.9	1.9	-0.3	1.8						
Spain	2.6	1.4	0.8	0.0						
Sweden	1.4	2.5	–	1.8	1.6	3.2	3.8	2.1	-1.4	3.0
Switzerland	0.3	0.5	–	–						
Turkey	2.5	2.0	0.8	1.3						
United Kingdom	1.9	1.7	–	1.4						
United States	1.2	1.7	0.6	–	1.3	3.1	1.6	2.0	-1.1	-0.4

Notes
Columns 1: Real GDP per person employed.
Columns 2: Real value added in services per person employed.
Columns 3: Labour productivity growth in the services sector: wholesale & retail trade, restaurants and hotels.
Columns 4: Labour productivity growth in the services sector: transport, storage and communication.
Columns 5: Labour productivity growth in the services sector: finance, insurance, real estate and business services.

Sources: Columns 1, 2: OECD (2000b); Columns 3, 4, 5: OECD (2001).

based on a price competitiveness due to lower labour costs. This catching up may have been boosted by some growth in human capital, but at least for Portugal (the most likely case) this expansion is not extraordinary.[17] Again in Portugal the use of ICTs equipment as a percentage of GDP is quite close to average (which is a relative performance) but most other figures, like the percentage of employment in high-tech services and of Internet users, are noticeably low,[18] as is the growth rate of productivity in services (see OECD Historical Statistics, 1999). The patterns of development of Portugal thus seems still highly dependent on old forms of markets and only progressively entering the type of growth pattern that we described.

Ireland is another case in point. Its sustained growth rate of productivity stems from a peculiar position in international trade, as a dispatching centre for many ICTs equipment goods. The real growth in exports and imports over the 1990s (respectively 14 per cent per year and 12 per cent per year) is very telling, bringing the ratio of exports to GDP to some 88 per cent by year 2000. This role as an intermediary of high-tech products in international trade would be enough to account for the rapid growth of this small country. In effect it remains one of the less tertiary OECD countries with services accounting only for 56 per cent of total value added when the same statistics is an OECD average of some 70 per cent, with Turkey at 55 per cent and Korea at 52 per cent (all data from OECD Historical Statistics, 1999).

Only when we consider the Nordic countries such as Finland, Norway and Sweden do we have cases of successful real tertiary economies (with value added in services amounting respectively to 64 per cent, 63 per cent and 70 per cent in 1999 to compare with 73 per cent in the USA). Still each country has a specificity of its own in its growth pattern. Norway can dispose of an important natural resource (oil); Finland has been closely associated with the impressive development of a mobile phone company (after being left in an awkward position in the early 1990s with the dismantling of the USSR); Sweden went through a crisis of its highly developed welfare state and experienced slow growth for two decades in the 1970s and 1980s. Nevertheless, all these northern countries displayed a specifically dynamic adjustment to the new growth pattern. Among the pre-eminent figures we find exceptionally good rates of innovation, alone or in cooperation, for small and medium manufacturing firms, together with an extensive diffusion of ICTs among firms and households.[19] These are the only countries with significant lifelong learning schemes, together with an average of schooling years in their population close to 12 years (close to the UK) but less than in the USA, Germany and Canada where the same figure is around 13 years. If one looks more closely at services they display good rates of internationalization (see for instance the share of foreign affiliates in total turnover, where they rank high with nearly 20 per cent as opposed to around 10 per cent for France and the USA) (see OECD,

2001 p. 25). If one looks at the productivity gains in various service activities in the 1990s, again the results of Finnish and Swedish industry are remarkable (see Table 5.3). One could wonder why Denmark, which has many similar features, did not succeed so well in the 1990s. First, following our criteria of a 2 per cent growth rate of GDP per person employed over the 1990s, Denmark just missed selection with a 1.8 per cent score. If one is to look for the few cases where Denmark gets a less good ranking than the other Nordic countries one finds that government R&D expenditures as a percentage of GDP is less than EU average and chiefly that the contribution of manufacturing to GDP growth is much lower than in Sweden or in Finland (see OECD, 2001, p. 20). With 72.1 per cent of GDP in services as against 70.5 per cent in Sweden, 66.3 per cent in Finland and 65.9 per cent in Norway, all in 1997, Denmark appears to be even more of a tertiary economy than the other Nordic countries.[20] Still Denmark ranks second, just after the USA, regarding the share in GDP of the value added in ICTs industries (see OECD, 2000b, p. 200).

Therefore, from the perspective that we took the whole Nordic group of countries turns out as following a relatively successful new growth pattern which seems (providing we can take further the empirical investigation) to respond to the main features of growth we retained: a balanced innovative development between the 'learning processes' on the production side, and on the consumption side where service activities play a key role in adjusting to the specific needs of a country the long-term structural changes in technologies, education and internationalization.

This characterization remains highly tentative and the period of the 1990s still belongs to a phase of transition. The analysis of growth patterns can be further clarified by looking at what one should consider as relative counter-performances from some countries such as the USA, Canada and the UK which were favourites in the race.[21]

According to our criterion (GDP per person employed over the 1990s) the Anglo-Saxon countries have not fared too badly, with a similar 1.7 per cent rate for all three.[22] Those indicators where the Anglo-Saxon countries really rank in the first places are those regarding education (see OECD, 2000c, p. 161) and the production and diffusion of ICTs (with the USA well ahead). ICTs equipment for instance contributes to some 14 per cent of the output growth of these Anglo-Saxon countries (see Schreyer 2000). These economies are also fully tertiary economies with respectively 73.2 per cent, 72.1 per cent and 71.4 per cent of the total value added in service activities. In fact had the criteria been used on GDP growth instead of productivity the US and Canada would have appeared among the fastest growing countries (with the UK slightly lagging behind) with respectively 3.0 per cent and 2.3 per cent average yearly growth over the 1990s (1.9 per cent for the UK). But this points to the extensive nature of the growth process in these countries, which is somewhat at odds with the more quality-oriented new growth model that was expected. The indicators where Anglo-Saxon countries display average or low figures mainly concern the nature and dynamics of the service sector (and more precisely the inter-mediation sector sketched in section 2). The productivity gains for the composite FIRB (finance, insurance, real estate and business services) sector are thus very low (see Table 5.3)[23] while the level of internationalization of services, at least for the USA, also appears rather weak (noticeably more than in manufacturing), contrary to what is observed in the UK. It suggests that it would be useful to look in the direction of the service sector, and of its articu-lation with the rest of the economy, to find out about the small handicap shown by Anglo-Saxon countries.

By contrast a set of continental European countries have been doing rather poorly in the last decade in terms of productivity growth; taking together France, Germany and Italy, with the addition of Japan (see Table 5.3). And if these countries display above average stocks of educated people (but very little in the way of lifelong training schemes), their results in terms of diffu-sion of ICTs, both within firms and households, are rather poor (see Table 5.1). The productivity gains in some service sectors (more precisely in distribution and in FIRB) are also rather poor, all of which would mean, if we take these measures for granted, that for this last group of countries the transformation of the intermediation sector is still underway. Somehow this observation applies across the board in all countries where the current structural transformation does not yet seem to have brought the productivity gains it did in the manu-facturing activities. Over these same years, growth in manufacturing produc-tivity is overall much stronger than the one observed at the level of the whole economy (as can be inferred from Table 5.3). In other words the growth of productivity in service activities did not, by and large, so far meet expecta-tions. One can see many reasons for that, including, in the first place, a prob-lem of measurement. The estimation of real terms growth in services is noticeably hazardous (see Gadrey, 1996), especially in business services, but also in intermediation services which are right at the heart of the modern trans-formation underlined above.

This problem of measurement may lead to some underestimation of the overall growth rate of the economy, a case largely debated after the Boskin report (1996). As we are mainly focusing on the transformation of intermedi-ary service activities it should not bias the measure of GDP, although it could prevent us tracking down what kind of transformation is taking place and whether or not the process is comprehensive and completed.

It is all the more binding that our observation of three groups of countries did effectively look as if they were at various phases of their transformation, the Nordic countries forging ahead and adjusting rapidly while the continental European economies seemed to lag behind, with the Anglo-Saxon group in the middle. Somehow this suggests that a strong social cohesion as in the Nordic group, or, on the contrary, a wide range of inequalities in the case of the Anglo-Saxon group tends to facilitate the adjustment of the economies, while a mild social cohesion, as in continental Europe hampers it.[24]

But this does not tell what the end of the process will be. It may be the case that slower and more comprehensive adjustment (caring to avoid lasting discrimination in access for instance or saving as far as possible human capital from rapid obsolescence) will bring larger gains in the end.

To answer such a question one precisely needs to be able to follow the various steps of the transformation. The transformation of the broad sector of services seems both to take time and to affect to different extents and at different speeds the various branches of services. In other words the logistics of intermediation we aimed at is not homogeneous in its improvement. There are good old Schumpeterian reasons for that: old technologies and organizations are in different positions to block, slow down or bias the adjustment. Some countries undertook wide programmes of reforms led by an ideological stand of liberalization which oversimplified some issues (long-term investment, security and so on), forgetting that deregulation could only be a re-regulation of some kind. Instances of such drawbacks are given by the railways in the UK and the utilities in the USA.[25]

Consequent to the complexity of the transformation of what we called the intermediation sector it is difficult to link to it the resumption of manufacturing productivity that seems to emerge in the late 1990s.

Beyond this complex transformation of the logistics of intermediation another relevant issue has been neglected in the above discussion which regards the upkeep of human resources. There is a clear need to go beyond rapid assessments of levels of initial education. Studies on literacy (see OECD, 2000a) have pointed out that in the late 1990s the obsolescence of these initial investments had to be accounted for, and all the more so that the new growth regime was more innovative, more open to external competition and to a financial governance. All these risks affect the expected trajectories of workers on labour markets and the skills required. The contemporary stress on competencies instead of skills precisely underlines this new quest for reactivity from the workers to changes in their environment, be it product market changes or financial organization or even dismissal. To take these requirements into account one needs a comprehensive management of human resources which goes beyond what firms can do on their own. Lifelong learning schemes are few. Considerations of health care and leisure on a lifelong basis are still largely absent from this debate on human resources. On many grounds this is fully part of the challenge that any new growth regime based on knowledge, quality and innovation has to answer. It may well be the capacity of economies to find innovative and progressive institutional answers to this required adjustment of the wage labour nexus that will decide the success in the long run of the different blends of new growth regime that we defined above.

NOTES

1. CEPREMAP, CNRS, 142 Rue du Chevaleret, Paris 75013 tel 33 1 40778416; email: pascal.petit@cepremap.cnrs.fr
2. The share of trade or of capital flows in GDP was effectively greater at the end of the nineteenth century for countries such as the Netherlands and the UK.
3. The OECD studies on literacy do lead to observations on a wide range of capabilities and obsolescence rates among people with various levels of education (OECD, 2000a).
4. The finding itself much depends also on the number of categories retained. Most studies refer to a dichotomy between qualified and non-qualified workers. Results are more telling on the nature of the change in work organization when skills are distinguished in 3 or 5 categories (see Howel and Wolf, 1992).
5. Which is finally close to the posture taken by Romer (1986), although in a different perspective as he was looking for a proxy of human capital.
6. For example, the factor to be increased to release the constraint set on economic growth.
7. A conclusion reached by Gurgand (2000) in a survey on the measurement of the effect of education on economic growth.
8. But net of products which may be considered as intermediary by the households in the more complex process through which they organize their consumption plan, as will be explained later on.
9. It supposes that productivity gains can be measured which is often problematic (see Gadrey, 1996) but could be improved by taking into account the quality indicators that we introduce hereafter.
10. This hypothesis is highly disputable at least in a transition period when the very measure of productivity is not straightforward and cannot be retained by the agents as the conventional basis to their wage settlements. Still at a macroeconomic level a relation should hold between productivity gains and wage increases, even if the share of profits has noticeably increased in the meantime.
11. On the new embeddedness of markets, see Callon (1998).
12. That one may consider as intermediate consumption in the more elaborated process of welfare production in which consumers are engaged in a more complex world. This distinction, whereby all consumptions are not put at the same level by the consumers, is a key issue in assessing the creation of wealth, with all the measurement problems it raises.
13. Again the quality indicator of the intermediation sector could be different concerning the consumption of the various products but this distinction may be of a second order of importance in the simplified scheme we retained which already raised rather intricate issues for the statistical material one can dispose of to calibrate these indicators.
14. Taken once again in the perspective of a Kaldorian cumulative growth pattern.
15. Even if the complementarity between the use of ICTs and the use of skilled workers is less developed in services than in manufacturing.
16. Source OECD Historical statistics, average 1989–1999.
17. According to OECD (2000c, p. 161), the increase in the average number of schooling years between 1970 and 1998 seems even smaller than in most other countries (from 6.5 to 7.5 when in the UK the same figure rose from 9 to 12).
18. Cf. the European Trend Chart, Innovation Scoreboard, October 2000.
19. Data source: The European Innovation scoreboard, October 2000.
20. Which also explains that it is the country where the largest share of business R&D, that is, 32 per cent, goes to services (after Canada), OECD (2001, p. 26).

21. A claim very much linked with the speculation around a New Economy mainly based on the speculative bubble which developed in the late 1990s in the financial markets.
22. If we extend the group of Anglo-Saxon countries, Australia scored well with an average growth rate of productivity of 2.2 per cent, but New Zealand, which could be added, did badly with a mere 0.6 per cent.
23. Again it may derive from country specific measurement conventions but in an organizational perpsective this is also meaningful.
24. It might be more relevant to speak in terms of types of welfare state instead of social cohesion, even if so far we did not discuss much the welfare aspect of the transformation, which is obviously involved in the transformation we schematized if only to inform on the upkeeping of human capital, where we only mentioned lifelong learning schemes when lifelong health care is also an important issue for instance.
25. A short list to which the events of September 2001 have rapidly added many issues regarding banking regulations, transport security, communication control and fair labelling in distribution.

REFERENCES

Acemoglu, D. (1998), 'Why Do New Technologies Complement Skills? Directed Technical Change and Wage Inequality', *Quarterly Journal of Economics*, 113, November, 1055–89.

Amable, B., J.B. Chatelain and O. De Bandt (1997), 'Stability and Efficiency of the Banking Sector and Economic Growth', mimeo presented at the Royal Economic Society Meeting, University of Stoke on Trent, UK, March.

Atkinson, A., L. Rainwater and T. Smeeding (1995), 'La distribution des revenus dans les pays de l'OCDE: documentation tirée du Luxembourg Income Study', in *La distribution des revenus dans les pays de l'OCDE*, Etudes de Politique Sociale, no. 18.

Ashauer, D.A. (1989), 'Is Public Expenditure Productive?', *Journal of Monetary Economics*, March, 177–200.

Ashauer, D.A. (1994), 'Public Capital, Productivity, and Macroeconomic Performance: A Literature Review in Infrastructure in the 21st Century Economy', Federal Infrastructure Strategy Program, 48(2), January, 391–406.

Barro, R. (1990), 'Government Spending in a Simple Model of Endogenous Growth', *Journal of Political Economy*, 23, 103–25.

Berndt, E.R. and B. Hanson (1992), 'Measuring the Contribution of Public Infrastructure Capital in Sweden', *Scandinavian Journal of Economics*, Supplement, 94, 151–72.

Boskin, M. (ed). (1996), 'Towards a More Accurate Measure of the Cost of Living', Final Report to the Senate Finance Committee, December.

Bradford De Long, J. and L. Summers (1991), 'Equipment Investment and Economic Growth', *Quarterly Journal of Economics*, 106(2), May, 445–502.

Braudel, F. (1985), *Civilization and Capitalism 15th–18th Century*, Harper Collins, p. 800.

Callon, M. (1998), *The Laws of the Market* (Oxford: Blackwell).

Chandler, A. (1977), *The Visible Hand*. The Managerial Revolution in American Business, Harvard: Harvard University Press.

European Commission (2000), 'European Trend Chart on Innovation', The European Innovation Scoreboard, Directorate General Enterprises, Innovation and SME Programme, October.

Gadrey, J. (1996) *Services: la productivité en questions* (Paris: Desclée de Brouwer).

Gallouj, C. and F. Gallouj (1996), *L'innovation dans les services* (Paris: Economica).

Gibbons, M. et al. (1994), *The New Production of Knowledge* (London: Sage).

Gurgand, M. (2000), 'Sait-on mesurer le rôle économique de l'éducation?', *Revue Française d'économie*, no. 2, 121–156.

Howell, D. and E. Wolff (1992), 'Technical Change and the Demand for Skills by US Industries', *Cambridge Journal of Economics*, 16, 128–46.

Kaldor, N. (1972), 'The irrelevance of Economic Equilibrium', *Economic Journal*, 82, December, 1237–55.

Lucas, R. (1988), 'On the Mechanics of Economic Development', *Journal of Monetary Economics*, **22**(1) July, 3–42.

Lundvall, R.A. (1988), 'Innovation as an interactive process. From use-producer interaction to the national system of innovation,' in G. Dosi, C. Freeman, R. Nelson, G. Silverberg and L. Soete (eds), *Technical Change and Economic Ttheory*, London: Pinter Publishes, 349–369.

Machin, S. and J. Van Reenen (1998), 'Technology and Changes in Skill Structure: Evidence from Seven OECD Countries', *Quarterly Journal of Economics*, November, 1215–44.

Morrison, C.J. and A.E. Schwartz (1996), 'State Infrastructure and Productive Performance', *American Economic Review*, December, 1095–111.

Moulton, B. and K. Moses (1997), 'Addressing the Quality Change Issue in the Consumer Price Index', *Brookings Papers on Economic Activity*, vol 1, 305–49.

Munnell, A. (1992), 'Infrastructure Investment and Economic Growth', *Journal of Economic Perspectives*, fall, 189–98.

OECD (1998), *Science, Technology and Industry Outlook* (Paris: OECD).

OECD (1999) Historical Statistics, Paris.

OECD (2000a), *Literacy in the Information Age* (Paris: OECD).

OECD (2000b), *Economic Outlook*, June, Paris.

OECD (2000c), *Economic Outlook*, December, Paris.

OECD(2001), *Innovation and Productivity in Services* (Paris: OECD).

Pack, H. (1994) 'Endogenous Growth Theory: Intellectual Appeal and Empirical Shortcomings! *Journal of Economic Perspectives*, **8**(1), winter, 55–72.

Petit, P. (1999), 'Les aléas de la croissance dans une économies fondée sur le savoir', *Revue d'Economie Industrielle*, June, 41–66.

Petit, P. and L. Soete, (2001), 'Is a Biased Technological Change Fueling Dualism?', Working paper, CEPREMAP, no. 2001–03.

Röller, L. and L. Waverman (1996), 'The Impact of Telecommunication Infrastructives on Economic Development, in Howit P. *The Implications of Knowledge Based Growth for Micro Economic Policies*, Industry Canada Research Series, Calgary, University of Calgary Press, 363–87.

Romer, P. (1986), 'Increasing Returns and Long-Run Growth', *Journal of Political Economy*, **94**(5), October, 1002–37.

Romer, P. (1990), 'Endogenous Technical Change', *Journal of Political Economy*, 98, 71–102.

Schreyer, P. (2000) 'The Impact of Information and Communication Technology on Output Growth', OECD Working Paper, 2000/2.

Sichel, D. (1997), *The Computer Revolution: An Economic Perspective* (Washington, DC: The Brookings Institution Press).

Storper, M. (2000), 'Lived Effects of the Contemporary Economy: Globalization, Inequality, and Consumer Society', Special issue of *Public Culture* on 'Millenial Capitalism' edited by Jean and John Comaroff.

6. Networks, distributed knowledge and economic performance: evidence from quality control in corporate legal services

Emmanuel Lazega

This chapter examines the relationship between distributed knowledge and economic performance in a professional, or 'collegial', organization. It identifies a few conditions under which the pattern of knowledge flows is most productive for firms stressing quality professional services. In such organizations, the production of services for clients is difficult to routinize, professional expertise and advice cannot be easily standardized, and therefore 'internal' transaction costs related to flows of resources, including knowledge, can be assumed to be a large part of total costs for the firm as a whole. The practical problem for professional services firms can be represented as reducing complexity and constructing certainties in order to provide quality advice (Dingwall and Lewis 1983; Lazega, 1992b; Sciulli, 1986) for clients. In order to achieve such knowledge-intensive work on a regular basis, intelligence is shared in two types of situation at least: in common work on cases or in case-related advice relationships. Saying that intelligence is 'shared', however, does not do justice to what really happens in social exchanges and in the flows of knowledge and experience. The important characteristic of such flows is shown to be that knowledge as a resource is efficiently distributed/allocated through two processes: selection of exchange partners (social niche seeking) and concentration of the authority to know (through status competition). Some members emerge as having the authority to know, although such status is fragile (Blau, 1964). These processes of knowledge allocation are micropolitical processes because they multiply the number of authorities and trigger status competition, but they are efficient too. Efficiency can be measured, I argue, in statistical evidence concerning the relationship between crude measurements of economic performance and position in social networks related to this allocation of knowledge. An empirical study of a medium-sized north-eastern US corporate law firm is used for that purpose. Distributed knowledge is measured through two types of networks: a network of co-workers with whom the 'Whole Picture' of the case is shared; and the advice network within the firm. Members' individual performance data (hourly rates, number of hours worked, fees brought in) are analysed as an effect of position in these networks. Dependence of economic performance on the overall pattern of ties in the two networks is also established. This suggests that proxy measurements – based on social network analysis – of productivity are possible in knowledge-intensive organizations, a thorny issue in contemporary economics (Gadrey, 1996). This approach to productivity, however, must recognize that knowledge and 'learning goods' in general are massively produced, allocated and circulated in society (and particularly in an organizational society) through politicized social exchanges that differ from market processes.

QUALITY CONTROL FOR KNOWLEDGE-INTENSIVE WORK

Maintaining quality through capitalization of authorized knowledge and sharing experience is not an easy process in knowledge-intensive organizations. A professional services firm (PSF) is usually not a capital-intensive organization producing material goods and relying on economies of scale in an industrial sense. It produces knowledge-based services evaluated by their level of quality. But quality is difficult to measure. There are formal mechanisms, such as official peer review committees, that can perform this task; but these mechanisms raise suspicion of being politicized. The question is then: does such a firm rely on its own multi-level social exchange system to provide an informal mechanism of overall peer review and quality control? If so, how does it ensure accumulation and distribution of authorized knowledge and experience?

Lawyers' work, for example, is knowledge intensive in the sense of 'knowledge-in-action' (Flood, 1987; Gallouj, 1992; Lazega, 1992a) accumulated by experience, or 'judgement' – a word often used by members to characterize the quality of a colleague's legal work. This experience is necessary to the provision of legal advice to corporations. This task often requires designing new solutions to complex problems, taking risks, and sometimes persuading the client to adopt untested strategies. For this kind of innovative work, often invisible and not very spectacular, one needs a certain accumulation of knowledge-in-action or experience. Managing this capital of expertise means using all the available information technology (libraries, online services, a firm electronic memory and so on), but also – and most importantly – recruiting the best possible attorneys, keeping them, and helping them manage and update their knowledge base. Management consultants often call this the 'human capital' of the organization. Members must build and convert tacit and innovative knowledge into a shared instrument, and perhaps eventually into more codified and routinized knowledge where pieces of information are already related to one another. Tacit knowledge can only be mobilized at the local level, in a decentralized way, between individual members. Indeed, if tacit knowledge and what collective learning produces are difficult to capitalize in a database, actors' 'live' and educated thinking must be taken into account.

Among members, concern for quantity is widespread, but the solution is relatively simple: the more partners and associates work (especially partners because their hourly rates are high), the more revenue they bring in. Concern for quality is also permanent, but here the solution cannot be standardized (by definition of a profession). Legal practice being knowledge intensive, based partly on a series of information management tasks, formal instruments are available (such as library, computer memory and standard documents). But there is no predefined standard of quality for this type of work. Much of it consists of using past experience to adjust to new problems through individual and collective learning (Gadrey, 1994; Gadrey and De Bandt, 1994; Favereau, 1994; Hatchuel, 1994a and 1994b; Starbuck, 1992). Thus it has to be done in common: cognitive efforts are more or less shared in brainstorming processes familiar to knowledge-intensive organizations. To avoid using the cognitive psychologists' term of 'distributed cognition', I use here the expression distributed knowledge.[1] Recall that partners, and to a lesser extent associates, are strategic in their effort to choose quality and loyal co-workers. They are constrained by specialization and (other) partners' decisions. Instead of an elusive predefined standard of quality, brainstorming processes include an informal quality control through common monitoring and through advice seeking. Thus economic performance and quality control depend on a social mechanism supporting individual efforts and competencies. The exchange system within and beyond social 'niche' boundaries is shown to provide a structural solution to problems of motivation and supervision in the absence of strong hierarchy.

In the light of this definition of professional work, distributed knowledge (as an organizational response to environmental complexity) is supposed to help. But contrary to what is asserted by many PSF specialists, information technology and human capital are not sufficient to ensure a high level of quality. Activities driven by market reaction do not necessarily encourage innovation and creativity (Alter, 2000; Gallouj, 2002); they can develop short-term adaptation. This raises the issue of quality control as a social process, and that of sharing experience in order to improve the quality of work when needed. The way in which the firm manages this issue is often called 'peer review'; it is the starting point of empirical analysis in this article. Many partners in PSFs tend to consider formal peer review to be costly, difficult to implement and inefficient. But informal peer review also takes place in order to try to maintain a high level of quality. Members observe each other's performances and evaluate (mostly informally) each other's production: they praise big successes, and indirectly sanction (that is, criticize and gossip about) blunders and mistakes (Bosk, 1979; Reynaud, 1989; Wittek and Wielers, 1998).[2] In the first section, I examine how members of a corporate law firm conceive of peer review, in particular peer review of the quality of work.

Spencer, Grace & Robbins, a Corporate Law Firm

Fieldwork was conducted in a north-eastern US corporate law firm, Spencer, Grace & Robbins (71 lawyers in three offices located in three different cities, comprising 36 partners and 35 associates) in 1991. All the lawyers in the firm were interviewed. In Nelson's (1988) terminology, this firm was a 'traditional' one, without formally defined departments, as opposed to a more 'bureaucratic' type. Interdependence among attorneys working together on a file could be strong for a few weeks, and then weak for months. As a client-oriented, knowledge-intensive organization, it tried to protect its human capital and social resources, such as its network of clients, through the usual policies of commingling partners' assets (clients, experience, innovations) (Gilson and Mnookin, 1985) and the maintenance of an ideology of collegiality. Informal networks of collaboration, advice, and 'friendship' (socializing outside), were key to the integration of the firm (Lazega, 1992b).

It was a relatively decentralized organization, which grew out of a merger, but without formal and acknowledged distinctions between profit centres. Although not departmentalized, the firm broke down into two general areas of practice: the litigation area (half the lawyers of the firm) and the 'corporate' area (anything other than litigation). Sharing work and cross-selling among partners was done mostly on an informal basis. Given the classical stratification of such firms, work was supposed to be channelled to associates through specific partners, but this rule was only partly respected. A weak administration provided information, but did not have many formal rules to enforce. The firm had an executive committee comprising a managing partner and two deputy-managing partners who were elected each year, renewable once, among partners prepared to perform administrative tasks and temporarily transfer some of their clients to other partners. This structure was adopted during the 1980s for more efficient day-to-day management and decision-making. The current managing partner was not a 'rainmaker' and did not concentrate strong powers in his hands. He was a day-to-day manager who made recommendations to functional standing committees (finance, associate, marketing, recruitment and so on) and to the partnership.

Partners' compensation was based exclusively on a rigid seniority system without any direct link between contribution and returns. The firm went to great lengths – when selecting associates to become partners – to avoid individuals who may not 'pull their weight'. Partners could argue informally about what contribution might 'fairly' match one's benefits, but the seniority system mechanically distributed the benefits to each once a year. Great managerial resources were devoted to measurement of each partner's performance (time sheets, billing, collecting, expenses and so on), and this information was available to the whole partnership. A low performance could not be hidden for long. However, the firm usually made considerable profits, which could help partners overlook the fact that some voluntary contributions to shared benefits were not always consistent with the successful pursuit of narrow self-interest.

The firm did not have a formal peer review system that could provide intermediate steps between lateral control and formal court procedures. Before expulsion, partners had the power to 'punish' each other seriously by preventing a partner from reaching the next seniority level in the compensation system. A partner could be expelled only if there was near-unanimity against him/her. Buying out a partner was very difficult and costly. Therefore, despite the existence of direct financial controls, the firm did not have many formal ways of dealing with free-loading. The harm that a single partner could inflict on others might become very substantial in the long run. Conversely, partners could try to insulate one of their own informally by, at the very least, not referring clients, not 'lending' associates, not providing information and advice.

Avoidance of Formal Peer Review

Among organizational processes that collegial firms (as well as others) deal with, peer review, that is, the evaluation of one's partners' work, is certainly one of the most sensitive and sometimes upsetting. Even more so when the review applies to the quality of work, not only to the economics of productivity. Some firms have a peer evaluation mechanism that looks at every person's 'professionalism' and tries to improve it. Especially under pressure from malpractice insurers, professional firms recognize the need for maintaining or upgrading their overall level of professionalism. Financial incentives are given to firms by these insurers to implement quality control. The financial incentives are tied for instance to in-house continuing legal education courses, or to intake policies which allow the firm to stay out of work that is likely to cause insurance claims. Despite a tradition of Yankee individualism and a belief that they are part of the elite of the profession, the firm had raised the issue, and was trying to find a methodology for helping partners look at what other partners do.

At the time of the study, it had not implemented a formal peer review system for the quality of work in which some partners go and check through other people's files and determine whether 'they did the matter right'. They relied on a less systematic or informal system (complaints). The main official argument against a more formal system was its high cost. It costs the client or the firm money to put two lawyers on a matter where one will suffice, where one is seen as just serving as a shadow of the other. Resistance to the implementation of formal review mechanisms was widespread. The more senior lawyers did not welcome any change that seemed to detract from the informality of earlier practice. Many partners said that they did not worry about the quality of work of their colleagues, that the problems were with partners who were not working hard enough or taking in lousy business. Many were sceptical about quality peer review, either because of practical difficulties or because of more substantive ones, such as defining the quality of service rendered:

> The peer review that we have right now is everyone sits down in the partners' meeting and you have in front of you the printout that shows you how many hours I worked, how many hours I billed, how many hours I collected and how outstanding my account receivable is, and then you get people grumbling at the meeting about the account receivables going up and not coming down. But as far as whether I am doing a good job on my work, unless they get a call from a client complaining about me, some kind of peer review as to quality of work, I think that will be hard to implement. I suspect it would be resented by many, and at least at the stage we are at, I don't think I want to be reviewing somebody else's work and decide whether it is good or not. I am too busy, I don't want to do somebody else's work, I want to do my own. The managing partner will have a hard time implementing a systematic second opinion. (Partner 29)

Rather, the firm counted on a proactive form of quality control. By this I mean: (1) the fact that its members shared the *whole picture* of the cases with their co-workers; and (2) the fact that they sought each other's *advice* or second opinion and shared their experience before they made decisions or sent opinions out to clients. From the perspective of the organization, relationships between members were necessary to share knowledge and experience. Especially in situations where members worked together, they depended on each other for these resources. Knowledge could be capitalized in members' individual live memory, but its use also depended on their work and advice relationships. Indeed reasoning exclusively in terms of human capital, presupposes that, once in business, members freely share their knowledge and experience with one another. We know that this is not an obvious fact, especially since Blau (1964) showed that status is central to such games.[3]

Proactive Quality Control: Sharing the Big Picture?

How do members of a PSF share knowledge with co-workers? In task forces, members combine cooperation, status competition and knowledge management in various ways, depending on their experience of this competition with specific co-workers. In order to show that quality control was ensured by the multiplex exchange system in the firm, it is important to show that members shared knowledge in their brainstorming processes and competed for professional status derived from 'knowing best' in their deliberations (Lazega and Pattison, 1999). Additional data was collected about this topic. Specifically, the lawyers were all asked with whom they had intensive work relationships within the firm; then they were asked to check the names of their co-workers with whom they felt that they usually *shared the whole picture of the cases* on which they worked together. A sub-network of co-workers, the 'Whole Picture network' was thus identified: it included the subset of colleagues with whom knowledge and expertise was felt to be shared. Arguments were then provided to explain why sharing did or did not take place. These arguments were examined for elements concerning social niche seeking and status competition.

In other words, I assume that members try to work in social niches (Lazega, 1999b), but also that in such niches this issue of knowledge sharing and quality control is often connected to the issue of the authority to know. A partner handling the case was often in a position to select among his colleagues those with whom he or she will allow professional status competition to take place. When a partner did not share the whole picture of the case with a colleague who also worked on this case, there could not be much status competition.[4] Someone who does not know enough about a case cannot display professional judgement. When a partner shared selectively the whole picture of the case with one colleague working on this case, but not with another, status competition was usually limited to a dyadic tournament.

Status and knowledge were also combined in associates' attitudes to work. The analysis of the arguments provided by associates to justify their sociometric choices in this vignette shows that associates were quickly made particularly aware of such issues because the firm could not guarantee a partnership to all of them. In the absence of a career prospect within the firm, they were told that they would receive training and develop skills and competencies which would help them manage their own career elsewhere if they did not reach the coveted position. In other settings, members are told that they need to think about their 'employability' on the labour market; permanent training and learning are presented as the way to increase it. Traditionally, associates complain about lack of training, about being kept in the dark, about not really knowing how what they do fits into the whole picture of the case. They may work very hard to make urgent deadlines, they sometimes do not know why things have to be done in a hurry and what is the scope of the project, or the gameplan. The decision as to whether they were getting the whole picture was the partners', not theirs. Such complaints also reflected the frustration of not being able to participate in the professional status competition. They came almost exclusively from junior associates. But more senior associates usually had the feeling that they participated much more: some could sometimes be choosy with regard to the cases in which they would like to get seriously involved. They were particularly selective. Some cases were not worth any professional status competition, some were.

Thus, the decision to share was surrounded by reasoning about partners' personal style, about the nature of the task, and about control. A very unclear division of labour existed in the sharing of background information. The deliberation process was qualified here in various ways, and the ongoing attempts at control of the authority to know, and indirectly at control of decisions, was made explicit several times. In the case examined here, partners were never accused of mistreating associates. They were sometimes accused of not playing the status competition game in a way that provided the associate with an opportunity to increase his/her professional status.

The analysis of the Whole Picture network shows that respondents were selective in their identification of knowledge sharers. But the density of the network was still 0.16, which was not much lower than that of the co-workers and advice networks (respectively 0.22 and 0.18). Analysis of the aggregated choices confirms that sharing knowledge did take place in social niches. The formal dimensions of firm structure were used as identity criteria by members who felt that they shared knowledge with their co-workers. They tended to consider that they shared the whole picture with colleagues in the same office who shared their speciality, although this was the case for Office I members much more than for Office II members. Litigators felt that they shared mostly with other litigators, mainly in Office I, and almost equally for partners and associates. The same was true with corporate lawyers, although a little less obviously so. When lawyers felt that they shared with members of other offices, it was mainly with partners – another indicator confirming the stratification of the system. One interesting result is that status differences did not prevent partners from feeling that they shared within the same office, although it did across office boundaries. At least, overall, partners felt more often that they shared mostly with other partners, but that effect is not statistically significant. It seems that, for partners, status did not matter as much as one would expect when sharing the whole picture. Status mattered much more for associates, who felt that partners who worked intensively with them also shared background information much more than other associates did. Associates who felt that they shared with other associates were mainly litigators from Office I.

Centrality measures in the network show that many partners and senior associates were identified as background information sharers by many others. Senior partners even tended to underestimate the extent to which they shared, when compared to what their younger co-workers felt about the issue: many co-workers considered that these senior partners did share the whole picture with them, whereas the latter said that they did not! In contrast, a few partners (for example Partners 15, 24 and 26) strongly overestimated the extent to which they shared: they asserted that they shared with almost all their co-workers, whereas only one-third of the latter confirmed this assertion.

In conclusion, the analysis of the Whole Picture network shows that status differences were temporarily downplayed in the deliberation process with one's immediate co-workers, and were more salient (overplayed) with other members of the firm. Next, in order to understand such status games more clearly, I analyse the advice network as the key network combining status and knowledge.

Informally Distributed Knowledge and Competition for the Authority to Know

The second way in which knowledge was circulated was through the advice network. In order to recognize the importance of social exchanges for quality control, one has to accept that quality of production is not a manifest variable (White, 2002). It is grasped as an implicit ranking, a local information inferred from status and rank. Transfers and exchanges of advice reflected this specific pecking order and form of status in the firm – a fragile order since everyone was allowed to hope to climb the professional ladder by impressing his/her colleagues. Indeed, competition for professional status was one reason why the fact of providing advice was kept so distinct from that of collaborating on a case. Moreover, personalized access and multiplex ties to sought-out and selective advisers could help advice seekers in stretching advice as much as possible before it became collaboration.

It was in members' collective economic interest to share information and experience as much as possible, but it was also in their individual interest – given status competition – to do so while increasing as much as possible their individual credit and stressing the value of their own knowledge and experience. Knowledge was not necessarily 'freely' or randomly shared under task force relational pressure. It was shared by the prospect of increasing one's firmwide and more general professional status. Once they had been provided with resources and with a sense of their interests beyond the short term, members needed another level of social approval if they wanted to increase their status within the firm. This form of status could be called 'professional authority or reputation'. Whereas individual economic performance was strongly associated with team membership and relational constraint (Lazega, 1999a), professional reputation was also based on the capacity to be recognized beyond local niches. The firm as a multi-level exchange system was thus a form of productive social mechanism when it helped members extend beyond their niches. In this section, I also look at how they concentrated the authority to know in the professional status of a few select partners. I argue that much of the proactive quality control was performed by seeking these members' advice on task related matters. Professional status allows members to push and sometimes impose their standards and criteria of quality.[5]

The main actors in the advice network of the firm – who had acquired a form of status that attracted some deference – are identified below.[6] Several local rules related to the circulation of advice within the firm have already been extracted from the analysis, among which the most important identified above is that one does not seek advice from people 'below.' This concentration of the authority to know may be puzzling in an organization where members were jealous of their professional discretion and individual intellectual autonomy. It is less so when considering the problems raised by formal peer review of quality of work – problems already sketched above. This social process of capitalization and sharing of knowledge was inextricably related to quality control through professional status and epistemic alignment. It was a complex process: it was necessary, but also costly. Protecting this expertise from opportunistic behaviour was a permanent preoccupation.[7]

The joint analysis of members' indegree (that is, the simple count of the number of times each member is chosen as an adviser by all the others) centrality scores and prominence scores confirms precisely that multilevel dimension of professional status. Indegree centrality scores show that members cited most often (more than 25 times) were the following: Partners 4, 12, 13, 16, 17, 19, 20, 22, 24, 26, 27, 28, 30, 31, 34, and Associates 40, 41, 42, 55, 65 and 66. This list includes a few senior partners, in particular those with an open door policy, either for senior associates, or even, as for Partner 13, for everyone. Senior associates and younger ones with high scores were mostly cited by other associates below or near them, with exceptions that will be examined below. However, Burt's (1982) prominence scores, which include a measurement of the importance of the people who cite the focal member, identify Partners 1, 2, 4, 6, 12, 13, 15, 16, 17, 20, 21, 24, 26, 28 and 34 as the most prominent. The difference between the two measures shows that Partners 1, 2, 6, 15, and 21 were cited by few colleagues, but by colleagues who were themselves important ones, mainly partners and senior associates. In addition, prominence scores for top partners are increased by the fact that, while being heavily sought out, they themselves sought out fewer people.[8] Partners 13 and 34 are still in the list but with relatively lower scores because they attracted a heavy volume of associates' citations (women associates for Partner 34, who was one of the three women partners).

Peer evaluation of quality is in the task-related advice network, and the way in which the advice network was stratified is a useful characteristic for our purpose.[9] Since quality in this context is linked to knowledge and experience, a reputation 'market' was created in the firm. We also know that the advice network had both hierarchical (or centre/periphery) and clustering tendencies with an emphasis on hierarchical arrangement.[10] Advice was sought within and across social niches; requests for advice and professional status recognition converged towards positions of partners, with senior associates as exceptions. Seniority in general was important here for achieving cognitive alignment or co-orientation around a common definition of the situation in collective action, that is, for the legitimacy of a certain course of action. Members rarely sought advice from others below them on the seniority scale: thus the longer you were in the firm, the more people came to you for advice (and the less you sought advice). They also tended to seek advice from others in their own niche, that is, from members similar in office and speciality. However, given the number of seniority levels in the pecking order, it was unlikely that junior associates would seek advice from senior partners. The latter would be overwhelmed with questions below their status. Therefore, it was very likely that members would seek advice from more senior members closer to them on this ladder.

In sum, professional status is an important form of status in knowledge-intensive organizations which count on members' capacity to innovate and maintain informal quality control; and a centre-periphery structure shows the existence of firmwide professional status. This implies a convergence of requests for knowledge in the system of 'distributed knowledge'. The distribution of the authority to know – produced by the multi-level exchange mechanism – inferred from the pattern of the advice network provides a clearer picture of the informal quality control process that took place in the firm as a result of avoidance of formal peer review. A few central members were key to this form of informal and indirect control. In a collegial environment, distributed knowledge not only means stratification of this relational structure. It also means multiplication and competition between top professional authorities; such a multiplication characterizes the learning process in knowledge-intensive firms. The next section stresses the fact that the dynamics underlying the quality control process examined here had a visible impact on economic performance.

INFORMALLY DISTRIBUTED KNOWLEDGE AND ECONOMIC PERFORMANCE

In any organization, measurements of performance are intrinsically difficult to interpret and their informative value can change from one year to another.[11] Managers know that performance data are never as 'hard' and indisputable data as one often expects them to be (Granovetter 1985; Nohria and Eccles 1992; Meyer, 1994).[12] A narrow conception of organizational efficiency ignores the fact that no measurement of actor's performance goes unchallenged within the organization. Therefore using performance measurements as a dependent or independent variable is not easy, and rarely provides spectacular results. Nevertheless, in this chapter, I propose a test of the idea that specific relational patterns shaping the flows and distribution of knowledge in organizations are correlated with various measures of economic performance.

Many factors account for members' individual performance. These factors can be external or environmental (some areas of practice provide more work, some markets are currently more lucrative) and individual (some attorneys are personally more motivated or hard working). For these reasons, the following analyses link information on members' economic performance – narrowly understood, for example, as the amounts of fees brought into the firm at the end of the year – with information on social status and *relationships* among them. Differences in such performance may be explained, in part, in terms of relationships within the firm, for instance because relational factors can help gain access to needed resources, reduce 'transaction costs' with co-workers, or help pressure colleagues back to more productive behaviour. To examine such effects on performance, I used information collected about each attorney's (partner and associate) relationships within the firm and combined it with information on their individual performance for the year before the study was conducted.

To study the effect of position in firm structure on this type of economic performance, I use regression models with measurements of such performance as dependent variables, and various social factors related to firm structure, work process, and members' ties in the year of fieldwork as independent variables. I first use as covariates three dimensions of formal structure of this firm that were expected to be the most important (status, office, speciality), as well as two attributes of members defined from outside the firm (gender and lawschool attended). Table 6.1 presents the distribution of lawyers in this firm per variable.

The first covariate is formal status, a variable with two levels, partners and associates. We can hypothesize that status matters for economic performance in the sense that firm rules required associates to put in more time than partners. This variable is elaborated upon in the second covariate, seniority. We can hypothesize that seniority matters for economic performance in the sense that the more senior members were, the higher the hourly rates systematically charged to clients. This second covariate is a variable with eight levels, indicating the three possible levels of seniority for a partner,[13] and five levels of seniority of associates. For associates, seniority had the meaning of being a member of a cohort recruited the same year. We can thus look at gradual effects of numerical rank on economic performance. Office membership and practice are the third and fourth covariates. Office is a variable with three

Productivity and performances in services

Table 6.1   Distribution of lawyers per variable

Formal Status	Partner	Associate	
Seniority level 1	14	7	
Seniority level 2	13	10	
Seniority level 3	9	5	
Seniority level 4		7	
Seniority level 5		6	
Office I (Boston)	22	26	48
Office II (Hartford)	13	6	19
Office III (Providence)	1	3	4
Speciality: Litigation	20	21	41
Speciality: Corporate	16	14	30
Man	33	20	53
Woman	3	15	18
Lawschool: Ivy-League	12	3	15
Lawschool: New-England Non-Ivy-League	11	17	28
Lawschool: Other	13	15	28
Total	36	35	71

levels, Office I, II and III; practice with two levels, litigation and corporate. They are expected to have an effect on economic performance as indicators of variations in market demand. The next covariates are other actors' attributes, gender and lawschool attended. These attributes are included as control variables representing two characteristics of the outside world that could have an influence on economic performance. In this firm, women attorneys were mostly associates and often felt that they needed to work harder than their male colleagues to reach the same economic results, for example because they mostly had to deal with male clients or partners. Lawschool attended is a variable with three levels, indicating whether a lawyer went to an Ivy League lawschool, to a New England non-Ivy League lawschool, or to another lawschool. This variable is introduced in the model to examine the extent to which a form of prestige acquired outside the firm may have an effect on the extent to which one was assigned work with extra-lucrative clients.

To locate members in the informal relational structure of the firm, I use two kinds of variable (indegree centrality scores and constraint scores) derived from standard sociometric information on three types of relations collected in this firm in 1991: co-workers, advice and friendship ties. First, their individual indegree centrality scores in these networks. As already mentioned, indegree centrality represents a measurement of the extent to which members are 'popular' in these networks and therefore accumulate resources circulating in them (Wasserman and Faust, 1994, pp. 169–219). One can therefore hypothesize that they will be in a better position to perform economically. Second, their individual constraint scores as defined by Burt (1992) in the same networks. For Burt, network constraint measures 'social capital' as a form of network structure. Specifically, constraint is a function of network size, density, and hierarchy (that measures the extent to which relations are directly or indirectly concentrated in a single contact). A contact in which relations are concentrated is a 'knot' in the network, making it difficult for negotiations to proceed independently in separate relationships. Constrained networks leave little opportunity for individual initiative, little chance to withdraw from difficult relationships. Difficult relations persist because they are interlocked with cooperative relations. The higher the constraint, the fewer opportunities for alternatives offered by one's contacts or contacts' contacts, and the lower the performance. In our case, constraint represents a measurement of the extent to which colleagues can exercise unobtrusive but insistent pressure on a member. High constraint in a specific network means that clique members in that network have high investments in each other and high expectations from each other. The denser a member's personal network of co-workers, for example, the more co-workers can coordinate their informal efforts at prodding him/her back into performing more (Lazega, 1999a). They can, for instance, try to increase their own collaborations with him/her, and exercise unobtrusive but insistent pressure to put in more time.

Using these covariates, several models were estimated to explain economic performance measured as the amount of fees brought to the firm (managing partner not included) in the year of fieldwork. It is important to realize that not all the covariates representing various dimensions of position in firm structure can be used at the same time, because of strong dependency between them. This is typically the case for status and seniority; in the models, the most refined covariate, seniority, is used. In addition, status and seniority overlap with the number of hours worked and hourly rates as explanatory variables. The more senior, the more attorneys charged per hour. Associates worked longer hours than partners. Therefore, to avoid this problem, analyses below test the robustness of relational capital effects using three different models. This multi-colinearity will be taken into account in the interpretation of results. In terms of economic and relational variables, the best overall models achievable with this dataset predicting the number of hours worked and the amount of hours worked and the amount of dollar fees brought in are presented in Table 6.2.

The significant effect of centrality in the advice network in Models 2 and 3

Table 6.2   *Variables explaining economic performance measured by the number of hours worked (model 1) and by the amount of fees brought into the firm (models 2 and 3) in 1990 (OLS regression models)*

Effects	Standardized estimates		
	Model 1	Model 2	Model 3
Seniority	0.01	0.76***	
Hourly rates			0.78***
Time input[a]			0.40***
Office	0.24**	0.15*	0.05
Speciality	–0.16*	0.01	0.07
Gender	–0.03	0.00	0.02
Lawschool attended	–0.14	–0.03	0.02
Centrality friendship	–0.27*	–0.11	–0.01
Centrality co-worker	0.17	0.01	–0.02
Centrality advice[b]	**–0.02**	**0.27***	**0.23***
Constraint friendship	–0.81***	–0.15	0.11
Constraint co-worker	0.23*	0.16*	0.13*
Constraint advice	**–0.04**	**–0.05**	**0.04**

Notes
*** $p<0.001$, ** $p<0.01$, * $p<0.05$. Adjusted R-squares are 0.66, 0.86 and 0.89 respectively. The managing partner, who concentrates on firm policy and administrative work, and is not a time keeper during his tenure, was not included in the computations of these parameter estimates.
a. Including the interaction effect of time input and hourly rates does not provide additional insights here because senior partners who charge the highest rates are not among the members who put in the greatest number of hours.
b. Centrality in the advice network represents the concentration of informally distributed knowledge examined in the text.

in Table 6.2 suggests that seniority and concentration of requests for knowledge was a determinant of strong performance in this case. This effect is added to that of higher hourly rates for senior partners and to that of constraint in one's workgroup (or task force). Recall that members got their advice in social niches, but also outside the niche, among partners with a specific form of status: it was not only technical expertise, but authority based on experience and willingness to risk an already well established reputation. Partners with high indegree scores in the advice network had high hourly rates ($r = 0.47$) and brought in more fees (in terms of dollars collected; $r = 0.42$).[14] Being sought out for advice was strongly correlated with being senior ($r = 0.46$), with years spent in the firm ($r = 0.48$), with age ($r = 0.43$), with being a partner (as differentiated from senior associates, who were also sought out for advice; $r = 0.30$)

and with coming from an elite lawschool ($r = 0.28$). Members sought out for advice tended to seek others for advice less (correlation between indegree and outdegree centralities is negative: $r = -0.28$), which confirms a status competition effect (one does not seek advice from people below). In short, processes connected to social status as well as to density of one's work relationships were key to the efficient distribution of knowledge.

CONCLUSION: LEARNING GOODS AND SOCIAL EXCHANGE

The problem of quality control, which was used to examine the distribution of authoritative knowledge and experience in a professional services firm, is a structural problem to which social exchange systems in PSFs provide a structural solution. Formal peer review being highly problematic, the focus was on yet another way in which this system remains productive: by allocating knowledge and helping members share experience – a crucial resource, too often considered to be exclusively individual 'human capital' – in spite of well-known professional status competition processes. The social exchange system provided a functional equivalent of peer review, an informal mechanism of quality control. In particular, the analysis of the pattern of advice network in the firm shows how the distribution of 'professional status' concentrated the authority to know in the hands of a few partners; it functioned as an informal quality control mechanism providing a form of allocation of knowledge and co-orientation. In such a knowledge-intensive organization, such a relational mechanism is even more important for collective action than it is in other types of organization. The pattern of advice relationships sustains quality through co-orientation by distribution of professional authority, while providing a social solution to the problem of capitalization of knowledge and experience.

Finally, this chapter studied the relationship between distributed knowledge and economic performance in order to show that it is worth studying the logic of social exchange of learning goods in order to understand productivity. In the professional, or 'collegial', organization under examination, the conditions under which the pattern of knowledge flows was most productive for firms stressing quality professional services included the existence of two processes: selection of exchange partners in the co-workers network (social niche seeking) and concentration of the authority to know in the advice network (through a form of professional status competition). Some members emerged as having the authority to know, although such status was fragile. This allocation of knowledge is a micropolitical process, but it was efficient too. This efficiency can be partly measured, I argued, in statistical evidence concerning the relationship between crude measurements of economic performance and position in social networks related to the allocation of knowledge.

This understanding of the process through which non-standardizable knowledge-intensive work is carried out provides insights into productivity. In effect, when combined with other results concerning economic performance, the existence of a consistent link between social networks (that of cooperation and advice) and economic performance opens up an avenue for proxy measurements of productivity in knowledge-intensive organizations, a thorny issue in contemporary economics (Baumol and Wolff, 1983; Gadrey, 1996). This approach to productivity, however, must recognize that knowledge and 'learning goods' in general are massively produced, allocated and circulated in society (and particularly in the organizational society) through politicized social exchanges that differ from market processes.

NOTES

1. This distinction is not simply cosmetic. The idea of distributed knowledge rests upon a different conception of actors' cognitive work. It is driven by what can be called 'appropriateness judgements' (Lazega, 1992a), which involve ingredients such as status and authority, two concepts entirely absent from cognitive psychologists' (and sometimes even cognitive sociologists'!) work. In my view, transforming individual knowledge into social and shared knowledge raises issues familiar to economists interested in the production of collective goods. This can only be dealt with by bringing in a different behavioural theory, one that takes into account the existence of competition between various kinds of legitimate authority.

2. In the law firm examined here, Goffman-like stories circulated about big mistakes. For example

   There is really a distinction between the people who were there from older generations, or because their father was the president of a big utility company, often very decent human beings but sometimes not very smart. One often used to make terrible mistakes; he was not a very good trial lawyer. I realized that at the time so I would frequently save his ass; I always pushed our clients to settle their case rather than let him screw their case in court. (A former partner)

3. See Burt (1992) and Flap (1999) and Flap et al. (1998) for the general idea that, in many ways, returns on human capital depend on members' relational capital.

4. From the individual partner's point of view, autonomy with regard to shaping one's own practice and with regard to hierarchy went together with a certain form of opacity of activities in the firm. In their cooperation with one another, members reduced this opacity. But they could still choose whether or not to go beyond a simple reduction of opacity and share background information (thus transfer or exchange knowledge and experience more systematically), or instead rely on the capacity of the partner in charge to divide the work among his co-workers.

5. This is possible by a relational mechanism that I have called elsewhere 'epistemic alignment' or 'co-orientation' (Lazega, 1992a), which is based on the interactive dimension of members' 'appropriateness judgements'. Quality control is thus more generally related to epistemic dimensions of collective action.

6. In their epistemic behaviour, individuals producing together legal help act as members of the firm *and* as members of a profession. Individuals must share similar categorizations in order to work together. Similar categories are created and maintained by people with power, who create categories and category orderings which are favourable to them.

7. PSFs recognize that protecting their knowledge is next to impossible, which is why members are encouraged to publish it and use it to be recognized as specialists, in a mix of academic and marketing approach.

8. Some interpreted this as a form of professional 'arrogance' or complacency. However, recall that this law of seniority also limited their pool of available advisers.

9. General density of the advice network is 0.17. Answers varied considerably in quantitative terms. At both extremes, we have a partner who said that he did not need nor ask anyone for advice, and another partner who declared seeking advice from 30 other colleagues. For extensive use of network diagrams and analyses to illustrate the social relationships described in this chapter, particularly the centralized nature of this advice network and the effect of status competition in it, see Lazega (1995). For a general introduction to network analytical tools, see Wasserman and Faust (1994).

10. Based on various statistical models (Lazega and Van Duijn, 1997; Lazega and Pattison, 1999) we know that the local organization of advice relations has positive parameters for transitivity and reciprocity, but the latter are weaker than for other types of tie, mainly because of status competition. 3-cycles (that is, generalized exchange with indirect reciprocity) were unlikely in the advice network. Parameters for 2-in-stars, 2-out-stars and transitive triads are positive (as well as the parameter for reciprocated ties) and the parameter for advice ties of length 2 is negative. The contribution of the advice out-star configuration is to suggest the tendency for an individual to seek advice from multiple, unrelated others, while the contribution of the advice in-star parameter is to suggest the likelihood that an individual may receive requests for advice from several unrelated individuals. It is interesting that the parameter for paths of advice ties of length 2 is negative, while the parameter for transitive triads is positive, and it is tempting to hypothesize that paths of advice ties created the potential for new advice ties. Certainly, the collection of important substructures of advice ties is consistent with a relation that exhibits tendencies both to clustering and hierarchy but, as noted above, with an *emphasis on informal hierarchical arrangements*.

11. For example, given the way a partner was compensated in the firm, focusing on the amount of fees actually collected in one year does not indicate exactly how productive this attorney was during that year. Work done in one year could be compensated the following year (or perhaps even later) and such overlaps made it difficult to disentangle an attorney's productivity in one year as opposed to his/her productivity in another year.

12. In addition, this type of temporary workgroup structure in which partners keep their autonomy in their negotiation of means and ends makes it difficult for a centre to identify and appropriate real or potential productivity gains. Therefore governance of these teams, when work is not defined as a standard process in the Taylorian way, also means that work is evaluated based on other standards, more local and subjective ones (in partners' minds).

13. Seniority is defined by the rank of partners in the letterhead, which is mainly based on age and years with the firm (with the exception of four partners who were hired away from other firms). Coding of seniority levels in *senior, medium seniority* and *junior* partners is based on cutoffs between Partners 14 and 15 (a difference of 8 years in age) and between Partners 27 and 28 (a difference of 9 years in age). These categories were explicitly used by the partners themselves.

14. Note that this is consistent with Frank's (1985) economic approach to labour markets, which asserts that incentives such as specific compensation systems take care of the negative effects of status differences. Thus, low performers and low status members tend to be overcompensated relative to the value they produce, whereas high performers and high status members tend to be undercompensated relative to the value they produce: they pay a price for being recognized as high status members. The firm's seniority system could therefore be considered to be a mitigation device for status competition among partners. A large majority of partners supported it because they believed that it prevented yearly conflicts among themselves, especially conflict about each member's value to the firm.

REFERENCES

Alter, Norbert (2000), *L'Innovation Ordinaire* (Paris: Presses Universitaires de France).
Baumol, William J. and E.N. Wolff (1983), 'Feedback from productivity growth to R&D', *Scandinavian Journal of Economics*, 85, 147–57.
Blau, Peter M. (1964), *Exchange and Power in Social Life* (New York: John Wiley).
Bosk, Charles (1979), *Forgive and Remember* (Chicago: The University of Chicago Press).
Burt, Ronald S. (1982), *Toward a structural Theory of Action* (New York: Academic Press).
Burt, Ronald S. (1992), *Structural Holes: The Social Structure of Competition* (Cambridge MA: Harvard University Press).
Dingwall, Robert (1976), 'Accomplishing Profession', *Sociological Review*, 24, 331–49.
Dingwall, Robert and Philip Lewis (eds) (1983), *The Sociology of the Professions* (London: Macmillan).
Favereau, Olivier (1994), 'Règle, organisation et apprentissage collectif', in André Orléans (ed.), *Analyse Economique des Conventions* (Paris: PUF), Collection: Economie, pp. 113–37.
Flap, Hendrik D. (1999), 'Creation and Returns of Social Capital: A New Research Program', *The Tocqueville Review*, 20, 1–22.
Flap, Hendrik D., Bert Bulder and Beate Völker (1998), 'Intra-organizational Networks and Performance: A Review', *Computational and Mathematical Organization Theory*, 4, 1–39.
Flood, John A. (1987), 'Anatomy of Lawyering: An Ethnography of a Corporate Law Firm', PhD Dissertation, Department of Sociology, Northwestern University.
Frank, Robert H. (1985), *Choosing the Right Pond: Human Behavior and the Quest for Status* (Oxford: Oxford University Press).
Gadrey, Jean (1994), 'La Modernisation des services professionnels: rationalisation industrielle ou rationalisation professionnelle?', *Revue française de sociologie*, 35, 163–95.
Gadrey, Jean (1996), *Services: La productivité en question* (Paris: Desclée de Brower).
Gadrey, Jean and J. De Bandt (eds) (1994), *Relations de service, marchés de services* (Paris: Editions CNRS).
Gallouj, Faïz (1992), 'Le Conseil juridique français: d'une logique professionnelle à une logique d'entreprise', in J. Gadrey, (ed.), *Manager le Conseil* (Paris: Mc-Graw Hill), 105–134.
Gallouj, Faïz (2002), 'Knowledge-Intensive Business Services: Processing Knowledge and Producing Innovation', in F. Gallouj, and J. Gadrey, (2002), *Performances and Innovation in Services: Economic and Socio-Economic Approaches* (Cheltenham: Edward Elgar).
Gilson, Ronald J. and Robert H. Mnookin (1985), 'Sharing among Human Capitalists: An Economic Inquiry into the Corporate Law Firm and How Partners Split Profits', *Stanford Law Review*, 37, 313–92.
Granovetter, Mark S. (1985), 'Economic Action and Social Structure: The Problem of Embeddedness', *American Sociological Review*, 91, 481–510.
Hatchuel, Armand (1994), 'Modèles de service et activité industrielle: la place de la prescription', in J. Gadrey and J. de Bandt (eds), *Relations de service, marchés de services* (Paris: Editions CNRS) 63–84.
Hatchuel, Armand (1995), 'Apprentissages collectifs et activité de conception', *Revue française de gestion*, July–August.

Lazega, E. (1992a), *The Micro-Politics of Knowledge: Communication and Indirect Control in Workgroups* (New York: Aldine-de Gruyter), 237–265.

Lazega, E. (1992b), 'Analyse de réseaux d'une organisation collégiale: les avocats d'affaires', *Revue Française de Sociologie*, 33, 559–89.

Lazega, E. (1995), 'Concurrence, coopération et flux de conseils dans un cabinet américain d'avocats d'affaires: Les échanges d'idées entre collègues', *Revue Suisse de Sociologie*, 21, 61–84.

Lazega, E. (1999a), 'Generalized Exchange and Economic Performance', in Roger Leenders and Shaul Gabbay (eds), *Corporate Social Capital and Liabilities* (Boston: Kluwer).

Lazega, E. (1999b), 'Le Phénomène collégial: Une théorie structurale de l'action collective entre pairs', *Revue Française de Sociologie*, 40, 639–70

Lazega, E. and Marijtje Van Duijn (1997), 'Position in Formal Structure, Personal Characteristics and Choices of Advisors in a Law Firm: A Logistic Regression Model for Dyadic Network Data', *Social Networks*, 19, 375–97.

Lazega, E. and Philippa E. Pattison (1999), 'Multiplexity, Generalized Exchange and Cooperation in Organizations: A Case Study', *Social Networks*, 21, 67–90.

Meyer, Marshall W. (1994), 'Measuring performance in economic organizations', in Neil Smelser and Richard Swedberg (eds), *Handbook of Economic Sociology*, (Princeton: Princeton University Press and Russell Sage Foundation), 556–578.

Nelson, Robert L. (1988), *Partners with Power: The Social Transformation of the Large Law Firm* (Berkeley: University of California Press).

Nohria, Nitin and Robert G. Eccles (eds) (1992), *Networks and Organizations* (Boston, MA: Harvard Business School Press).

Reynaud, Jean-Daniel (1989), *Les Règles du jeu : L'action collective et la régulation sociale* (Paris: Armand Colin).

Sciulli, David (1986), *Theory of Societal Constitutionalism* (Cambridge: Cambridge University Press).

Starbuck, William H. (1992), 'Learning by Knowledge-Intensive Firms', *Journal of Management Studies*, 29, 713–40

Wasserman, Stanley and Katherine Faust (1994), *Social Network Analysis: Methods and Applications* (Cambridge: Cambridge University Press).

White, Harrison (2002), *Markets from Networks* (Princeton: Princeton University Press).

Wittek, Rafael and Rudi Wielers (1998), 'Gossip in Organizations', *Computational and Mathematical Organization Theory*, 4, 189–204.

PART II

Innovation in Services and through Services

7. Services as leaders and the leader of the services

William J. Baumol[*]

[A]lthough international trade widens the market attainable by a successful innovator and thus raises the incentive to do research, it also raises the cost of research by making labor more productive in manufacturing, with effects that tend to offset each other. (Aghion and Howitt, 1998, p. 5)

1.   R&D AS SERVICE: *PRIMUS INTER PARES*

Not so long ago, particularly in economic theory, the services were regarded as a backwater of the economy. Agriculture was king, and manufacturing was next in the line of succession. In the famous zigzag graph of the *Tableau Économique,* services do not even appear, and as late as *Das Kapital* they continue to be assigned a distinctly minor position. In today's industrial world this has changed dramatically. In the USA, for example, services account for nearly three-quarters of total employment. Services, most of which were formerly difficult to transport, are increasingly exported. Indeed, one of them, entertainment, in the form of movies and television programmes is one of my country's leading exports, to the distress of chauvinists in the importing countries. At the same time, the USA increasingly imports a variety of technician services from remote places such as India. All signs point to the services' very substantial and growing significance for the economy.

But there is one service that, from the point of view of the state of the economy and its future prospects, stands ahead of all the others. That service is research and development, which has so critical a role for economic growth. One can well argue that R&D is primarily responsible for the incredible rise in living standards and productivity since the Industrial Revolution, and that its magnitude and its degree of success will influence future income levels and the competitive position of firms and economies more than any other activity. In short, R&D has become the current king of the services and perhaps even of the economy as a whole, at least in the industrial countries.

This chapter will focus on this activity, telling a feedback story, indicating how activity in this field affects the productivity performance of the economy and how, in turn, the economy's degree of success in productivity growth affects the magnitude of R&D activity. The result will be the skeleton of a model of the interactions of growth and R&D that is truly endogenous and, moreover, unlike most theoretical analyses in this arena, is not ahistorical. This contrasts with the deservedly noted models of endogenous innovation that have appeared in recent years. In those models, the endogeneity of innovation simply takes the form of the public-good properties of investment in human capital and in R&D, so that the R&D in a particular industry becomes a function of that in the entire economy. There is nothing wrong with this assertion, but it applies just as much to the economies of ancient Rome and medieval China as it does to ours. Moreover, the formulation is something of a black box; the assumed innovation process is endogenous, but it works in mysterious ways. The model toward which I will be working represents an attempt to make the endogenous determination of innovation somewhat more explicit, and to endow it with some features of the market mechanism of the free enterprise economies. After all, its unparalleled record of growth and innovation is surely one of the main features of the market that have recently led to moves in the direction of free enterprise systems in so many parts of the world. Ahistoric models that do not distinguish one type of economic system from another are, to say the least, handicapped in dealing with this issue.

2. PRODUCTIVITY AS FUNCTION OF R&D, INNOVATION AS INTERMEDIATE INPUT AND THE OULTON THEOREM

Our story, then, is constructed around the two sides of the feedback process: the effect of R&D on productivity growth and the effect of productivity growth on R&D. I begin with the first of these. There is clearly a relationship between the volume of R&D and the rate of growth of productivity in the economy. That is, we can assume $g_{t+1} = f(y_{rt}, \ldots)$, where g_{t+1} is the growth rate of productivity in the economy in period $t + 1$ and y_{rt} is the volume of R&D expenditure in the economy in the previous period and, presumably, the partial derivative of g with respect to y is positive. The function no doubt contains other variables such as past expenditures on education, as well as other variables cited in the literature.

So far, the story is trivial and well known. However, there are a number of crucial complications that are, in fact, the main focus of my discussion. The complications I will discuss relate to the second side of the story, the effect of productivity growth on R&D. They stem from the cost disease of the services that are resistant to productivity growth, services which I call 'stagnant' or 'asymptotically stagnant'. I will argue later that R&D is among the economy's asymptotically stagnant services, meaning that it has a tendency to fall ever further behind the rest of the economy in terms of productivity growth. Assuming, at least for the moment, that this is true, two consequences would appear to follow, though, as it turns out, only one of them is, in fact, correct. The first consequence is that the cost of R&D can be expected to rise cumulatively, relative to the economy's rate of inflation. We will see later how this is likely to influence the demand for R&D, that is, the amount that the economy is willing to spend on this activity. But this will be left for later consideration. The second apparent consequence follows the premise that productivity in the rest of the economy moves steadily ahead of that in R&D. Then, if R&D's output is not to fall very far behind the economy's growing output, labour and other inputs will persistently have to be transferred into R&D from the sectors of the economy where productivity growth is rapid. So far, this is mere tautology. If there is no increase in the share of the economy's inputs that goes to sectors with relatively slow productivity growth, by definition, the relative output of those sectors must fall constantly. The next step in this chain of inference is where the trouble lies. I, along with a number of other theorists, used to conclude that if there is indeed a fall in the input share of sectors with rapid productivity growth with a concomitant rise in employment in the slow-growing sectors, the result must be a downward drag on the productivity growth of the economy overall. Recent work, however, has shown that this is not necessarily so, and that the apparent exceptions are actually the rule, rather than the exception.

Here, there is an important new theorem by Nick Oulton of the Bank of England (Oulton, 1999). His theorem shows that, in the cost-disease model, *if the stagnant sector supplies only final products*, it is indeed true that a shift of the economy's inputs from the 'progressive sector' (the sector with rapid productivity growth) to the slow-growth 'stagnant sector' can be expected to reduce the average productivity growth of the economy. This result seems quite obvious intuitively, and it is generally, indeed trivially, correct. However, if the stagnant service in question turns out to be an intermediate product – an input to progressive services – then, counter-intuitively, transfer of other inputs from the progressive to the stagnant services will actually enhance the economy's overall productivity growth. That is what the Oulton theorem tells us.

The theorem is important in practice because a significant share, perhaps even the bulk, of the shift of the labour force into the stagnant services, is not a move into the production of final products but into the supply of intermediate goods. This is certainly true of applied R&D, on the continuing assumption that R&D is a stagnant service, at least asymptotically. More generally, the evidence indicates that most of the substantial rise in jobs in the USA since the Second World War has been provided by information-related services, whose outputs are used substantially, if not predominantly, by other industries, as inputs to their own activities. In sum, a substantial share of this shift of the labour force has been into intermediate goods, rather than final products. Specifically, as Oulton points out, much of the growth in input use by the stagnant sector does, indeed, occur in business services and other intermediate-output sectors of the economy.

It is here that Oulton's surprising and significant result applies. We have:

Proposition 1 (Oulton): A shift of primary inputs, such as labour or raw materials, from the progressive sector to the portion of the stagnant sector that produces intermediate outputs rather than final products tends to *increase* the economy's growth rate of productivity. Moreover, the larger the input shift, the larger the resulting productivity rise will be. This will be true so long as the stagnant sector has any positive growth in its productivity, however small.

The result is counter-intuitive, because it suggests that productivity growth can be raised by increasing the share of the economy's primary inputs used *in the slow-growth sectors*. The explanation of the result is, however, straight-forward. Suppose there is some growth of the productivity of a primary input turning out a stagnant sector's intermediate product that is used, in turn, in the progressive sector. This increases the growth rate in the net productivity *of the primary input* used both directly and indirectly by the progressive sector. It does so by reducing indirectly the primary input (say, labour) per unit of stagnant input used by the progressive sector, which serves as a supplement to the independent labour-productivity growth rate within the progressive sector. I illustrate the argument using a two-sector model, with relatively stagnant sector 1 providing intermediate input to progressive final-product sector 2. I assume perfect competition, for simplicity.

Let

y_i = the output of sector i

L_i = the primary input quantity used by sector i, where $L_1 + L_2 = L$ (constant)

p_i = the price of the sector's output

G_i = the growth rate of the productivity of the primary input used directly by sector i (with $0 < G_1 < G_2$, so that sector 1 is the relatively stagnant sector)

w = primary input price, and

$*$ denote the (natural logarithmic) growth rate of the pertinent variable.

Then we have for the production functions of the two sectors

$$y_1 = F_1(L_1, t) \qquad y_2 = F_2(y_1, L_2, t).$$

The growth rate of productivity in the economy is

$$(y_2/L)^* = y_2{}^* - L^* = y_2{}^* = (1/y_2)(\delta y_2/\delta t) + (y_1/y_2)(\delta y_2/\delta y_1)(1/y_1)(\delta y_1/\delta t)$$
$$= G_2 + (p_1 y_1/p_2 y_2)G_1 = G_2 + (wL_1/wL)G_1 = G_2 + (L_1/L)G_1.$$

This is Oulton's result. It shows that the economy's growth rate of primary-input productivity is a rising function of L_1/L, the share of primary input in the stagnant sector, provided that $G_1 > 0$. The last line of algebra follows from the perfect-competition assumption, which tells us that relative output price equals the marginal rate of transformation of the two outputs, $p_1/p_2 = y_2/\delta y_1$, and the zero profit condition, $p_1 y_1 = wL_1$ and $p_2 y_2 = wL_2 + p_1 y_1 = wL$.

The implication is that the growth of overall productivity contributed by R&D activity may be greater than might otherwise have been expected. The theorem adds substance to one side of our story, the influence of R&D expenditure on productivity growth in the economy. Next we must turn to the other side of our feedback relationship, the effect of overall productivity growth on the volume of R&D activity.

3. COST, DEMAND AND THE VOLUME OF R&D ACTIVITY

There probably is no definitive list of the main endogenous influences that affect the volume of innovative activity. Here, the discussion will focus on only two of these variables, the demand for products that use the results of R&D and other innovative activity, and the cost of such innovative effort.

Demand

Schmookler (1966) offers extensive evidence indicating that the amount of innovation is affected by the size of the market for related final products. That is, the flow of patented inventions in a particular industry appears to parallel closely the volume of sales of a product both over the business cycle and in terms of longer-run trends. It follows that both growing population and expanding GNP can speed up the pace of innovation. In terms of our arms race ratchet model of innovation, this and other evidence on the role of demand suggest an influence in addition to a technical breakthrough that can lead firms in an industry to exceed the current norm in R&D spending. It can move the industry to a new and higher norm – an enhanced level of expenditure on innovation that firms in the industry feel it is necessary to adopt in order to stay abreast of their rivals.

But while enhanced demand seems to make a clear contribution to the magnitude of R&D activity in an industry, the role of Keynesian aggregate demand in the economy is not so straightforward. Ester Fano, the distinguished

Italian economic historian, has provided a powerful example. She reports that in the USA during the Great Depression the employment of scientists and technicians *grew* markedly. She tells us, 'the evidence shows that industrial research underwent such a sustained boom in the 1930s that it could be expected to produce, in addition to cost-reducing devices, a large number of new products as well'. More specifically, she reports that,

> Between 1921 and 1938 industrial research personnel rose by 300%. In 1927 approximately 25% of its employees reportedly worked on a part-time basis; by 1938 this proportion had fallen to 3%. Laboratories rose from fewer than 300 in 1920 to over 1600 in 1931 and more than 2,200 in 1938; the personnel employed increased from about 6,000 in 1920 to over 30,000 in 1931 and over 40,000 in 1938. The annual expenditure, from about $25,000,000 in 1920 to over $120,000,000 in 1931, to about $175,000,000 in 1938. In 1937, industrial research on an organized basis in the United States ranked among the 45 manufacturing industries which provided the largest number of jobs. (1987, pp. 262–3)

Surely, there is no more dramatic case than that of the Great Depression to test (and reject) the proposition that weakness of aggregate demand invariably handicaps innovative activity.

A plausible explanation of Fano's observation, which I believe to be the key to the story, is cost. The Great Depression was a period in which the earnings of scientists, engineers and technicians were extremely low. Since R&D is a labour-intensive activity, the low remuneration meant a major reduction in cost. This brings us to the influence of cost on innovative activity, the central element of the model of this chapter.

Cost of Innovative Activity

Routinized innovation, the innovation carried out by business firms as a standard business activity, now accounts for some 70 per cent of R&D outlays in the USA. Such expenditure on R&D and other innovative activities is just another of the types of investment that the firm can use as an input of its production process, that is, as an instrument for the acquisition of revenues and profits. If the relative prices of such inputs change, we can expect substitution to take place, with some degree of replacement of the input whose relative cost has risen by another input whose price has fallen. This at once suggests that the derived demand for investment in innovation has a non-zero elasticity that, as Fano's evidence indicates, may well be substantial. In particular, sharp increases in the earnings of technical personnel can lead to a significant cutback in real investment in innovation.

This may appear to conflict with my conclusion elsewhere (Baumol, 2002) that, in a sector of the economy that is (oligopolistically) competitive, often innovation and counter-innovation become primary competitive weapons, along with prices and advertising. The firms then are driven into what amounts to an arms race in terms of the resources devoted to it. Innovation expenditure is sticky downward, because in an innovation arms race no firm dares to cut its R&D outlays unilaterally. With no firm willing to take the first step, no such reduction will take place.

However, there is a significant influence that modifies this conclusion. It is also part of my hypothesis that the R&D investment norms are calibrated in *nominal* rather than *real* terms, if not entirely, at least to a considerable degree. That is, when the costs of R&D rise because wages of technical personnel or other costs increase, the R&D norms will not rise immediately and by the fully corresponding amount. It is highly implausible, given what we know of business responses to changing cost and price levels, that expenditures of the firm will be adapted fully and without any lag. It is even conceivable that for some interval of time nominal expenditures will not be adjusted at all, so that the price elasticity of demand for innovation investment will be unity.

It will be argued next that in the innovation process the changes in R&D cost on which I will focus are neither fully exogenous nor exclusively random. On the contrary, the flow of innovation itself has a critical influence on these prices and costs. It follows from the effects of innovation on the rate of productivity growth in the economy as a whole, as well as the persistence of differences in productivity growth rates of different sectors of the economy.

4. THE COST-DISEASE MODEL AND INNOVATION: INTUITIVE SUMMARY

The issue of trends in the cost of R&D brings us back to the 'cost disease' of the technologically stagnant personal services, which can affect research in roughly the same way that it does education, legal activity, the performing arts and a number of other services. As already noted, I will argue that innovation is such an activity. The act of thinking is a crucial input for the research process, but there seems to be little reason to believe that we have become more proficient at this handicraft activity than Newton, Leibnitz or Huygens. The productivity of labour has probably risen at an annual rate of slightly less than 2 per cent compounded since roughly 1830, when the Industrial Revolution really took off, so that the real product of an hour of labour has been multiplied by a factor of perhaps 20 since that time. This means that the opportunity cost of an hour devoted to the technologically stagnant process of thinking must have risen by about 1900 per cent! If R&D is interpreted as just another input in the production process, such a rise in its relative price must have cut back its derived demand – inducing some substitution away from this input and toward other inputs whose real cost was reduced by technical change. The cost disease of the stagnant component of research, then, may conceivably be a major impediment to acceleration of innovation.

The way in which this works out is best shown with the aid of a model of the feedback relationship between the production and dissemination of information and the rate of growth of productivity in industry. Here, R&D is considered to be a sector of the economy that is engaged in the production of information. The magnitude of its information production clearly influences the rate of productivity growth. However, as we will see, that growth rate in turn will affect the output of information, thereby closing the feedback loop, with effects on the trajectory of innovation that may not be obvious without a formal model.

In brief, the analysis has three elements (three sequential steps): (i) Production of new information through R&D activity stimulates productivity growth *in industry*. (ii) As a result, the price (real cost) of *information production and dissemination* rises. This is because these activities are what my colleagues and I have called 'asymptotically stagnant' – characterized by productivity growth that is initially high, but with the passage of time, for reasons to be explained, tends to lag further and further behind that of industry. (iii) As information grows relatively more costly, other inputs tend to be substituted for information in the production process. For example, when R&D costs have risen, a firm that wants to increase its output may decide not to invest more in R&D designed to increase the productivity of its machines but, instead, to buy additional machines of the current type. Thus, rising cost of the innovation process can cut the derived demand for innovative activity. That, in turn, impedes productivity growth, thus reversing the first of the three steps of the intertemporal process in its next iteration.

5. THE COST-DISEASE MODEL EXTENDED: ASYMPTOTIC STAGNANCY

The least familiar of the components of our model is the second – the effect of rising productivity in the economy generally upon the cost of production and dissemination of knowledge. To show how productivity growth can raise costs in sectors such as R&D, some years ago my colleagues and I introduced the concept of asymptotic stagnancy (Baumol et al., 1989). In the underlying model, the economy is taken to be composed of three sectors: a progressive sector, 1, in which productivity grows exponentially; a stagnant sector, 2, in which productivity remains constant; and a sector 3 which uses as inputs, in fixed proportions, the products of the other two sectors. For simplicity, there is a single primary input, labour. With labour quantities L_j used by sector j, the outputs of sectors 1 and 2 are given by

$$y_1 = c\,L_1 e^{rt}\ y_2 = b\,L_2. \tag{7.1}$$

Sector 3, the *asymptotically stagnant* sector is, as noted, composed of activities that use in (more or less) fixed proportions two different types of input, one produced by progressive sector 1, and the other of which is either obtained from stagnant sector, 2 or is composed of pure labour (or some combination of the two).[1] Now, let y_{13} and y_{23} be the inputs of the other two sectors used in the production of y_3. With input-output proportions assumed absolutely fixed (for simplicity) we can then write

$$y_{13}/y_3 = k_1,\ y_{23}/y_3 = k_2, \tag{7.2}$$

where by choice of units we can set $k_2 = 1$. We then obtain for the average cost of sector 3

$$AC_3 = k_1 AC_1 + k_2 AC_2 = k_1 w/ce^{rt} + AC_2. \tag{7.3}$$

Measured in terms of labour units, that is, holding w constant, the first term of (7.3) must approach zero asymptotically. Consequently, the behavior of AC_3 over time will approach that of the stagnant sector, 2.

Thus, we have

Proposition 2:   The behaviour of the average cost of an asymptotically stagnant sector will approach, asymptotically, that of the stagnant sector from which the former obtains some of its inputs.

What is surprising about the phenomenon we are discussing is that the sectors of the economy suffering from the asymptotic stagnation problem in its most extreme form include, in reality, some of those providing the most 'high tech' activities – those in the vanguard of innovation and change, such as computing. That this is predicted by the theory should be clear from 7.3, which shows that the more rapid the rate of productivity growth of the sector 1 input, that is, the greater the value of r, the more rapidly will the intertemporal behaviour of AC_3 approach that of the non-progressive sector.

The intuitive reason also explains what underlies the attributes of asymptotically stagnant cost behaviour. The falling cost of the progressive sector input accounts for the initial fall in the real unit-cost of the asymptotically stagnant sector. But the very fall in the cost of that input reduces its *share* in the total costs of the asymptotically stagnant sector, leaving the behaviour of those costs to be determined largely by the course of the stagnant sector input. Hence, an initial period of decline in the cost of the asymptotically stagnant sector is followed by a future of rising relative cost.

Computer *usage* was just cited as an example of a sector 3 activity and the behaviour of its cost provides a truly striking example of our conclusion. The heterogeneity of the products involved makes it difficult to arrive at precise figures, but it has been estimated that the hardware cost of memory and of a given amount of computation may be decreasing at a compounded annual rate somewhere between 30 and 50 per cent. This, surely, is not what we expect of a stagnant sector. Yet, a second set of figures indicates the obverse side of this picture. It has been estimated that the pure labour cost of the computation process rose from some 5 per cent of a microprocessor system cost in 1973 to some 80 per cent of the total in 1978 (see Kubitz, 1980, p. 143). There is no reason to doubt that this trend has since continued. Thus, the budgets of operations such as computer centres come rapidly to be dominated by the stagnant input components, and one should not have been surprised when this activity soon exhibited symptoms of the cost behaviour of the stagnant sector.[2]

A similar phenomenon is to be observed in broadcasting. It has been suggested that the transition from live performance to television broadcasting may represent the single largest leap in productivity in the twentieth century. Using virtually the same number of person hours as a live performance, (broadcast-technician time versus ticket sellers, theater ushers, operators of means of public transportation, and so on), a live performance of a drama is fortunate to have an audience of 1500. In contrast, a television broadcast of the same performance may reach 20 million persons – more than a ten-thousand-fold increase in productivity. Yet, presumably because of the very rapid growth of productivity in the process of transmission, technical costs have been reported to constitute as little as 11 per cent of the cost of broadcasting.[3] This means that even though it is a hi-tech industry it, too, for all practical purposes, may be joining the stagnant sector. The data confirm that its overall costs are rising correspondingly.

So far, it has been assumed for simplicity that there is a fixed ratio between the input quantities sector 3 derives from the progressive and the stagnant sectors. But this premise was used only for expository convenience. It is easy to show that over a broad range of patterns of behaviour of input proportions the same sort of cost problems arise for the asymptotically stagnant sector.

6. R&D AS ASYMPTOTICALLY STAGNANT ACTIVITY

There is reason to presume that cost trajectory of R&D activity falls somewhere between those of a sector that is purely stagnant and one that is asymptotically stagnant. R&D may be taken to use, preponderantly, two types of input, which can be described as mental labour (that is, human time) and technological equipment such as computers, making it an activity approximating the characteristics of sector 3, though one with some intertemporal variation in input proportions. That the input proportions did vary is indicated by the fact that while R&D expenditures by private industry increased by 36 per cent between 1967 and 1980 in real terms, the number of FTE (full-time equivalent) scientists and engineers they employed increased by only 21 per cent. All of this indicates why R&D activity can be expected to behave very much like an asymptotically stagnant sector.

But this conclusion also suggests others. One of the immediate implications is that, depending upon the price (and income) elasticity of the (derived) demand for R&D, it is possible that its rising relative cost will reduce its use relative to other inputs, with the passage of time. Moreover, it can be shown that, with time, in our model (a) output of R&D may decline, and (b) total expenditure on R&D may rise, both absolutely and as a share of GDP.

7. FEEDBACK MODEL: PRODUCTIVITY GROWTH AND ENDOGENOUS INNOVATION[4]

So far we have assumed that in the progressive sector the productivity of labour grows at a constant percentage rate, g. However, that premise ignores a crucial relationship – that between R&D (information production) and the technical change in sector 1 that is the source of its productivity growth. Thus, instead of g being a constant, it must be a function of y_{31}, the quantity of information produced by R&D that is used as an input by sector 1.

To combine all of the resulting relationships and determine their effects we must modify our formal model further. In the notation the sector subscripts will no longer be needed. We let

g_t = the rate of growth of productivity *outside* R&D (information-producing) industries in period t
y_t = the output (level of activity) of R&D activity
p_t = the price of the product of R&D
h = a parameter of independent R&D activity.

I will assume that R&D comes from two sources and will refer, correspondingly, to price sensitive R&D, y_{pt}, (which is generated by routine business activity) and price-insensitive R&D, y_{it}, so that

$$y_t = y_{pt} + y_{it}. \tag{7.4}$$

Then one can formulate the following illustrative relationships:

$$g_{t+1} = s + by_t \text{ (R&D contributes to productivity growth)} \tag{7.5}$$

$(p_{t+1} - p_t)/p_t = vg_{t+1}$ (price of R&D output grows proportionately to g_t);
$$(7.6)$$

and for the case where price insensitive R&D is zero, so that $y_{pt} = y_t$,

$$(y_{t+1} - y_t)/y_t = -E(p_{t-1} - p_t)/p_t \text{ (the R\&D demand function)}, \quad (7.7)$$

where E is a bastard intertemporal demand elasticity which, for simplicity of illustration, is assumed to be constant.[5] For simplicity, I will also adopt as the price-insensitive R&D output function

$$y_{it+1} = hy_t. \quad (7.8)$$

This implies that R&D activity encourages and facilitates independent R&D activity, and that the relationship is proportionate. Later, I will briefly consider some alternative forms of the relationship (7.8).

Then, substituting (7.5) and (7.6) into (7.7), we have at once

$$(y_{t+1} - y_t)/y_t = -k(s + by_t), \text{ where } k = vE > 0, \text{ or} \quad (7.9)$$

$$y_{t+1} = (1-ks)y_t - kby_t^2 \quad (7.10)$$

that has the two equilibrium points, at which $y_e = y_t = y_{t+1}$,

$$y_e = 0 \text{ and } y_e = -s/b.$$

Next, dealing with the case in which there is price insensitive R&D as given by (7.8), I assume that its amount is set using some average or target share, a, of total R&D as a base, so that the demand function becomes, instead of (7.7)

$$(y_{pt+1} - ay_t)/ay_t = -E(p_{t-1} - p_t)/p_t$$

so that

$$y_{t+1} = y_{pt+1} + y_{it+1} = (1 - ks)y_t - kby_t^2 + hy_t, \quad (7.11)$$

which is now our feedback relationship, yielding a trajectory whose properties are studied next.

Setting $y_e = y_{t+1} = y_t$ we now obtain the two equilibrium values

$$y_e = 0 \text{ and } y_e = (h/kb - s/b).$$

To test for their stability we note that by (7.11)

$$dy_{t+1}/dy_t = 1 - ks + h - 2kby_t \qquad (7.12)$$

which equals

$$1 - ks + h \text{ where } y_t = y_e = 0 \qquad (7.13)$$

and

$$1 + ks - h \text{ where } y_t = y_e = h/kb - s/b. \qquad (7.14)$$

We adopt the assumption that $vEs \equiv ks < 1$. This seems plausible since, apparently, $v \cong 1$ in (7.7); E, the information elasticity of demand, is likely to be considerably smaller than 2 (indeed, our ratchet model for *nominal* expenditure implies E is near unity); and s, the productivity growth rate when information output is zero, is probably very small.

The parameter s is presumably positive, meaning that in the absence of all endogenous information flow output productivity will nevertheless continue to grow at what we may call *autonomous rate*, s. Then (7.13) tells us the equilibrium point $y_e = 0$ will be monotonic and stable if h is very small (slope of the graph of (7.10) will be positive but less than unity), and monotonic and unstable if h is sufficiently large. Similarly, by (7.14) equilibrium point $y_e = h/kb - s/b < 0$ will be negative and unstable if h is sufficiently small and so the path will tend toward the origin, moving monotonically toward zero R&D and productivity growth rate s. If h is somewhat larger this equilibrium point will take a positive value and become stable. With h sufficiently large, so that dy_{t+1}/dy_t becomes negative, the trajectory will grow oscillatory, finally lapsing into explosive oscillation with cycles of increasing amplitude. Ultimately, it may well lead to a limit cycle, to the left of the maximum of the parabola that is the graph of our feedback relationship (7.10) (see Figure 7.1 below). It is even possible that h will reach a value at which a chaotic regime results.

Intuitively, the cycles are generated by the sequence generated by an initial leap in R&D activity. This, thereafter, substantially increases the productivity growth of the economy, causing a sharp rise in the cost of R&D, which in turn slows down productivity growth, and so on and on.

8. GRAPHIC ANALYSIS OF THE FEEDBACK MODEL

It is perhaps possible to get a clearer picture of the behaviour of the model with the aid of the standard pseudo-phase diagram for a difference equation. Figure 7.1 depicts the case in which no price-insensitive R&D is generated, that is, in which $h = 0$. Then, the basic feedback equation (7.10) can be represented in

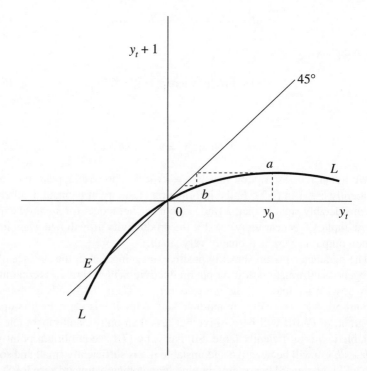

Figure 7.1   A feedback model with h = 0

(y_t, y_{t+1}) space as the parabolic locus *LL* in Figure 7.1. The equilibrium points are, of course, the points 0 and *E* where *LL* intersects the 45° line, that is, where $y_t = y_{t+1}$. Since E lies to the left of the vertical axis, this equilibrium represents a (nonsensical) negative amount of R&D activity, and is really irrelevant. What is much more to the point is what happens after beginning with an initial position $y_o > 0$, (as is patently true in reality). We see that with the relationships as shown in Figure 7.1, with the 45° line above *LL*, there will be a time path $y_o ab$ . . . that leads monotonically, that is, without any deviation, toward $y = 0$, period after period.

Figure 7.2 shows how matters change when the economy also provides some price-insensitive R&D whose quantity follows the expression $y_{it+1} = hy_{it}$, $h>0$, as assumed in our illustrative model. Since this last relation is obviously represented by a positively sloping straight line through the origin, its addition to (7.10), to obtain (7.11) simply results in a counter-clockwise rotation of the Figure 7.1 *LL*, around the origin, moving it to the position of *LL* in Figure 7.2. We see that this tends to move the position of equilibrium point *E* to the right. For *h* sufficiently large it transfers *E* to the right of the origin, as shown in

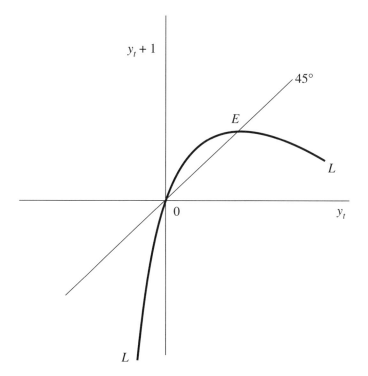

Figure 7.2   A feedback model with h > 0

Figure 7.2. The new equilibrium point, with its positive level and growth rate of R&D, can be stable since at that point *LL* can cut the 45° line from above.

The significant role of price-insensitive innovation activity makes it important to emphasize that in our model it can be taken to refer to more than the work of the lone dedicated inventor who works fanatically in attic or basement. It also can include, for example, the unexpected breakthrough originating in a bureaucratically-run corporate R&D facility that induces the firm to undertake a substantial increase in the resources it devotes to innovation. While this will obviously differ from industry to industry, and can only be expected to occur sporadically, if at all, in any particular firm, in the economy as a whole its expected value may conceivably be fairly predictable.

The discussion of the graphs also indicates how one can analyse cases in which price-insensitive R&D activity is described by possibly more complicated relationships than $y_{t+1} = hy_t$. For example, one may want to explore non-linear relationships with diminishing returns as enhanced current R&D diminishes the stock of possible innovations that it is easy to explore and develop in the future. Or, alternatively, one can consider the possibility of increasing returns as successful innovation makes further innovation activity less costly and more powerful. Since, in analysing such relationships, they are added to the part of (7.10) that describes routine business R&D activities, one need merely see what happens when the graph representing such a relationship is added to *LL* in Figure 7.1.

9. CONCLUDING COMMENT

The analysis here indicates that if there really is a feedback relationship between information activity and productivity growth in industry, this raises the possibility of a non self-terminating trajectory, with monotonically declining productivity growth and information production. In this model we see that this danger can be overcome, but only if h is sufficiently large. This can be interpreted as saying that it all depends on the occurrence of significant breakthroughs, either from truly independent innovators or from routine business R&D activities. If $h = 0$, so that only the steadier but non-breakthrough products of business generated R&D remain, the model as described here will move the economy inexorably and steadily toward zero R&D as its rising cost extinguishes the business demand for it. Of course, in the end this result can be attributed more to the oversimplifications of the model than to the full workings of the market mechanism's innovation process. But it does call attention to a side of the process that is clearly not irrelevant and that may yet prove of substantial importance.

However, the primary purpose of the model has been to show how one can analyse somewhat more explicitly the ways in which outlays on R&D and rate of growth of productivity can be determined endogenously and simultaneously. I have sought to bring more of the process outside the black box and to make the analysis less ahistorical in character. The model has also indicated that the approach is capable of providing concrete results. This is perhaps the main implication of its suggested possibility that the very success of the R&D sector may conceivably sow the seeds of a future price impediment to demand for its output.

NOTES

* I am extremely grateful to the Russell Sage Foundation and to the C.V. Starr Center for support of this work. I also am deeply indebted to my colleagues, Edward N. Wolff and Sue Anne Batey Blackman, for their contributions to the analysis.

1. It makes no difference to the analysis whether sector 3's second input is y_2 or is labour itself, since both costs behave similarly. That is, $AC_2 = w/b$, and the average cost of labour to industry is simply w. Indeed, we can aggregate the supply of y_2 and labour to industry 3 into a

single broader sector which offers them both and which is clearly stagnant. If sector 3 uses L_3 hours of labour and y_{23} units of y_2 per unit of y_3 produced, then writing $y_{23} = aL_{23}$ it is clear that a unit of output 3 requires $L_3 + L_{23}$ hours of labour altogether. Thus, we may invent a fictitious output $y_2{}^*$ satisfying $y_2{}^*/a = L_3 + L_{23}$ as the product of the aggregated stagnant sector which supplies both labour and y_2 to sector 3.

2. Of course, one must expect attempts to offset these rising costs to whatever extent is financially feasible. In computing, for example, effort has been devoted to the design of equipment and software that reduces the expenditure of time on the creation and modification of software. Some observers have even expressed hope that this can lead to a progressive reduction in the share of wages and salaries in the cost of computation. However, if hardware costs continue to fall at their current rate, it is hard to believe that the *proportion* of cost devoted to wages and salaries can decline for any protracted period.

3. 'Television Financial Data 1980, FCC Financial Figures', *Broadcasting*, 101, 10 August 1981, p. 51.

4. This model is based on earlier writings by Baumol and Wolff (1983).

5. This negatively sloping demand curve for R&D activity seems an obvious assumption. It is supported by some evidence (see, for example, Schmookler, 1966, and, as described above, in the work of Fano). The assumption is also employed elsewhere in the literature, for example in Grossman and Helpman (1991). It should also be noted that the equation is a generalization of the premise that oligopolistic competition forces firms to fix their *nominal* R&D expenditure, K. For then (omitting subscripts) $y = K/p$ so that $y'p = -p'y$, and hence $y'/y = -p'/p$.

REFERENCES

Aghion, Philippe and Peter Howitt (1998), *Endogenous Growth Theory* (Cambridge, MA: MIT Press).

Baumol, W.J., S.A.B. Blackman and E.N. Wolff (1989), *Productivity and American Leadership* (Cambridge, MA: MIT Press).

Baumol, W.J. and E.N. Wolff (1983), 'Feedback from Productivity Growth to R&D', *Scandinavian Journal of Economics*, 85, 147–57.

Fano, Ester (1987), 'Technical Progress as a Destabilizing Factor and as an Agent of Recovery in the United States Between the two World Wars', *History and Technology*, 3, 249–74.

Grossman, G.M. and E. Helpman (1991), *Innovation and Trade in the Global Economy* (Cambridge, MA: MIT Press).

Kubitz, William J. (1980), 'Computer Technology, A Forecast for the Future', in F. Wilfred Lancaster, ed., *Proceedings of the 1979 Clinic as Library Applications of Data Processing: The Role of the Library in an Electronic Society*, Urbana-Champaign: University of Illinois Graduate School of Library Science, 135–161.

Oulton, Nick, (1999) 'Must the Growth Rate Decline: Baumol's Unbalanced Growth Revisited', Bank of England, (Working Paper 107).

Schmookler, Jacob (1996), *Invention and Economic Growth* (Cambridge, MA: Harvard University Press).

8. Services innovation: towards a tertiarization of innovation studies

Ian Miles

INTRODUCTION

This chapter examines the current state of play in the study of services innovation. This field of study, after a long period of neglect, has attracted the attention of a large number of serious scholars in recent years. However, their work remains fragmented and disciplinary and national 'flavours' of study are still striking. The growing volume of work demonstrates clearly, first, that services do innovate, both technologically and organizationally. There are (naturally) substantial differences in innovation propensity and style across different classes of service firm and sector, and indicators of R&D and (technological) innovative effort do suggest that on average service firms are rather less active than comparable manufacturers. But to characterize all services as 'supplier-driven' is inappropriate: many are extremely proactive.

Much of the analysis from services researchers has stressed the specificities of services – though equally there is much attention to the heterogeneity of service firms and industries. Despite the variety of services, services innovation does appear to frequently display features that suggest that our understandings and indicators of innovation, being manufacturing-centred, are missing significant phenomena and processes. However, this does not mean that a sharp demarcation thus needs to be drawn between services and manufacturing innovation. The 'tertiarization' of innovation studies referred to in the title stems from the view that services innovation has great implications for studying innovation right across the economy. This has several elements: one is that many of the 'service' activities of manufacturers are themselves subject to innovation (and innovation that evades the standard categories of product and process innovation). Another element involves the rise of knowledge-intensive business services (KIBS), that play a wide range of important roles in facilitating innovation across the economy.

The rise of the service economy is leading to changes in innovation processes more generally. In other words, the implications of the tertiarization of the economy need to be examined by innovation research. Innovation studies accordingly need to systematically address innovation in service functions; and the role of services in innovation systems and their contributions to innovation in all sectors. A tertiarization of innovation studies is required, and there are many signs that this is now gaining momentum.

PHYSIOCRATS AND POST-INDUSTRIALISTS

Physiocrats have gone down in history as an early school of classical political economists who argued that all wealth comes from the land, from agriculture and related activity. Our basic requirements are satisfied by the products of extractive industries; in the words of the popular song, 'the farmer is the one who feeds us all' – and clothes us, warms us and so on. All of the factories that were sprouting up as the Industrial Revolution gathered pace were simply battening off the real sources of value creation. They might help consumers extract the value of agricultural and other extractive products in ways that were useful for them, but this was aiding consumption rather than producing new value.

According to conventional histories of economic thought, the physiocrats were overwhelmed by industrialisation. The wealth of products that poured forth from factories, the impressive new materials, machines and consumer goods that were generated from manufacturing sectors, meant that it was simply implausible to see the land – or natural resources, or farming – as the source of value. Instead, debate raged about whether value originated in labour, in scarcity, or in the utility of products. Physiocracy was (fittingly) buried.

But in reality, physiocracy simply discarded its farmer's garments, and put on the blue collar and work clothes of the new industrial workforce. Manufacturing industry became esteemed as the source of true wealth, as industrial capitalism established itself as a central economic and political force. Services, meanwhile, were discounted as contributing no value of their own. There were always dissenting voices, but the lack of attention received by services was remarkable. It is notable that while Marx himself in *Das Kapital* is far from unequivocal on the point, the great majority of Marxists regarded services as contributing no (surplus) value – though contributing to its redistribution. The apotheosis of this was the Soviet Union's use of the Net Material Product indicator in place of the decadent West's use of Gross National Product, which included the output of services.

But even in the West, while the statistical systems of national accounts were being established, services were regarded as constituting a tertiary or residual sector, superimposed upon the primary extractive and secondary constructive sectors. It was only in the 1960s and 1970s that serious attention began to be directed toward further explication of the roles of services – some authors wrote of quaternary and even quinary sectors, while Singlemann (1979) had a long-lasting impact with his identification of distributive, community, consumer and producer services sectors. These attempts at more precise analysis of services activities were limited by the very poor resolution of statistical systems where it came to services. While branches of manufacturing industry that were very small in terms of employment and output were charted in exquisite detail, many diverse sets of service activities were swept into large residual categories; likewise the delineation of different occupational groups in services sectors was nothing like as precise as that applying to manufacturing.

Gradually these problems began to be widely conceded, and, for example, a long process of restructuring industrial and occupational classification systems to cope with the new realities was embarked upon. As services overtook manufacturing in their share of output and employment in many Western countries it became increasingly difficult to regard them as unproductive. (Though the debate about this remained lively into the 1980s, at least.) Perhaps the change in opinion also reflected the erosion of the traditional manual working class, and the decline in its salience as a (more or less) cohesive political force.

Analysis of services innovation has lagged behind the recognition of services as economic forces and influences on the political landscape (if not necessarily the focus of new service classes, as some commentators suggested). Services might stabilize societies, by providing the knowledge for political and economic steering (as in Daniel Bell's (1973) post-industrial society), by providing sources of consumer satisfaction for more demanding citizens (the sociology of leisure), by absorbing labour displaced by the automation of manufacturing industry (Daniel Bell again). But very few researchers considered the possibility of innovation in services – even while there was much media interest in such new (or newly diffused to mass markets) services as civil aviation, television, distance learning and computer software. These were new services, perhaps, but they relied upon new manufactured goods.

These were also, perhaps, seen as exceptions – exceptionally modern. Most services were in contrast seen as unmodernized activities. The division of labour in most service activities had not progressed anything like as far as in manufacturing industry. There were few equivalents to the assembly line – even in activities like sorting items of mail for post office services, the staff were having to decipher addresses and make judgements as to how to file them, as opposed to carrying out the same sequence of activities on each item of equipment. The work organization often featured a craft-like system: sometimes involving work that was regarded as relatively low-skilled (catering, cleaning) sometimes involving far more professional work and expertise (law, medicine). Many services were run as very small and/or family firms (corner shops, many professional practices), others were large-scale public services (education, health – the precise boundaries of public services varied considerably across countries). Such factors were believed to be implicated in the telling fact that the productivity growth of services as displayed in economic statistics was low compared to that of other sectors.

One important line of analysis, that represents perhaps the first coherent account of services innovation, was that which stressed the 'industrialisation' of services (see Levitt, 1976). Organizational innovations that could establish regimented division of labour, and standardized service products, might be key to enhancing service productivity. And, who knows, just as organizational innovation and division of labour in factories paved the way for technological innovation in manufacturing, services might be able to embark upon more sustained patterns of innovation on the basis of such developments. Perhaps new technologies were in the offing that could benefit services in the same way that steam and successive power systems had been used to transform manufacturing industry.[1]

The scope for applying Information Technology (IT) to services had already been hinted at by Bell (1973), Kahn (1972) and others, but the microelectronics revolution that emerged in the 1970s inspired increasing numbers of observers to consider options for services innovation. In his earliest studies Gershuny (1978) was already speculating about the application of IT to services. But his starting point was actually one that saw services as largely non-innovative. Whereas Bell and other post-industrialists had attributed the growth of services as being largely a matter of growing consumer demand, Gershuny was struck by the displacement of services by 'self-services'. (Ironically, of course, the term derives from the organizational innovation employed in some cafeterias and restaurants that became the norm in many areas of retail as supermarkets and hypermarkets mushroomed. Self-service saved on staff labour; they were no longer employed to fetch desired items – instead the consumer loaded them onto a tray or into a shopping basket or trolley. This shift to unpaid labour was not on the whole rejected, since it usually meant a speedier, and sometimes a socially less awkward, process: one that might not always even be regarded as laborious.)

Gershuny noted that quite frequently, people were moving to forms of consumption that did not rely on traditional services. They were decorating their own homes ('do-it-yourself'), driving cars, watching TV, using new household appliances like washing machines and so on. Some of these are activities that, like retail self-service, involve substantial inputs of unpaid labour; others do not (watching TV requires considerably less effort than going to the cinema). Meanwhile, some consumer services – like cinemas and laundries – faced dwindling markets. Data on consumer expenditure confirmed these observations. For some major classes of consumption activity (for example, entertainment, transport), there was not the expected trend for demand for services to outstrip that for manufactures. In many such consumption classes, the opposite was the case. There was a shift of expenditure away from purchase of services to achieve consumer goals, and towards purchase of goods for the 'self-service' production of final services.

What explained this trend, and how could it be reconciled with the growth of services in Western economies? Gershuny hypothesized that lower levels of innovation in services than in manufacturing were responsible. If services were systematically less innovative – as was the common wisdom – then this would explain their lower productivity growth. This would have two implications. First, it would mean relative increases in the cost of services as compared to goods aimed at similar functions. It was possible to demonstrate such a trend in relative prices; one would anticipate another consequence as being lower levels of quality improvement in services. Second, with labour productivity gains being lower in services than in manufacturing, and with total levels of demand tending to increase with economic growth, the relative share of service employment could still grow, despite the shifts in consumer demand. An additional factor is that the aims to which expenditure is directed evolve alongside economic growth, and the 'more sophisticated requirements' that affluent consumers express more of are liable to be for classes of activity that have higher levels of service content – to put it crudely, away from sandwiches and houses, and towards self-realization and holidays.

Gershuny adopted the conventional wisdom that services have tended to be non-innovative, and was more interested in exploring the state of post-industrial society and the prospects for service employment than in explaining this situation. In keeping with this forward-looking orientation, however, he was open to the scope for new IT to transform services costs and quality. Gershuny and Miles (1983) attempted to generate a systematic analysis of such innovations, some already evident and some much more speculative. Not all services are as obviously ripe for IT-based transformation as, say, education and media. But it was clear that the informational components of many services could be the site of application of new IT. At least these elements of services – often very central ones – could be subject to efficiency and quality gains.

IT-based innovations in services in the 1980s were also being examined by another British researcher. Barras (1986) paid somewhat more attention to innovation processes and trajectories. While much attention to IT in services at this time concerned the impacts on employment – with many estimates of the job losses that new information systems might occasion – Barras developed a conceptual model of stages of IT use in services. His work is resonant of the information systems literature, in which several elaborate theories of stages of systems development within organizations have been propounded. Barras's model is effectively an industry-level version of these intra-organizational studies: based on brief case studies of several organizations in each sector studied. Its popularity benefited from being labelled the 'reverse product cycle' (RPC) model.

The specific features of services innovation alluded to in the RPC account relate to the *information-intensity* of services. In this account, the application of new IT in services is initially undertaken for reasons of back-office efficiency – to handle the extensive information processing requirements of large service organizations. IT effectively brings services into the industrial era – they begin to use an industrial technology appropriate to their information-intensive activities; and as they learn about its capabilities, they come to organize important parts of their work around it. Organizational learning means that service operatives and managers come to recognize the scope for applying the new technology in innovative ways. These move on from efficiency gains to service product quality improvements, and eventually to new service products. Service organizations become independent innovators in their own right, having been set on this course by initially adopting innovations from the manufacturing sector. The view of services innovation as typically being supplier-driven, was clearly expressed in Pavitt's (1984) highly influential effort to classify firms and sectors in terms of innovation dynamics.[2] But Barras implies that this view describes a phase of services innovation. Supplier-driven services could move on to become more innovative, and such was becoming a reality for many information-intensive services.

Barras identified three phases of services innovation – *Improved Efficiency*, *Improved Quality*, and *New Services* – as roughly characterizing the 1970s, 1980s and (prospectively) 1990s respectively. Examples of this evolution are: in *insurance* (from computerized policy records to online policy quotations, and on to complete online services); in *accountancy* (from computer audit to internal time recording, computerized management accounting, and on to fully automated audit and accounts); and in *local government* (from corporate financial systems, for instance for payroll, to departmental service delivery as in housing allocation, and on to online public information services). These examples were telling, and many researchers could recognize parallels in sectors and cases that they had studied – thus the RPC perspective provided a conceptual framework to understand these cases and more generally to relate services innovation to innovation in manufacturing (see Barras, 1986, 1990). The obvious importance of IT-related innovation in services, and more generally, and the growth of IT-related social research and policy analysis also meant that Barras's perspective became highly influential.

The RPC perspective suggests that many services may (still) be non-innovative, but history was rendering this an increasingly obsolete appraisal of services as a whole. The popularity of the RPC account helped establish a view of services as potentially, and often actually, innovative – especially through the application of new IT. Barras saw IT as effecting a technological revolution in services – but why should services be particularly receptive to the technology? The answer lay in their information-intensity, a feature also raised in Gershuny's work.

While anglophone analyses of services were beginning to examine services innovation (especially in the context of new IT), and stressed information-intensity,[3] francophone studies placed more emphasis on (what an anglophone might call) *interactivity* – the relation between service firms and their clients. Interactivity certainly does involve information flows (more so in information services like counselling, consultancy and education, less so in services performing physical and biological functions like transport, cleaning, surgery and hairdressing) – but it also depends on many other features of social relations.

Researchers at IFRESI in Lille, for example, produced many studies with the service relationship as the focal point of analysis.[4] Other researchers coined the term 'servuction' to describe the processes underpinning service relationships: the activities and procedures involved in producing and sustaining supplier–client relations, believed to be typically more important to service firms than those in other sectors. The terminology clearly contrasts with material production activities and procedures transforming objects – and thus studied by most innovation researchers. One study of innovation in services (Belleflamme et al., 1986) suggested that innovations could involve servuction, production, or a combination of both, and classified a sample of innovations from service companies accordingly. The study did not assume that these would necessarily be IT-centred innovations, and did accept that that services could be sources of innovation in their own right. Surprisingly, few services innovation studies have followed up this particular approach, though the role of service relationships continues to be emphasized by francophone researchers.[5] These studies also link to a large body of work on service quality, which we cannot review here, in which there are important Scandinavian and American contributions alongside the French literature. It is worth noting, however, that attention to quality has served as a trigger to services innovation in many cases. Such attention has led to the identification of problem areas where innovation is required; and by 'decomposing' the service process into component parts for quality control, has fostered an analysis of the engineering of these component elements.

A third body of work that grew markedly in the 1980s was particularly elaborated in The Netherlands (and often by geographers, who continue to be very active in this area). This examined producer services, in marked contrast to the Gershuny focus on consumer services. Here we have the interesting phenomenon of rapid growth in firms supplying business services to other parts of the economy – many analysts saw this as an 'externalization' or 'outsourcing' of service functions to enterprises and public sector organizations, a process that is in direct contrast to the internalization of consumer service functions within households described in the 'self-services' literature. Dutch researchers addressed several themes in their studies, including the nature of the service relationships between business services and their clients (for example, Tordoir, 1996 – while he published many earlier studies, this is an accessible reference) and the functions that were being implemented by these firms (Lambooy and Tordoir, 1985). Though few of these studies were centrally focused on innovation (Krolis, 1986, is an exception), they did draw attention to the emerging roles of producer services, and their contributions to technological (and organizational) innovation among their clients.

THE EVOLUTION OF SERVICES INNOVATION STUDIES

By the end of the 1980s a substantial number of studies of innovation in services had been amassed. Over the 1990s the case that services innovation is an important and neglected phenomenon gradually gained ground, meaning that a tertiarization of innovation studies was underway. It would require an exhaustive and exhausting literature review to survey all of the lines of study that emerged over the 1990s, with many specialized lines of study developing – innovation indicators, management of technology, software engineering studies, outsourcing decisions, health services technology assessment, and many more. Rather than set off on such an encyclopaedic course, this chapter will examine a number of significant shifts in services innovation research that are apparent from the vantage point of 2001.

Alternative Models of Services Innovation

Sometimes it has appeared that the reverse product cycle (RPC) model is *the* model of services innovation, especially in the English language literature (in Europe – it does not seem to have been taken up much in the USA – perhaps there is not enough high philosophy in it!). Conventional models of product and industry cycles have been subject to many critiques over the years (though since they have been useful benchmarks, if nothing else, they have remained highly influential). In contrast, the RPC model was subject to little critical analysis for a long time: the lack of rigour of most IT literature will have done little to stimulate critique of the RPC account. Some studies did address how different types of service industry were using IT, but the effort to examine the processes involved, and their relation to the RPC, was limited.[6]

Recently, a sustained critique of the RPC approach has been elaborated by Uchupalanan (1998, 2000). He studied IT innovations in banking services – a sector which Barras often wrote about (though it did not constitute one of his original case studies) – in Thailand.[7] Effectively all Thai banks' activities, over a period of more than a decade, in respect of five IT-based innovations, were studied.[8] Uchupalanana uncovered not a general RPC trajectory, but rather found that different firms displayed a diverse range of innovation strategies, and furthermore that these strategies and the resulting trajectories also varied across innovations within the same organization. The relationships between innovations were also important – banks were influenced by competitors' strategies, and strategies with respect to one innovation were influenced by other innovations that they had undertaken (or intended to undertake).

This is only one of a number of studies to propose alternatives to the RPC approach. But it is the most sustained detailed analysis yet undertaken, and it certainly demonstrates that the processes of innovation within service organizations rarely conformed to the RPC framework. This is despite the RPC model's apparently being a useful benchmark for describing IT-related innovation trajectories. While Uchupalanan's case studies might be affected by a particular national context (indeed, he drew attention to the regulatory factors shaping IT innovations in banking), his conceptual critique was also telling. His study makes a strong case for the interrelation of market competition and innovation dynamics, showing that the innovation processes in particular firms are shaped by their particular competitive and technological circumstances.

Other studies similarly suggest that we should anticipate a variety of services innovation processes, in which the RPC model may be only one of several empirically identifiable configurations. Maintaining a focus on technological innovation, den Hertog (2000) considers that innovations may focus on four very different elements of services production and delivery. These are (1) the service concept (where innovations are influenced by the characteristics of competing and existing services); (2) the client interface (influenced by the characteristics of current and potential clients); (3) the service delivery system (influenced by the capabilities, skills and attitudes of service workers); and; (4) the technological options confronted. Specific innovations, and the overall dynamics of innovation processes, are shaped by the interplay of organizational capabilities that mediate the links between these dimensions. Den Hertog illustrates different types of innovation, and identifies distinctive patterns such as supplier-led innovation, client-led innovation, innovation in services, innovation through services and paradigmatic innovations.

This analysis, focused on particular innovations and innovation processes, is clearly influenced by several lines of work. One is the study of the contribution of business services' to innovation ('innovation through services') to which we return later. Another is the range of efforts that have been made to describe the patterns and trajectories of innovation characteristic of different services firms and sectors. A particular stimulus was Soete and Miozzo's (1989) service-oriented reinterpretation of Pavitt's innovation taxonomy. They do recognize that some firms and sectors are largely *supplier dominated* – for example, public or collective services (education, health care, administration), and personal services (food and drink, repair businesses, hairdressers, and so on), together with the retail trade.[9] But they also argue that the range of innovative practices in services is as wide as that in manufacturing, and that there are several categories of innovative service businesses.

These include *production-intensive scale-intensive sectors* where IT can be applied to large-scale back-office administrative tasks (following Barras, this is, initially, at least, aimed at reducing costs). Some (*network sectors*) are dependent on physical networks (for example, transport and travel services, wholesale trade and distribution); others on elaborate information networks (for example, banks, insurance, broadcasting and telecommunication services). Such services are important in shaping IT networks, and play a major role in defining and specifying innovations, rather than being simply supplier-driven. Another category is *specialized technology suppliers and science-based sectors*, such as software and specialized business services, laboratory and design services.[10] The main source of technology is the innovative activity of the services themselves. The innovations tend to be 'user dominated'.

This study presented a plausible but largely impressionistic overview of different services sources of technological innovation. Evangelista and Savona (1998) went on to explore this topic from a wider empirical base – a specialized Italian survey of services. They used factor and cluster analysis to group the service sectors into four groups:[11]

1. *Technology users* This least innovative group is the effective equivalent of 'supplier-dominated' services, being reliant on technologies from external sources (particularly manufacturing). This category comprised the large majority of service firms sampled, and contributed more than half of the employment: this scale helps explain the persistence of the 'supplier-driven' view of services. The sectors within this group were: waste, land and sea transportation, security, cleaning, other business services, legal services, other financial services, travel, and retail.[12]

2. *Interactive services* This is where innovation is achieved through close interaction with clients, rather than through internal R&D or technology acquisition. Heavy reliance is placed upon developing software and/or acquiring know-how. This is another large group – it and the first group together account for three-quarters of services employment. Sectors here included advertising, banks, insurance, hotels and restaurants.

3. *Science and technology-based services*   These generate new technologi-
    cal knowledge, which they diffuse to other firms. Their innovation is typi-
    cally 'up-stream', with close interaction with public and private research
    institutions. The sectors involved included R&D, engineering, and
    computing and software. While a small group (less than 5 per cent of
    services employment), it contributed 30 per cent of services total innova-
    tion expenditures.
4. *Technical consultancy services*   These combine characteristics of the
    science and technology-based and interactive sectors – they undertake
    internal innovation efforts but also draw considerably on client knowl-
    edge. Their services involve generating and helping to implement techni-
    cal answers to the specific problems of their clients.

We can expect to see increasing analysis of different services innovation
patterns based on such survey studies in the near future, as services are more
regularly included in such innovation surveys. But how appropriate is it, to
apply innovation survey instruments, originally designed for studying manufacturing innovation, to services? If what is at stake is a matter of degree, these
may be perfectly adequate; if we confront qualitative differences, they may
fail to give us sufficient leverage to grasp the major features.

Evangelista and Savona compared their survey results for services with
those of an earlier survey of manufacturing firms, and concluded that there
were more similarities than differences between sectors, with respect to the
basic dimensions of innovation (that the survey allowed them to examine) (see
also Sirilli and Evangelista, 1998). While accepting that in-depth investigation
could reveal more areas of divergence between sectors, they interpret their
results as confirming the ability of innovation instruments, originally designed
to cover manufacturing innovations, to address service innovations. The study
certainly does demonstrate that the conventional instruments can cast light on
services innovation – not least demonstrating the importance of relationships
with clients for some groups of service. But, as is inevitable for any large-scale
survey, it is highly constrained; though many of these constraints reflect the
origins of the instruments in studies of manufacturing, rather than being
unavoidable features of survey tools. For example, 'delivery innovations' (or
indeed 'servuction' innovation at the service provider–client interface more
generally) is poorly captured in the conventional product innovation/process
innovation dichotomy. New IT is particularly well suited to application to the
information exchanges at the supplier–client interface, and has become a
major focus of innovative effort. Unfortunately, conventional instruments
either neglect this area, or force respondents to see it as either product or
process innovation.[13] Innovations like cash machines, online banking, e-
commerce, and even pizza delivery and self-service shops and cafes show how

pervasive this category is in services. But, significantly, it is far from unknown in manufacturing industry – for example in after-sales and marketing functions.

We shall consider some more results from survey studies shortly, but first let us introduce another line of argument that should warn us against thinking that they are providing anything like the whole picture. Several authors, perhaps most systematically Gallouj (2000), have criticized the (excessive?) focus that has been given to technological innovation, by most innovation researchers who have turned their attention to services innovation. The point is not that technological innovation is unimportant – it is simply that it is not the whole story, and that it cannot be understood completely without a broader analysis of innovation dynamics in services.

An example of the value of such a broader approach, showing avenues of evolution and influences upon innovation additional to those highlighted in the more technology-oriented accounts reviewed above, is Sundbo and Gallouj's (2000) account of several distinctive service innovation patterns (see also Gallouj and Weinstein, 1997; Gallouj and Gallouj, 2000; Gallouj, 2000; and Sundbo, 2000). While we can see strong echoes of the den Hertog, Soete and Miozzo, and Evangelista and Savona taxonomies here, there are quite distinctive elements introduced in the classification below – not least in that the 'supplier-driven' category begins to disappear:

- The *classic R&D pattern* – coming in traditional/Fordist, and neo-industrial variants – is mainly found in large firms producing standardized operational services dealing with material or information – large-scale data processing, building maintenance and so on.[14]
- The *service professional pattern*, displayed by services who use their specialized expertise and related technical capabilities for problem solving for clients, and whose professional staff often follow professional norms and adopt methods diffused through professional channels in what the authors consider a collective innovation process. This especially characterizes medium-sized professional services, such as consultancy and engineering, the fourth of Evangelista and Savona's groups.
- The *organized strategic innovation pattern* – this features in many large service firms not captured in the earlier groups. They do not have organized R&D departments, but the generation of innovative ideas is a widely diffused task, and their development (typically requiring more concentrated effort and time), is undertaken by ad hoc project teams. Thus orientation toward being innovative is integral to the firm's strategy.
- The *entrepreneurial pattern* describes small service firms created around a radical innovation, which they then produce and market as their main

activity – in other words, new technology based small firms, but ones specialized in services. These firms do not have an R&D department. After their formation, innovation processes are generally focused on the improvement of the initial radical innovation. Many IT services take this form, and we could add environmental services and those around biotechnology and other major technologies as other branches with many entrepreneurs of this sort. (Some of the smaller firms in the Evangelista and Savona group 3 are found here.)

*   The *artisanal pattern* is closest to the supplier-driven pattern, and accordingly applies especially to the many small firms involved in operational services (cleaning, security, hotels, restaurants and so on), who have little if any innovation strategy. When undertaken, innovations are generally either supplier-driven, or else small incremental ones that are rarely reproduced more widely.
*   Finally, a *network pattern* involves a common resource – a professional organization similar to the industrial research associations in manufacturing and construction – established by a group of service firms, with the objective of developing innovations for the member firms. This sort of model can apply, for example, in tourism (often with government support) and in some financial services.

Like Uchupalanan, Sundbo and Gallouj note that a given firm or industry may follow different patterns for different innovations. Similarly, some patterns are seen to be more common than others; and some of these are becoming dominant in specific contexts (the organized strategic innovation and, in specific areas, the service professional and artisanal patterns). And while some of the forms of innovation mentioned above might not be very common in manufacturing industries, it is by no means implausible that many are. There is little a priori reason to believe that the models outlined are restricted to services.

Increasing attention has been given to services in innovation surveys since the mid-1990s. The particular tools that are most commonly used were developed in the context of manufacturing. However, these data may illuminate at least some features of services innovation, and how they relate to – and shed light on – manufacturing sector innovation. Some aspects of the organization of innovation within services can be examined. Case study analysis has frequently reported on the specificities of this organization – at least, as compared to high-tech manufacturing. Services rarely contain the procedures and institutions typically described for (large and/or science-intensive) manufacturing firms – that is, R&D departments and specialized research managers and management tools (Sundbo, 1998).

Analysis of the CIS-2 (Community Innovation Survey) dataset for the UK in 1997 confirms these accounts. Overall, the UK services put proportionally more effort than do manufacturing firms into technology development activities other than R&D (Miles and Tomlinson, 2000). Some service sectors (close to the Italian science and technology-based services group) do have very high R&D intensities; they are in many respects similar to the high-tech manufacturing sectors in this and some other ways. Thus, R&D services, computer services, and business activities, which are among the top sectors for total technology spend, also have unusually high expenditures on training, machinery and (business activities excepted) on market introduction of innovations. Financial and other information-processing services (including business services) emerge as major consumers of 'other external technology' – presumably largely a matter of software and related systems, and associated with their high IT use. There is considerable diversity within services sectors, as usual, and it should be noted too that there is fairly high correlation between the various expenditures on technological innovation at firm level. Nevertheless, marked sectoral difference among these different categories are evident – see Table 8.1.

Again, the diversity of services is confirmed. And while the organization of services been contrasted with that of manufacturing, it appears that the more important contrast is between high-tech firms in any sector (especially of course those sectors usually regarded as intrinsically high-tech) and others. The high-tech firms are not the only ones with a strategic orientation to innovation, but their innovations are particularly bound up with the knowledge generated in R&D. (They are also, we will see, particularly linked in to organized innovation systems.) Other firms may be highly innovative, but the familiar patterns of R&D organization do not appear to be central sources of the new knowledge. As indicated in the Sundbo and Gallouj approach, sources of novelty may derive from professional organization, from skilled workforces generating new approaches, and so on. The survey data also points to the importance of market-related activities to some services: a dimension that warrants more detailed examination.

So, a tertiarization of innovation studies has been underway. The study of services innovation had grown and given rise to substantial contributions around the turn of the millennium. One of the main achievements of these contributions was the recognition and explication of the diversity of innovation styles, trajectories and processes across different services sectors and firms. This has been informed by comparative case studies and large-scale surveys. It widens and adds to the range of practices described in studies of manufacturing industry. Another achievement, which will be returned to shortly, is the beginnings of an effort to locate services innovation within wider innovation systems – this is apparent in most of the contributions reviewed above. This effectively means a tertiarization of our understanding of innovation systems –

Table 8.1 UK services technology activities, CIS-2 data, 1997 (percentage of turnover, ordered by final column)

Sector	R&D		Innovation-related acquisition of				Total technological innovation spend
	Intramural	Extramural	Machinery & equipment	Other external technology	Training	Market introdution of innovation	
73. Research & Development	24.60	3.24	6.87	0.81	0.65	7.08	46.86
67. Aux.Financial Intermediaries	0.10	0.03	4.01	14.85	0.10	0.03	25.48
71. Renting of Machinery	*0.01*	*0.00*	*1.32*	*1.39*	*0.01*	*0.00*	*16.95*
74. Business Activities	2.37	0.00	4.15	2.62	0.46	0.04	12.25
72. Computer & Rel. Activities	6.40	0.25	1.56	0.66	0.57	0.54	12.19
37. Recycling	0.63	0.08	1.96	0.01	0.01	0.00	5.83
51. Wholesale	0.08	0.00	0.12	0.91	0.63	0.81	4.94
65. Financial Intermediaries	0.14	0.00	0.12	1.38	0.36	0.00	4.46
66. Insurance & Pensions	0.00	0.00	0.16	2.51	0.04	0.02	3.85

Industry							
64. Post & Telecomms	0.32	0.00	0.84	1.38	0.21	0.50	3.71
60. Land Transport	0.00	0.00	1.29	0.13	0.06	0.02	3.00
61. Water Transport	0.00	0.00	0.04	0.15	0.05	0.00	2.99
55. Hotels & Restaurants	0.02	0.00	0.01	0.01	0.02	0.00	2.01
70. Real Estate	0.17	0.02	0.29	0.23	0.05	0.04	1.80
45. Construction	0.05	0.01	0.07	0.01	0.02	0.00	1.35
52. Retail	0.00	0.00	0.02	0.01	0.00	0.02	1.08
40. Electricity, Gas and Water	0.04	0.01	0.37	0.08	0.00	0.00	0.85
62. Air Transport	0.03	0.00	0.02	0.03	0.01	0.10	0.67
50. Sale of Motor Vehicles etc	0.04	0.00	0.00	0.25	0.01	0.00	0.57
41. Collection, Purification	0.07	0.05	0.10	0.05	0.01	0.00	0.47
Entire Population, inc. manufacturing	*0.73*	*0.05*	*1.25*	*0.58*	*0.15*	*0.30*	*6.75*

Source: Miles and Tomlinson (2000).

though to date the systems literature remains dominated by studies with a manufacturing interest. We have moved away from a view of *all* services as non-innovative, and away from the one-size-fits-all RPC account of services innovation, and are beginning to understand how services innovation relates to the (changing) location of services in the knowledge-driven economy.

Another study that documents the very different patterns of innovation in services, using a survey instrument but encompassing organizational as well as technological innovation, used results from an industrial innovation survey covering private services in Germany (Hipp et al., 2000). This study does pay attention, too, to the 'service relationship', giving a first survey-based inkling of the very wide range of such relationships displayed by different firms and sectors.

This survey asked about organizational innovation alongside product (service) and process innovation. Using open-ended responses about the innovations, Hipp was able to examine how far the firms' own designation of innovations in terms of these three groups corresponded with her own more standardized account. A first result was that these German service firms understood innovation in broadly similar terms to the standard (but arguably manufacturing-biased?) understanding of innovation researchers. There was over 90 per cent agreement between her identification of firms as innovators or non-innovators and their self-identification. Hipp disagreed more with the firms' classifications for what types of innovations were involved, especially problems reflected in differentiating between process and organizational innovations (compare also Preissl, 2000) – for example, many firms saw intra-company communications networks as organizational innovations, but some saw them as process or procedural changes.

Hipp's own definition of organizational innovation is a narrow one. Simple procedural changes, such as total quality management or ISO 9000, were excluded, (though often seen by respondents as organizational, Hipp classified them as process innovations). Organizational innovations are taken to be innovative changes in the structure of the organization, such as establishing a new profit centre, or amalgamating divisions within a company. Technologies usually play a marginal role here. In Hipp's reclassification:

- process innovation (80 per cent agreement with firms' own classifications) was most frequent,
- followed by service (product) innovation (77 per cent agreement),
- and with organizational innovation (63.5 per cent agreement) well behind.

The distinction between service and process innovation is thus reasonably robust (though we might still question as to where innovations at the client interface should be classified). That between process and organizational innovation is more problematic.[15] This survey examined how far the service function is tailored to specific client requirements by different firms: respondents were asked how much of their output was standardized, how much adapted to specific clients. These researchers demonstrated that while services subsectors vary in broad terms, firms also vary within sectors, between those whose output is much more standardized, and those who are more specialized (Hipp et al., 2000; see also Tether et al., 2000; and for a more general discussion of the survey in question, Licht et al., 1995). This is obviously only one aspect of the complex relationships that terms like 'interactivity' and 'servuction' point to, but even from this vantage point we can see a huge diversity across services firms. Standardized, customized and bespoke orientations were distinguished, as follows:

- *Wholly standardized* – 535 firms whose sales were entirely 'standardized services'. (This does not, of course, mean that there are no 'servuction' elements to their activities – interaction with clients may be very important in standardized services such as some transport activities.)
- *Largely standardized* – 900 firms, with more than two-thirds (but not all) of their sales being standardized services.
- *Bespoke* – the smallest group, 159 firms with more than a third of sales being 'bespoke services'.
- *Customized* – the 567 remaining firms, mainly with a relatively large proportion of their sales being of 'partially customized' services.

These orientations are distributed in significantly uneven ways across sectors and firm sizes. Table 8.2 displays exemplary results. To provide a very rough summary, the indication is that smaller and more technology-oriented services are more likely to tailor their services to specific client requirements.

The pattern of innovative activities was related to such variables as firm size, service branch and these service orientations. The results were complicated, but some of the interrelationships can be highlighted:

- *Wholly standardized* firms in Trade, Transport and Communications, Technical Service and Other Business Service sectors feature below average levels of innovation (especially service and process innovation).
- Other Trade, Transport and Communications firms, and the 'Other Services' firms, are close to the average in terms of innovation. In contrast, Transport and Communications firms providing Customized and Bespoke services are more likely to innovate (particularly process innovation).

Innovation in services and through services

Table 8.2   Firm size, sector and standardization–particularization

Size and sector	Standardized		Customised (%)	Bespoke (%)	N
	Wholly (%)	Largely (%)			
All Firms	24	42	26	7	*2150*
1–9 employees	27	↓↓34	↑30	↑10	*387*
10–49 employees	24	↓39	28	8	*747*
50–249 employees	22	↑↑48	↓24	7	*588*
250+ employees	27	↑46	24	↓↓5	*423*
Other Services	↑↑31	42	24	↓↓4	*482*
Trade	↑↑29	44	↓↓21	↓5	*602*
Transport & Comm.	26	44	27	↓2	*314*
Banking/Insurance	22	↑49	23	↓4	*189*
Other Business services	↓↓18	45	28	10	*204*
Other Financial services	↓↓14	↓↓22	↑↑46	↑↑18	*100*
Technical Services	↓↓11	↓35	28	↑↑27	*149*
Software	↓↓6	↓↓33	↑↑44	↑↑18	*110*

Notes
The arrow symbols indicate that the data differ significantly from what would be found if 'standardization–particularization' did not vary across size classes and sectors. Upwards arrows (↑) indicate the observed proportion was significantly greater than would be expected; downward arrows (↓) that it was significantly smaller than expected. Single arrows indicate significance levels between 5 and 10 per cent, double arrows between 0 and 5 per cent.

Source: Hipp et al. (2000).

- Banking and Insurance and Software firms (including the Wholly Standardized firms) are high innovators (particularly service and process innovation – and for Banking and Insurance firms organizational innovations).
- Technical Services are unusual – there is little variation of innovation propensity across the size distribution of firms.[16] Apart from the sector's Wholly standardized firms, small Technical Service firms are more likely to innovate than similarly sized firms in other sectors, while large Technical Service firms are more like large firms in other sectors.

Few innovation surveys have addressed features of the service relationship, and it would of course be most intriguing to examine the standardization–specialization dimension in the manufacturing sectors, too. Do manufacturing firms that are more specialized have more in common with similar services than with other manufacturing firms? What of organizational innovation across sectors? Unfortunately, so far the survey instruments remain heavily rooted in their origins as tools to examine manufacturing innovations. It would be desirable to have data on all sorts of innovations – in intra-organizational and interorganizational relations, in marketing and other service relationships, in techniques and routines as well as in technologies and organizational forms. So far, the tertiarization of innovation surveys has been more a matter of extension of the sample scope of the surveys than a re-evaluation of their content.

A TERTIARIZATION OF INNOVATION SYSTEMS?

We have so far mainly been talking about innovation *within* services firms. As with innovation studies more generally, the study of services innovation has been increasingly concerned with the role of innovation networks and systems.[17] Innovation systems researchers have from the start recognized that services organizations – such as higher education, training services, and specialized research and technology organizations – play an important role in such systems. One question is whether the role of such intermediaries is growing or changing, and whether there are new intermediaries to consider – for example, the specialized marketing industries, spin-off consultancies from many other sectors. Innovation systems may be tertiarized in the sense of such services organizations playing more significant parts as links and steering agents in networks. And another element to consider is the extent to which services innovation is facilitated or shaped by the degree of development of relevant innovation systems. Because of the importance of services intermediaries, services innovation is already recognized as a topic that can be analysed in terms of, and that can contribute to the understanding of, such systems.

Innovations are typically produced in competitive environments, in which individual actors attend to the strategies of others, and employ a range of informational and other sources to inform and organize their innovative efforts – as was apparent in Uchupalanan's study (1998, 2000), for example. The 'systems' view draws attention to the connections and information flows between these interacting agents. An associated point is that many innovations are essentially the result of collaborative activity in networks and systems, ranging from joint ventures, through collaborative R&D projects, to collective efforts to set standards, and to build and mobilize the socio-technical constituency required to bring an interdependent complex of innovations to market at the same time.

It is widely believed that services – other than innovative KIBS and very large companies – are poorly articulated into innovation systems. One source of evidence for this comes from an analysis of the first round of the UK (Technology) Foresight Programme in the mid-1990s (Miles, 1999). Foresight was meant to enhance the networking capacity of innovation systems, between engineers, marketers, finance, policymakers and academics; it thus serves as some indicator of how far firms are engaged in such networking. Some pieces of evidence were:

- In a sample of 'innovating firms' roughly half of manufacturing firms were involved in or aware of Foresight, but only a quarter of service firms.
- Of actors actually involved in Foresight exercises, those services that were traditionally not technology-intensive – though they are liable now to be making use of IT – seem to have more problems in accessing technological expertise. It would seem that their technology vision is relatively short term too.
- In contrast, highly IT-based services (for example, communications) are more like manufacturing in terms of their access to innovation systems. Those reliant on motor power and other traditional technologies (construction and transport) display a mixed pattern – transport appears to be relatively well-networked, while construction appears more disarticulated (corresponding to familiar complaints about the sector).[18]

Another source of evidence suggests that even knowledge-intensive business services (KIBS) may not universally be well-linked into innovation networks. New technology based KIBS are liable to differ from more traditional firms. Table 8.3 (based on a small UK sample of three types of KIBS) suggests that accountants' linkages to other sorts of organizations are worse than those of the more technologically-oriented KIBS.

There are exceptions to this generalization: they have already been implied by the Sundbo and Gallouj approach, whose professional service innovation model indicates that professional/trade associations can play a vital role in advancing innovation as well as legitimizing and providing quality control for the profession. These data suggest that this route could apply to accountants and architects, who find such associations important sources of knowledge. Accountants' low links to universities are notable – the low contact between the academic and practical professions in the UK is revealed in academics' comments that in this sector, university accountancy departments generate innovation, while practitioners are conservative – and shown in the lack of interest of some accountancy firms in employing graduates from accountancy departments. Larger firms, predictably, appear better networked than smaller ones.

Table 8.3   Where three types of KIBS gain knowledge

Types of organization and no. of employees	KIBS sector		
	Accountants	Architects	Engineers
University/higher education institutes			
1–14	20.0	42.3	78.7
15–49	11.5	42.1	81.3
50+	33.3	66.7	95.0
A similar company (to respondent's own)			
1–14	60.0	53.8	71.4
15–49	34.6	36.8	68.8
50+	33.3	50.0	65.0
Professional/trade associations			
1–14	80.0	96.2	50.0
15–49	100.0	100.0	87.5
50+	100.0	100.0	95.0
Government sponsored organizations or programmes			
1–14	30.0	34.6	50.0
15–49	38.5	52.6	68.8
50+	46.7	66.7	75.0
Consultants			
1–14	60.0	84.6	64.3
15–49	80.8	94.7	75.0
50+	66.7	100.0	80.0

Note: Percentages (in size classes) of UK firms (roughly 10+ per group) citing each type in response to the question: 'In addition to clients and suppliers, which of the following types of organization do you interact with to gain knowledge?

Source: Miles et al. (2000)

The really large service firms, in many sectors, do play important roles as orchestrators of innovation in their supply chains – driving innovations in manufacturing (for example, railway companies shape the activities of the suppliers of locomotives and carriages), in IT systems (banks shape ATM and network hardware and software), and agriculture and forestry (food and furniture retailers have influence on the environmental practices of farmers and wood suppliers, as well as on the food manufacturing sectors). Harvey (1999) and colleagues are generating highly interesting analyses of the interplay of supermarkets, biotechnology companies, food manufacturers and others, in the divergent courses of development of genetically modified tomato products.[19]

Thus it is possible to make some very crude and broad generalizations about services, as follows:

1. Some KIBS play extremely important roles as intermediaries in innovation systems – especially technology-based producer services. We take up this theme below.
2. Some services are well-networked into innovation systems, and may even play important roles as orchestrators of innovation across supply chains. For example, large supermarket chains may dictate the use of e-business systems among their suppliers. Just as motor car manufacturers have notoriously brought their component suppliers into an electronic supply chain, large retailers have prompted their suppliers of consumer goods (and their own intermediate requirements) into dealing with them through online networks. It is thus not uncommon for a supply chain that is ultimately providing such consumer goods as foodstuffs or household consumables, to be turned into a network governed by e-business systems. Other innovation pressures derive from large retailers, too: for example, towards environmentally-sensitive production or sourcing on the part of their suppliers.
3. But many services are not well-linked into the standard technology-oriented innovation systems. The main systemic impetus to innovation they receive may be a more or less weak one coming from professional associations and similar network structures, for whom research and innovation are liable to be minor functions.

The relatively poor articulation of many services into innovation systems may help to explain why in some studies, and in some countries, the rates of innovation among services recorded in CIS-type surveys are typically lower than for manufacturing. Even while we may dispute these indicators, features of many services (intangible products, knowledge- and client-intensive production and so on) may play a role. And even if, as we suspect, there is a general tendency for services to become more like other sectors in terms of innovative capacity and effort they may lack the systemic supports to realize this potential fully. The legacy of a manufacturing-oriented 'knowledge infrastructure' may still inhibit the innovativeness of (some) service firms and sectors.

For example, in innovation systems terms, the institutional and informal structures that support innovation may be poorly developed for services as compared to other sectors. The familiar systems for production of knowledge resources are relatively rarely oriented to services – consider the industrial research associations, university departments and research groups, and scholarly journals devoted to manufacturing and its sub-branches as compared to those aimed at services. Systems for protection (and diffusion) of innovation-related knowledge are similarly manufacturing-oriented (Miles et al., 2000; Andersen and Howells, 1998).

The analysis of the location of services in innovation systems requires much more development (compare Hauknes, 2000). If many services are, for whatever reason, disarticulated from key elements of the national innovation system, they will often lack access to knowledge, human resources, and networks to help guide their use and creation of new technologies and organizational practices. This structural problem may contribute to lower rates of innovation, which would otherwise be expected to converge more rapidly with those of other sectors as their technology-intensity increases. We may expect policy interventions and spontaneous network development in the future: and thus, probably, an accelerated rate of services innovation.

KIBS have recently come to be seen as playing important roles in innovation systems (Miles et al., 1995). It has been long established that these are among the most, if not the most, intensive adopters of new IT: they are leading *users* of innovation from other sectors, and as vanguard users of highly configurable technologies they have played important roles as pioneering agents in the shaping of IT software and systems. They can be *sources* of innovation, generating new knowledge, as in contract R&D services. Furthermore they can be *agents* of innovation, playing critical roles in the processes somewhat misleadingly known as technology transfer (and the parallel transfer of techniques and other organizational innovations). In other words, the issue is not just how far these services are themselves innovative, but also whether KIBS are critical for innovation in manufacturing and other industries! From being portrayed as at best lagging elements or peripheral outposts in innovation systems, such services are now recognized as being able to perform important roles as intermediaries and nodes in such systems.

Such services roles in facilitating innovation across the economy have been until recently neglected by innovation studies.[20] Contract R&D services form a particularly dramatic example, having received very little attention, even though they now account for a considerable share of industrial R&D. In one study of these services, Howells (1999) has suggested that their role is evolving both quantitatively and qualitatively. Not only are they becoming more numerous and active, as more users outsource R&D requirements, their role is also becoming more strategic, moving from very simple laboratory testing and basic technical functions to far more active involvement in technical specification and design; indeed, there are cases of such firms taking the lead in defining product innovations, and then mobilizing a constituency of manufacturers and retailers to realize the innovation.

But many other services – including the much-maligned management consultancies, alongside such obvious candidates as IT facilities management, training, engineering and design services – also play important roles in supporting the selection and implementation of new technologies by their clients. Den Hertog points out that often they are more than stores of knowledge about available technologies and their use, though the roles of locating, selecting and translating knowledge resources can be vital ones (den Hertog, 2000; den Hertog and Bilderbeek, 2000). As well as being 'carriers' of innovation, some KIBS facilitate innovation processes within companies by helping to confront organizational and cognitive barriers to change. And some KIBS go further in terms of *co-producing* innovations with their clients. This can range from helping achieve a fusion of industry- or firm-specific knowledge with more generic knowledge (about the characteristics of technological solutions to problems such as those confronted by the clients) to actually generating new knowledge in areas such as environmental impacts of industrial wastes, properties of materials, software for virtual reality and other advanced IT applications and so on. (Parallel social knowledge is, perhaps, generated by some market research and marketing companies.)

The e-commerce field is a particularly interesting example. Here, KIBS play roles ranging from aesthetic design to creation of leading-edge software, from helping to configure in-house databases with standard frameworks of representation of trade data to managing and maintaining fileservers and interactive interfaces that are pushing at the limits of available technology (Bolisani et al., 1999). Den Hertog, like Bolisani, examines KIBS in terms of models of knowledge processing, and this seems to be a very promising approach for such innovation studies. Beyond the intriguing development of classifications of different types of knowledge-related activity, he and his colleagues go on to suggest that we need to think of KIBS as more than just being interesting agents of innovation, or even as crucial bridges in innovation systems. The argument is that KIBS are gradually evolving into a second 'knowledge infrastructure', partially complementing and partially displacing the intermediary roles traditionally played by the more institutionalized, knowledge infrastructure of government labs, Research and Technology Organizations (RTOs) and Higher Education Institutions. They hypothesise that the traditional distinction between public and private knowledge-based (advisory) services will gradually erode. We can thus anticipate innovative boundary-straddling organizational forms to emerge, as the tertiarization of innovation systems proceeds.

CONCLUSIONS: TERTIARIZATION OF INNOVATION STUDIES

Research on services, and research on services innovation, has become a lively area, with fragmented lines of enquiry coming together and conventional wisdom challenged. The diversity of services, of their innovation processes, of their roles in innovation systems, is beginning to be acknowledged and explored. Services innovation research is increasingly articulated into the broader trends in innovation studies, and its challenges to some of the mainstream assumptions and instruments are being accepted – or at least debated. This reflects two aspects of the tertiarization of innovation studies. The first is the acceptance of the services as sites of innovation that need to be studied, whether with an orientation to their specificities or their commonalties with received wisdom. This reflects the growth of service sectors in the economy, and their changing involvement in innovation processes and systems (only partly a matter of the introduction of IT). The second is the growing recognition that services innovation has points of relevance for studies of innovation across the whole economy. This reflects the importance of service functions in all sectors – whether as activities performed in-house, or as services to be outsourced.

Much of the literature on services innovation has stressed its *distinctiveness*. As we have seen, case study work often stresses its divergence from received accounts of innovation patterns and dynamics, while innovation survey research, however, has demonstrated many points of similarity (though some points of difference) between innovation in services and in other sectors. One possibility is that surveys have elided the distinguishing features of services innovation, underestimating the extent to which it is shaped by points of difference – simply because the indicators employed do not really address such points as the extent of interactivity, the role of 'delivery' innovations, the regulatory context, the intangibility of many products, Intellectual Property Rights regimes and so on.

But to what extent are these specific features of service sectors? It is plausible that these are aspects of (or areas for) innovation across the economy, but ones that are generally neglected in innovation studies and surveys. After all, all sectors are acquiring similar characteristics, as they mutate away from their traditional forms – the adoption of new IT and of various new management styles is token of this. Managers in all sectors are repeating the litany that what they are really doing is providing customers with services. Innovation in manufacturing and in services does not necessarily have to be sharply demarcated.

But this may mean some refocusing of attention. The features of innovation that characterize service firms often characterize services functions in manufacturing industries. Conventional R&D departments have tended to emphasize very narrowly defined product and process innovation. There has been less attention (among managers as well as academics) to organization of innovation of 'service' functions – like distribution, management of transactions, marketing, design and so on – in manufacturing and extractive sectors. It is likely that innovation in such activities is an increasingly prominent feature of innovative efforts more generally – evidence for this is the growth of e-commerce and e-business. (Managers often think of innovation in such functions not in terms of 'R&D' but rather as 'project development', quality management, or 'business re-engineering' – just as in service firms' innovations.) We should move beyond the polarized assertions that there is either nothing new about services innovation, or that its study requires a complete rethink of the established wisdom, to consider the variety of innovation dynamics across and within all sectors – and, indeed, within different parts of firms.

This suggests that there is considerable scope for further elaboration of (empirically verifiable) taxonomies of (service) innovators, innovations and innovation processes. These should encompass not only IT-related innovations, but also other technological innovations and innovations in organizational innovations structures and practices. One topic to examine in this context is how the (changing) nature of service relationships affects innovation processes. As well as the general relevance to services, this becomes especially interesting in the context of KIBS interactions with clients in innovation-related service transaction. The issues of knowledge management and protection of IPR are also raised here. This is not just an issue that concerns individual firms: often when KIBS are involved in innovative activities, they do so as part of teams. It is common to find numerous service suppliers working together, in a complex division of labour, where there are large or technically challenging projects. Such 'distributed innovation processes', are (probably increasingly) common in many large and complex activities – such as the introduction of e-commerce systems, online financial services (like those described by Uchupalanan), the environmental and engineering dimensions of major projects (for example, in construction activities) and public health services. Knowledge has to be 'managed' across several organizations, and we can anticipate that problems will occur at the interface of intra-organizational knowledge management systems just as they have occurred when there have been efforts to 'automate' design, transactions and so on. The processes of interaction in groups of innovating agents, and the ways in which innovation in the tools used to mediate such interactions is developing and has influenced the interaction process, also make a fertile topic for study.

With the tertiarization of innovation studies, the need for such analyses should increasingly be recognized by, and their results reflected in, the mainstream innovation literature. Increased dialogue between specialists in services and mainstream innovation researchers will result in a richer analysis of innovation processes. Several elements of this tertiarization can be identified:

- The acceptance that services innovation should be considered an intrinsic and revealing part of innovation studies,
- *and* that these studies reveal that some elements of services innovation can be understood in conventional terms,
- *but* that they also point to neglected themes and topics.
- The adoption of instruments and tools from innovation studies into the services field,
- *but* also the modification of such methods to take into account issues highlighted in the study of services innovation.

These are beginning to be addressed systematically in innovation studies, though as always some institutionalized activities (like the production of statistics, or the design of innovation surveys) prove far more resistant to change than others. Taken together with other empirical developments (globalization, new technologies and business practices), and the emergence of new analytic approaches (the focus on knowledge, the use of research techniques ranging from ethnography through to web-based network analysis), we can expect the products of tertiarized innovation research to be highly interesting. Perhaps, as in other services, we will even see more attention to 'service relationships' from innovation studies themselves – to questions being asked that reflect the interests of users of the research, and to answers being presented in ways that these users can more readily understand! That would really be tertiarization!

NOTES

1. Over the 1980s, the European Community's FAST Programme (FAST = Forecasting and Assessment of Science and Technology), funded many research studies on services – with its orientation to technology issues meaning that many of these studies had an innovation studies element. Barras, Belleflamme, Gershuny, Howells and Tordoir, whose work is discussed below, all participated in FAST activities. A major theme of much European work on services has been the contribution of producer services to regional development, a theme heavily represented in later phases of the FAST programme: in addition to such conference and working papers as Lambooy and Tordoir (1985), see the books by Howells (1988), Howells and Green (1989) and Illeris (1989). Relevant initiatives in other countries include that of the National Academy of Engineering in the USA, whose activities included a major conference on innovation in services in the mid-1980s, which resulted in the volumes by Guile and Quinn (1988a, 1988b).
2. Pavitt (1984) provides the classic account. In a subsequent paper (1994) – probably influenced by Barras – Pavitt added a category of 'information intensive' firms which included finance, retailing, travel and publishing service sectors; and software appeared in the 'specialized supplier' group.

3. US researchers also featured such a focus: see, for example, Faulhaber et al. (1986).
4. A fairly recent study is Gadrey & de Bandt (1994). IFRESI (Institut Fédératif de Recherche sur les Économies at les Sociétés Industrielles, Centre National de la Recherche Scientifique, Universités de Lille).
5. Gallouj and Weinstein (1997) provide a useful review, comparing 'servuction' to a number of other formulations.
6. Miles (1999a) differentiates between physical, informational and human services, demonstrating their very different histories and circumstances of technology and IT in particular use. Some early analysis of IT use in services, which informed the development of this approach, can be found in Miles (2000)
7. The emergence of studies from developing countries is another important trend in services innovation studies.
8. The innovations were: Interbranch On-line services, Automated Teller Machines, Credit Card services, Remote Banking, and Electronic Funds Transfer at Point of Sales.
9. Note, however, that the rise of major retail service firms, in some cases to be large transnational chains, has meant that these can exercise sufficient market power to be significant sources of direction for their suppliers. Thus UK supermarket chains are able to set quality standards and identify new products for their suppliers. They have had a considerable impact, for example, in promoting various environmental practices, organic foods – and recently, in first promoting and then inhibiting the use of genetically modified organisms.
10. The 'R&D Consultancy, technical testing and analysis' branch of services accounts for around 10% of current UK R&D - cf. recent issues of *Business Monitor MO14* London, HMSO.
11. A limitation of the study is that the authors were constrained to work with aggregated data, and thus were unable to examine intra-sectoral variation, firm size issues and so on. Some other studies now in preparation, using similar data sets for other counties, will display rather different detailed results at the firm level. Postal and telecommunications services appeared to operate at the crossroads of the four main clusters, perhaps because of the huge diversity between the two main groups collapsed together here.
12. Note that a brief consideration of the list of sectors here reveals many that feature highly innovative firms – airports, supermarket chains and so on.
13. The Italian researchers also suggest that service managers have relatively few problems in distinguishing product and process innovations. Service researchers have often argued that product and process, and indeed consumption, are closely interwoven for many services, so more confusion might have been expected. See the Hibb et al., (2000) study.
14. Less standardised services such as large software and telecommunications companies could be added to this list.
15. Sirilli and Evangelista (1998) argued from their study of innovation in Italian services, that most firms could distinguish service from process innovation
16. Similar results appear to apply in the UK CIS-2 survey results, in as yet unpublished work by Tether and colleagues at The Centre for Research in Innovation and Competition at the University of Manchester (CRIC) who are analysing the CIS-2 data set for the EC. Indeed, IT services seem to display a negative relationship between propensity to innovate and size – a rare result indeed.
17. A recent collection that takes up this theme is Metcalfe and Miles (2000).
18. There is of course a mixture of manufacturing and other non-service firms in these groups.
19. A book on *The Tomato* by Harvey et al. is awaited with relish; it should be available in 2002.
20. An exception in the technology transfer literature is Bessant & Rush (2000).

BIBLIOGRAPHY

Andersen, B. and J. Howells (1998), 'Innovation Dynamics in Services: Intellectual Property Rights as Indicators and Shaping Systems in Innovation', CRIC

Discussion Paper no. 8, University of Manchester, available at http://les.man.ac.uk. cric/.

Barras, R. (1986), 'Towards a Theory of Innovation in Services', *Research Policy*, **15** (4), 161–73.

Barras, R. (1990), 'Interactive Innovation in Financial and Business Services: The Vanguard of the Service Revolution', *Research Policy*, **19**, 215–37.

Bell, D. (1973), *The Coming of Post-Industrial Society* (London: Heinemann).

Belleflamme, C., J. Houard and B. Michaux (1986), 'Innovation and Research and Development Process Analysis in Service Activities', Brussels, EC, FAST, Occasional papers no. 116.

Bessant, J. and H. Rush (2000), 'Innovation Agents and Technology Transfer', in M. Boden and I. Miles (eds), *Services, Innovation and the Knowledge Economy* (London: Continuum).

Bolisani, E., E. Scarso, I. Miles and M. Boden (1999), 'Electronic Commerce Implementation: A Knowledge-Based Analysis', *International Journal of Electronic Commerce*, Spring 1999, **3** (3), 53–69.

Bryson, J.R. and P.W. Daniels (eds) (1998), *Service Industries in the Global Economy* (2 vols) (Cheltenham: Elgar).

Coombs, R. and I. Miles (2000), 'Innovation, Measurement and Services: The New Problematique', in J.S. Metcalfe and I. Miles (eds), *Innovation Systems in the Service Economy* (Dordrecht: Kluwer), pp. 83–102.

Coppetiers, P., J.-C. Delaunay, J. Dyckman, J. Gadrey, F. Moulaert, and P. Tordoir, (1986), The Functions of Services and the Theoretical Approach to National and International Classifications, mimeo, Lille, Johns Hopkins University Centre.

De Bandt J. and Gadrey, J. (1994), *Relations de service, marchés de service* (Paris: CNRS éditions).

Den Hertog, P. (2000), 'Knowledge-Intensive Business Services as Co-Producers of Innovation', *International Journal of Innovation Management*, **4** (4), December, 491–528.

Den Hertog, P. and R. Bilderbeek (2000), 'The New Knowledge Infrastructure: The Role of Technology-Based Knowledge-Intensive Business Services in National Innovation Systems', in M. Boden, and I. Miles (eds), *Services, Innovation and the Knowledge Economy* (London: Continuum).

Evangelista, R. and M. Savona (1998), 'Patterns of Innovation in Services: The Results of the Italian Innovation Survey', paper presented to the 7th Annual RESER Conference, Berlin, 8–10 October; revised version forthcoming in *Research Policy*.

Faulhaber, G., E. Noam and R. Tasley (eds) (1986), *Services in Transition: The Impact of Information Technology on the Service Sector* (Cambridge, MA: Ballinger).

Fuchs, V. (1968), *The Service Economy* (New York: National Bureau of Economic Research).

Fuchs, V. (1969), *Production and Productivity in the Service Industries* (New York: National Bureau of Economic Research).

Gallouj, F. (2000), 'Beyond Technological Innovation: Trajectories and Varieties of Services Innovation', in M. Boden, and I. Miles (eds), *Services, Innovation and the Knowledge Economy* (London: Continuum).

Gallouj, C. and F. Gallouj (2000), 'Neo-Schumpeterian Perspectives on Innovation in Services', in M. Boden, and I. Miles (eds), *Services, Innovation and the Knowledge Economy* (London: Continuum).

Gallouj, F. and O. Weinstein (1997), 'Innovation in Services', *Research Policy*, **26**, 537–56.

Gershuny, J.I. (1978), *After Industrial Society? The Emerging Self-Service Economy* (London: Macmillan).

Gershuny, J.I. and I.D. Miles (1983), *The New Service Economy: The Transformation of Employment in Industrial Societies* (London: Pinter).

Greenfield, H.C. (1966), *Manpower and the Growth of Producer Services* (New York: Columbia University Press).

Guile B.R. and J.B. Quinn (eds) (1988a), *Managing Innovation: Cases from the Services Industries* (Washington, DC: National Academy Press).

Guile, B.R. and J.B. Quinn (eds) (1988b), *Technology in Services* (Washington, DC: National Academy Press).

Harvey, M. (1999), 'Genetic Modification as a Bio-Socio-Economic Process: One Case of Tomato Purée', CRIC Discussion Paper no. 31, University of Manchester, available at http://les.man.ac.uk. cric/.

Hauknes, J. (2000), 'Dynamic Innovation Systems: What is the Role of Services?', in M. Boden, and I. Miles (eds), *Services, Innovation and the Knowledge Economy* (London: Continuum).

Hipp, C., B. Tether and I. Miles (2000), 'The Incidence and Effects of Innovation in Services: Evidence from Germany', *International Journal of Innovation Management*, **4** (4), December, 417–54.

Howells, J. (1988), *Economic, Technological and Locational Trends in European Services* (Aldershot: Avebury).

Howells, J. (1999), 'Research and Technology Outsourcing', *Technology Analysis and Strategic Management*, **11**, 591–603.

Howells, J. and A. Green (1989), *Technological Innovation, Structural Change and Location in UK Services* (Aldershot: Avebury).

Illeris, S. (1989), *Services and Regions in Europe* (Aldershot: Gower).

Kåhn, H. and B. Bruce-Briggs, (1972), 'Things to Come New York', Macmillan.

Kleinknecht, A.H., J.O.N. Reijnen and J.J. Verweij (1990), *Innovatie in de Nederlandse industrie en dienstverlening: een enquête-onderzoek* (Beleidsstudies Technologie Economie nr 6) Amsterdam, SEO.

Krolis, H.P. (1986), 'Producer Services and Technological Change: The Internationalisation Issue', Brighton, SPRU MSc dissertation, published at Delft by TNO Research Centre for Urban and Regional Planning.

Krolis, Hinne Paul, Pieter. P. Tordoir and P.T. Tanja, (1990), *Informatietechnologie voor de Dienstensector: de waarde van samenwerking: Een oriëntatie op ontwikkelingen, vraagstukken en visies binnen de commerciële dienstverlening in Nederland*, Delft, INRO-TNO.

Lambooy, J. and P. Tordoir (1985), 'Professional Services and Regional Development', mimeo, presented at FAST Conference, Brussels.

Levitt, T. (1976), 'The Industrialization of Services', *Harvard Business Review*, 50, 63–74.

Licht, G., M. Kukuk, N.Janz, S. Kuhlmann, G. Münt, C. Hipp, M. Smid, and D. Hess, (1995), 'Results of the German Service-Sector Innovation Survey', ZEW, Mannheim, and FhG-ISI, Karlsruhe.

Metcalfe, J.S. and I. Miles (eds) (2000), *Innovation Systems in the Service Economy* (Dordrecht: Kluwer).

Miles, I. (2000) (revision of 1988 paper), 'Sectoral and Organisational Patterns of Use of Information Technology: UK Data on Services in the 1980s', online publication available at http://les.man.ac.uk/cric/Ian Miles/Papers/yap.htm.

Miles, I. (1999a), 'Services in National Innovation Systems: From Traditional

Services to Knowledge Intensive Business Services', in G. Schienstock and O. Kuusi (eds), *Transformation towards a Learning Economy: The Challenge to the Finnish Innovation System* (Helsinki: Sitra). 57–98 (Finnish National Fund for R&D)

Miles, I. (1999b), 'Services and Foresight', *Service Industries Journal*, **19** (2), 1–27.

Miles, I., B. Andersen, M. Boden and J. Howells (2000), 'Services Processes and Property', *International Journal of Technology Management* 20, 95–115.

Miles, I., N. Kastrinos (with K. Flanagan) and R. Bilderbeek, P. den Hertog (with W. Huitink and M. Bouman) (1995), *Knowledge-Intensive Business Services: Users, Carriers and Sources of Innovation*, Luxembourg, European Innovation Monitoring Service, Publication no. 15 (ed./d-00801 mas).

Miles I. and M. Tomlinson (2000), 'Intangible Assets and Service Sectors: The Challenges of Service Industries', in A. Jacquemin (ed.), *Intangible Assets and the Competitiveness of the European Economy* (Aldershot: Edward Elgar).

Murphy, M. and G. Vickery (1999), *Strategic Business Services* (Paris: OECD).

Pavitt, K. (1984), 'Sectoral Patterns of Technical Change: Towards a Taxonomy and a Theory', *Research Policy*, **13** (6), 343–73.

Pavitt, K. (1994), 'Key Characteristics of Large Innovation Firms', in M. Dodgson and R. Rothwell (eds), *The Handbook of Industrial Innovation* (Aldershot: Edward Elgar).

Preissl, B. (2000), 'Service Innovation: What Makes it Different? Empirical Evidence from Germany', in J.S. Metcalfe, and I. Miles (eds), *Innovation Systems in the Service Economy* (Dordrecht: Kluwer: Kluwer Academic, Publishers).

Rubalcabo-Berenejo, L. (1999), *Business Services in European Industry* (Luxembourg: European Commission).

Singelmann, J. (1979), *From Agriculture to Services* (Beverly Hills: Sage).

Sirilli, G. and R. Evangelista (1998), 'Technological Innovation in Services and Manufacturing: Results from Italian Surveys', paper presented to Conceptualising and Measuring Services Innovation Workshop, CRIC, University of Manchester, 20–21 May.

Soete, L. and M. Miozzo (1989), 'Trade and Development in Services: A Technological Perspective', Working Paper No. 89–031, Maastricht, MERIT.

Sundbo, J. (1998), *The Organisation of Innovation in Services* (Aldershot: Edward Elgar).

Sundbo, J. (2000), 'Organisation and Innovation Strategy in Services', in M. Boden, and I. Miles (eds), *Services, Innovation and the Knowledge Economy* (London: Continuum).

Sundbo, J. and F. Gallouj (2000), 'Innovation as a Loosely Coupled System in Services', in S. Metcalfe and I. Miles (eds), *Innovation Systems in the Service Economy* (Dordrecht: Kluwer).

Tether, B.S., C. Hipp, and I. Miles (2000), 'Standardisation and Particularisation in Services: Evidence from Germany', mimeo, CRIC, Discussion Paper No. 30 at http//les1.man.ac.uk/cric/Pots/dp30.pdf.

Tordoir, P.P. (1986), 'The Significance of Services and Classifications of Services', in P. Coppetiers, J.-C. Delaunay, J. Dyckman, J. Gadrey, F. Moulaert and P. Tordoir, The Functions of Services and the Theoretical Approach to National and International Classification, mimeo, Lille, Johns Hopkins University Centre.

Tordoir, P. P. (1996), *The Professional Knowledge Economy: The Management and Integration of Professional Services in Business Organizations* (Dordrecht: Kluwer Academic).

Uchupalanan, K. (1998), 'Dynamics of Competitive Strategy and IT based Product-Process Innovation in Financial Services: The Development of Electronic Banking Services in Thailand', DPhil thesis, University of Sussex, Falmer, Brighton.

Uchupalanan, K. (2000), 'Competition and IT-Based Innovation in Banking Services', *International Journal of Innovation Management*, **4** (4), December, 455–90.

Wyatt, S. (2000), 'ICT, Innovation in Central Government: Learning from the Past', *International Journal of Innovation Management*, **4** (4), December, 391–416.

9. Demand, innovation and growth in services: evidence from the Italian case

Maria Savona

INTRODUCTION[1]

The economics of services has never found a proper systematization within the body of economic analysis, despite service activities representing nowadays a major component of advanced economies, accounting for between 50 and 75 per cent of jobs in most OECD countries (OECD, 2000). The various theories of economic growth have rarely explicitly embodied service industries in their domain of analysis.

A stylized reading of the literature suggests that service growth has been approached either in terms of *service supply,* that is the specificity of service production processes and its *impact* on productivity growth, or in terms of *(final) demand* shifts, as the main *determinant* of services growth. These dimensions cut across the usual dichotomy between mainstream and non-conventional theories of economic growth. Moreover, among the non-marginalist streams of analysis which have tried to incorporate the role and impact of technological change on economic growth (Nelson and Winter, 1982), the absence of an explicit and consistent extension to the domain of service industries is even more severe. As argued in the next section, a polarization in terms of methodological approaches also occurs in the most recent contributions which look at the economic impact of technological change on services. A conceptual framework encompassing the link between the demand side, technological change and growth in services is still missing.[2]

This work draws therefore on two main considerations. On the one side, the role of demand is generally taken to be exogenous and outside the domain of analysis in science, technology and innovation studies. In particular, the neo-Schumpeterian approaches tend to focus on firms' strategies and, in general, on the supply side, thus privileging the firm level as the main domain of investigation. Very little effort has been devoted to detecting whether and to what extent the demand, both in terms of level and composition, interacts with supply factors and impacts on innovative behaviours, and to what extent such mechanisms have positive feedback on the dynamics of growth at an inter-sectoral level. Such a gap is even more severe as far as service industries are concerned.

On the other side, the literature on innovation in services, in the absence of robust empirical evidence, mainly focuses either on micro-level evidence based on sector-specific case studies, or on largely aggregate pictures, which overlook the heterogeneous nature and impact of technological change on growth across service sectors.[3]

In this chapter some empirical issues relating to the link between demand, innovation and growth in services are addressed, based on the case of Italy. In particular, the analysis focuses on the joint role of the sectoral composition of demand for services and their innovative profiles in determining the different patterns of growth in services, trying to answer the following question:

> Is it possible to disentangle the role of supply and demand factors, that is the technological opportunities and their impact on differing sectoral innovative profiles vis-à-vis the sectoral composition of demand, in explaining the different patterns of growth in services?

It is argued here that it is the sectoral composition of demand for services, besides the widening of technological opportunities provided by the Information and Communication Technologies (ICTs), that accounts for the diverse patterns of growth in services. In particular, a sectoral specialization towards intermediate producer demand (within the manufacturing sector and business services sector themselves) is a necessary condition for a positive growth performance. On the other side, the exploitation of the opportunities provided by the new ICT paradigm is not a sufficient condition for a positive growth performance when service industries are specialized in final and intermediate distributive demand (trade and finance sectors). Our conjecture is that the presence of an intermediate demand-pulling mechanism is the main determinant of the growth differentials among intermediate producer, intermediate distributive and consumer (final) services.

It is not planned here to get into the old debate on technology push vis-à-vis demand pull determinants of technical change (Schmookler, 1962; Mowery and Rosenberg, 1979). Such debate mainly revolves around the influence of changes in the *level* of market (final) demand on *inventive activity* as an incentive in the context of firms' strategies and performance. Rather, the focus is on the *sectoral composition* of demand, that is the difference between intermediate and final demand as a sector-specific characteristic, in explaining the growth patterns in services. Neither do we focus on the difference between *product (service)* and *process* innovation (Simonetti et al., 1995), which still presents a certain degree of ambiguity as far as services are concerned (Gallouj and Weisenstein, 1997). Rather, the different types of innovation are more likely (and less problematically) to be linked to the degree of *standardization vs. specialization* of service production and delivery (Sundbo, 1995). We come back to this issue in the next section.

The empirical analysis, based on the case of Italy, will be structured as follows.

1. The sectoral composition of demand for services by different destination markets (primary, manufacturing and market service macro sectors, public services and final consumers) will be considered as a picture of the sectoral division of labour between services and other branches of the Italian economy. The data used come from the Italian Sectoral Census of Manufacturing and Service Enterprises (ISTAT, 1995a; ISTAT, 1995b; ISTAT, 1995c).
2. The sectoral aggregated data provided by the Italian Innovation Survey of Service Enterprises (ISTAT, 1997) will be used to identify the main innovative profiles, thus highlighting the diverse impact of technological change on service sectors' innovative performance.
3. Finally, an overall picture of the dynamics of growth experienced by service industries in the years 1991–1996 is provided. The data come from the series of Census of Manufacturing and Services Enterprises (ISTAT, 1998).

The three sets of descriptive evidence will then be used in a regression framework, to explore the links between demand factors, innovation and growth. The role of demand and innovation is therefore endogenously taken into account to explain sectoral differences in the rate of growth across service industries.

The chapter is structured as follows. The next section briefly maps the selected contributions which have dealt with the growth of the service sector, on the basis of a demand-side or supply-side approach. A brief reassessment of the most recent attempts to analyse the role and impact of technical change on economic performance in services is also provided. In the following section the descriptive evidence on the sectoral composition of demand and innovative profiles is explored. The presence and the extent of the links between the composition of demand, innovation patterns and growth is empirically tested in the following section. The final section provides a summary of the main findings and concluding remarks.

THE DEBATE ON THE ECONOMICS OF SERVICES: A MAP OF ITS EVOLUTION

In this section a stylized reading of the evolution of the debate revolving around the growth of services is proposed, which reclassifies the different

Table 9.1 Services in economic thought by field of analysis

Evolution of the debate	Fields of Analysis	
	Supply side (specificity of services production processes: impact on productivity growth)	Demand side (specificity of service product: determinants of services growth)
The classical tradition	Smith (1776)	Smith (1776)
Three sectors split model (1930s to 1950s)	Clark (1940) Fourastié (1949)	Fisher (1935) Kuznets (1957)
Post-industrial vis-à-vis neo-industrial society approaches (1950s to 1980s)	Cohen and Zysman (1974) Baumol (1967) Fuchs (1968) Petit (1986)	Bell (1973) Browning and Singelmann (1978) Gershuny (1978)
Services and technology change: reverse product life cycle model and new approaches (1980s onwards)	Barras (1986, 1990) Miles (1994, 1995) Miozzo and Soete (1999) Evangelista (2000)	Barras (1986, 1990) Gallouj and Weisenstein (1997)

contributions according to the main focus of the analysis. Table 9.1 locates the various contributions.

Since the earliest debates over the growth of services, the main determinants and impact of service growth have been investigated in terms of either *service supply* or *service (final) demand*. The former approach was mainly devoted to the analysis of the specificity of service production processes and its implications for productivity growth. The latter focused on the specificity of service products and the implications for the shifts in (final) demand, considered as the main factor accounting for the growth of service activities. Across the different stages of the debate and behind the dichotomy between supply and demand approaches, a polarization of concerns about the growth of services also occurred. The opposition between the 'pessimistic neo-industrialism' view and the 'optimistic post-industrialism' one well represents the nature of the debate.[4]

Among the 'pessimistic' supply-side approaches, a theoretical line including Smith, Clark, Fourastié, Baumol and Cohen[5] can be identified. Smith was concerned with the process of erosion of capital accumulation due to the increasing presence of 'unproductive hands'. Clark and Fourastié provided a definition of service activities based on the different 'scale of production' and the lower average growth of productivity in services compared to primary and manufacturing activities. These contributions were implicitly based on a three-sector split of the aggregate economy: they *assumed* a lower rate of productivity growth in services rather than considering such evidence as the object of their analysis.

Within the 'neo-industrial society' approach, Cohen and Zysman were sceptical about the 'third stage of development' and formulated the hypothesis of a strong interrelation between the role played by some service industries and the mode of production in the manufacturing sector. The growth of high-wage services and the evolving capabilities in manufacturing activities are thus *complementary* rather than *substitutive*. The implication is a need for a re-conceptualization of the linkages examined.

Among the 'optimistic' demand-side approaches, Fisher (1935), Kuznets (1957), Bell (1973) and Gershuny (1978) represent a second broad line of theoretical analysis. The Smithian notion of division of labour is also located within the demand-side approaches to service growth. Although adopting different perspectives, each of these contributions was mainly concerned with the role of (final) demand linked to the growth of service activities. The stages of growth theory, the post-industrial society approach, and, within the latter, the hypothesis of a self-service economy, are devoted to exploring the nature and the shift in the patterns of final demand as a determining factor accounting for the growth of services. The final demand was expected to become more concentrated in the 'superior' services (eventually becoming perfect substitutes for 'inferior' manufactured goods). In the case of Gershuny, a progressive substitution of final demand for service products by capital goods accounts as well for a successive decline of the aggregate added value in services.

The interest has over time shifted from the *tertiary sector* to *service activities*, with the aim of creating a conceptual framework able to account for the high heterogeneity across service sectors. Further, the level of analysis has also shifted from the macro to the meso level. The new analytical purpose was more often aimed at classifying rather than interpreting the nature of services. The notion of an 'advanced tertiary sector' emerges, as compared to the traditional branches of service activities (Barbieri and Rosa, 1990). Yet little place in these accounts is left for the role of intermediate demand in explaining the growth of service industries within a context of structural change of the economy.

Only recently, with the widespread influence of the 'ICT revolution', has a new shift of interest led to extending to the service sector the analysis of the impact of technological change on the specificity of service innovation as well as on service growth and economic performance. Among others, the contributions by Barras (1986, 1990), Miles (1994, 1995), Soete and Miozzo (1989, 1999), Gallouj and Weisenstein (1997) and Evangelista (2000) tried to disentangle the complex issue of innovation in services, using different methodological approaches. In particular, Miles, Soete and Miozzo and Evangelista adopt a taxonomic approach, with the aim of highlighting the diverse nature of technological change across service sectors. On the other side, Gallouj and Weisenstein and Barras aim at providing new conceptual tools to tackle the complex issue of innovation in services, focusing on the peculiarities of services products and production processes with respect to manufacturing products.

In particular, Barras's contribution represents one of the first attempts to explicitly provide a theory of innovation in services. In his reverse product cycle model, Barras argues that ICTs represent the 'enabling technology' created elsewhere and adopted by the service sectors, which accounts for their innovation potential. Three evolving stages are identified: one of incremental process innovation, one of radical process innovation, and finally, one of product innovation. In this regard, Barras argues that the nature of the innovation introduced depends upon the different stages of adoption of the ICTs, and the existence of a learning curve behind the adoption process. He also assumes that a service innovation represents, in some respects, a more radical process innovation.

Nevertheless, the difference between product and process still presents a certain degree of ambiguity as far as services are concerned, due to the characteristics of intangibility and coterminality between production and consumption of services. This makes it even more difficult to disentangle the nature of innovation in services, as the distinction between product and process innovation in services becomes less clear-cut. Rather, the specific nature of innovation in services can be identified as the ability to *adapt a generic technology to specific applications*. Therefore, besides the rate of adoption of the enabling technology, what matters is the specific nature of user needs, which in turn affects the nature and type of innovations carried out in service firms. The specificity of service production and delivery processes can be considered in terms of different degrees of standardization vs. specialization, according to the nature of users' needs, in particular the distinction between intermediate and final users. Most of the final users are likely to be more price-sensitive (pulling firms towards service standardization and cost-reduction strategies) than intermediate users, which in general are more sensitive to technological and quality competitiveness factors (pulling firms towards strategies of customization and specialization of the service delivered). In this regard, recent attempts have been made to encompass the role of *users' learning* in affecting the nature of innovation in services (Tchervonnaia, 2001).

If the distinction between intermediate and final users is crucial for the individual firm's innovation strategies, at the sectoral aggregate level the composition of demand plays a role in determining the specific sectoral innovative pattern. It is not just a matter of providing an enabling technology but also of application of its functions through specific activities. The 'ICT revolution' itself does not theoretically justify the new demand for knowledge functions; nevertheless it has to be considered within the context of an increasing division of labour at the inter-sectoral level. There is also strong empirical evidence which shows that the emergence and growth of service sectors tightly linked to intermediate producer markets have been particularly striking (Karaomerlioglu and Carlsson, 1999).

From a macro-level perspective, few contributions have looked explicitly at service growth as a result of structural change. Among these, it is worth recalling the work of Momigliano and Siniscalco (1986) and Prosperetti (1986), as well as the contribution by Notarangelo (1999). These works all attempt to include the effect of demand in determining the structural dynamics of the economy which have led to the growth of service industries, trying to encompass in a unified framework demand and supply effects. Nevertheless, as argued above, each of these contributions focuses on the service sector as a whole, thus overlooking the differentiated impact of service sectors' growth on the whole economy.

The empirical exercise proposed here represents a first attempt to account for the joint role of demand and technological innovation in impacting on sectoral differences in service growth, as well as to explain the functioning of the intermediate demand-pull mechanism mentioned above. This latter may be represented by a change in the elasticity of intermediate demand for services, which amplifies the increase of final demand, due to price-decreasing effect, in response to the technological shock of the adoption of ICTs at various levels of the vertical chain. What is argued, and the empirical evidence aims at testing, is that such a structural change and the consequent increase of intermediate demand, is a necessary condition for the positive growth performance of some services. On the other side, a technological (supply-side) shock alone is not able to explain the sectoral differences in the growth rate. Again, such a mechanism is not argued as being substitutive to the price-led increase of the level of final demand; rather, it may be considered as complementary, when not dominant, in explaining the differentiated service sectors' growth.

DEMAND, INNOVATION AND GROWTH IN SERVICES: THE EMPIRICAL EVIDENCE

The Sectoral Composition of Demand in Services

The 1991 Italian Sectoral Census of Manufacturing and Service Enterprises provides the distribution of users of service activities, broken down by the main macro-sectors of the economy. In particular, for 21 service sectors (labelled as Input Sectors), the Census provides the number of firms purchasing services, broken down by the macro-sectors of the economy which they belong to (labelled as Destination Markets). These latter include:

- farming industries;
- manufacturing industries;
- market service industries, which are in turn disaggregated into the main service branches (transport and communication, financial services, trade, hotels and restaurants, business services);
- public services;
- final consumers.

The Input Sectors are classified on the basis of the Classification of Economic Activities, as last revised in 1991.

The Input Sector Market Share has been obtained as a ratio between the number of purchasing firms from each input sector and the number of total purchasing firms. The Demand Concentration by Destination Market has been obtained as a ratio between the number of purchasing firms in each destination market and the number of total purchasing firms.

The Demand Specialization Index (DSI) of each input sector in each destination market has therefore been obtained as a ratio between the number of purchasing firms from each input sector in each destination market, weighted by the Input Sector Market Share, and the Demand Concentration by Destination Market. This allows taking jointly into account both the weights in terms of market share of each input sector within the whole service sector and the magnitude of the demand represented by each destination market. As with any market specialization index, a DSI above 1 indicates a relative specialization of each input sector in each destination market. Symmetrically, a DSI below 1 indicates a relative de-specialization in the demand expressed by each destination market.

It is worth clarifying that the Demand Specialization Index is neither based on the value of the services purchased, nor weighted by the size of the single firm purchasing services. The data at our disposal do not provide information about the extent of demand expressed by each firm purchasing services: small and big firms purchasing services have actually the same weight. Nevertheless, the DSIs measure the degree of interdependence between services and their destination markets, and can therefore be considered as proxies of the sectoral division of labour between services and the other branches of the economy, including services themselves as destination markets.

Table 9.2 shows the sectoral composition of total demand by service industries. Across the 21 service sectors, each column shows the DSIs in each destination market. The simple percentages of purchasing firms out of the total number of purchasing firms by each input sector are also reported. The last columns in the table report respectively the Input Sector Market Shares and the total number of purchasing firms by input sectors. The last row shows the Demand Concentration by destination markets. The input sectors are ranked according to the DSIs in the manufacturing sector. As mentioned above, these latter are proxies of the degree of interdependence between services and the manufacturing sector as a whole. This allows an empirical-based classification of services among intermediate producer services (DSI above 1 in manufacturing), intermediate distributive services (DSI close to 1 in manufacturing) and final services (DSI below 1 in manufacturing).

The highest share of firms purchasing services belongs to the service sector itself (51.2 per cent), followed by the final demand (18.2 per cent) and the manufacturing sector (17.1 per cent). The concentration of demand from public services and the primary sector is instead rather marginal (respectively 7.1 per cent and 6.1 per cent). Only a few service industries are specialized in final demand, especially retail trade (DSI 2.25), hotels and restaurants (DSI 2.16) and trade and repair of motor vehicles (DSI 1.16). Most of the service industries are in fact specialized in manufacturing demand (14 out of 21 sectors) and in farming demand (13 out of 21 sectors). Despite market services themselves representing the largest share of services demand, the DSIs in

Innovation in services and through services

Table 9.2   Sectoral composition of total demand by service industries, 1990

Input service sectors	DSI Farming industries	%	DSI Manufacturing industries	%
Intermediate producer services				
Technical consultancy	1.85	11.30	2.22	37.97
Land transportation	1.06	6.49	1.74	29.72
Engineering	1.11	6.77	1.68	28.82
Shipping and sea transportation	0.47	2.85	1.66	28.46
R&D	1.91	11.65	1.59	27.18
Advertising	0.69	4.23	1.47	25.11
Travel and transport services	0.62	3.79	1.42	24.29
Waste disposal	1.19	7.25	1.34	22.87
Cleaning	0.29	1.77	1.27	21.78
Computing and software	0.81	4.95	1.24	21.28
Legal, accounting	1.14	6.92	1.17	20.03
Other business services	1.37	8.38	1.16	19.93
Intermediate distributive services				
Wholesale trade (excel. motorv.)	1.12	6.82	1.07	18.26
Trade and repair of motorvehicles	1.37	8.33	1.00	17.19
Other financial services	1.66	10.11	0.93	16.00
Post and tele-communication	0.17	1.05	0.91	15.61
Security	1.07	6.55	0.91	15.58
Banking	1.77	10.77	0.88	15.04
Insurance	1.53	9.35	0.83	14.29
Final services				
Hotel and restaurants	0.42	2.57	0.58	9.91
Retail trade	0.64	3.92	0.48	8.29
Demand concentration by destination market (%)	1.00	6.10	1.00	17.11

Destination markets: DSI – Demand Specialization (Number of firms purchasing services on total

Notes
*The Demand Specialization Index has been obtained as a ratio between the number of purchasing firms of each destination market from each input sector, weighted by the Input Sector Market Share (Total Purchasing Firms by Input Sector out of the Total Purchasing Firms) and the Demand Concentration by Destination market (Total Purchasing Firms by Destination Market out of the Total Purchasing Firms).
An index above 1 indicates a relative specialization of each input sector in each destination market.
The index below 1 indicates a relative de-specialization of each input sector in each destination market.

Source: Italian Census of Manufacturing and Service Enterprises (ISTAT, 1995a, 1995b, 1995c).

Index* ranked by manufacturing users purchasing firms by input sector (%))

DSI Service industries	%	DSI Public services	%	DSI Final consumers	%	Input sector market share (%)	Total purchasing firm by input sector
0.67	34.49	1.63	11.59	0.26	4.64	0.16	345
1.01	52.02	0.82	5.81	0.33	5.97	4.43	9 664
0.75	38.51	2.33	16.60	0.51	9.30	1.92	4 181
1.07	55.28	0.80	5.69	0.42	7.72	0.11	246
0.68	34.95	3.14	22.33	0.21	3.88	0.14	309
1.18	60.65	1.22	8.66	0.07	1.35	0.95	2 079
1.09	56.16	0.77	5.45	0.57	10.31	3.08	6 734
0.71	36.46	3.21	22.87	0.58	10.65	0.50	1 089
0.95	49.17	2.85	20.28	0.39	7.00	2.64	5 768
1.26	64.87	0.92	6.57	0.13	2.32	5.97	13 038
1.15	59.44	0.50	3.59	0.55	10.02	9.68	21 123
1.05	54.01	1.14	8.11	0.53	9.58	1.53	3 331
1.14	58.76	1.05	7.45	0.48	8.72	22.47	49 053
0.92	47.12	0.88	6.28	1.16	21.07	14.04	30 657
1.00	51.33	0.69	4.93	0.97	17.64	3.16	6 901
1.23	63.50	1.84	13.08	0.37	6.75	0.22	474
1.11	57.24	1.53	10.86	0.54	9.77	0.92	2 016
1.07	55.09	0.83	5.92	0.73	13.18	3.44	7 502
1.06	54.67	0.67	4.76	0.93	16.93	0.26	567
0.84	43.15	0.72	5.14	2.16	39.23	9.28	20 254
0.76	39.05	1.10	7.85	2.25	40.90	15.11	32 993
1.00	51.49	1.00	7.11	1.00	18.18	100.00	218 324

Table 9.3 Structural composition of service demand by service industries, 1990

			Destination markets: DSI – Demand Specialization (Number of firms purchasing services on total			
Input service sectors	DSI total service industries	%	DSI Transport communication	%	DSI Financial services	%
Computing and software	1.26	64.87	1.25	7.78	1.86	8.25
Post and tele-communication	1.23	63.50	2.07	12.87	3.46	15.40
Advertising	1.18	60.65	0.82	5.10	2.08	9.24
Legal, accounting	1.15	59.44	1.20	7.44	1.72	7.65
Wholesale trade (excl. motorv.)	1.14	58.76	0.47	2.89	0.49	2.18
Security	1.11	57.24	0.87	5.41	3.08	13.69
Travel and transport services	1.09	56.16	2.81	17.45	0.57	2.52
Shipping and sea transportation	1.07	55.28	3.99	24.80	0.27	1.22
Banking	1.07	55.09	1.51	9.38	1.88	8.38
Insurance	1.06	54.67	1.42	8.82	3.49	15.52
Other business services	1.05	54.01	0.78	4.86	1.10	4.89
Land transportation	1.01	52.02	3.29	20.43	0.37	1.62
Other financial services	1.00	51.33	1.22	7.58	2.74	12.19
Cleaning	0.95	49.17	0.58	3.57	2.27	10.09
Trade and repair of motorvehicles	0.92	47.12	1.50	9.31	0.66	2.92
Hotel and restaurants	0.84	43.15	0.59	3.69	0.95	4.24
Retail trade	0.76	39.05	0.31	1.94	0.55	2.46
Engineering	0.75	38.51	0.49	3.04	0.89	3.95
Waste disposal	0.71	36.46	0.53	3.31	0.62	2.75
R&D	0.68	34.95	0.47	2.91	0.58	2.59
Technical consultancy	0.67	34.49	0.28	1.74	0.72	3.19
Demand concentration by destination market (%)	1.00	51.49	1.00	6.21	1.00	4.45

Notes
*The Demand Specialization Index has been obtained as a ratio between the number of purchasing firms of each destination market from each input sector, weighted by the Input Sector Market Share (Total Purchasing Firms by Input Sector out of the Total Purchasing Firms) and the Demand Concentration by Destination market (Total Purchasing Firms by Destination Market out of the Total Purchasing Firms).
An index above 1 indicates a relative specialization of each input sector in each destination market.
The index below 1 indicates a relative de-specialization of each input sector in each destination market.

Source: Italian Census of Manufacturing and Service Enterprises (ISTAT, 1995a, 1995b, 1995c).

Index* ranked by total service users
purchasing firms by input sector (%))

DSI Trade	%	DSI Hotels and restaurants	%	DSI Business services	%	Input sector market share (%)	Total purchasing firm by input sector
0.95	21.17	1.11	9.18	1.81	18.48	5.97	13 038
0.66	14.77	0.67	5.49	1.47	14.98	0.22	474
0.99	22.13	0.93	7.70	1.62	16.50	0.95	2 079
0.83	18.57	1.17	9.65	1.58	16.13	9.68	21 123
1.72	38.42	1.04	8.54	0.66	6.74	22.47	49 053
0.78	17.36	1.22	10.07	1.05	10.71	0.92	2 016
0.81	18.12	0.48	3.98	1.38	14.09	3.08	6 734
0.45	10.16	0.69	5.69	1.31	13.41	0.11	246
0.65	14.49	1.10	9.04	1.35	13.80	3.44	7 502
0.56	12.52	0.98	8.11	0.95	9.70	0.26	567
0.98	22.01	0.59	4.89	1.70	17.35	1.53	3 331
0.88	19.60	0.30	2.46	0.77	7.91	4.43	9 664
0.71	15.98	1.01	8.29	0.71	7.29	3.16	6 901
0.50	11.23	0.91	7.49	1.64	16.78	2.64	5 768
0.98	21.92	0.49	4.00	0.88	8.97	14.04	30 657
0.38	8.49	2.19	18.05	0.85	8.67	9.28	20 254
0.90	20.17	0.95	7.80	0.65	6.68	15.11	32 993
0.41	9.14	0.63	5.17	1.69	17.22	1.92	4 181
0.48	10.65	0.91	7.53	1.20	12.21	0.50	1 089
0.46	10.36	0.35	2.91	1.58	16.18	0.14	309
0.58	13.04	0.21	1.74	1.45	14.78	0.16	345
1.00	22.38	1.00	8.24	1.00	10.22	100.00	218 324

services for each input sector are not very high. According to the DSI values, the sectors with the highest degree of specialization are waste and disposal (3.21 in public services), R&D (3.14 in public services), engineering (2.33 in public services), cleaning (2.85 in public services) and technical consultancy (2.22 in manufacturing).

Table 9.3 shows the demand specialization in the different branches of market service industries. The input sectors have been ranked here according to the DSI in total services. The largest share of demand of service industries comes from the trade compartment (22.4 per cent), followed by the business services (10.2 per cent). The highest specialization is found in financial services, the destination market with the highest DSIs. It is worth noting that most of the service industries with a high DSI in manufacturing (technical consultancy, R&D, engineering, computing and software) also have a high DSI in business services, showing a high similarity of the demand expressed by the manufacturing and the business service sectors.

The evidence shown in this section allows for a picture of the sectoral division of labour between service industries and the whole economy, by different branches of activities. In particular, the Census data allow identifying the sectoral composition of demand on the basis of the number of firms purchasing services from each input sector considered. On the basis of the DSI in manufacturing industries, it is also possible to give an empirical dimension to the traditional classification of service industries as between intermediate producer, intermediate distributive and final services (see Table 9.2). The sectoral DSIs, considered as a proxy of sectoral composition of demand, will be used as an explanatory variable, jointly with the sectoral innovative profiles, to explain the different patterns of growth at the sectoral level.

The Characteristics of Innovation in Services

The previous section has clarified the boundaries and nature of the demand-side factors to be considered within the scope of our analysis. The sectoral composition of demand for services is used as a proxy of the sectoral division of labour between services and all the branches of the economy.

As far as the supply-side factors are concerned, the specificity of technological regimes and innovative profiles across sectors are explored on the basis of the sectoral aggregate data provided by the Italian innovation survey of service enterprises. The survey, carried out by the Italian National Institute of Statistics (ISTAT) in 1997 and covering the period 1993–95, provides a rich set of innovation indicators. It represents one of the first large-scale statistical attempts to collect systematic information on innovation activities in the service sector, on the basis of the guidelines indicated in the Revised Version of the OECD 'Oslo Manual' (OECD–EUROSTAT, 1997). The survey has been carried out on a sample of more than 6000 service firms, drawn from a universe of 19 300 market service enterprises with more than 20 employees. The data cover 21 sectors classified according to the Classification of Economic Activities as last revised in 1991 and it is therefore possible to match them with the evidence provided by the Census and shown in the section above.

A factor analysis on different sets of quantitative and qualitative variables[6] has been performed, with the aim of highlighting the different dimensions of innovative performance and identifying the main innovative profiles. The results of the analysis are reported in Tables 9.4 and 9.5.

Three sets of variables have been considered in the analysis:

1. type of interactions used as sources of information for innovation;
2. type of strategies pursued when innovating;
3. type of innovation expenditure (R&D, design, know-how, training, marketing, ICTs and investments).

In turn, three main kinds of interactions have been identified on the basis of the number of firms which consider very important and crucial different information sources included in the survey questionnaire:

i.   firms which establish 'upstream' kinds of interactions, with public research institutes, universities and conferences as external sources, and rely on their own R&D internal departments (upstream interactions);
ii. firms which tend to establish informal types of interactions with clients and users, with such interactions integrated with the information provided by the internal production departments (downstream, informal interactions);
iii. firms which tend to rely on downstream sources of information more formally and continuously, that is through their internal marketing departments and external consultant enterprises (downstream, formal market-oriented interactions).

Three kinds of strategies can be identified, on the basis of the number of firms which consider very important and crucial different objectives of the innovation introduced:

i.   market-oriented strategies, among the firms which aim at entering new markets or increasing their market share;
ii. diversification strategies, aiming at modifying or extending the service range offered;
iii. cost-reducing strategies, aiming at improving production flexibility and reducing production and delivery costs.

Table 9.4   Goodness-of-fit of the factor analysis

Principal components	Initial eigenvalues	% of variance explained	% of cumulative variance explained
1	4.90	37.40	37.40
2	2.50	19.60	56.90
3	1.50	11.50	68.40

Note: Extraction Method: Principal Component Analysis.

Table 9.4 confirms that the factor analysis has been quite effective in interpreting the different profiles on the basis of the variables considered, explaining almost 70 per cent of the total variance through three principal components, shown in Table 9.5.

The first component captures the sectors that mostly rely on upstream interactions, that is universities and public research institutes as well as their own R&D departments. As far as the innovation strategies are concerned, the results show a high negative correlation with rationalization and cost-reduction strategies. Further, the innovative effort is concentrated in R&D, design, know-how and training. This suggests that this profile presents most of the characteristics of the *science-based* sectors (Pavitt, 1984). When related to growth performance, this profile is expected to have a positive impact, typically science and innovation (supply) pushed.

The second component has been labelled as *market-oriented*. It identifies a different innovative mode, with a prevalent tendency to pursue market strategies when innovating, and mostly relying on downstream interactions (formal and informal) to innovate. Accordingly, the innovative expenditures are concentrated in marketing. These sectors do not seem to rely particularly on the exploitation of technological opportunities. As far as growth performance is concerned, these sectors are likely to be more demand-pulled, as they orient their innovative strategies towards the creation and expansion of demand.

The third component has been identified as mostly *standardization-oriented*. The sectors belonging to this profile do not seem to rely on any particular source of information to innovate. Besides, the strategies behind their innovative efforts mainly aim at process rationalization and cost reduction, which turn out to be complementary to diversification strategies. Further, the sectors captured by this profile seem to pursue this kind of strategy mainly by investing in ICT-related technologies. This might suggest that the exploitation of the ICT paradigm in most of the (Italian) service industries is mainly

Table 9.5   The main innovative profiles in services – rotated component matrix

Variables included	Principal components		
	1 Science- based	2 Market- oriented	3 Standardized- oriented
Interactions			
Upstream	0.845	0.38	0.0003
Downstream, informal user	0.273	0.549	0.157
Downstream, formal market-oriented	−0.009	0.91	0.182
Strategies			
Market oriented	−0.102	0.532	0.002
Diversification	0.008	0.002	0.791
Rationalisation/cost reduction	−0.432	−0.425	0.453
Innovation expenditures			
In R&D per employee	0.907	−0.003	−0.168
In design per employee	0.955	−0.002	0.102
In know-how per employee	0.774	−0.006	0.324
In ICTs per employee	0.006	0.368	0.692
In training per employee	0.843	0.272	0.003
In marketing per employee	0.228	0.942	−0.104
In investments per employee	0.641	0.0002	−0.0001

Note: Extraction method: principal component analysis; rotation method: varimax.

Source: Italian Innovation Survey of Service Enterprises (ISTAT, 1997).

aimed at standardizing production and delivery processes, to enhance the price-competitiveness of the services provided. The sectors belonging to this profile are likely to be those traditionally affected by the so-called 'cost disease' (Baumol, 1967), which are now exploiting the opportunities provided by ICTs to increase labour productivity and reduce costs and prices. It is therefore likely that the growth performance of most of these sectors is mainly dependent on the trends of final demand, and, in general, on the price-elasticity of the different components of total demand.

A similar exercise has been performed by Evangelista and Savona (1998), and a taxonomy of the service sectors according to different innovative profiles has been obtained. A detailed description of the individual sectors within the taxonomy has been developed in Evangelista (2000). In this particular context the factor scores are used for further predictive purposes. Namely, they will be considered as proxies of the different impact of technological change at the sectoral level, and used as explanatory variables, together with the Demand Specialization Indexes illustrated above, to explain different sectoral employment growth rates.

An overview of the growth differentials experienced by the Italian service industries during the years 1991–96 is provided below.

The Sectoral Patterns of Growth in Services (1991–96)

The series of censuses of manufacturing and services enterprises, recently made comparable and carried out by ISTAT, allows for a detailed picture of growth patterns across 22 service sectors, at the same level of aggregation considered in Tables 9.2 and 9.3 above.

Figure 9.1 shows the compound annual growth rate of employment over the period 1991–96, considered as a proxy of the growth patterns experienced by service sectors over the same period. The time-span considered is consistent with the aim of exploring both the impacts of the different innovative profiles, as drawn from the analysis of the 1993–95 Innovation Survey, and the structural composition of demand, as a result of the 1991 Census of Service and Manufacturing Enterprises and illustrated above.

Overall, the service sector as a whole has not shown a positive employment trend of growth. Nevertheless, the sectoral patterns of growth have been highly differentiated. Most of the sectors classified above as intermediate producer services have shown positive rates of employment growth, whereas all the financial and trade compartments, that is the intermediate distributive services, as well as most of the transport services except shipping and sea transport, have shown a negative employment growth trend. The highest growing sectors over the period considered are other business services, cleaning and sea transport, as well as all the intermediate producer services, such as engineering, R&D, technical consultancy, and computing and software. In particular, we find that sectors which do not present particularly high innovative profiles (such as cleaning, other business, and legal and accounting services) nonetheless experience high employment growth rates. On the other hand, we find sectors, which are supposed to be pushed by high technological

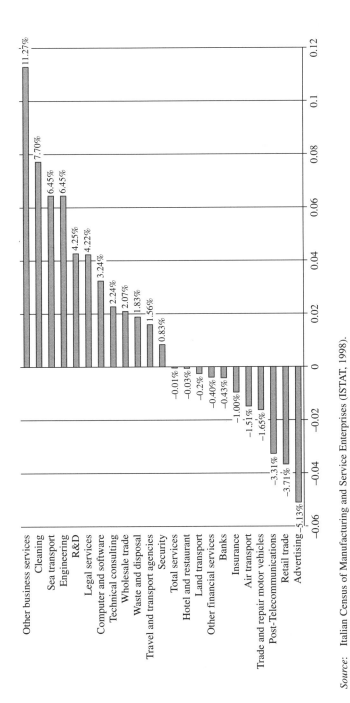

Source: Italian Census of Manufacturing and Service Enterprises (ISTAT, 1998).

Figure 9.1 Sectoral patterns of growth in services (compound annual rate of employment growth, 1991–96)

opportunities (such as post and telecommunications, air transport, as well as the financial compartment) that show negative trends of employment growth. This confirms that it is crucial to try to disentangle the role of demand and supply-side factors as determinants of growth at the sectoral level.

DEMAND, INNOVATION AND GROWTH IN SERVICES: THE CAUSAL LINKS

The previous section has set out the descriptive evidence on demand, innovation and growth in services. In the present section we aim at testing the extent of a causality relationship between the sectoral composition of demand for services and the innovative profiles on the one hand, and the different patterns of growth on the other. For this purpose, the factor scores and the DSIs have been entered as independent variables in a linear regression model, against the sectoral compound annual growth rates of employment in services (1991–96). The particular regression method used (backward stepwise) allows identification of the best-fit independent variables against the particular dependent variable. In other words, we are willing to test which kind of innovative profile, represented by the factor scores, and which kind of demand specialization, represented by the DSIs, best explain the differences in the growth rates experienced by service industries from 1991–96.

Table 9.6 reports the results of the regression analysis. The first part of the table illustrates all the explanatory variables regressed against the compound annual growth rate of employment. Two sets of explanatory variables have been considered, the *DSI* and the *INNPROF* variables, respectively indicating the different demand specialization and the innovative profiles illustrated in the previous sections. Among the different services branches (see Table 9.3) we have chosen to include the *DSI*s relating to business services and trade services, which cover the largest market shares within the whole service sector as a destination market. Further, the business and trade services represent respectively part of the intermediate producer demand (together with manufacturing) and part of the intermediate distributive demand (together with the financial sector, which however covers only 6 per cent of the whole service sector as a destination market).

The second part of the table reports the results of the regression model, firstly when all the explanatory variables are entered (original model), and secondly in the case of the best-fit model, that is when the best-fit explanatory variables are econometrically selected. The best-fit model shows a rather good explanatory capacity (R-square 0.55), despite the constraint due to the low number of observations (21 service sectors). The coefficients of the best-fit explanatory variables are all statistically significant at the 95 per cent level, the constant included.

Table 9.6   Sectoral composition of demand, innovative profiles and growth
          patterns in services – regression estimates

Dependent variable	
Compound annual rate of employment growth in services (1991–96)	*Growth9196*
Eplanatory variables	
Demand Specialization Index in farming services	*DSI Farming*
Demand Specialization Index in manufacturing industries	*DSI Manuf.*
Demand Specialization Index in business services	*DSI Bus. Serv.*
Demand Specialization Index in trade services	*DSI Trade*
Demand Specialization Index in public services	*DSI Public*
Demand Specialization Index in final demand	*DSI Final*
Factor's scores Comp. 1 (Science-based)	*INNPROF1*
Factor's scores Comp. 2 (Market-orient.)	*INNPROF2*
Factor's scores Comp. 3 (Standard.-orient.)	*INNPROF3*

Original model[a] – Model fit (R-square): 0.70 – no. of observations: 21

Dependent variable	Explanatory variables	B coeff.	Sig.(.05)
Growth9196	*Constant*	−22.86	**
	INNPROF1	−1.28	
	INNPROF2	−2.72	**
	INNPROF3	−0.85	
	DSI Farming	2.98	
	DSI Manufacturing	5.47	*
	DSI Business	8.17	**
	DSI Trade	2.64	
	DSI Public	0.52	
	DSI Final	2.73	

Best-fit model[a] – Model fit (R-square): 0.55 – No. of observations: 21

Dependent variable	Best-fit explanatory variables	B coeff.	Sig.(.05)
Growth9196	*Constant*	−8.73	**
	INNPROF2	−2.29	**
	DSI Manufacturing	4.18	**
	DSI Business	4.28	**

Notes
[a]For the regression analysis, Linear Backward Entry Method has been used (criterion: Probability F to Remove equal or higher than .1).
** = significant at 95% level; * = significant at 90% level.

Sources: Italian Census of Manufacturing and Service Enterprises (ISTAT, 1995a, 1995b, 1995c, 1998; Italian Innovation Survey of Service Enterprises (ISTAT, 1997).

As far as the supply side in our model is concerned, the different innovative profiles identified above are expected to have different potentialities in terms of impact on the growth performance. Namely, we would expect a positive growth performance by the science-based and the market-oriented service sectors. The former are likely to have the ability to exploit the technological opportunities provided by the current paradigm, whereas the latter would tend to actively create their own demand or better exploit cycles of demand expansion. Regarding the standardization-oriented sectors, their growth performance is likely to be more demand-constrained compared with the market-oriented sectors, due to the fact that their competitiveness is typically linked to price factors and the high price-elasticity of the peculiar components of demand they serve.

As far as the demand side in our model is concerned, a specialization towards intermediate producer components of demand (the manufacturing and business service sectors themselves) is argued as being a necessary condition to assure positive growth performance, as well as to exploit the technological opportunities provided by the current paradigm.

The results of our model confirm in part our conjectures. The coefficients of the *INNPROF* variables turn out negative in our model, though only *INNPROF2* is statistically significant. On the contrary, all the *DSI* variables coefficients are positive, though only the *DSI Manufacturing* and *DSI Business* services are significant and quite high (4.18 and 4.28 respectively). This confirms that the sectoral composition of demand for services does matter, particularly the different specialization in intermediate producer, distributive, public and final demand. Overall, the demand side seems to fit our model better than the supply side, that is the different innovative profiles proxied by the components' factor scores, which seem to be negatively related to the different growth rates.

According to the results of our empirical model, it is therefore the structure of the economy, rather than the ability (or inability) of each sector to exploit the technological opportunities, that accounts for the growth performance in services. In particular, the results show that a specialization in intermediate producer demand does explain the (positive) growth performance experienced by these specific sectors (technical consultancy, engineering, sea transport, R&D, travel and transport services, waste and disposal, cleaning, computing and software, legal services, other business services), though they belong to different innovative profiles. The only exception is represented by the advertising, post and telecommunication and land transport sectors. Symmetrically, it can be inferred that a de-specialization in intermediate producer demand (or a specialization in final and distributive demand, that is for all the financial services, retail trade, hotel and restaurants, trade and repair of motor vehicles) explains the negative growth performance. Also in this case, the demand-side explanatory power seems to be higher than the supply-side one, as the sectors involved have different innovative profiles. These findings are supported by the role of the *INNPROF2* proxy, which shows a negative relation to the dependent variable. This can be interpreted as follows: the innovative effort (in this case strongly market oriented) is not sufficient to assure positive growth trends when not associated with the specialization towards intermediate demand, whereas a positive growth performance can be achieved regardless of the presence of innovative effort.

CONCLUDING REMARKS

A stylized reading of the literature on the growth of service sectors as part of the process of structural change occurring in the last few decades has been proposed. The analytical approaches, as well as the main emphasis on the determinants of service growth, appear to be polarized, in terms of processes/supply and product/demand. While there have been some attempts at bringing the role of intermediate demand to attention, they do not seem to encompass in a unified framework the effect of the composition of demand on *sectoral differences* of growth trends. On the other side, the most recent contributions, which have aimed at accounting for the role and impact of technological change on innovation and growth performances in services, seem to have neglected the importance of the demand side, generally taken to be exogenous. In particular, the sectoral composition of demand for services, together with the innovative profiles, has rarely been taken into account to explain cross-sector differentials in terms of growth rates.

The empirical evidence proposed in this chapter has aimed at disentangling the role of demand and supply factors, considered as sector-specific characteristics, in explaining the different growth trends experienced by services in the last decade. In particular, the sectoral composition of demand and the different innovative profiles, taken respectively as proxies of the sectoral division of labour between services and the rest of the economy and the different impact of technological change on innovative performance, have been taken into account. Within a regression framework, it has been shown that a specialization in the intermediate producer components of demand (the manufacturing and business service sectors) does matter in explaining the different patterns of growth. On the contrary, different innovative profiles are not able to explain differences in the growth patterns.

The results of the empirical analysis seem to confirm our conjecture on the different role and impact of demand vs. supply factors in determining different patterns of growth in services. In particular, a sectoral specialization towards intermediate producer demand (manufacturing sector and business services sector) is a necessary condition for a positive growth performance. On the other hand, the exploitation of the technological opportunities provided by the new ICT paradigm and emphasized by most of the literature on innovation in services is not a sufficient condition for a positive growth performance when service industries are specialized in final and intermediate distributive demand (trade and finance sectors).

The picture emerging represents a first step towards the main claim of this chapter, and further research is necessary to account for the role of both supply and demand side in explaining sectoral differences of service growth. Nevertheless, the results of our empirical analysis seem to be consistent with the conjecture of an intermediate demand-pull mechanism as the main determinant of service growth. The structural change in the elasticity of intermediate demand amplifies the increase of final demand, due to the price-decreasing effect of the adoption of ICTs at various levels of the vertical chain, and represent the dominant mechanism able to explain sectoral differences in services' growth.

NOTES

1. This research has been carried out with the Research Programme 1999 funded by the MURST (Italian Minister of University, Research and Technology). I thank Giulio Perani (ISTAT) for having provided the data used in this work. I also thank Faiz Gallouj, Fabio Montobbio and Rinaldo Evangelista for their comments on earlier drafts of this chapter, based on the paper prepared for the International Conference, 'The economics and socio-economics of services: international perspectives', held in Lille-Roubaix on the 22 and 23 June 2000. The usual disclaimers apply.
2. A few attempts have been made to encompass the role and impact of (final) demand within the analyses of technological change and economic growth (see Vivarelli, 1995; Pianta, 2001), yet none of them has explicitly extended the analysis to service industries, mainly focusing on the manufacturing sector.
3. The few exceptions are the taxonomies of technological change in service sectors proposed in Soete and Miozzo (1989), Miles (1994) and Evangelista (2000), though only the latter is carried out on an empirical base.
4. Delaunay and Gadrey (1992) propose a detailed historical review of the various contributions to the economics of services.
5. See Smith (1776), Book Two, *Of the Nature, Accumulation and Employment of Stock*; Clark (1940); Fourastié (1949); Cohen and Zysman (1974); Baumol (1967). The work of Cohen and Zysman actually belongs to the following 'generation' of the debate, concerned with the myth of the post-industrial society. A pure chronological criterion would suggest considering it alongside the well-known contribution by Bell (1973). However, the reclassification proposed here is based on the main field of analysis and the relationship towards the *supply side* or *demand side* in determining the growth of services and its implications.
6. See Evangelista and Savona (1998) and Evangelista (2000) for a detailed description of the various indicators provided by the Italian Innovation Survey of Service Enterprises.

REFERENCES

Barbieri, G. and G. Rosa (1990), *Terziario avanzato e sviluppo innovativo* (Bologna: Il Mulino).

Barras, R. (1986), 'New Technologies and the New Services', *Futures*, December 1996, 748–86.

Barras, R. (1990), 'Interactive Innovation in Financial and Business Services: The Vanguard of the Service Revolution', *Research Policy*, 19, 215–37.

Baumol, W. (1967), 'Macroeconomics of Unbalanced Growth: The Anatomy of an Urban Crisis', *American Economic Review*, 57, 415–26.

Bell, D. (1973), *The Coming of Post-Industrial Society. A Venture in Social Forecasting* (New York: Basic Books).

Browning, H.S. and J. Singelmann (1978), 'The Transformation of the US Labour Force: The Interaction of Industries and Occupation', *Politics and Society*, 3–4, 481–509.

Clark, C. (1940), *The Condition of Economic Progress* (London: Macmillan).

Cohen, S.S. and J. Zysman (1974), *Manufacturing Matters – The Myth of Post-Industrial Economy* (New York: Basic Books).

Delaunay, J.C. and J. Gadrey (1992), *Services in Economic Thought – Three Centuries of Debate* (Boston/Dordrecht/London: Kluwer Academic Publishers).

Dodgson, M. and R. Rothwell, (eds), *The Handbook of Industrial Innovation*, Cheltenham: Edward Elgar.

Evangelista, R. (2000), 'Sectoral Patterns of Technological Change in Services', *Economics of Innovation and New Technology*, 9, 183–221.

Evangelista, R. and M. Savona (1998), 'Patterns of Innovation in Services. The Results of the Italian Innovation Survey', VIII Annual RESER Conference, Berlin, 8–10 October.

Fisher, A.G. B. (1935), *The Clash of Progress and Security* (London: Macmillan).

Fourastié, J. (1949) *Le grand espoir du XX siècle* (Paris: PUF).

Fuchs, V. (1968), *The Service Economy* (New York: National Bureau of Economic Research).

Gallouj, F. and O. Weisenstein (1997), 'Innovation in Services', *Research Policy*, 26, 537–56.

Gershuny, J. (1978), *After Industrial Society? The Emerging Self-Service Economy* (London: Macmillan).

ISTAT (1995a), '7° Censimento Generale dell'Industria e dei Servizi–Imprese e Unità Locali – Settore Commercio Alberghi e Pubblici Esercizi', Rome: ISTAT.

ISTAT (1995b), '7° Censimento Generale dell'Industria e dei Servizi – Imprese e Unità Locali – Settore Industria', Rome: ISTAT.

ISTAT (1995c), '7° Censimento Generale dell'Industria e dei Servizi – Imprese e Unità Locali – Settore Trasporti Credito Assicurazioni e altri Servizi', Rome: ISTAT.

ISTAT (1997), 'Indagine sull'innovazione tecnologica nelle imprese di servizi in Italia (1993–1995)', Rome: ISTAT.

ISTAT (1998), 'I Censimenti delle Attività Producttive dal 1951 al 1991', Rome: ISTAT.

Karaomerlioglu, D. and B. Carlsson (1999), 'Manufacturing in Decline? A Matter of Definition', *Economics of Innovation and New Technology*, 8, 175–96.

Kuznets, S. (1957), 'Quantitative Aspects of the Economic Growth of Nations, II: Industrial Distribution of National Product and Labour Force', *Economic Development and Cultural Change* (Supplement, July).

Miles, I. (1994), 'Innovation in Services', in Dodgson, M. and R. Rothwell, (eds) *The Handbook of Industrial Innovation*, Chelteham: Edward Elgar.

Miles, I. (1995), 'Knowledge Intensive Business Services – Users, Carriers and Sources of Innovation', European Innovation Monitoring System Publication n. 15. EIMS.

Miozzo, M. and L. Soete (1999), 'Internationalisation of Services: A Technological Perspective', 3rd International Conference on Technology Policy and Innovation 30 August–2 September, Austin, USA.

Momigliano, F. and D. Siniscalco (1986), 'Mutamenti nella Struttura del Sistema Produttivo e Integrazione tra Industria e Terziario', in L. Pasinetti (ed.), *Mutamenti Strutturali del Sistema Produttivo e Integrazione tra Industria e Terziario* (Bologna: Il Mulino).

Mowery, D. and N. Rosenberg (1979), 'The Influence of Market Demand upon Innovation: A Critical Review of Some Recent Empirical Studies', *Research Policy*, 8, 102–53.

Nelson, R. R. and S.G. Winter (1982), *An Evolutionary Theory of Economic Change* (Harvard: Belknap Harvard).

Notarangelo, M. (1999), 'Unbalanced Growth. A Case of Structural Dynamics', *Structural Change and Economic Dynamics*, 10, 209–23.

OECD (2000), 'Science, Technology and Industry Outlook', OECD, Paris.

OECD–EUROSTAT (1997), 'Proposed Guidelines for Collecting and Interpreting Technological Innovation Data – Oslo Manual', OECD, Paris.

Pasinetti, L. (eds.), (1986) *Mutamenti Strutturali del Sistema Producttivo e Integrazione tra Industria e Terziario* (Bologna: Il Mulino).

Pavitt, K. (1984), 'Sectoral Patterns of Technical Change: Towards a Taxonomy and a Theory', *Research Policy*, 13, 343–74.

Petit, P. (1986), *Slow Growth and the Service Economy* (London: Pinter).

Petit, P. and L. Soete (eds) (2001), *Technology and the Future of European Employment* (Cheltenham, UK and Brookfield, US: Edward Elgar).

Pianta, M. (2001), 'Demand, Innovation and Employment', in P. Petit and L. Soete (eds), *Technology and the Future of European Employment* (Cheltenham, UK and Brookfield, US: Edward Elgar).

Prosperetti, L. (1986), 'Servizi e Sviluppo Economico: un Riesame di Alcuni Modelli', in L. Pasinetti (ed.), *Mutamenti Strutturali del Sistema Producttivo e Integrazione tra Industria e Terziario* (Bologna: Il Mulino).

Schmookler, J. (1962), 'Economic Sources of Inventive Activity', *Journal of Economic History*, March, 1–20.

Simonetti, R., D. Archibugi and R. Evangelista (1995), 'Product and Process Innovations. How Are They Defined? How Are They Quantified?', *Scientometrics*, 1, 77–89.

Smith, A. [1776] (1997), *The Wealth of Nations* (London: Penguin Classics).

Soete, L. and M. Miozzo (1989), 'Trade and Development in Services: A Technological Perspective', Maastrich Economic Research Institute on Innovation and Technology (MERIT), Working paper no. 89–031.

Sundbo, J. (1995), 'Standardisation vs. Customisation in Service Innovations', SI4S Topical Paper, Oslo: STEP Group.

Vivarelli, M. (1995), *The Economics of Technology and Employment* (Cheltenham, UK and Brookfield, US: Edward Elgar).

Tchervonnaia, O. (2001), 'Consumer Skills and Learning in Services', paper presented at the PhD course on 'Technological Practices and Innovation in Services', Roskilde University, 3–5 May.

10. Co-producers of innovation: on the role of knowledge-intensive business services in innovation

Pim den Hertog

1. INTRODUCTION

For a long time services were simply seen as part of a very undifferentiated residual sector, a wide group of 'non-manufacturing industries'. The issues of whether, to what extent, and how service firms and service organizations innovate, and how this differs from manufacturing industries were not central research questions nor significant features of the (innovation) policy agenda. However, as the discussion on the knowledge-based society unfolds, the attention directed at services is increasing. Policymakers and researchers alike seem to have discovered that services do matter. With large majorities of the workforce in some developed economies employed in service industries or for that matter in service occupations, and with ICT-based innovation a prominent feature of many service organisations, it is evident that a better appreciation and understanding of the role of services in innovation is indeed needed. This chapter aims to contribute to this understanding.

First some existing approaches in the services' literature towards the question what it means to produce a service are briefly reviewed (section 2). Then a four-dimensional model is presented aimed at improving the understanding of the interaction of technological and non-technological factors in service innovation (section 3). Then, still at a rather general level, a distinction is made between five basic service innovation patterns (section 4). Subsequently, the focus will shift towards a sub-category of services, namely knowledge-intensive business services (KIBS). It is argued that these services can play a substantial role in innovation processes, especially in client firms, by functioning either as facilitator, carrier or source of innovation (section 5). It is further argued that KIBS and their client firms may develop an almost symbiotic relationship. This relationship in practice is shaped by a multitude of tangible and discrete knowledge flows, but equally important intangible and more process-oriented knowledge flows. This leads to the notion of KIBS as co-producers of innovation (section 6). Adopting a more dynamic perspective a three tiered model is presented in which the formerly separate worlds of the public knowledge base and the private knowledge base are seen to be inter-mingling and developing into networks of interconnected service profession-als. This approach is linked to the wider discussion of the production of knowledge and associated institutional changes – in particular the distinction between 'mode 1' and 'mode 2' knowledge production in science and tech-nology as provided by Gibbons et al. (1994). KIBS can be perceived as a specific example of the 'mode 2' variety of knowledge production (section 7). At the end of this chapter some challenges for further research into service innovation and the role of KIBS herein are formulated (section 8).

2.   WHAT DOES IT MEAN TO PRODUCE A SERVICE?

Before entering into a discussion on service innovation and its modalities, it seems worthwhile to look into the question included in the title of this section. Gadrey et al. (1995), who raised this question, have formulated their answer as follows:

> to produce a service . . . is to organise a solution to a problem (a treatment, an oper-ation) which does not principally involve supplying a good. It is to place a bundle of capabilities and competencies (human, technological, organisational) at the disposal of a client and to organise a solution, which may be given to varying degrees of precision. (Gadrey et al. pp 5–6)

This answer is appealing for various reasons. In the first place it makes clear that apart from technological capabilities, human and organizational capabilities are important for providing services well. Secondly, it allows for a differentiation between highly standardized service products or service formulas with quasi good characteristics (for example the well-known retail chains), and the more customized services that are much harder to pinpoint (such as the majority of the various new types of knowledge business services that have emerged over the last decade). It is especially the latter category of services that is often based on more tacit forms of knowledge and knowledge exchange. What is characteristic about these services is, that not only the service itself, but also the innovation process underlying their constant renewal is often the result of a co-production between the actual service provider and its client. This makes many of the services that in section 5 will be labelled as KIBS into important vectors of change and knowledge diffusion in innovation systems.

Many contributions in the past decades on the economic role of services start by telling a story of neglect and gross generalizations. Luckily this no longer seems to be the case. Although it was not that long ago that as soon as innovation came into play the majority of innovation scholars seemed to turn almost automatically to analysing technological innovation in manufacturing, reducing service firms to passive users of technological innovations originating from manufacturing industries. When Pavitt introduced in 1984 his by now well-known sectoral taxonomy of technological change, services industries were mainly labelled as supplier-dominated sectors.[1] In a similar vein the important theoretical contributions of Barras on service innovation (1986; 1990) still portray most service sectors as initially supplier-dominated, and as receiving an impetus from manufacturing in order to be able to embark on subsequent phases of the innovation process.

However, especially during the 1990s, when the field of services innovation studies had been gradually expanding, two important changes occurred in the way services and innovation in services were perceived. First, the fact that services do play an often substantial role in innovation processes has been increasingly recognized. Services at last were not automatically portrayed as merely passive recipients of others' innovations. Second, attention on non-technological elements in innovation and innovation processes started to grow, shifting attention to service innovation. Various lines of research such as the ones on the 'peculiarities' of services (Miles, 1993), on service management (Normann, 1991; Quinn, 1992), on the significance of interaction with clients (and of clients' competencies; compare also Kline and Rosenberg, 1986), on the importance of recombination of existing elements in new services (Henderson and Clark, 1990) came to the fore. Gradually more general approaches towards innovation have been developing that could be equally used for describing services as well manufacturing innovation. This is illustrated by the total of six innovation models as discerned by Gallouj and Weinstein (1997). They distinguish between radical innovation, improvement innovation, incremental innovation, ad hoc innovation, recombinative innovation and formalization innovation.

A comprehensive model for understanding innovation that sensibly accommodates service innovation, however, is still lacking. There is a need for such a model as service functions abound in the economy. Service innovation can be said to be equally relevant for manufacturing firms as these increasingly use innovation in service functions and features to differentiate their products. Likewise, some business processes in service firms resemble those in manufacturing, for example administrative processing in back offices. Therefore, a continuum rather than a strict distinction between manufacturing firms and service firms – and the innovation models used for them – seems appropriate when discussing firm innovation. The heuristic model to be introduced in the next section can be used for discussing service innovation in both manufacturing and service firms.

3. A FOUR-DIMENSIONAL MODEL OF SERVICE INNOVATION

Service innovation is seldom limited to a change in the characteristics of the service product itself. Innovation often coincides with new patterns of product distribution, client interaction, quality control and assurance and so on, though there are huge differences in the specific patterns involved. What is important for introducing one new product onto the market might be totally irrelevant for other products. Offering a completely new service may differ considerably from offering an existing service using a new distribution channel. In practice most innovations appear to be a mixture of major and minor changes and adaptations of existing (service) products.

In order to discuss, map and analyse the diversity of innovations in greater detail and in a structured way, a four-dimensional model of service innovation is introduced (Figure 10.1). Although conceptual, it is concrete enough to map service innovations and discuss their practical development. First the four dimensions are presented, before touching upon the linkages between them.[2]

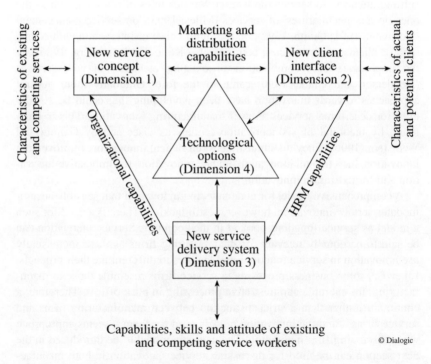

Figure 10.1   A four-dimensional model of service innovation

Dimension 1   The Service Concept

Manufactured products (and processes) are typically highly tangible and visible. This is often not the case with services. Some service innovations are highly visible, especially where delivery of the product is involved. However, frequently it is not so much a physical product but a much more intangible characteristic of a new service, like a new idea or concept of how to organize a solution to a problem. Although a particular service concept may already be familiar in other markets, the key thing is that it is novel in its application within a particular market. As usual in innovation research, there are thorny problems concerning when a product, function or concept is really new. Judgements can vary according to whether and when it is new to the providing firm, new to the client, to the regional, national or global market and whether it involves new logic or scientific knowledge.

Some examples of conceptual innovations are:

- Green or 'ecologically sound' banking products such as investment schemes aimed at environmentally friendly projects, or 'green power' as marketed by electricity manufacturers.
- Call centre services – these install, organize and recruit staff for clients' call centres – which have emerged from temporary staffing offices on the basis of their initial involvement with providing temporary labour for call centres.
- Environmental accounting or intercultural management advice – these are new types of services offered by accountancy or consultancy firms which developed into completely new markets quite recently. Accountants help firms in reporting their efforts to run their business in a more environmentally friendly way. Management consultants found out that misunderstandings deriving from differences in cultural backgrounds are quite common in increasingly internationalized firms and have developed intercultural advice into a specialist consultancy area.
- Development of a particular style of shopping outlets, currently the rise of mono-brand stores to give the brand name its own character, to create a specific shopping environment that is recognizable for their clients.

Although not all service innovations have a strong novel conceptual element, conceptual innovations are much more likely to be found in service firms (or, better, service functions) than in pure manufacturing firms. Such innovations are usually highly intangible – meaning that while in some cases the service itself may have quite tangible elements, the new features have less to do with material artefacts.

Dimension 2   The Client Interface

A second element of service innovations is the design of the interface between the service provider and its clients. These interfaces are the focus of a good deal of service innovations, though innovation studies, with their focus on mass manufacturing, have tended to overlook the changes occurring in these interfaces. As a quite general phenomenon across a wide span of services, product offerings are increasingly marketed and even produced in a client-specific way (even with client-specific pricing) and delivered electronically as far as they have informational components.

In business services in particular, clients are often also part and parcel of the production of the service product. The way the service provider interacts with the client can itself be a source of innovation. Increasingly, there is no clearly identifiable point where the producer's activity stops and the user's activity begins. This is of course particularly true where the business service itself is offering support for innovation, for example in R&D and design services. With the high degree of co-design and co-production of service products, it may be difficult to locate the innovation within service supplier or client: it is not unusual, for instance, for service firms to site their staff within client organizations for periods of time.

Examples of client interface innovations include:

- The large-scale introduction of account management systems in professional organizations such as economic consulting or IT firms can in some cases be interpreted as a renewal of the client interface.
- The Internet has developed into a new distribution channel in quite a number of trades, be it retailing, banking or the travel industry. The major change is that clients for selected services do not interact any longer with individuals, but are guided by well-designed and self-explanatory graphical interfaces. Service innovations quite often are about new ways of interacting with clients and about their integration with other channels (multi-channelling).

Dimension 3   The Service Delivery System/Organization

The third dimension – involving service delivery system and organization – is often directly related to the previously discussed dimension – the linkage between the service provider and its client (the client interface). The delivery is indeed one specific type of interaction across the client interface (others including financial transactions, design inputs, after sales, and so on). However, dimension 3 is different. It refers to the internal organizational arrangements that have to be managed to allow service workers to perform their jobs properly and to develop and offer innovative services. It is closely related to the question of how to empower employees, to facilitate them so that they can perform their jobs and deliver service products adequately. On the one hand, new services may require new organizational forms, (inter)personal capabilities, and skills. On the other hand, an organization can be designed, and employees can be trained, so as to leave room for innovations and non-conventional solutions to practical problems.

Examples of delivery system and organizational innovations include:

- The large-scale introduction of home shopping services – or consumer e-commerce – not only causes a substantial change in the ways in which service provider and client relate, but requires the redesign of the logistics, IT systems and skills required.
- Organizations promising customers an unusually fast service – be it a fast food meal ready in a few minutes or having tyres changed within 20 minutes – mostly utilize innovative ways of workflow management and human resources management.
- In more traditional shopping environments, the lengthening of retailer opening hours may have serious consequences for the type of customers attracted, the type of products on offer, the management of the workforce and so on.

Dimension 4   Technological Options

The fourth dimension is the centre of much analysis and debate, especially concerning the degree to which service firms themselves, in practice, are giving shape to technology development. Clearly, service innovation is possible without technological innovation; technology is not always a dimension. Nonetheless, in practice there is a wide range of relationships between 'technology' and 'service innovation'. These vary from technology mainly playing a role as a facilitating or enabling factor, to something much closer to supply-push, technology-driven innovation.

Service firms also differ in their awareness of relevant available technological options, the degree to which they posses the necessary technology themselves or have access to the necessary knowledge and the degree to which they can act as demanding customers and articulate their technological needs. Many innovations are driven by downstream service sectors and can surely be considered user-dominated. In fact, users may play a crucial role in developing and implementing new services, although some of the required technologies may come from suppliers.

Although ICT is certainly not the only relevant technology in service innovation, it is particularly pervasive. The numerous information processing tasks to which it may be applied, include many that are intrinsic to almost all economic activities. ICT is thus often perceived as the enabler of service innovation. Many commentators who recognize the profound implications of ICT for services still, however, consider this technology as typically supplier-dominated. It is true that many smaller and less innovative service firms are relatively less proactive where it comes to incorporating new ICT, though even here there is rarely the purely passive process of absorption implied by the term 'diffusion'. However, in many larger and/or more advanced firms there is an extremely active process of technological development going on.

Examples of technological innovations include:

- automatic ordering systems in supermarkets to prevent empty shelves, or scanning cash registers in large retail stores;
- tracking and tracing systems which enable transport service providers to monitor the progress of their fleet and thus to manage their transport services more closely;
- handheld wireless devices as used in cafes and restaurants to efficiently take orders without running back and forth between kitchen and table.

These examples of ICT utilization illustrate that service firms are not necessarily supplier-dominated as some of these systems are developed (partly) in-house or require intense advanced user-producer linkages in their development phase. This is especially true in the case of ICT services themselves, like software houses. To a certain degree software firms have to adapt their activities to new products from hardware companies, for example new generations of chips. This involves near continual updating and – typically – expansion of software to exploit the facilities of new equipment. But the process of developing new applications, new functionality, new interfaces and so on is much more in the software firms' hands. It is also evident that sectors with a long experience of ICT investment are major sources of innovation – in the shape of new configurations of hardware, new software and applications, new interfaces and so on. A good example is the financial sector, which is a huge employer of software and networking staff.

Service innovation is a multi-dimensional phenomenon. A complete new service usually means the introduction of a new service concept, new distribution channels or ways of interacting with clients, new service delivery systems in the form of new working routines, new organizational concepts or back office set up, the need for new generations of ICT or customized software packages and so on. Apart from the meaning of these four dimensions separately as discrete vectors of change, the linkages between these dimensions may be of even more significance.

Often these cross-linkages are forged in practice by those responsible for marketing, organization development and distribution. For instance, launching a new service concept (for existing or new clients) requires marketing expertise. Similarly, creating an adequate interface with clients, and adapting the service delivery system, requires knowledge of how services are distributed (both in terms of where they are produced and of how they are delivered). The decision as to whether to develop new services requires also organizational knowledge: can the current organization deliver the new service? What organizational changes might be needed?

The point is that a particular service innovation may be characterized by one dominant feature related to one of the above-mentioned dimensions; quite likely, this particular feature will prompt a set of changes in other dimensions, in order to bring about a successful innovation. Consider an example from the retail service sector. Intelligent cash registers and advanced data warehousing are widely used by large companies, and these are basically technological innovations (that is dimension 4). They allow for the creation of detailed client profiles and personalized product offerings. However, these applications cannot be bought off the shelf and simply be implemented. They need to be combined with the specific characteristics of the shop formula at hand (dimension 1), the way the retailer wants to communicate with its clients (dimension 2), the way the employees are trained (dimension 3), and so on.

In practice, it may be the combination of the four dimensions that ultimately characterizes each particular service innovation. The weight of the individual dimensions, and the importance of the various linkages between them, varies across individual services, innovations and firms. Similarly, the inputs required to link the dimensions in practice differ according to the type of service, and the extent to which the search and selection process (inherent in all innovation processes) is formalized.

By way of illustration innovation in retailing is given in a stylized way in Table 10.1 below using the four dimensions introduced above. From this table it is hard to judge which of the four dimensions is most important for innovation as most innovations appear to be combinations of conceptual, technological and organizational innovations, often combined with new ways of relating to the consumer. It does however illustrate that innovation in retailing is much more than just technological innovation.

4. PATTERNS OF SERVICE INNOVATION

The four dimensional model as described in the preceding section sketches out the various ingredients of service innovations. It is most suited for mapping service innovation in a particular firm (micro-level) or industry (sectoral level). At a somewhat more aggregated level and focusing more on the role of

Table 10.1 Innovations in retailing using the 4D-model (den Hertog and Brouwer, 2000, p. 11)

Dimension	Innovations
1. New service concept New formulas (marketing, brands), new locations, new combinations, new assortments aimed at specific groups of clients	• Mono brand stores (MEXX, Vanilla, GAP, Nikeworld) • Out of town retailing (e.g. factory outlets) • Non-store retailing (e.g. e-commerce) • New shop formulas on new locations with specific product assortment and opening hours (e.g. shops in railway stations revamped local supermarkets or other new formulas aimed at e.g. cash rich/time poor consumers) • Mixtures of shopping, entertainment and restaurants aimed at increasing the duration of the visits (integration of floral centres, pet shop, cafes; specialized shopping malls • Combinations of retailers and non-retailers (bank counters in supermarkets; travel insurance offered in travel agencies and outdoor centres) • Life 'experiences' in stores (climbing wall in outdoor equipment shop, cooking lessons offered by supermarkets) • New services on the basis of strong brandname (e.g. credit cards issued by TESCO) • Packages adapted to smaller households or products aimed at the elderly (smaller portions, special diet food, etc.) • Green products • E-commerce/M-commerce
2. New client interface How do clients experience the interaction with the retailer, i.e. forms of dehumanization and	• Smart routing in stores (e.g. discount corridor, convenience corners etc.) • E-commerce (e.g. electronic purchasing and delivery of information) • Semi-standardized (personalized) list of groceries or suggested reading or music on the basis of your personal preferences • User-friendly interactive retailing and virtual client interfaces (how is the interface of e-shops and e-malls shaped?)

humanization, shaping of virtual or interactive retailing through personalization, new electronic interfaces	• Client-specific product offerings on the basis of loyalty programmes and client cards (personalized product offerings send home) • Home delivery services and development of 'pick up centres' (e.g. pick up your ordered products at the petrol station) • Self-scanning check outs
3. New service delivery system Intra- and extra-organizational changes and new skills needed to supply (re-)new(ed) retailing services. Clients are co-producers and at the same time expect more personal service	• Innovations in logistical chain (JIT, replenishment, status information, etc.) as rate of circulation increases and stocks are kept to a minimum • Self-scanning check outs • Click-and-mortar strategies (combinations of virtual and physical retailing, e.g. extra after sales services, extra product information) • Various forms of self-service (weighing, scanning, payment) • More personal advice on products • Home based services and home delivery (e.g. goods ordered electronically) • Additional services (transport, installation, instruction, etc.)
4. Technological options New ICT systems allow for optimization of logistics, consumer profiling, self-service devices and development of (personalized) e-commerce applications	• Inventory control systems/replenishment systems allow for active stock management • Intelligent packaging, tagging and scanning • Scanning cash registers • Authentication and access technology, electronic payment systems • Client profiling (allowing one-to-one marketing) and data-mining • Data navigation products and electronic interfaces • Multimedia hard and software for e-commerce/M-commerce as well as specific applications (e.g. 3D models for trying clothes, one click buying technology) • E-shops, e-malls and platforms for e-procurement

Source: Den Hertog and Brouwer (2000, p. 11).

services and service firms in innovation processes there still is a need to reflect on the supposed supplier-dominated character of much service innovation. This section considers different patterns of service innovation. It is argued that although supplier-dominated innovation is characteristic for some service firms and some service industries, there are many more roles of service firms in innovation processes than just passive users of (technological) innovations stemming from capital good industries. This is much more likely, of course, if we are prepared to include non-technological aspects of innovation in our analysis. Some services, which will be looked into more thoroughly in subsequent sections, can even be said to function as co-producer of innovation in the operations of their clients. First , a typology[3] of innovation patterns will be presented. The typology demonstrates the wide variety of roles of service firms in innovation processes. A central variable is the way in which suppliers of inputs (equipment, capital, human resources and so on), service firms and clients (end consumer or intermediate user) interact.[4] Each of the five patterns discerned displays a different mix of linkages between these three types of actors. The influence that the client firm or final consumer exerts on the innovation process, gradually increases from pattern 1 to 4. Pattern 5 represents a somewhat different situation as all actors in the value system contribute to a particular innovation or are forced to accommodate it.

Pattern 1 Supplier-Dominated Innovation

Services innovations have traditionally been depicted as following this pattern where innovations (as a rule technological innovations in the form of new technical equipment) are largely based on primarily technological innovations as supplied by hardware manufacturers. These innovations from external suppliers are disseminated and implemented by service industry users, who in their turn satisfy the needs of their clients. Examples of this pattern include:

- microwave ovens in catering, whose introduction has greatly extended the possibilities for food preparation (and reheating) in cafes and restaurants;
- cash registers and mobile phones assimilated into many small firms that otherwise use little new technology;
- introduction of interactive TV.

There are many similar examples, with a clear 'technology push'. Typical for this pattern is, at least initially, little scope for user industries to influence the actual product supplied by the supplier. The adopting firm often has to bring about some organizational changes in order to be able to use the innovation – to adapt its organization, train its employees and so on – and to offer more efficient and higher quality services as a result.

Pattern 2   Innovation within Services

Here the actual innovation and implementation is initiated and takes place in the service firm itself. Such innovations may be technological, non-technological, or (as in many cases) a combination of the two. Typical examples of this pattern involve a new product, product bundle, or delivery system, that is thought up in the service firm itself (for example, by a new business team) and implemented throughout the organization, possibly with 'innovation support' from outside. Examples of this pattern are:

- introduction of new shop formulas by retailers;
- new pension and saving schemes as introduced by financial service providers;
- new tools for assessing applicants looking for a temporary job in staffing agencies.

These are the sort of innovations that have been overlooked for a long time as typically they have quite often a more conceptual character.

Pattern 3   Client-Led Innovation

In this case the service firm is responding to needs clearly articulated by its clients. While, in a sense, every successful innovation is a reaction to a perceived market need, for some service innovations this is more clear-cut than for others. Some examples:

- door-to-door public transport services aimed at the business traveller, a clear answer to the often heard complaint 'we would like to use public transport (the train) more often, but that pre- and post-train transport is too time consuming';
- green banking services, to appeal to a growing number of individuals that want to invest their (saved) money in a 'socially responsible' way.

In these cases the demands are expressed by segments of mass markets. In many other cases the influence may come from a single client, which is often the case in business services: for instance, a client may propose that a training firm back up its face-to-face sessions with computer-based aids.

Pattern 4   Innovation through Services

In this more complicated pattern, service firms influence the innovation process taking place within the client firm. The provider of intermediate services may provide knowledge resources that support the innovation process in various ways, such as:

- providing an expert project manager with the necessary skills to implement an innovation;
- providing an innovative tailor-made software package;
- providing training or written advice regarding product selection and implementation;
- an engineering consulting firm supporting an oil and gas company wanting to drill and explore in a 'protected' area by helping them to find new operational methods to meet the strict environment protection rules, by reviewing existing practice, proposing new operations, designing new methods and so on, eventually facilitating the innovation process at the client firm (see Hofman et al., 1998).

Pattern 5   Paradigmatic Innovations

When complex and pervasive innovations profoundly affecting all actors in a value chain are involved one might phrase these as paradigmatic innovations. When driven by fundamentally new technologies these can be labelled technological revolutions or new technology systems (Perez and Freeman, 1988). But they may also be driven by regulations, resource constraints, and other dramatic changes that require innovation to take place across many elements of the value chain, implying completely new infrastructures, new types of knowledge and adaptation on the part of intermediate and final users. For example:

- If in a very densely-populated area the regular transport of goods is no longer possible and the decision to switch to underground transport was taken, parties across the value chain would have to innovate and change practices. Manufacturers of transport equipment would have to provide completely new transport equipment; transport companies would have to change their service offerings, retrain their personnel, market their product in different ways; users would have to change their behaviour and use of transport facilities.
- Similarly, the switch from a few public TV channels towards multi-channel pay-per-view regimes require innovations and change of behaviour on many fronts.
- The large-scale introduction of multi-functional chipcards would be another example of a paradigmatic innovation.

After having in more general terms conceptualized services innovation as well as innovation patterns in which service (functions) may play different roles the focus in the remainder of this chapter will be on KIBS as co-producers of innovation. Subsequently the role of KIBS in innovation, the knowledge resource flows they are involved in and the development towards networked KIBS service professionals are dealt with.

5. KIBS AS CO-PRODUCERS OF INNOVATION

KIBS are an important category in at least two ways. First, they consist of service firms that are often highly innovative in their own right. Second, they play a facilitating role in innovation in other economic sectors, including both industrial and manufacturing sectors. In what is believed to be the first study in which the phrase KIBS was used Miles et al. (1995) defined KIBS industries as:

- private companies or organizations;
- relying heavily on professional knowledge, that is, knowledge or expertise related to a specific (technical) discipline or (technical) functional domain; and,
- supplying intermediate products and services that are knowledge-based.

They further concluded that the range of service industries that can be classified as KIBS is considerable. Many professional services for instance, whether technology-based or not, can be considered to be knowledge-intensive.

A closer analysis of how KIBS operate and contribute to innovation processes brings into focus the co-production of knowledge in which KIBS are involved. The production of services by KIBS is often the result of a joint effort of service provider and client. In this process of *co-production* the quality of the resulting service product largely depends on the nature of the interaction between the KIBS firm and the client firm as well as on the quality of the communication process that is involved. KIBS stand out in providing a point of fusion between more general scientific and technological information, dispersed in the economy, and the more local requirements and problems of client firms. KIBS can be said to function as catalysts who promote a fusion of generic and quasi-generic knowledge, and the more tacit knowledge located within the daily practices of the firms and sectors they service. One result of this interaction is that feedback from clients can shape innovations in service firms, just as much as service firms can influence their customers' innovation.[5] This two-way learning process is prominent where KIBS are concerned, including the category of wholesale and retail trade of machinery and equipment.[6] IT support services, management consultancy, and technical engineering, for example, when providing their services interact with their clients quite intensively and in many ways as we will see later in this chapter. Client firms and KIBS providers work together, to find solutions to problems and challenges. Through this interaction the client's knowledge base changes, while the KIBS provider also gains more experience, learning more about the characteristics of a specific industry. KIBS providers are thus enabled to refine and differentiate the services offered and methods used, to learn about new business opportunities, upgrade track records, and so on.

As innovation processes involve parties with various gaps in resources and in innovation management capabilities, intermediaries (including various KIBS) may be employed directly to fill these gaps, or less directly to help bridge them. Bessant and Rush (1998) discerned various types of bridging such as:

- Expert consulting, providing particular solutions to particular problems.
- Experience-sharing, transferring what is learned in one context to another.
- Brokering, putting different sources and users in contact across a wide range of services and resources.
- Diagnosis and problem-clarification, helping users articulate and define the particular needs in innovation. Many user firms lack the capability to understand or prioritize their problems into a strategic framework for action and outside agencies may be able to assist in this process.
- Benchmarking, where the process of identifying and focusing on 'good practice' can be established through an intermediary.
- Change agency, where organizational development can be undertaken with help from a neutral outside perspective.

Earlier on, and more specifically focusing on KIBS, a distinction was made between three roles played by KIBS in supporting innovation in client firms (Miles et al., 1995; Bilderbeek and den Hertog, 1997), namely:

1. *Facilitator*   A KIBS firm is a facilitator of innovations if it supports a client firm in its innovation process, but the innovation at hand does not originate from this KIBS firm, nor is it transferred (from other firms) by this KIBS firm to the client firm. A management consultant helping a client to introduce a new account management system or developing a new services distribution channel is an example. Another example would be a technical engineering firm seconding a team of its engineers to work with the technical engineers of the client to co-produce an innovative solution in, for example, offshore platform construction or subsoil building.

2. *Carrier*   A KIBS firm is a carrier of innovation if it plays a role in trans-
    ferring existing innovations from one firm or industry to the client firm or
    industry, even though the innovation in question does not originate from
    this particular KIBS firm. An IT firm implementing and customizing
    advanced and innovative ERP software (SAP, BAAN) in a client firm –
    but not developing these packages themselves – would be a typical exam-
    ple of this role. A technical engineer specializing in CAD/CAM applica-
    tions helping a major client (a shipyard) to specify the exact user needs
    and technical specifications of a new CAD/CAM programme, and subse-
    quently to implement it would be another illustration of this role.
3. *Source*   A KIBS firm is a source of innovation if it plays a major role in
    initiating and developing innovations in client firms, usually in close
    interaction with the client firm. Relevant examples here include an adver-
    tising agency developing and implementing a complete new Internet-
    based campaign for a client for the first time or a provider of innovative
    call centre solutions advising and actually installing a new call centre
    concept at a client.

6.   KNOWLEDGE FLOWS BETWEEN KIBS AND CLIENT FIRMS

This section focuses on the various types of knowledge flows that are relevant
to the process of co-production between KIBS and their clients.[7] Key to the
functioning of KIBS is that, in addition to discrete and tangible forms of
knowledge exchange, process-oriented and intangible forms of knowledge
flows are crucial in their relationship with client firms. In practice knowledge
flows between KIBS and their clients are manifold. Some examples are given
in Table 10.2. Sometimes these resources – solutions to a (perceived) problem
– are (in part) very concrete and tangible. This is the case, for example, when
the service product delivered is a software programme, written report, drawing or design, advertisement campaign, temporary expert, project plan, benchmark, or advice on a new organization structure. However, more often than not
the outcomes of the interaction between service provider and client firm are
much more complex and hard to pinpoint. More fuzzy outcomes or process-
oriented forms of knowledge exchange can be important by-products of the
more concrete resources just mentioned, since explicit knowledge is often
accompanied by tacit knowledge. In other cases knowledge resources are
developed and exchanged in the course of the cooperation between KIBS
provider and client firm. Examples of the more fuzzy results that this can
achieve are: improvement of a management team's internal communications
(they have been able to build knowledge of shared language, metaphors,

Table 10.2   Some examples of knowledge flows between service provider and client firms

Discrete/Tangible knowledge flows	Process-oriented/Intangible knowledge flows
• Written report • Project plan • Drawing/design • Advice • Computation • Diagnosis • Training • Benchmark • Project management • Software package • Advertisement campaign • Product documentation • Secondment of a temporary expert • Use of an R&D facility	• Routine problem-solving as part of everyday project work • Improved capability to collaborate in project teams • Instruction when installing new machinery • Articulation/specification of needs • Sparring partner (testing of ideas suggested by client firm) • Introduction to new networks of professionals/user groups • Information on performance competitors • Market information • Coupling to new partners • Knowledge on how to create support for innovations • Insight on how to access research and technology organizations, higher education institutes and government

visions, objectives), better understanding of potential markets, know-how for applying equipment/systems, improved negotiating capabilities for discussing plans and actions with partners, creation of R&D collaborations, building increased support (inside or outside the firm) for a solution to a problem, improved reputation, new personal contacts, introduction to expert network, knowledge institutions or policymakers.

In their landmark book, Nonaka and Takeuchi (1995)[8] provide a model of organizational knowledge creation and knowledge conversion modes that has become well known. In practice the functioning of KIBS and more in particular the KIBS-client interface are found to be much in line with this model. Some of the relevant insights include the following:

1. The observation that the more tacit forms of knowledge flows are at least as important as the explicit, codified forms of knowledge exchange. Various case studies of the relationships of KIBS to their clients (Bilderbeek et al., 1994; Miles et al., 1995) indicate that the more tacit forms of knowledge flows are at least as important as the explicit, codified forms of knowledge exchange.

2. The importance of interaction between individuals, team members and employees from various organizations in creating knowledge new to the firm. Studies of the functioning of, for example, engineering services (Hofman et al., 1998; Vlaar et al., 1997) provide many examples in which the knowledge base of the client firm is constantly enriched by confronting it with the knowledge base of the KIBS provider. This mainly involves personal interactions between professionals. In the client firm, professionals must be available who can maintain and enrich this dialogue.

3. The dynamic nature of knowledge conversion processes. The various forms of tacit and explicit knowledge are constantly mixed, redefined, linked, exchanged, reshaped and enriched in the course of interaction.[9] This is what typically happens where KIBS and their clients interact. KIBS can trigger and strengthen processes of knowledge conversion in clients (and vice versa). Often, when a client hires a KIBS, new project teams are set up, employees are forced to interact, to make tacit knowledge explicit, to think about new combinations of knowledge and their mental models are challenged. KIBS, in other words, contribute to firm-level learning processes. They can provide new knowledge, certainly, but they may also act as catalysts, which help internal communication and knowledge conversion.

Nowhere near all services provided by KIBS can be packaged in the form of a written report or a piece of software. Even when they can, it is quite common to find various forms of more direct interaction that are needed for actually implementing the service provided. The content and quality of the service as provided by a KIBS is to an important degree defined by the quality of this interface between KIBS and client firm: how well and how effectively do service professionals in the client firm and the service provider relate to each other?

Below a more structured view of the ways in which KIBS providers and client firms interact is offered. The four dimensions discerned earlier when introducing the four-dimensional model of service innovation (section 3) are related to four dichotomies of knowledge resource flows, namely:

1. discrete/tangible versus process-oriented/intangible knowledge;
2. human embodied versus non-human (capital, written information) embodied forms of knowledge resources;
3. explicit/codified knowledge versus tacit/non-codified knowledge;
4. contractual versus non-contractual forms of knowledge.

Dimension 1   Discrete/Tangible versus Process-Oriented/Intangible Knowledge Resource Flows

Intangible or process-oriented knowledge resource flows are as important as their more tangible or discrete equivalents. As just indicated, the two are often

Table 10.3 *Examples of tangible and intangible knowledge resource flows between service provider and client on the four dimensions of the services innovation model*

	Service concept	Client interface	Delivery system	Technolgoical options
Tangible knowledge flows	Campaign of an advertising company for positioning a new shop formula on the market	Report delivered by marketing bureau on market prospects for an electronic home shopping service	Marketing training for front office service employees	Installation of a new data-mining software programme
Intangible knowledge flows	Experience of hired expert on similar campaigns in the industry	Invitation to present the new service on an international marketing conference (new networks, new contacts)	Hired expert acts as a mirror, e.g. by confronting the client firm with the quality of the 'service encounter' as perceived by competitors	In-house software team brainstorms with hired expert on new business opportunities using the new software

co-produced. A KIBS provider that offers a software solution to a client firm will not only produce a knowledge flow in the form of a ready made software package. The software developers will learn about the firm in which it will be applied, establish a working relationship with the in-house experts, possibly advise, en passant, on other topics, introduce the client to a network of other users of similar software and so on. The software provider may use the client as a reference (helping to maintain his reputation) and, for example, fine tune the software package further. Table 10.3 outlines some discrete and some more process-oriented knowledge flows for each of the four dimensions of service innovation.

Dimension 2   Human Embodied Knowledge versus Non-Human (Capital, Written Information) Knowledge Resources

Another way of discriminating between various types of knowledge flows is by judging whether they are embodied in humans. Human embodied knowledge flows require face to face interaction between service provider and client firm. Disembodied knowledge flows are typically written down (a report, an action plan, an article in a magazine, an electronic database) or incorporated in a capital good or piece of equipment. Human embodied knowledge flows are generally thought of as relatively important in services in general. However, from the example (see Table 10.4) it can be gathered that written communication and technology do play an important role as well, most often in combination with human embodied knowledge flows.

Dimension 3   Explicit/Codified Knowledge versus Tacit/Non-Codified Knowledge

The Nonaka and Takeuchi model stresses the conversion processes in which tacit knowledge becomes explicit, recombined and is again internalized (in an enriched version). This is what actually happens at the interface between KIBS and client firms. However, discussions on economic transactions usually only bring explicit knowledge to mind. But while it is hard to put a price tag on exchange of tacit forms of knowledge (which are much harder to pinpoint), they are at least as important in the interaction between KIBS and their clients. Table 10.5 gives some examples, again differentiating between the four dimensions of service innovation.

Dimension 4   Contractual versus Non-Contractual Forms of Knowledge

A fourth and final way of differentiating between the various knowledge flows between KIBS and client firms is by differentiating between knowledge flows

Table 10.4 Human and non-human embodied knowledge flows between service provider and client: examples in terms of the four dimensions of the services innovation model

	Service concept	Client interface	Delivery system	Technological options
Human embodied knowledge flows	Ask a management guru in a face-to-face meeting to give a vision of electronic commerce-based service concepts	Organize a user panel with a firm's clients to test a prototype service	Employees of the client firm receive on-the-job training (by external experts) on dealing with customers	An instruction by a maintenance worker on how to handle the new copier
Non-human embodied knowledge flows	Reading a report on state of the art on service innovation strategies in service firms	Install a website to communicate with (potential) clients	An action plan by a management consultant for reorganizing the firm into well focused strategic business units	A CD-ROM containing an interactive demo of the e-commerce encounter

Table 10.5   Examples of explicit and tacit knowledge flows between service provider and client firm on the four dimensions of the services innovation model

	Service concept	Client interface	Delivery system	Technological options
Explicit/codified knowledge flows	Read a chapter on launching new service products in the latest service management book	Purchase a customer relations module from an ERP software company	Obtain the requirements for obtaining an ISO 9000 certificate for the service organization	Read the product documentation on how to handle the new colour photocopier
Tacit/non-codified knowledge flows	Two friends – one working for a insurance firm, the other in space research – discuss their weekly cafe visit financial constructions for financing satellites	Sharing the feeling between the external and internal inter-active designer of what 'feels' an appealing website design	Participate in a one-day seminar on data warehousing and discuss new opportunities with a software sales representative	Engineers of the contracted engineering firm and oil company share best practices during their two months at sea installing a new oil rig

Table 10.6 Examples of contractual and non-contractual knowledge flows between service provider and client firm on the four dimensions of the services innovation model

	Service concept	Client interface	Delivery system	Technological options
Contractual knowledge flows	Contract an external designer to design a new line of differently positioned products	Hire a marketing research firm to assess how many customers might switch to e-commerce.	Order consultancy firm to improve client friendliness of after sales service department	Contract an engineering firm to help procure a piece of machinery/hardware
Non-contractual knowledge flows	Discuss new business opportunities during a meeting of a professional association	A software bureau specialized in 'call centres' suggests contacting a specialized temporary work agency for pool management	A trainer discusses after the training with the management the situations he/she experienced with competitors	Experience as an expert the advantages of an electronic boardroom session and decide to use it in one of their own projects

which are mediated by contracts and those which are not (Table 10.6). Most often, contractual and non-contractual forms of knowledge exchange coincide, and especially when KIBS have a more or less steady relationship with a client the contractual knowledge flows are liable to be supplemented with more informal types of knowledge flows. This is not only the result of KIBS trying to link client firms, but also a matter of experts or professionals of both KIBS and client firm developing (trustful) relationships and gradually – as will be hypothesized in the following section – developing professional networks in which borders between different organizations are increasingly fuzzy.

7. A THREE-TIERED MODEL ON THE ROLE OF KIBS IN INNOVATION SYSTEMS

Within innovation systems KIBS can develop into a valuable asset. They can be perceived as a clearing house of knowledge where various types of knowledge are confronted, enriched and translated into practical solutions for client firms and vice versa. They might function as dissemination agents of best practice among their clients – carrying their professional knowledge and experience from client to client and, at the same time, feeding back problems encountered in their day-to-day practice to academic research or fellow KIBS. They do so typically by managing a wide network of contacts, but also through employees of KIBS who combine positions at, for example, universities and industry or simply via high human mobility rates. KIBS can be perceived as typical intermediaries or 'translators' that are deeply involved in various kinds of tangible and intangible knowledge flows that are so important in the knowledge-based economy. These roles played by KIBS have much in common with the roles of organizations within the public knowledge infrastructure such as research and technology organizations (RTOs) and higher education institutions (HEIs) which are increasingly urged – especially by policymakers – more actively to share their knowledge with and be more sensitive to the needs of industrial and non-industrial users. RTOs and HEIs also play a role in diffusing knowledge to the various firms and organizations they work with through contract research, educating students, and providing training to personnel of client firms.

It has been argued (den Hertog and Bilderbeek, 1997b, p. 31; den Hertog, 2000, pp. 518–23) that, given their role as co-producers of knowledge and innovation with client firms, KIBS develop into an informal (private) 'second knowledge infrastructure' or knowledge base partially complementing and partially taking over the intermediary role traditionally played by parts of the more institutionalized, formal (public) 'first knowledge infrastructure'. This of course is in stark contrast with the (traditional, but persistent) view of service firms as innovation followers.

However, this notion of the development of a 'second knowledge infrastructure' can be put into a more dynamic perspective by perceiving this as a transitory/temporary phase in a development where eventually the traditional distinction between public and private knowledge-based (advisory) services will disappear or become obsolete altogether. In this view the process of blurring of boundaries would then eventually result in a more flexible capacity of external KIBS professionals cooperating with internal KIBS professionals in providing knowledge-intensive business services. Ultimately not firms and institutions, but networked service professionals – irrespective of the formal organization to which they belong – would increasingly act as facilitators, carriers and sources of knowledge flows. This dynamic view on the role of KIBS in innovation systems has been summarized in a three-tiered model as given in Table 10.7. While the shift from phase 1 to phase 2 is relatively well substantiated, phase 3 is much more an extrapolation from a few apparent vanguard developments. For instance, networks are emerging in which professionals operate rather loosely between organizations, sometimes combining various assignments, and there seems to be increasing mobility of personnel between the various organizations in the (now broadly defined) knowledge infrastructure. Given these trends, and the gradual shift from the first phase to the second phase of KIBS development; it will be well to be prepared for developments toward the third phase.

At first sight this notion of a 'second knowledge infrastructure' might resemble the distinction made earlier between 'mode 1' and 'mode 2' knowledge production in science and technology – as provided by Gibbons et al. (1994). Their basic argument is that a distinctly new set of cognitive and social practices in the production, legitimization and diffusion of knowledge is emerging. This so-called 'mode 2' is different from those practices governing the largely Newtonian model of 'mode 1' or what many would label as science (pp. 2–3). The argument cannot easily be summarized in one table,[10] but Table 10.8 outlines some characteristics of the two modes of knowledge production.

KIBS can be seen as a specific example of the 'mode 2' variety of knowledge production. KIBS share many of the characteristics of the 'mode 2' way of producing knowledge, most notably its organizational diversity, orientation to applications, and transdisciplinarity. The characterization of 'mode 2' for example as 'problem solving capability on the move' (Gibbons et al., 1994, p. 5) very neatly describes what KIBS in practice are. However, the notion of KIBS as a 'second knowledge infrastructure' has a more institutional connotation indicating that a specific category of business services in a innovation systems perspective may serve as facilitators, carriers and sources of innovation. Seen from that perspective they can be looked upon as co-producers of innovation.

There is some evidence of a blurring of the boundaries between services

Table 10.7   Some characteristics of the individual phases in the three-tiered model

---

Phase 1: 'Embryonic' stage of KIBS development

- Limited interaction between the public and private knowledge base
- Limited number of intermediary knowledge institutions (mainly public) and firms
- Emphasis in innovation processes on generating new knowledge
- Predecessors of KIBS functions mainly coupled to well-established categories of professional staff (R&D, accounting, marketing, legal affairs, etc.) and to a substantial degree provided within the firm
- Knowledge mainly interpreted as formal technical expertise (R&D)
- Sectoral knowledge orientation dominates
- Innovation policies mainly focused on supporting R&D/increasing knowledge bases

Phase 2: 'KIBS as second knowledge infrastructure'

- Interaction between public and private knowledge bases increasingly considered essential ('economies of scope in S&T')
- Increasing number of intermediary knowledge institutions and firms
- Emphasis in (interactive) innovation processes on generating new knowledge and diffusion
- KIBS increasingly identified as a separate category of knowledge generators/diffusers, although a clear separation between public and private KIBS remains
- Explicit 'make or buy' decision concerning provision of KIBS functions
- Broadened definition of knowledge, various kinds of formal knowledge and tacit knowledge (intangibles)
- Knowledge orientation crosses sectoral boundaries. Network and cluster perspective starts to develop.
- Broadening of innovation policies (more aspects, more actors)

Phase 3: 'Networked "KIBS" service professionals'

- Increasingly non-separable and overlapping public and private knowledge bases
- KIBS recognized as significant intermediate actors in innovation processes in public and private sectors
- Increasing combination of innovative service functions in new products and services.
- Normalization of innovation in service functions.
- Public and private organizations and firms develop knowledge management systems and seek actively the help of KIBS
- Well developed user–producer linkages between internal and external KIBS professionals
- KIBS professionals increasingly combine various roles (enterpreneur, scientist, consultant, staff member) and function in a network of service professionals
- Tasks traditionally performed by public policymakers increasingly performed by semi-public (at arms length) or private KIBS professionals

---

Sources: den Hertog and Bilderbeek, 1997b; den Hertog, 2000, p. 522.

Table 10.8   Some characteristics of 'mode 1' and 'mode 2' knowledge production

'Mode 1'	'Mode 2'
Problems set and solved in a context governed by the (academic) interests of a specific community	Knowledge produced in the context of application
Disciplinary	Transdisciplinary
Homogeneity	Heterogeneity
Hierarchical organization	Organizational diversity
More socially accountable and reflexive	More socially accountable and reflexive
Quality determined mainly through peer review judgements on a disciplinary basis	More composite, multidimensional quality control process

Source: Gibbons et al. (1994, pp. 3–8).

offered by the public knowledge infrastructure and KIBS services. However, the two infrastructures generally still play different roles within innovation systems. Universities primarily have relations with large R&D intensive manufacturing firms and (in the case of social and administrative knowledge) the public sector. KIBS firms have a much broader spectrum of clients, including public authorities, larger service firms and some smaller firms. Large firms benefit disproportionately from both types of knowledge infrastructures, whereas SMEs (small and medium-sized enterprises) with their relatively low levels of internal competence, and limited financial resources, often lack capabilities for making effective use of KIBS, and typically rely on public or semi-public sources for external knowledge.

8.   THE ROLE OF KIBS AS CO-PRODUCERS IN INNOVATION SYSTEMS: A RESEARCH AGENDA

From the preceding sections it has become clear that service innovation involves various non-technological dimensions that cannot be ignored any longer if we are to understand and measure service innovation properly. Further, a typology of five innovation patterns was presented illustrating that services cannot be simply set aside with regard to their role in innovation processes as mainly 'supplier-dominated'. Subsequently the notion that at least some KIBS act as co-producers of innovation in interaction with their client firms in some innovation systems was put forward. Some illustrations as to how KIBS are interacting with their client firms to co-produce innovation were provided. It was also shown that this basically two-way knowledge exchange involves a great number of tangible and intangible knowledge flows. Finally it was hypothesized that KIBS might act as a second knowledge infrastructure next to the formal and institutionalized first knowledge infrastructure. In a more dynamic perspective this might even be perceived as a temporary phase before public and private knowledge bases start intermingling further into networks of KIBS service professionals that together help innovate service functions in service and manufacturing firms as well as non-profit organizations.

It is obvious that many questions as to the exact functioning of KIBS in innovation systems remain unanswered. Do industries differ, for example, in their actual 'consumption' of KIBS, and if so how? Which are the vanguard KIBS industries; and which KIBS industries are most likely to follow a similar development pattern in the near future? How do in-house and outsourcing strategies, both in KIBS and client firms, affect the scope for co-production of innovation? What type of appropriability strategies do KIBS use themselves and how do KIBS firms take stock of the lessons learned in the interaction with client firms? Particular attention is also needed for cross-country – or should we say cross-innovation systems – differences in terms of institutional set up and the degree to which KIBS and their client firms are integrated.

Additionally, some more policy-related research questions pop up. KIBS play a role in transferring knowledge in innovation systems and this might have consequences for the way in which innovation policy is shaped as well. Given indications that (some) service industries are particularly prone to use the services of KIBS, innovation policymakers might consider the scope for using KIBS for realizing their policy goals. This is especially so as 'traditional' institutions within the public knowledge infrastructure seem less able to function in the service economy, and seem thus far to be more geared towards servicing established manufacturing industries. Are KIBS for example better suited than traditional research organizations to co-produce innovation in services? How accessible are the services offered by KIBS for SMEs and how country-specific are these patterns? Other policy-related research issues that seem worth exploring include the complementarity or competition between KIBS and more traditional or at least more established bridging institutions. How do other bridging institutions – such as applied research organizations, government research labs, transfer agencies and universities – cope with the rise of KIBS? To what extent can KIBS be used to perform knowledge transfer and innovation support programmes for government? And how can this be done?

Paying attention to these and other challenging research themes related to service innovation will hopefully fuel further the debate and do justice to the role of services, and particularly KIBS, in innovation.

NOTES

1. A helpful extension of the well-known Pavitt taxonomy is provided by Soete and Miozzo (1989). They differentiate between supplier-dominated, scale-intensive physical networks and information networks and specialized/science-based services. However, this taxonomy is largely a technology-based (and sectoral) taxonomy.
2. Although most examples provided below are taken from service industries, service innovation is equally relevant for manufacturing industries.
3. This is to be considered a mapping device: quite possibly more patterns can be found.
4. Many more variations on these innovation patterns can be found in practice, for example when a particular service function is taken as a point of departure. Two such examples are provided in den Hertog (2000, p. 504).
5. 'Interactive learning' and 'user-producer linkages' (see for example Lundvall, 1988 and 1992) are important notions for the study of service (mediated) innovation.
6. These to an increasing degree are providing services 'surrounding' the hardware, which is often as important as the hardware itself for implementing especially complex systems and machinery.
7. A first quantitative assessment of the development of IT services, business consultancy and engineering services, their role in knowledge transfer and their use by industry is included in den Hertog (2000, pp. 516–19).
8. In den Hertog (2000) the Nonaka and Takeuchi model of knowledge creation and how it relates to the knowledge flows in which KIBS are involved in is dealt with more extensively.
9. KIBS – especially management consultancies – are often (and sometimes justly) criticized for reselling the client's own knowledge back to the client. However, the process of conversion and reconversion of knowledge may not be entirely fruitless! The sheer act of interacting with the KIBS can help processes such as socialization, externalization and combination. The interaction between clients and KIBS can establish a field in which knowledge resources are exchanged and dialogue established between various functions/experts (for example, creating multidisciplinary project teams). This can allow for combining existing pieces of knowledge already present inside and outside the company. And the tacit tricks of the trade can be interchanged just through the process of performing tasks together (for example, when in-house software developers are working together in project teams with external IT consultants).
10. Their wide-ranging analysis covers interaction between those involved in 'mode 1' and 'mode 2' knowledge production and the role of IT in this; the expansion of both knowledge providers and knowledge users; the implications for 'traditional' knowledge generating institutions such as universities, government research organizations and industrial laboratories, and the shaping of innovation policy.

BIBLIOGRAPHY

Barras, R. (1986), 'Towards a Theory of Innovation in Services', *Research Policy*, 15, 161–73.

Barras, R. (1990), 'Interactive Innovation in Financial and Business Services: The Vanguard of the Service Revolution', *Research Policy*, 19, 215–37.

Bessant, J. and H. Rush (1995), 'Building Bridges for Innovation: The Role of Consultants in Technology Transfer', *Research Policy*, 24, 97–114.

Bessant, J. and H. Rush (1998), 'Innovation Agents and Technology Transfer', report prepared for the TSER-SI4S project, Brighton, CENTRIM/Brighton University.

Bilderbeek, R.H. and P. den Hertog (1992), 'Innovatie in diensten. Position paper', Apeldoorn, TNO Centre for Technology and Policy Studies.

Bilderbeek, R. and P. den Hertog (1996), 'Innovation in Knowledge-Intensive Business Services. Lessons from Case Studies', paper presented at the SI4S Roskilde seminar on Innovation in Business services, Roskilde University.

Bilderbeek, Rob and Pim den Hertog (1997), 'The Interactiveness and Innovative Role of Technology-Based Knowledge-Intensive Business Services (T-KIBS)', TSER-SI4S-project, TNO-SI4S report no. 3, Apeldoorn, TNO Strategy, Technology and Policy.

Bilderbeek, Rob and Pim den Hertog (1998), 'Technology-Based Knowledge-Intensive Business Services in The Netherlands: Their Significance as a Driving Force behind Knowledge-Driven Innovation', *Vierteljahrshefte zur Wirtschaftsforschung*, **67** (2), 126–38.

Bilderbeek, Rob, Pim den Hertog and Nabila Chehab (1998a), 'Management van vernieuwing in diensten. Verslag van een workshop voor ondernemers op 22 april 1998', Utrecht/Apeldoorn, Dialogic/TNO Strategy Technology and Policy.

Bilderbeek, Rob, Pim den Hertog and Nabila Chehab (1998b), 'Innovation and Services, Report of an Expert Workshop for the Dutch Ministry of Economic Affairs', Utrecht/Apeldoorn, Dialogic/TNO Strategy Technology and Policy.

Bilderbeek, R.H., P. den Hertog, W. Huntink, M. Bouman, N. Kastrinos and K. Flanagan (1994), 'Case Studies in Innovative and Knowledge-Intensive Business Services', Apeldoorn, TNO Centre for Technology and Policy Studies.

CBS (2000), *Kennis en Economie 2000* (Voorburg/Heerlen: Centraal Bureau voor de Statistiek).

Gadrey, J., F. Gallouj and O. Weinstein (1995), 'New Modes of Innovation. How Services Benefit Industry', *International Journal of Service Industry Management*, **6** (3), 4–16.

Gallouj, F. and O. Weinstein (1997), 'Innovation in Services', *Research Policy*, 26, 537–56.

Gibbons, M., C. Limoges, H. Nowotny, S. Schwartzman, P. Scott and M. Trow (1994), *The New Production of Knowledge. The Dynamics of Science and Research in Contemporary Societies* (London: Sage Publications).

Hales, M. (1997a), 'Producer Services and Manufacturing Production', report for the OECD STI Group, Brighton, CENTRIM/University of Brighton.

Hales, M. (1997b), 'Make or Buy in the Production of Innovations – Competences, Fullness of Service and the Architecture of Supply in Consultancy', contribution to the SI4S project, Brighton, CENTRIM/University of Brighton.

Henderson, R.M. and Clark, K.B. (1990), 'Architectural Innovation: The Reconfiguring of Existing Product Technologies and the Failure of Established Firms', *Administrative Science Quarterly*, **35** (1), 9–30.

Hertog, P. den (2000), 'Knowledge-Intensive Business Services as Co-Producers of Innovation', *International Journal of Innovation Management*, **4** (4), 491–528.

Hertog, P. den and R. Bilderbeek (1997a), 'Recent Innovation Patterns in Services in The Netherlands', TNO-SI4S report no. 1, Apeldoorn, TNO Strategy, Technology and Policy.

Hertog, P. den and R. Bilderbeek (1997b), 'The New Knowledge Infrastructure: The Role of Knowledge-Intensive Business Services in National Innovation Systems', report prepared within the framework of the SI4S-project and reprinted in Mark

Boden and Ian Miles (eds) (2000), *Services, Innovation and the Knowledge-Based Economy* (London and New York: Continuum), pp. 222–46.

Hertog, P. den and R. Bilderbeek (1999), 'Conceptualising Service Innovation and Service Innovation Patterns', paper phase 1 for the Research Programme on Innovation in Services (SIID) commissioned for the Ministry of Economic Affairs, Utrecht, Dialogic.

Hertog, P. den, R. Bilderbeek and S. Maltha (1997), 'Intangibles, the Soft Side of Innovation', *Futures*, **29** (1), 33–45.

Hertog, P. den, Rob Bilderbeek, Goran Marklund and Ian Miles (1998), 'Services in Innovation: Knowledge-Intensive Business Services (KIBS) as Co-Producers of Innovation', SI4S synthesis paper no. 3, published by STEP, Oslo.

Hertog, P. den and E. Brouwer (2000), 'Innovation Indicators for the Retailing Industry: A Meso Perspective', paper phase 1 for the Research Programme on Innovation in Services (SIID) commissioned by the Ministry of Economic Affairs, Utrecht, Dialogic.

Hofman, Y., P. den Hertog and Rob Bilderbeek (1998), 'The Intermediary Role of Engineering Firms in Innovation Processes in Offshore Industry. TSER-SI4S-project, TNO-SI4S report no. 5, Apeldoorn, TNO Strategy, Technology and Policy.

Kline, S.J. and N. Rosenberg (1986), 'An Overview of Innovation', in R. Landau and N. Rosenberg (eds), *The Positive Sum Strategy: Harnessing Technology for Economic Growth* (Washington DC: National Academy Press), pp. 275–305.

Lundvall, B.A. (1988), 'Innovation as an Interactive Process: From User–Producer Interaction to the National System of Innovation', in G. Dosi, C. Freeman, R. Nelson, G. Silverberg and L. Soete (eds), *Technical Change and Economic Theory* (London: Pinter Publishers).

Lundvall, B.A. (ed.) (1992), *National Systems of Innovation: Towards a Theory of Innovation and Interactive Learning* (London: Pinter Publishers).

Miles, I (1993), 'Services in the New Industrial Economy', *Futures*, **25**(6), 653–72.

Miles, I. (1998), 'Environmental Services and European Regulations', paper presented at the Europeanisation and the Regulation of Risk SPSG Conference at London School of Economics, 27 March.

Miles, I., N. Kastrinos, R. Bilderbeek, P. den Hertog with K. Flanagan and W. Huntink (1995), 'Knowledge-Intensive Business Services: Their Role as Users, Carriers and Sources of Innovation', Luxembourg, report to the EC DG XIII Sprint EIMS Programme.

Nonaka, I. and H. Takeuchi (1995), *The Knowledge-Creating Company. How Japanese Companies Create the Dynamics of Innovation* (Oxford and New York: Oxford University Press).

Normann, R. (1991), *Service Management. Strategy and Leadership in Service Business* (2nd edition) (London: John Wiley).

OECD (1998), *Science, Technology and Industry Outlook 1998* (Paris: OECD).

Pavitt, K. (1984), 'Sectoral Patterns of Technical Change: Towards a Taxonomy and a Theory', *Research Policy*, 13, 343–73.

Perez, C. and C. Freeman (1988), 'Structural Crisis of Adjustment: Business Cycles and Investment Behaviour', in G. Dosi, C. Freeman, R. Nelson, G. Silverberg and L. Soete (eds) *Technical Change and Economic Theory* (London: Pinter Publishers).

Quinn, J.B. (1992), *Intelligent Enterprise: A Knowledge and Service Based Paradigm for Industry* (New York: Free Press).

Soete, L. and M. Miozzo (1989), 'Trade and Development in Services: A Technological Perspective', Maastricht, MERIT 89–031.

Vlaar, L. and M. Bouman with the cooperation of P. den Hertog and R.H. Bilderbeek (1997), 'The Role of Technology-Based Knowledge-Intensive Business Services in the Dutch Environmental Production and Service Cluster (EPSC). A Study in the Subclusters Water and Waste', report prepared within the framework of the SI4S-project, Apeldoorn, TNO Centre for Technology and Policy Studies.

Windrum, P. and M. Tomlinson (1999), 'Knowledge-Intensive Services and International Competitiveness: A Four Country Comparison', *Technology Analysis and Strategic Management*, **11**(3), 391–408.

11. Knowledge-intensive business services: processing knowledge and producing innovation

Faïz Gallouj

INTRODUCTION

Services constitute a challenge to economic theory, both conceptually and methodologically. It is not always easy, indeed, to define the outputs of service activities. They are often indissociable from the process by which they are produced and have to be considered within different time frames: that in which the service itself is produced and that in which the effect of the service makes itself felt. As a result, it is difficult to define innovation, evaluate performance and analyse markets.[1]

In knowledge-intensive business services (KIBS), that is research, consultancy and engineering business services, these difficulties are compounded by those associated with another problematic area of economic theory, namely that of knowledge. Knowledge is also a concept that has multiple meanings, and one that poses important theoretical and methodological problems. Nor is it always clear where the boundary lies between knowledge and other notions such as data, information, competences, capabilities and so on.

One of the fundamental characteristics of what is called 'the knowledge-based economy' is the spectacular growth in economic transactions relating to knowledge itself (Maskell and Malmberg, 1999; Antonelli, 1999). KIBS firms are organizations that are particularly representative of this economy, since knowledge constitutes both their main input and output. These firms are both processors and producers of knowledge. The aim of this chapter is to examine the modes of knowledge processing and production used in such firms and their implications for the question of innovation produced *in* and *through the use of* KIBS. These two aspects of innovation in KIBS are not independent of each other: the first denotes the processes of innovation within KIBS firms, while the second relates to the contribution of KIBS providers to innovation in their client organizations.

This chapter is divided into three parts. The first is given over to a summary of the economic debate on the nature of knowledge and on the distinction between information, knowledge and competences. In Section 2, we examine the basic mechanisms of knowledge processing and production, firstly within the general framework of learning cycles or spirals (Noteboom, 1999; Nonaka, 1994; Nonaka and Takeuchi, 1995) and then more specifically in the context of KIBS transactions. In Section 3, we seek to mark out the boundary and establish the nature of the links between these modes of knowledge processing and innovation in and through the use of KIBS.

1.   DIFFERING CONCEPTIONS OF INFORMATION AND KNOWLEDGE

Knowledge, like services, continues to be a vague concept, despite the efforts of economic theorists to clarify matters. The boundaries between the notions of (1) data, (2) information, (3) knowledge, (4) competences and (5) capabilities are not always clearly delineated. Nevertheless, there is widespread agreement on at least two points.

1.   The semantic content (that is the extent to which context is taken into account) is generally considered to increase in the course of a move from category (1) to category (3). Thus a given category cannot be reduced to the mere summation of elements from the preceding category. For example, knowledge cannot be reduced to the sum of a sequence of discrete items of information, since different individuals can extract different knowledge from the same information and any one individual can, in different circumstances, extract new knowledge from that same information. Within a bounded rationality framework, the phenomena of 'interpretative ambiguity' (Fransman, 1994) and 'causal ambiguity' (Lippman and Rumelt, 1982) can be called on to interpret these distortions.

2.   The notions of competence and capability (often regarded as synonyms) open up a breach in the sequence of increasing semantic content, since they reflect an 'aptitude for performing (successfully) with confidence . . .'[2] (Nelson, 1994) that is based on data, information and knowledge. In other words, competences do indeed have a cognitive element but they also reflect other aptitudes such as manual dexterity and sensory capacities (Senker, 1995).

All these analytical categories apply to the service providers that are the object of analysis in this paper. Indeed, they can be defined as organizations that mobilize a certain number of competences in order to process data, information and knowledge that can be used to produce the data, information and knowledge that crystallize in various ways in what is termed a solution (to a problem).

Starting from the hypothesis that what ultimately concerns the client firm is the (direct or indirect[3]) acquisition of *meaning* in the hope of shedding light on changing internal and external environments,[4] we can say that it is *knowledge* (the category with the greatest semantic content) that lies at the heart of the activities of KIBS providers. The service provider's *competence* can be defined as an aptitude for *processing* that knowledge in different ways. The various forms this competence takes, with which this chapter is chiefly concerned and which are examined in Section 2, are closely linked to the particular characteristics of knowledge as a commodity. These characteristics can be considered from three different points of view: the object of the knowledge, its nature and its economic properties.

1.1   The Object of Knowledge

The object of knowledge may be an understanding of the physical and natural world or of the economic and social world. Thus this first point of view denotes the distinction between (1) scientific and technical knowledge (in the strict sense of the term), which describes the laws governing the functioning of the physical and natural world and which is the product of research, and (2) economic and social knowledge which, from the perspective of firms and organizations, relates to the states of the internal and external economic and social environments (including the technological environments). In reality, there is no reason why the first category (scientific and technical knowledge) should not also include knowledge relating to the principles governing the economic and social world when they too are the result of research activity (in economics, law, sociology or psychology).

Paradoxically, and with few exceptions (notably Hayek, 1945), economic theories of information and knowledge, whether in traditional economics (Arrow, 1962) or in the new economics of science (Dasgupta and David, 1994), focus essentially on the first category (in its strict sense). Thus Machlup (1984) himself identifies three types of knowledge: (1) technological knowledge, (2) useful non-technological knowledge and (3) 'dispersed' knowledge, that is information on unique and ephemeral events in economic life. However, as Ribault (1991) notes, he concerns himself essentially only with the first category, namely with scientific and technical knowledge.

The provision of KIBS can encompass the whole range of functions that constitute a firm's activity. Consequently, a KIBS provider may be required to assume responsibility for the dynamic of different environments: economic, legal, social, scientific and technological, and so on. Thus in any analysis of the activity of KIBS firms, account has to be taken of all existing types of knowledge and not simply of scientific and technical knowledge.

1.2 The Nature of Knowledge

The question of the nature of knowledge can be examined at various levels. Firstly, it should be noted that, like the notion of service itself, the term knowledge denotes both a process and an outcome. The various forms of knowledge also differ in the extent of their sphere of application. Thus there are general and specific forms of knowledge. Another distinction is made between declarative, procedural and causal knowledge in order to denote, respectively, the content, modalities and explanations of a given event (Cohen and Bacdayan, 1996). These three categories constitute a subset of the typology developed by Lundvall and Johnson (1994), in which four forms of knowledge are identified: *know-what*, *know-how*, *know-why* and *know-who*.

However, the most widely used distinction is the one frequently associated with Polanyi (1983), which contrasts tacit knowledge (sometimes known as implicit or embodied knowledge) with codified knowledge. Tacit knowledge is subjective and difficult to articulate and codify, that is to express in the form of language or written symbols. For Polanyi, it reflects the fact that individuals know more than they are capable of expressing. In reality, the tacit nature of knowledge can be considered not only at the level of the individual but also at that of the group or organization. More generally, it can be said that knowledge can be embodied in various media: individuals, organizations (in the form of procedures or routines) or technical systems. Conversely, codified knowledge can readily be expressed in the form of signs and verbal or written symbols.

As we shall see, the importance of this distinction lies in the differences between the various regimes of appropriation and in the ease with which knowledge can be transferred. Codified knowledge is easy to transfer and difficult to appropriate. Tacit knowledge can be transferred, but the process is slower and considerably more costly and the regime of appropriation higher. As Winter (1987) stresses, the ease with which knowledge can be transferred increases in line with other criteria: the opportunity to observe the knowledge in use, its simplicity and its relative autonomy (as opposed to its integration into a system). Moreover, the extent to which knowledge is codified may not be an accurate indicator of the ease with which it can be transferred. Indeed, the degree of codification may well be a reflection not of any intrinsic technical characteristic of the knowledge but rather of a transitory state that is likely to change in accordance with technical, intellectual or social conditions. Thus in order accurately to assess the ease of transfer, we have to focus on the following three continuums: tacit-articulable, teachable-not teachable and inarticulated-articulated, since even tacit knowledge can be more or less teachable (and therefore transferable) and articulable knowledge may or may not be articulated depending on the strategy or circumstances.

1.3   The Economic Properties of Knowledge

In the traditional economic literature, there is a general belief, derived in particular from the works of Arrow (1962), that knowledge (regarded as comparable to technological information) has two properties that distinguish it from traditional tangible goods but make it similar to public goods.[5]

1. Knowledge is a good whose exclusivity is difficult to maintain: it is a 'non-excludable' good. Despite firms' efforts to contain it, knowledge has a propensity to escape into the external environment, there to disperse itself through a variety of channels to the benefit (at no extra cost) of other economic agents. Thus the processing and production of knowledge give rise to positive externalities (spillover) that are difficult to control.
2. Knowledge is a good that is not exhausted in use. Each individual can consume knowledge without reducing others' consumption of it, however numerous those others may be. In order to consume such knowledge, economic agents do not enter into rivalry or competition with each other. Thus it is a non-rival good. The marginal cost of its consumption by an (additional) consumer is close to zero.

Taken in conjunction with each other, these two characteristics of the use of knowledge (non-excludability and non-rivalry) have certain economic consequences:

*   knowledge cannot be appropriated by its producer (or only at excessively high cost);
*   it can be transferred easily and at low cost between individuals and across time and space;
*   the sale of knowledge poses a difficult problem, since no such sale can take place without disclosure but disclosure renders the sale null and void.

This concept of knowledge is not without value for those seeking to understand knowledge-intensive business services. Some of the transactions involved do indeed relate to information that was either codified initially or became codified as a result of the service provider's intervention. However, this concept does not adequately describe the full diversity of forms taken by KIBS transactions.

The recently developed neo-Schumpeterian approach marks a break with this concept of knowledge as information and as a public good. It alters the economic characteristics of knowledge by attributing a significant role to tacit knowledge and to the nature of the relationships between tacit and codified knowledge and by emphasizing the cumulative and specific nature of knowledge. Tacit (or embodied) knowledge is considered, on the one hand, as a rival good and, on the other hand, as an excludable good, that is, one that is easily appropriated. In other words, such knowledge is a genuine private good. Whether tacit or codified, knowledge depends on context and introduces irreversibilities into learning processes. Thus knowledge can be stored, accumulated and capitalized, and the competitive advantage of external KIBS providers over internal specialists can be said to lie less in the reduction of transaction costs than in quantitative and qualitative differences and complementarities relating to knowledge, what Noteboom (1992) calls external economies of cognitive scope.

2. DIFFERENT BASIC MECHANISMS FOR PRODUCING AND PROCESSING KNOWLEDGE

Since the activity of KIBS providers can be said to consist of the production of knowledge from knowledge, their competences can be said to reside in their aptitude for processing and producing knowledge on behalf of a client. Thus any attempt to investigate the competences of KIBS providers must seek to clarify the content of the general terms processing and producing. Although they are not directly concerned with KIBS, the economics and organization science literatures contain some interesting studies of basic knowledge-processing mechanisms that might shed some light on our analysis of the competences of KIBS providers. However, the competences mobilized within a KIBS relationship cannot be considered independently of the mechanisms located within the 'black box' of knowledge-intensive business services (and particularly those related to the accumulation of knowledge).

2.1 The Basic Knowledge-Processing Mechanisms

Although the literature contains many studies of knowledge processing, there have been few attempts to focus in a precise and articulated way on the basic procedures by which knowledge is processed. We outline below two of the exceptions to this general rule (Noteboom, 1999; Nonaka, 1994; see also Nonaka and Takeuchi, 1995).

1. *Noteboom* (1999) sets out to investigate the way in which firms attempt to reconcile continuity and change or, in other words, incremental and radical

innovation or even uncertainty and risk. The problem here is one of *abduction*,[6] in the sense of the term defined by Peirce (1957) as he sought to understand the mechanisms that facilitate the transition from one practice to another. Drawing his inspiration from the works of Piaget (1970) on individual cognition, Noteboom (1999 p. 132) describes five (heuristic) principles of abduction which, taken in succession, constitute a learning cycle.

(i)   *Generalization*   This first principle of abduction describes the application of a tried and tested practice to new but adjoining contexts. While it satisfies the demands of current production, this principle also reveals the limits of generalization and triggers the following principle.

(ii)   *Differentiation*   This denotes the adaptation to the local context of practices whose limits have been revealed by generalization. Differentiation represents an attempt to circumvent these limits. Once again, it allows current production to continue while at the same time introducing new adaptations in accordance with another principle of abduction, namely reciprocation.

(iii) *Reciprocation*   This is the principle whereby, in any given context, different but parallel practices are compared with a view to exchanging the most effective elements in those practices. Thus metaphor and analogy are principles of reciprocation.

(iv)   *Accommodation (or combination)*   Repeated implementation of the principles of differentiation and reciprocation may weaken the practice in question and impact adversely on its efficiency and effectiveness. The opportunities for standardization and realizing economies of scale gradually decline and the practice becomes more complex, losing its coherence as it is adapted and augmented. Once a certain stage has been reached, a more fundamental restructuring becomes necessary. This restructuring consists of establishing a new practice by combining elements derived from different practices. This principle of accommodation or combination leads to the creation of novelty in an indeterminate form.

(v)   *Consolidation*   This principle involved the transformation of an indeterminate novelty into a 'dominant design', in the sense of the term used by Abernathy and Utterback (1978). Once this dominant design has been established, a new learning cycle (initiated by the generalization principle) can get under way.

The learning cycle outlined above gives rise to several comments.

• It applies not only to individuals but also to organizations, industries and even countries.

- It has to be considered as a heuristic procedure and not as a logical sequence. Some principles may be superimposed on each other, others may be absent, and so on.
- It links the principles of continuity, exploitation and equilibrium, or first-order learning (consolidation and generalization), with those of exploration and disequilibrium, or second-order learning (differentiation, reciprocation and accommodation).

2.   The studies by *Nonaka* (1994) and *Nonaka and Takeuchi* (1995) also offer a potentially very fruitful perspective on the modes of knowledge processing. Although they too are interested in the emergence of innovation, these authors put the emphasis not on the diversity of the principles of abduction but rather on the variety of 'social interactions between tacit and explicit knowledge'. These social interactions, which constitute different modes of knowledge conversion or transfer, fall into one of four categories.

(i)   *Socialization*   This mode of conversion denotes social interactions in which tacit knowledge is exchanged. Socialization is based on and contributes to the construction of a knowledge base that is shared by the group or organization in question. It is closely linked to the notion of experience, in the sense that tacit knowledge is acquired through experience.

(ii)   *Externalization*   This denotes the conversion of tacit knowledge into codified knowledge. This form of knowledge processing, which goes hand in hand with a certain loss of meaning, may take the form of metaphors, analogies, concepts, hypotheses or models.

(iii) *Combination*   This is a mode of knowledge conversion in which explicit knowledge is combined with more explicit knowledge and fed into the common base of explicit knowledge. The process of combination is facilitated by the use of various media: written documents, communications networks, and so on.

(iv)   *Internalization*   This denotes the transformation of explicit knowledge into tacit knowledge. Internalization is often synonymous with learning by doing (imitation, experience).

These four modes of knowledge conversion (socialization, externalization, combination and internalization) are not independent of each other. Sequenced as above, they constitute a learning spiral.

The studies outlined here deal with the question of knowledge processing from two different but complementary angles. The first puts the emphasis primarily on the principles of abduction. A distinction is made between exploration and exploitation mechanisms (in the sense attributed to the terms by

March, 1991), depending on how far the mode of knowledge processing in question leads the individual or organization away from the initial cognitive state. The second stresses the epistemological dimension of knowledge, that is its tacit or explicit nature.

These studies express the view that the learning cycle or spiral can be considered at various levels of analysis (the individual, the group, the organization, and so on) or that analysis of it has to be conducted at several different levels. We are concerned here with one particular situation, namely service transactions involving a client and a KIBS provider. Our purpose, therefore, is to examine the modes of knowledge processing deployed in this particular situation.

2.2   The Competences of KIBS Providers

Drawing on the definition of services proposed by Gadrey (2000), we can say that the activity of KIBS providers consists of *placing at the disposition of clients capabilities for processing information and knowledge*. These capabilities are what we call the *competences* of KIBS providers. Our aim here is to highlight the various forms that these competences take. In so doing, we will draw on the studies examined above while at the same time seeking to remain close to the actual forms of knowledge processing deployed by KIBS providers.

A KIBS transaction can be said to bring three elements into play (Figure 11.1):

1.   the source (S) of the input knowledge;
2.   the receiver (R) of the output knowledge;
3.   the processor (P) of the input knowledge and the (co)-producer of the output knowledge.

This representation in Figure 11.1 is an extremely simplistic one. It covers a number of more complex configurations.

Thus the receiver of the knowledge (R) may denote the individual client, a group within the organization or the client organization as a whole. The service provider itself is also a receiver, to the extent that it seeks to store the knowledge that emerges from each new transaction in its organizational memory in order to use it later as input knowledge (compare section 2.3).

The source of the knowledge (S) is also a heterogeneous category encompassing (a) the client itself (that is the receiver in the various senses of the term), (b) the client's external environment and (c) the processor, considered as a database of knowledge accumulated in the course of repeated KIBS transactions. While it is possible that just one of these components may be brought into play in a KIBS transaction, it is more usual for them all to be mobilized.

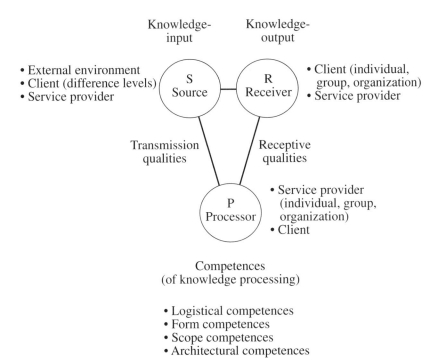

Figure 11.1   The KIBS transaction as a form of knowledge processing

The processor (P) is the service provider, which may also be regarded as an individual, a project group or an organization. The client itself is a knowledge processor, particularly when the service is co-produced and not simply subcontracted.

Some of the components of a KIBS transaction (S, R, P) may merge with each other. In this case, they indicate the existence of reflexive relationships: for example, an individual or a group may be both the source and the receiver of knowledge. Usually, however, their very heterogeneity means that these various components bring different sub-units into contact with each other. For example, it is commonly the case in large firms that the source of knowledge is different from the receiver. In particular, as Cohendet et al. (1999) stress, the problem facing large international firms today is how to ensure that (localized) knowledge circulates internally between different sites.

The main activity of the service provider as a processor of knowledge is to transfer, as effectively and efficiently as possible, the knowledge crystallized in a solution from a source to a receiver. The term transfer denotes both a physical movement and the economic circulation of a good (with all the difficulties of transferring ownership inherent in this particular commodity). The forms taken by this transfer equate to the interventions of the KIBS provider in the various aspects of the knowledge in question (Table 11.1): its (physical) circulation, its form, its scope and its structure. However, the quality of the various basic transfer mechanisms also depends on certain characteristics of the source and the receiver.

Table 11.1   The competences of KIBS providers (modes of knowledge processing)

KIBS provider's intervention in the various dimensions of knowledge	Competence	Definition
Circulation (logistical competences)	Basic logistical	Mechanical transfer of knowledge functioning as information
Intrinsic nature (competences of form, or 'shaping' competences)	Externalization	Competence involving the transformation of knowledge that is tacit at S into knowledge that is codified at R
	Internalization	Competence involving the transformation of knowledge that is codified at S into knowledge that is tacit at R
Reach or scope (competences of scope)	Generalization	Competences involving an increase in the degree of generality at R of knowledge that is local at S
	Localization	Competences involving an increase in the degree of localization at R of knowledge that is general at S
Structure or morphology (architectural or combinatory competences)	Association	Competences involving the association of knowledge existing at S in order to produce different knowledge at R
	Dissociation	Competences involving the dissociation of knowledge existing at S in order to produce different knowledge at R

2.2.1 The characteristics of the source and the receiver

The qualities of the *receiver* can be described, in very simple terms, as *receptive qualities*. They denote the cognitive aptitudes, the 'technical' conditions and the attitudes (behaviour patterns, strategies) that encourage the acquisition of knowledge. They reflect the additive and complementary nature of knowledge. The quality of a KIBS provider's intervention depends on the receptive qualities of the receiver. These qualities permit or facilitate communication and reduce informational asymmetries in the provision of the service. Thus these receptive qualities are weakened when a client organization does not have an internal department made up of experts in a given function (for example, a legal department in the case of the provision of a legal service). These receptive qualities may also be affected by internal disputes and by unfavourable individual or group behaviour (a refusal to learn), particularly when the receiver feels threatened by the new knowledge.

This question occupies a position of some importance in the economic and socio-economic literature, where it is known by various names. In economic analyses that draw their inspiration from the phenomena of percolation in the physical sciences, it is denoted by the term *receptivity* (Antonelli, 1996). In sociology (and particularly in the sociology of science), the term *translation capabilities* is used (Callon, 1986), while in the economics of technical change (Cohen and Levinthal, 1990), the term *absorptive capacities* is used. These absorptive capacities relate essentially to scientific and technical knowledge. Thus the receptive qualities that are the object of our analysis here can be interpreted as *extended* receptivity or *extended* absorptive capacity, since they relate to all the forms of knowledge that might be subject to processing by a KIBS provider (compare section 1.1). These receptive qualities are to some extent given, but they can also be improved by the interventions of the KIBS provider.

The source of the knowledge may also have a certain number of characteristics that facilitate the flow of knowledge to a greater or lesser extent. As opposed to the receptive qualities discussed above, the propensity of a source to deliver up its knowledge will be denoted by the term *transmission qualities*. These transmission qualities also denote the cognitive aptitudes, the technical conditions and the attitudes of a source, which may be more or less favourable to the transfer or, conversely, retention of knowledge. Thus these transmission capacities are dependent on the nature of knowledge in question, on the cognitive characteristics (aptitudes) of the various elements that make up the source and on the attitudes of those elements to the sharing of knowledge. The transmission qualities of the source are generally increased when the knowledge is codified. They decline when this knowledge is regarded as strategic by the source (or its various components) or when the purpose to which the knowledge is put is likely, in one way or another, to call into question the source itself.

Mistrust of this kind is not uncommon in audit services and, more generally, in knowledge-intensive business services of a therapeutic nature, that is those seeking to provide answers to what Kubr (1988) calls corrective problems.

These transmission capacities are also partly given, but the service provider's intervention may help to improve them. Since a source must exist before transmission can take place, the first form that such an intervention can take is to locate the source of the knowledge, what Gibbons and Johnston (1974) call 'knowledge about knowledge'. In fact, outside of the ideal-typical situation of the standard classical market, locating the source of the knowledge is not such an easy task. For this reason, the typology of knowledge drawn up by Lundvall and Johnson (1994), namely the *know-what*, *know-why*, *know-how* and *know-who*, needs to be supplemented by a fifth type of knowledge that we will denote by the term *know-where*. This additional type signifies the ability to identify and locate the place where the knowledge is to be found (that is the source).

2.2.2   Competences relating to the circulation of knowledge (logistical competences)

The circulation of knowledge may take a very simple basic form that we describe as the *linear transfer of knowledge* or *basic logistical competence*. Here, knowledge is reduced to the status of information. The service provider is regarded as a mere processor of information, a simple intermediary whose activity is limited to moving the information ('physically') from the source where it is located to the receiver who purchases it or who is designated by the purchaser. In this case, the knowledge is not modified as it moves from S to R: the input knowledge is identical to the output knowledge. Some market research services, the use of online databases and some aspects of recruitment consultancy or of the transfer of technical systems by IT consultants can be described in these terms.

This basic logistical competence is regarded here as an autonomous service. Usually, however, the transfer or circulation of knowledge includes some form of knowledge processing, or in other words more complex competences. In most cases, indeed, this basic logistical competence is *combined* with other competences that reflect an aptitude for modifying the nature of the knowledge and its economic properties.

The links between the basic logistical competence and the other competences are complex. They may be implemented before the knowledge is circulated, or they may succeed it, accompany it or merge into one with it. If the categories outlined above are examined alongside a number of empirical studies (Gallouj, 1991; Gadrey et al., 1992; Bessant and Rush, 1995; Miles et al., 1995; Bilderbeek and Den Hertog, 1997), it is evident that the activity of KIBS providers involved in a service relationship can be described relatively satisfactorily in terms of six basic competences. Although they are difficult to dissociate from each other within the framework of any given service, these competences can be separated out analytically. They can be broken down into three groups, each containing two opposing principles, which describe the changes of state the knowledge undergoes as it flows between the source and the receiver.

2.2.3 Competences relating to the form of knowledge (competences of form, or 'shaping' competences)

The first pair of competences describes the capacity to alter the form (codified or tacit) taken by the knowledge in question. It is largely coterminous with, though somewhat more extensive than, the conversion mechanisms that Nonaka (1994) denotes by the terms externalization and internalization.

Externalization is undoubtedly the most studied mode of knowledge processing, particularly because it is associated with the increasing importance of information technologies. Externalization is synonymous with formalization, with codification (that is, the 'conversion of knowledge into a message that can then be manipulated as information', Cowan and Foray, 1998 p. 301) or even with 'forms investments' (that is, the 'costly establishment of a relationship that remains stable over a certain period of time', Thévenot, 1988). In the context of a KIBS relationship, and to use terms coined by Nonaka (1994), externalization denotes the transformation of knowledge that is tacit at the source into knowledge that is codified at the receiver. This transformation of the knowledge makes it easier to manipulate and gives it a certain stability.

Nonaka's definition can be extended to include a particular case already alluded to above, namely a situation that arises frequently in large firms whereby (useful) knowledge that exists within an organization is not recognized as such by the organization, irrespective of its form (tacit or codified). It is, as it were, involuntarily concealed (or tacit) because it lies outside the firm's capacity for introspection. As Kirzner (1979, quoted in Maskell and Malmberg, 1999) observes, this type of knowledge highlights weaknesses in the standard theories of individual decision-making:

> Ignorance of knowledge that might be spontaneously, undeliberately absorbed can ... never be explained in terms of anything other than itself. Such ignorance is simply there. It cannot be accounted for on the grounds of high search and learning costs, since no searching or learning is needed at all even, to repeat, at zero cost ... Ignorance of knowledge that can be absorbed without decision is simply the expression and the evidence of a sheer failure to notice what is there to be seen. It can be given a name – lack of entrepreneurial alertness – but it cannot be explained in terms of the standard economics of micro-theory, the theory of deliberate individual decisions. (Kirzner, 1979, p. 145)

By deploying this particular externalization competence, and thereby making firms actively aware of knowledge they have hitherto ignored and helping them to rediscover and create it socially, KIBS providers are helping to stimulate what Kirzner (1979) calls 'entrepreneurial alertness'.

More generally, the aim of externalization is to facilitate the transfer of knowledge by reducing transaction costs (Zander and Kogut, 1995). Thus externalization facilitates the implementation of basic logistical competences. It facilitates the absorption of knowledge by the client (learning) and increases the service provider's pedagogical efficiency (teaching).

However, externalization poses problems of appropriation for the service provider. It makes imitation easier. It is unlikely that a service provider will be able to sell the same knowledge twice to the same client, and it may be very easy for the client to duplicate that knowledge and diffuse it internally. However, as Senker (1995) and Callon (1999) in particular stress, some of the codified knowledge thus created is learned and applied tacitly. Moreover, the process of externalization itself is based on tacit knowledge that exists within the service-providing organization. Externalization cannot be taken for granted: it always depends on the extent to which the knowledge can be codified, which varies from case to case.

Internalization denotes the transformation of knowledge that is codified at the source into knowledge that is tacit at the receiver. In this case, the service provider supports the client during the learning process (pedagogical function). Internalization requires the service provider to become involved voluntarily and actively in the client's imitation process. Internalization cannot be achieved without close interaction between the client and service provider. It enables the client to appropriate the knowledge more easily. Here, the logistical competence and the internalization process become one and the same thing. Internalization may have another advantage over externalization. The cost of codification may be too high, particularly when the practices described by the knowledge are recursive in nature. Internalization eliminates the need to explain and codify ad infinitum.

Internalization transforms a public good into a private good with a high rate of appropriation. However, the knowledge transferred by means of this internalization competence can be used effectively only by the front-office staff in the client firm, since it is difficult to diffuse it rapidly throughout the organization as a whole.

2.2.4 Competences relating to the scope of knowledge (competences of scope)

The second pair of competences reflects the evolution of the scope of knowledge. It contrasts competences relating to generalization with those relating to localization, which cover the same ground as but are not to be confused with the principles of generalization and specification developed by Noteboom (1999). Evolutionary theory, in particular, has attributed a key role to localized technological knowledge (Antonelli, 1996, 1999).

Generalization denotes the process whereby knowledge (tacit or codified) that is specific at the source is transformed into knowledge (tacit or codified) that is general when it reaches the receiver. This competence extends the range of application of a particular item of knowledge, or its audience (the scope of the 'knowledge about knowledge', as it were). Nonaka's notion of socialization could be regarded as a particular case of generalization, to the extent that it is an instrument for the generalization of tacit knowledge. This socialization requires a degree of interaction that is at least as high, if not higher, than that required for internalization. In implementing the generalization principle, KIBS providers are helping to reduce 'cognitive distance' (Noteboom, 1999) both inside and outside the receiving organization (the cognitive distance between and within firms if the organization is a firm). Thus it encourages what might be called 'cognitive alignment', which facilitates the exchange of knowledge.

Localization (or differentiation or specification) is the transformation of knowledge that is general at the source into knowledge adapted to the local context of the receiving organization. Again, this knowledge may be both tacit and codified. Localization increases the extent to which the knowledge can be appropriated by the client. Of course, this appropriation is made all the easier by the tacit knowledge put in place by the localization process. In this case, the solution proposed or co-produced by the service provider is an exclusive one shared by the client and the service provider. It is not widely diffused beyond the group. Nevertheless, it should be noted that localization makes such diffusion not only difficult and costly (particularly in the case of tacit knowledge) but sometimes also useless (because of the local nature of knowledge). In contrast to generalization, localization can be said to introduce 'cognitive distance' between the receiver and the external environment, which may reduce the diffusion of knowledge beyond the local level. If the receiving organization is a firm, localization increases the cognitive distance between firms but sharply reduces that within firms.

2.2.5 Competences relating to the structure or morphology of knowledge (architectural or combinatory competences)

In the course of a transaction, a KIBS provider may modify not only the form and scope of the knowledge in question but also its architecture. In order to highlight the two contrasting modes of the architectural or combinatory competence, we will replace the combination principle adopted by Nonaka (1994) and the accommodation principle developed by Noteboom (1999) with the association and dissociation principles.

Association involves supplying to the receiver, in combined form, items or sets of knowledge (of different forms) that were originally discrete. Although this is a fundamental principle of the production of innovation in the Schumpeterian model, association is being considered here in a more general and mechanical way as one of the basic knowledge-processing mechanisms, which does not necessarily produce innovation.

Association concerns not only codified knowledge (as in Nonaka's framework) but also tacit knowledge (the socialization mechanism comes into play once again here), as well as knowledge embodied in organizations, technical systems or individuals. Thus a range of different activities can be described by means of this basic mechanism: not only R&D, which involves the production of new knowledge (tacit or codified) from various combinations of old knowledge (tacit or codified), but also associations between different organizations (collaborations, alliances), and so on.

Like internalization, the tacit exchange of knowledge or the association of tacit knowledge (socialization) is a way of reducing the cost of codifying recursive knowledge.

Dissociation, conversely, involves separating out a set of knowledge (of whatever form) in order to produce a different set of knowledge to be supplied to the client. As with association, the knowledge may be embodied in individuals, in technical systems or in organizations, and the process of dissociation may relate to the knowledge itself or to the media that carry it.

The seven basic knowledge processing mechanisms outlined above represent the various aspects of a multi-faceted interactive process, namely learning.

Here, this complex process involves the client and the KIBS provider. It has to be understood positively (learning in the strict sense), negatively (forgetting or unlearning) and neutrally (remembering), in other words as a mechanism for accumulating knowledge, for destroying obsolete knowledge (unlearning) and preserving a stock of knowledge (maintaining it at a given level). Thus it may be part of a KIBS provider's remit to destroy knowledge. Or, to put it another way, if learning is a cumulative process, then that cumulativeness is selective, since learning is a social phenomenon which, from the client firm's point of view, does not preclude creative forgetting (a means of dealing with the obsolescence of knowledge), or just plain forgetting (Johnson, 1992). These two types of forgetting may prompt service providers to help the client either to 'forget' or, in the second case, to relearn or to remember.

This learning process must also be perceived from the perspective of the 'beneficiary' (service provider, client) and of the object of the process (knowledge and the modes of knowledge acquisition). From the point of view of the service provider, learning (or unlearning) may take a number of different forms:

- learning,
- teaching, that is imparting knowledge to clients through a variety of mechanisms, whether formalized (training) or not (learning by interacting);
- learning to learn (that is improving one's own absorptive capacity);
- teaching others to learn (that is improving their absorptive capacity).

These basic mechanisms, which describe some of the facets of the learning process, give rise to the following observations.

1. This typology of basic competences reconciles the typologies drawn up by Noteboom and Nonaka. It introduces a logistical competence that does not exist in these authors' typologies but which, on examination of the services actually supplied by KIBS providers, constitutes an important borderline case. It introduces the converse mechanism of association, which does not exist either in these two authors' typologies but which constitutes a not-insignificant mechanism for processing knowledge (and producing innovation) in KIBS, as well as in services in general. Generalization, association and dissociation are defined in such a way that they can be applied to both tacit and codified knowledge. Thus socialization does not disappear from our analysis but is incorporated into different principles.

2. The logistical competence always comes into play in the provision of KIBS, since what is involved is the transfer of knowledge from a source to a receiver. However, it is frequently incorporated into other mechanisms. This logistical competence (viewed independently) may also be regarded positively or negatively, since the transfer of knowledge may also be positive or negative (for example, redundancy, discarding of a software package).

3. Although the seven basic competences outlined above can be distinguished from each other in analytical terms, they are actually implemented in more or less complex configurations. Each of these competences can be mobilized independently. The competence in question then becomes one and the same thing as the service transaction. Thus the provision of a given KIBS may consist of the mere circulation of knowledge: certain market research or auditing services have already

been mentioned above by way of example. It may also involve the adaptation of a generic solution to a local situation, and vice versa. More usually, however, a range of different basic competences is mobilized during the provision of a KIBS. In such situations, these various basic competences may be related to each other in various ways. For example, they may be deployed simultaneously or successively. Thus the association, generalization or logistical principles are frequently proceeded by implementation of the externalization principle, during which the knowledge in question is codified. Localization often goes hand in hand with internalization, which explains why these two mechanisms are frequently confused in the literature.

2.3   The KIBS Firm as a Knowledge-Accumulation System

In the previous section, our analysis focused on the processing of knowledge within the framework of a given service relationship, that is at the interface between source and receiver. This processing affects the (physical) circulation, form, scope and morphology of the knowledge in question. Another aspect of knowledge must be taken into account, namely its cumulative nature (compare section 1.3). This aspect plays an extremely important role within KIBS firms, independently of any given service transaction.

Indeed, since the use of KIBS can be explained less by transaction costs than by cognitive differentials, the main objective of KIBS providers is to accumulate, capitalize and protect the knowledge derived from different service transactions, in other words to establish and maintain an organizational memory.

This organizational memory is important for several reasons. It constitutes one of the sources of knowledge that can be drawn on for input in any given service relationship (compare Figure 11.1). It can also be drawn on in situations in which the KIBS provider is helping a client with an innovation process. Finally, it constitutes an essential source of cognitive raw material for innovation within KIBS firms themselves. However, even while it is acting as a source of input knowledge in these three situations, the organizational memory is being further enriched by the knowledge crystallized in the solutions being developed.

The stock of knowledge on which KIBS providers draw for their main input is essentially the product of past experiences that have been memorized. Since they are the product of individual efforts, these experiences are embodied in individuals or groups of individuals. As a result, the organizational memory of KIBS firms is heavily dependent on the loyalty of its staff. The loss of certain members of staff produces an effect akin to amnesia or a cognitive haemorrhage. Stinchcombe and Heimer (1988), for example, described IT service providers as 'precarious monopolies', constantly prey to the risk that their best experts will leave, taking with them the expertise that is also publicized by the companies, which further increases the risk of defections.

However, a part of each individual experience exists in codified form. Documents, reports (as hard copies or in electronic form), software, films, recordings, models, prototypes and technical systems are constantly circulating among the various actors engaged in the provision of a given service. This type of knowledge is more easily accumulated. It transforms individual experiences into a collective memory that can be drawn on at any time and in any place by all the members of the organization. The largest KIBS firms, which are very conscious of the phenomena associated with knowledge localization and their perverse effects, particularly the formation of cliques that may cause the organization to fragment (Granovetter, 1973), routinely put in place codification or externalization strategies. These strategies may take various forms: the accumulation of knowledge derived from experience in databases, the use of structuring methods and so on.

However, it should not be concluded that the trade-off between externalization–generalization and internalization–localization is always resolved in favour of the first pair. In reality, there is a dialectical relationship between the two that can be interpreted by means of a paradoxical mechanism that Eisenberg (1984) calls 'unified identity', that is some degree of balance between two apparently contradictory mechanisms, namely a diversity of interpretations and their simultaneous unicity (that is the construction of consensus).

From the KIBS provider's point of view, what really matters is the establishment of a cognitive differential between the organization and its clients. In other words, it needs to expand its organizational memory. This is achieved through the combination of two knowledge-accumulation strategies:

1. Accumulation in individual memories, that is the training of individuals and the recruitment and outplacement of experts. Training may be formalized or take place on the job (internalization and socialization principles in Nonaka's sense of the terms). The recruitment of experts may expand the memory quantitatively or mechanically (recruitment of an additional expert in order to strengthen an existing speciality) as well as qualitatively (recruitment in a new area of expertise). Outplacement also reflects a qualitative change in the memory, particularly when 'up or out' strategies are being implemented.
2. The accumulation of knowledge on inanimate media, that is the codification of knowledge in libraries, databases, expert systems, methods, standard contracts, publications and so on.

The first of these knowledge-accumulation strategies produces diversity and creative ambiguity. The second produces unity, or common knowledge. Once combined, they generate 'unified diversity'.

3.   KNOWLEDGE PROCESSING AND INNOVATION *IN* AND *THROUGH THE USE OF* KIBS

The question of knowledge processing is closely linked to that of innovation, particularly in the evolutionary approach. Like innovation, KIBS are often defined as activities intended to resolve selected (and sometimes 'reconstructed') problems. However, the notion that all KIBS transactions are to be regarded as innovations should be rejected. Thus one important problem that has to be resolved in any economic analysis of KIBS is that of the boundary between a routine or standard service and an innovative service.

The link between innovation and KIBS can be considered from two different, though not unrelated perspectives, namely that of innovation produced *through the use of* KIBS and that of innovation *within* KIBS themselves.

3.1   Innovation Through the Use of KIBS

We are dealing here with the role that KIBS can play in assisting client firms to innovate. Two different scenarios can be envisaged.

In the first, the KIBS is mobilized in order to provide the knowledge-processing competences required for an innovation project (whether technological, organizational or strategic in nature) that has been fully identified as such by the client.

In the second, the KIBS is called on to play a part in a 'non-programmed' innovation that will be denoted by the term 'ad hoc innovation'. This scenario will be examined in greater detail in the following section, since it involves both innovation through the use of KIBS and innovation within KIBS themselves.

Whatever the scenario under consideration, this model of KIBS-assisted innovation can be broken down into four component parts (Gallouj, 2002; see Figure 11.2):

1.   The functions (F) of the client firm that are the object of the innovation. The innovation may concern one or more of the firm's functions (legal, IT, research and so on). A functional approach of this kind to the object of innovation has several advantages. It is consistent with certain KIBS typologies that define service providers in terms of the main function of the client firm on which they act in order to produce change (the legal

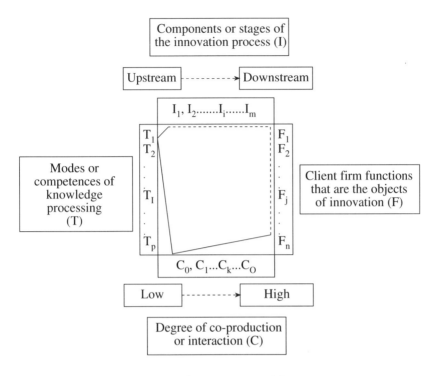

Figure 11.2   The KIBS-assisted innovation model

function in the case of legal consultants, for example). It also facilitates the introduction of a broadly-based, open concept of innovation, which encompasses not only new products and processes but also new strategies and new forms of organization. The adoption of a functional approach to the object of innovation makes it possible to analyse in much greater detail these last two categories (particularly organizational innovation), which very often serve as residual, catch-all categories. Moreover, this functional approach, located upstream of products and processes, can be used to explain innovation in manufacturing and services with a certain degree of consistency (whatever the possible differences in content between the corresponding product and process innovations).

2. The degree of interaction (C) between the service provider and client around the innovation project or emerging innovation. In the case of 'non-programmed' innovation, the degree of interaction around the innovation becomes conjoined with the degree of interaction involved in the provision of the service. In the case of an innovation project identified as such from the outset, the interaction revolves entirely around the innovation.

The client participates to a greater or lesser extent in the provision of the service. In many cases, a non-programmed innovation emerges out of an intense service relationship. When a service provider is taking part in a clearly identified innovation project, the degree of interaction is highly variable. In particular, it depends on the stage of the process at which the service provider is called in. Indeed, the service provider may be called on before the innovation project proper gets underway in order to supply simple codified information, such as that produced by market surveys, which does not require any real interaction.

3. The stages of the innovation process (I) at which the service provider is called in. This process can be conveniently represented in terms of the following traditional sequence: (i) the gathering of information and ideas, (ii) research (whether basic or applied), (iii) design and development (including testing or experimentation), (iv) the production of the solution, (v) the marketing of the solution (or its pseudo-marketing when it is to be diffused within an organization).

   From the client firm's point of view, this process of innovation is never a linear one. The sequence outlined above is merely a heuristic device: the various stages may not all take place, some may overlap (that is take place simultaneously) and others may merge with each other (in services, for example, production and marketing are frequently synonymous).

   From the service provider's point of view, this process (I) may also be approached in various ways. He may be called on to intervene in one stage only or in several stages. He may also be called on to take responsibility for the overall coherence of the project. Finally, several different providers may be called on to provide their own particular specialist services (marketing consultants upstream of the innovation, R&D laboratories, legal consultants downstream of the solution, and so on). The strategies adopted by the major international auditing and consultancy companies are designed to make available to their clients a whole range of services in an integrated way (Gadrey et al., 1992).

4. The various knowledge-processing competences (T). These competences are those outlined in section 2 above, that is the basic logistical competences, together with those of externalization, internalization, generalization, localization, association and dissociation.

A service provider called in to assist a client engaged in innovation may mobilize one, some or all of these competences. As Figure 11.2 shows, the model of KIBS-assisted innovation may take a multiplicity of configurations equating to sets (I, T, F, C). One particular configuration merits particular attention, namely the one that describes the mobilization of basic logistical competences within the framework of an innovation project. This configuration, which might be described as the standard configuration, consists of the simple transfer from source to receiver of codified information, without any real interaction between processor and receiver and irrespective of the various components of the innovation process and of the functions being considered.

The boundary between a KIBS provider's normal problem-resolving activities and his contribution to innovation is a fragile one. For example, legal services routinely provided by lawyers involve the processing of knowledge on behalf of clients. Such processing implies the implementation (in a multiplicity of configurations) of transfer, internalization, externalization, association, dissociation, generalization and localization competences. Even when he is producing a novel legal solution on behalf of a client (an innovation), a service provider is calling on the same knowledge-processing competences. In both cases, the competences mobilized are, to varying degrees, vectors of novelty, depending on whether they are exploitation competences (for example, generalization) or exploration competences (for example, association).

Thus it is not the modes of knowledge processing (that is the competences) that define innovation by services (innovation does not occur solely when the Schumpeterian combinatory mechanism is brought into play), but rather the existence, a priori, of a clearly identified innovation project or the recognition, a posteriori, of an innovation and its designation as such (what might almost be called its social construction). In our model of KIBS-assisted innovation (compare Figure 11.1), this innovation is represented by the [I] axis. This means that, when a service provider takes part in an innovation project with a client, the service provider is a (co)-producer of the innovation, even if the only competences mobilized are those that would ordinarily be mobilized when a normal service is provided. Thus there is no theoretical reason why the activities of external KIBS providers should be excluded from definitions of innovation indicators (as certain national and international statistical institutes do, for example, particularly the OECD).

3.2 Innovation in KIBS

Although KIBS providers assist their clients in the production of innovation, they may also innovate internally. In order to understand the nature of innovation in this type of activity, we must not allow ourselves to becoming entrapped in traditional categories. Rather we must seek to supplement and adapt them. Since KIBS providers process and produce knowledge, it seems to us appropriate to consider the innovation they produce in the same terms. Empirical studies (Gallouj, 1991) have revealed various types of innovations that can be inferred from a particular relationship to knowledge.

Innovation can be defined as the creation of new knowledge in order to resolve a problem. This new knowledge may be created intentionally, as is the case with 'new fields of knowledge innovation' and 'formalization innovation'. However, it may also emerge unintentionally out of various activities, as is the case with ad hoc innovation.

1. *Ad hoc innovation* is a solution (that is a set of knowledge) that allows a certain degree of new light (we are dealing here with an incremental innovation) to be shed on a firm's (legal, organizational, strategic, technical and so on) problem, without it necessarily being possible to transfer the solution *in toto* to other firms. Ad hoc innovation requires the service provider to have detailed knowledge of the client firm's problem, knowledge which is usually generated through an extremely interactive relationship. Thus ad hoc innovation is co-produced. It is also an innovation produced within KIBS and through the use of KIBS. It depends heavily on the competences of socialization, internalization and localization. As a result, it poses problems of appropriation and pricing. However, once this ad hoc innovation has been produced, the externalization and generalization competences are deployed in order to incorporate it into the service provider's organizational memory so that certain elements of it can be reproduced elsewhere. In this way, ad hoc innovation (output knowledge) is transformed into input knowledge.

2. *New fields of knowledge innovation*   By analogy with Schumpeter's categories, and in view of the fact that, for KIBS providers, knowledge is both input and output, we can say that 'new fields of knowledge' innovation encompasses (i) new products, (ii) new markets and (iii) new sources of raw materials. 'New fields of knowledge' innovation denotes the accumulation of input knowledge relating to emerging spheres of knowledge (the Internet is perhaps the best current example) with a view to providing services (output knowledge) in these new spheres. The degree of novelty here is greater than in ad hoc innovation.

    The principal (internal) competences deployed in this process of knowledge accumulation are characterized by their diversity: reciprocation (analogy, metaphors), combination and externalization. However, since the new sphere of knowledge is initially a quasi-public good, with the economic properties characteristic of this type of good, certain specification and consolidation activities are required in order to establish a dominant design that can then be appropriated.

3. *Formalization innovation*   This term denotes a heterogeneous group that includes all the mechanisms that serve to give form to the service in question (process, methods, organization and so on). It relies heavily, therefore, on all the knowledge-processing competences that give solutions a certain degree of 'visibility' and 'stability' (externalization, generalization and so on).

CONCLUSION

If firms are processors of knowledge, as some recent studies suggest (Fransman, 1994), then KIBS firms are the best possible exemplification of the thesis, since knowledge, in all its forms, is both their main input and their main output.

We have been concerned in this chapter with the activities of KIBS providers, the main objective of which is to make knowledge-processing capacities available to clients. These capacities can be described satisfactorily in terms of a certain number of basic mechanisms (which we have denoted by the term competence) that modify the spatial characteristics, form, scope or architecture of the knowledge in question.

These are the same basic mechanisms (competences) that are mobilized in innovation projects (whether ad hoc or identified as such). Nevertheless, it should not be thought that all KIBS transactions constitute innovations, and although the knowledge-processing competences may be either exploitation or exploration competences (March, 1991), what distinguishes a routine service from an innovative service is the existence of an innovation project or its 'social construction' or designation as such in the course of service delivery.

As far as innovation in KIBS is concerned, it cannot be said to be independent of innovation through the use of KIBS. Indeed, both forms of innovation draw on the same organizational memory and feed back into the same memory. Moreover, the highly interactive nature of many knowledge-intensive business services confuses the ownership regimes of certain forms of innovation.

There is some value in considering the nature of innovation in KIBS in cognitive terms by virtue of the cognitive nature of the input and, particularly, the output of such services. The various forms of innovation thus revealed are also related in specific ways to the various basic knowledge-processing mechanisms.

NOTES

1. For a recent assessment of these various issues cf. in particular C. and F. Gallouj (1996), Sundbo (1998), Gadrey (1996), De Bandt and Gadrey (1994) and Rubacalba-Bermejo (1999).
2. In the case of the 'aptitude for performing (successfully) better than others', the term 'core competences' is used (Teece, 1998).
3. When the service provider supplies raw materials that have to be processed by the client in order to produce meaning.
4. It is in fact the dynamic of the particular environment that justifies the use of service providers, and it is in the most dynamic environments, that is the most rapidly changing areas of expertise, that the use of KIBS is growing most quickly (Wolff and Baumol, 1987, cited in Starbuck, 1996).

5. For a review and more detailed discussion of these questions see in particular (to cite just a few recent studies) Dasgupta and David (1994), Cowan and Foray (1998), Callon (1999), Antonelli (1999) and Foray and Mairesse (1999).
6. Etymologically: 'lead or take away . . .'

REFERENCES

Abernathy, W. and J. Utterback, (1978), 'Patterns of Industrial Innovation', *Technology Review*, 80, June–July, 41–7.

Antonelli, C. (1996), 'Localized Knowledge Percolation Processes and Information Networks', *Journal of Evolutionary Economics*, 6, 281–95.

Antonelli, C. (1999), 'The Evolution of the Industrial Organization of the Production of Knowledge', *Cambridge Journal of Economics*, 23, 243–60.

Arrow, K. (1962), 'Economic Welfare and the Allocation of Resources for Invention', in R.R. Nelson (ed.), *The Rate and Direction of Inventive Activity: Economic and Social Factors* (Princeton, NJ: Princeton University Press).

Bessant, J. and H. Rush (1995), 'Building Bridges for Innovation: The Role of Consultants in Technology Transfer', *Research Policy*, **24** (1), 97–114.

Bilderbeek, R. and P. Den Hertog, (1997), 'The New Knowledge Infrastructure: The Role of Technologies-Based Knowledge-Intensive Business Services in National Innovation Systems', SI4S project, European Commission (DG XII), TSER program.

Callon, M. (1986), 'Eléments pour une sociologie de la traduction. La domestication des coquilles Saint-Jacques et des marins-pêcheurs dans la baie de Saint-Brieuc', *L'année sociologique*, 36, 169–208.

Callon, M. (1999), 'Le réseau comme forme émergente et comme modalité de coordination: le cas des interactions stratégiques entre firmes industrielles et laboratoires académiques', in M. Callon et al., *Réseau et coordination* (Paris: Economica), pp. 194–230.

Cohen, M. and D. Levinthal (1990), 'Absorptive Capacity: A New Perspective on Learning and Innovation', *Administrative Science Quarterly*, 35, 128–52.

Cohen, M.D. and P. Bacdayan (1996), 'Organizational Routines are Stored as Procedural Memory: Evidence from a Laboratory Study', in J. R. Meindl, C. Stubbart and J. F. Porac (eds), *Cognition between and within Organizations* (London: Sage Publications), pp. 341–67.

Cohendet, P., F. Kern, B. Mehmanpazir, and F. Munier (1999), 'Knowledge Coordination, Competence Creation and Integrated Networks in Globalised Firms', *Cambridge Journal of Economics*, 23, 225–41.

Cowan, R. and D. Foray, (1998), 'Economie de la codification et de la diffusion des connaissances', in P. Petit (ed.), *L'économie de l'information* (Paris: La Découverte), pp. 301–29.

Dasgupta, P. and P.A. David (1994), 'Towards a New Economics of Science', *Research Policy*, 23, 487–521.

De Bandt, J. and J. Gadrey (eds) (1994), *Relations de service, marchés des services* (Paris: CNRS Editions).

Eisenberg, E.M. (1984), 'Ambiguity as Strategy in Organizational Communication', *Communication monographs*, 51, 227–42.

Foray, D. and J. Mairesse (1999), *Economie de la connaissance*, mimeo Paris.

Fransman, M. (1994), 'Information, Knowledge, Vision and Theories of the Firm', *Industrial and Corporate Change,* 3(3), 713–57.

Gadrey, J. (1996), *Services: la productivité en question* (Paris: Desclée de Brouwer).

Gadrey, J. (2000), 'The Characterization of Goods and Services: An Alternative Approach', *Review of Income and Wealth*, **46**(3), 369–87.

Gadrey, J. et al. (1992), *Manager le Conseil* (Paris: Ediscience).

Gallouj, F. (1991), 'Les formes de l'innovation dans les services de conseil', *Revue d'économie industrielle*, 57, 25–45.

Gallouj, F. (2002), 'Interactional Innovation: A Neo-Schumpeterian Model', in J. Sundbo, and L. Fuglsang (eds), *Innovation as Strategic Reflexivity* (London and New York: Routledge) pp. 29–56.

Gallouj, C. and F. Gallouj, (1996), *L'innovation dans les services* (Paris: Editions Economica Poche).

Gallouj, F. and O. Weinstein (1997), 'Innovation in Services', *Research Policy*, **26**(4–5), 537–56.

Gibbons, M. and R. Johnston (1974), 'The Role of Science in Technological Innovation', *Research Policy,* 3, 220–42.

Granovetter, M. (1973), 'The Strength of Weak Ties', *American Journal of Sociology*, **6**(78) 360–80.

Hales, M. (1997), 'Make or Buy in the Production of Innovation: Competences, Fullness of Services and the Architecture of Supply in Consultancy', SI4S project, European Commission (DG XII), TSER program.

Hayek, F. (1945), 'The Use of Knowledge in Society', *American Economic Review*, **35**(4), 519–30.

Johnson, B. (1992), 'Institutional Learning', in B.A. Lundvall (ed.), *National Systems of Innovation* (London and New York: Pinter Publishers).

Kirzner, I. (1979), *Perception, Opportunity and Profit. Studies in the Theory of Entrepreneurship* (Chicago: University of Chicago Press).

Kubr, M. (1988), *Management Consulting: A Guide to the Profession* (Geneva: BIT).

Lippman, S. and R.P. Rumelt, (1982), 'Uncertain Imitability: An Analysis of Interfirm Differences in Efficiency under Competition', *Bell Journal of Economics*, 13, 418–38.

Lundvall, B.A. and B. Johnson (1994), 'The Learning Economy', *Journal of Industry Studies*, **1**(2), 23–42.

Machlup, F. (1984), *Knowledge: Its Creation, Distribution and Economic Significance*, Vol. III, *The Economics of Information and Human Capital* (Princeton, NJ: Princeton University Press).

March, J.G. (1991), 'Exploration and Exploitation in Organizational Learning', *Organization Science*, 2, 71–87.

Maskell, P. and A. Malmberg (1999), 'Localized Learning and Industrial Competitiveness', *Cambridge Journal of Economics*, 23, 167–85.

Miles, I., N. Kastrinos, K. Flanagan, R. Bilderbeek, P. den Hertog, W. Huntink, and M. Bouman, (1995) 'Knowledge-Intensive Business Services: Their Role as Users, Carriers and Sources of Innovation', PREST, University of Manchester.

Nelson, R. (1994), 'The Co-Evolution of Technology, Industrial Structure and Supporting Institutions', *Industrial and Corporate Change*, 3, 47–64.

Nonaka, S. (1994), 'A Dynamic Theory of Organizational Knowledge Creation', *Organization Science*, **5**(1), 14–37.

Nonaka, S. and N. Takeuchi, (1995), *The Knowledge-Creating Company* (New York: Oxford University Press).

Noteboom, B. (1992), 'Towards a Dynamic Theory of Transactions', *Journal of Evolutionary Economics*, 2, 281–99.

Noteboom, B. (1999), 'Innovation, Learning and Industrial Organisation', *Cambridge Journal of Economics*, 23, 127–50.

Peirce, C.S. (1957), *Essays in the Philosophy of Science*, (Indianapolis: Bobbs-Merrill).

Piaget, J. (1970), *Psychologie et épistémologie* (Paris: Denoël).

Polanyi, M. (1983), *The Tacit Dimension* (Gloucester, MA: Peter Smith) (1st edition 1966).

Ribault, T. (1991), 'Formes et limites de la marchandisation de l'information', PhD thesis, Lille University.

Rubalcaba-Bermejo, L. (1999), 'Business Services in European Industry, European Commission', report for DG III-Industry.

Senker, J. (1995), 'Knowledge and Models of Innovation', *Industrial and Corporate Change*, 4(2), 425–47.

Starbuck, W.H. (1996), 'Learning by Knowledge-Intensive Firms', in M.D. Cohen and L.S. Sproull (eds), *Organizational Learning* (London: Sage Publications).

Stinchcombe, A. and C. Heimer (1988), 'Interorganizational Relations and Careers in Computer Software Firms', *Research in the Sociology of Work*, 4, 179–204.

Sundbo, J. (1998), *The Organization of Innovation in Services* (Roskilde: Roskilde University Press).

Teece, D.J. (1988), 'Technological Change and the Nature of the Firm', in G. Dosi, C. Freeman, R. Nelson, G. Silverberg, L. Soete (eds) *Technical Change and Economic Theory* (London: Pinter Publishers), pp. 256–81.

Thévenot, L. (1988). 'Les investissements de forme', *Cahiers du Centre de l'étude et de l'emploi*, 2, 21–73.

Winter, S. (1987), 'Knowledge and Competence as Strategic Assets', in D.J. Teece (ed.), *The Competitive Challenge* (New York: Harper & Row), pp. 159–84.

Wolff, E.N. and W.J. Baumol (1987), 'Sources of Postwar Growth of Information Activity in the US', Unpublished manuscript, New York.

Zander, U. and B. Kogut (1995), 'Knowledge and the Speed of the Transfer and Imitation of Organisational Capabilities: An Empirical Test', *Organizational science*, 6(1), 76–92.

032
L80

Epilogue: towards innovation and high performance in research on services

Jean Gadrey and Faïz Gallouj

We would like to conclude this collaborative volume by touching on some of the questions that seem to us crucial if further progress is to be made in economic and socio-economic research on services. Most of these questions have already been addressed by the various contributors to the book. Our aim in this epilogue is to give them greater visibility, to introduce a little order and to add a few hypotheses. Of course, it is our own view of the priorities for such a research agenda that we are putting forward here, a view that may not be shared by all those who have contributed to the book. This epilogue is, therefore, intended as a very open contribution that seeks to prefigure some of the academic debates to be pursued in future.

We concentrate on three wide-ranging sets of 'fundamental' questions which, in our view, should be regarded as priorities:

- the concepts, typologies and methodologies that might serve to bring some order to the diversity of services, particularly with a view of measuring and evaluating results and performance;
- the role and social organization of knowledge and intelligence in the production, innovation, consumption and trading of services;
- the role of ICTs in the development of services and the rationalization of the processes whereby they are produced, as well as in innovation in services.

The first proposed area of research is immense and yet, in the current state of research, can be said to be underdeveloped. It is as if the majority of researchers, particularly economists, are happy to subcontract to national accountants the task of producing classifications and carrying out conceptual and methodological research into the evaluation of the output and performance of service activities.

We do not seek to imply that national accountants are unaware of the difficulties that exist, nor that they are reluctant to innovate. On the contrary, indeed, they have produced many new and useful tools. Nevertheless, it is our conviction that the two major paradoxes of today's service economies could be clarified and largely resolved by conceptual and methodological research into services and their results and quality. Some of the contributions to the present book point to some potentially stimulating directions for new research. Let us briefly outline the two major paradoxes of the service economy.

The first is 'Solow's paradox', which applies primarily to services, some of which are particularly paradoxical. It can be summarized by the following question: how can it be possible that (official) productivity figures have not displayed substantial productivity gains since the late 1970s, while investment in computers and related technologies has experienced a huge growth, especially in service sectors, such as banking and insurance, with poor productivity records? Economists have yet to provide a satisfactory answer.

The second paradox, partly connected to the first, is even more crucial to any attempt to understand the core structural change of developed economies during the second half of the twentieth century, namely the growth of services, which is reflected particularly in their share in employment and in nominal GDP. This paradox is summarized in the title of the first part of a recent book (Raa and Schettkat, 2001): 'The amazing vigour of services'. Why is this vigour paradoxical? The reason is that many services are characterized by 'cost disease' (to use Baumol's words), which has its origins in the 'productivity gap' between the production of goods (high labour productivity gains, as a result of the substitution of capital for labour) and that of services, in which productivity gains are low or non-existent, at least for that part of the service sector described as 'stagnant'. The vigour of such services is a paradox because final demand is constantly growing while costs are (seemingly?) exploding. And, what is more, the rate of growth of this demand exceeds, in nominal terms, that of total demand in the economy. Hence the rising share of service employment.

The book edited by Raa and Schettkat contains a number of valuable theoretical and econometric models concerning both the supply-side and the demand-side reasons for employment shifts towards services. However, most of these analyses rest on the hypothesis that output and productivity are not seriously mismeasured in services. And the result is that the bulk of the paradox remains unsolved. To quote the conclusion of the book: 'the possible underestimation of the real output of services industries leaves us with the puzzle that nominal demand for services rises with prices'. A radical doubt is even cast by one of the contributors: 'It may be that there is no real Baumol disease in services' (Raa and Schettkat, 2001, p. 117). But, in this book, such a doubt is not supported by any serious argument. It is our contention that the principal answers to the main paradox of the service economy will be found around these issues of the definition and measurement of the real output of services.

Some suggestions as to the orientation of future research are to be found in the present volume, particularly in the first three chapters, but the field for future research is vast. Some research has already been carried out in this area, but it has not been pursued with sufficient tenacity or resources. In 1992, a collaborative book edited by Zvi Griliches (Griliches, 1992) and published in the USA provided an impressive assessment of the uncertainties surrounding the measurement of the output of service industries in the United States (which at the time accounted for 70 per cent of the American economy). The fact that these uncertainties are mainly conceptual in nature (relating to the definition of output) is acknowledged in the book. In the introduction, Griliches writes: 'The conceptual problem arises because in many service sectors it is not exactly clear what is being transacted, what is the output, and what services correspond to the payments made to the providers'. Coming from one of the leading specialists in the area, this judgement should surely give pause for thought.

The second area of research we would prioritize concerns the role and the social organization of knowledge and intelligence in the service economy. Not all service activities are affected to the same extent by the increased knowledge intensity that characterizes the production and exchange of certain services. Many, however, are very directly affected. Economists and socio-economists cannot be accused of ignoring this aspect of services, far from it. At the moment, however, they are experiencing considerable difficulty in integrating the cognitive dimension of economic activities into traditional theories and models that were not conceived for that purpose. In the present volume, there are a number of new and stimulating approaches that demand further development. They include the conceptual approach to and tailor-made typology of knowledge-intensive activities outlined in Chapter 3 and the empirical approaches developed in Chapters 1 and 6 to the increase in knowledge workers and to the production of 'shared intelligence' in organizations that sell professional knowledge. Further examples are to be found in Chapters 5 and 7, whose authors develop new macroeconomic approaches to growth which, paradoxically again, has become more 'endogenous' in the era of globalization, and in Chapters 10 and 11, which present sectoral analyses of knowledge-intensive business services (KIBS) as activities in which knowledge is both input and output and where innovation and performance largely elude the traditional tools developed by industrial economists. These multifocal approaches to the knowledge economy, applied to services, are authentic innovations, and only through further research will we discover whether they stand up to the twofold test of juxtaposition with the facts and competition with other theoretical frameworks. In all cases, however, research on these issues should be accompanied by evaluative measures. This is the only way of producing durable academic work on issues that are contaminated by an ideology of the knowledge society that ignores the slowness, difficulties and social inequalities that currently characterize these processes of gaining access to 'shared intelligence'.

Such caution is even more necessary in the case of the third major area of research which, in our view, needs to be extended, namely the role of ICTs in the performance of services industries and the innovations they help to produce. Why is such caution required? The first reason is that, in economics, technological innovation is the main variable in determining economic and social progress – so much so, in fact, that the other variables are frequently ignored. The second is that powerful interest groups are working to propagate the belief that the only issue at stake in the modern world is how to gain access as rapidly as possible to a 'new economy' based on ICTs (computer and communications technologies, the Internet and so on).

However, what is clearly revealed by economic and socio-economic research that is both highly rigorous and firmly rooted in observation of the facts is that while ICTs are, it is true, an important factor, they are only one among several. Robert Gordon, for example, has produced some impressive work that can serve as a basis for more qualified assessments (Gordon, 1999 and 2000). Similarly, the most advanced research in services (see Part II of this volume) puts the notion that innovation is purely technological very much into perspective.

In order to clarify matters and provide a balanced diagnosis, we need theoretical and empirical research into the way in which ICTs provide support for the production and exchange of knowledge, service relationships and organizational change but, for all that, only as tools which, in many cases, supplement human intelligence – thereby improving service quality – but do not replace it.

We would like to examine in greater detail one of the difficulties encountered by those using traditional economic methods to resolve the following major question: what is the impact of ICTs on growth and on productivity gains? We will then see how more extensive empirical research into the modernization of services might lead to re-examination of those methods.

On the face of it, the question asked falls within the scope of traditional macroeconomics. It would seem to be a fairly typical problem that can be tackled with the standard tools of national accounting and neo-classical economic theory. With these tools, the following three-stage method suggests itself:

1. Isolate the new technologies (ICT) sector, with its own growth and productivity gains and hence its own contribution to GDP and to national productivity gains: it is a national accounting problem.
2. Isolate productive investment in new technologies: it is still a national accounting problem.
3. Evaluate, by means of a standard Cobb–Douglas production function, the

contribution of this investment to productivity gains and growth in the economy as a whole. This is where macroeconomics comes into play. The aim is to analyse the impact of the technical progress embodied in the investment, thereby making it possible to assess the contribution of various factors to growth and productivity.

Almost all the analyses produced in the United States and in Europe of the impact of ICTs on growth and productivity gains during the 1990s are based on one variant or another of a macroeconomic method of this kind. Frequently, however, little attention is paid to the number of assumptions that lurk behind the act of writing, almost without thinking, a Cobb–Douglas function with constant returns of the type:

$$Y = aK^s L^{1-s}$$

We have no intention of revisiting this long-standing and tricky question, and in any case it is our view that, under certain conditions, this method is a reasonable one for conducting economic analyses. However, we are very dubious about its efficacy as a means of isolating the impact of investment in ICTs on growth and productivity gains in the economy as a whole, and particularly in services. A macroeconomic production function of this kind is fairly well suited to analysis of the dynamics of substitution between production factors for a total output Y which, it is assumed, can properly be measured in constant prices, an assumption that implies that the components of Y do not undergo significant qualitative change. However, we have to ask ourselves what happened with the introduction of computer technology into firms, particularly in the service sector. There was a period, roughly from the 1960s to the 1980s, when centralized computer systems based on mainframes and then networked systems were introduced into firms and other organizations largely in order to achieve productivity gains, to substitute capital for labour and to process large volumes of standardized data, transactions, files, insurance policies, and so on. According to our own assessments, productivity gains greater than 10 per cent were achieved in the banking and insurance industries for these types of tasks over the course of this period (Gadrey, 1996). This was the 'Fordist' phase of computerization, analogous to the automation of manufacturing industry, when capital was simply subsituted for labour while the output was left more or less unchanged in qualitative terms.

This aspect of computerization did not disappear in the 1990s, but to judge from our observations in several service industries, the main impact of ICTs is now on the quality of the services provided (judged by various quality criteria), an impact mediated through the complementarity of IT assets and labour. At the microeconomic level, the nature of the production function has changed, in the sense that Y, the actual output, is progressing more in quality and service intensity than in quantity and that IT assets K, which rapidly increase in volume, are deployed to support a labour force L, which has itself been radically changed by the IT environment in which it works. In particular, there is greater functional flexibility, aided by computers, with a low level of capital/labour substitution. All this largely eludes a traditional production function and the measuring tools of accountancy.

This 'post-Fordist' model of 'servicing backed up by ICTs' has not led to the disappearance of the old, Fordist model of computerization, but it is gaining in importance virtually everywhere. Neither the techniques used to measure production nor standard production functions seem capable of capturing it, whereas it is perhaps here that the heart of the economics of the 'new economy' lies, if by 'new economy' we mean an economy that makes significant use of IT assets and networks such as the Internet in order to innovate.

Obviously the three main areas for future research outlined in this epilogue represent only part of the needs that are expressed today. The list could easily be extended to encompass, for example, skills, job quality and industrial relations in service industries, the economic geography of services or even the characteristics of the markets for services and the rules governing them. However, these three areas – concepts and measurement, knowledge and ICTs – are, in our view, the ones in which there is the greatest gap between (theoretical and policy) challenges and the current state of knowledge. It is these three areas, therefore, that require the most innovation and intellectual effort from researchers. We hope that this book will be a modest but serious contribution to that endeavour.

REFERENCES

Gadrey, Jean (1996), *Services: la productivité en question* (Paris, Desclée de Brouwer).
Gordon, Robert (1999), 'Has the "New Economy" Rendered the Productivity Slowdown Obsolete?', June, http://faculty-web.at.northwestern.edu/economics/gordon/indexmise.html
Gordon, Robert J. (2000), 'Does the "New Economy" Measure Up to the Great Inventions of the Past?', *Journal of Economic Perspectives*, 14, 49–74.
Griliches, Zvi (ed.) (1992), *Output Measurement in the Service Sector* (Chicago: NBER and University of Chicago Press).
Raa, Thijs ten and Ronald Schettkat (eds) (2001), *The Growth of Service Industries: The Paradox of Exploding Costs and Persistent Demand* (Cheltenham, UK and Brookfield, US: Edward Elgar).

Index